INSIGHT GUIDE
New York State

Discovery CHANNEL

APA PUBLICATIONS L

Part of the Langenscheidt Publishing Group

ABOUT THIS BOOK

Editorial

Managing Editor
Donna Dailey
Editorial Director
Brian Bell

Distribution

UK & Ireland
GeoCenter International Ltd
The Viables Centre, Harrow Way
Basingstoke, Hants RG22 4BJ
Fax: (44) 1256-817988

United States
Langenscheidt Publishers, Inc.
46–35 54th Road, Maspeth, NY 11378
Fax: (1) 718 784-0640

Canada
Thomas Allen & Son Ltd
390 Steelcase Road East
Markham, Ontario L3R 1G2
Fax: (1) 905 475 6747

Australia
Universal Press
1 Waterloo Road
Macquarie Park, NSW 2113
Fax: (61) 2 9888 9074

New Zealand
Hema Maps New Zealand Ltd (HNZ)
Unit D, 24 Ra ORA Drive
East Tamaki, Auckland
Fax: (64) 9 273 6479

Worldwide
**Apa Publications GmbH & Co.
Verlag KG (Singapore branch)**
38 Joo Koon Road, Singapore 628990
Tel: (65) 865-1600. Fax: (65) 861-6438

Printing

Insight Print Services (Pte) Ltd
38 Joo Koon Road, Singapore 628990
Tel: (65) 865-1600. Fax: (65) 861-6438

©2001 Apa Publications GmbH & Co.
Verlag KG (Singapore branch)
All Rights Reserved

First Edition 1985
Fourth Edition 2001

CONTACTING THE EDITORS

Please alert us to errors or out-
dated information by writing to:
**Insight Guides, P.O. Box 7910,
London SE1 1WE, England.**
Fax: (44) 20 7403-0290.
insight@apaguide.demon.co.uk

www.insightguides.com

This guidebook combines the interests and enthusiasms of two of the world's best known information providers: Insight Guides, whose titles have set the standard for visual travel guides since 1970, and Discovery Channel, the world's premier source of nonfiction television programming.

Insight Guides provide both practical advice and a broad understanding of a destination's history, culture, institutions and people. Discovery Channel and its Web site, www.discovery.com, help millions of viewers explore their world from the comfort of their own homes while also encouraging them to explore it first hand.

This fully revised and updated edition of *Insight Guide: New York State* is carefully structured to convey an understanding of New York's many varied regions as well as to guide readers through its sights and activities. Photographs are chosen not only to illustrate the major attractions of the state, but also to present a vivid portrait of New York's many faces and seasonal mood swings.

◆ The **Features** section, indicated by a yellow bar at the top of each page, covers the history and culture of the state in a series of informative essays written by experts.

◆ The main **Places** section, indicated by a blue bar, is a complete guide to the sights and areas worth seeking out. Places of special

EXPLORE YOUR WORLD

interest are coordinated by number with the maps.

◆ The **Travel Tips** listings section, with an orange bar, provides a handy point of reference for information on travel, hotels, shops, restaurants and more. An index to the section is on the back flap, which also serves as a bookmark.

The contributors

An experienced team of writers and editors was assembled to rewrite and expand the previous edition of the book. Managing editor **Donna Dailey**, an experienced American travel journalist, coordinated and supervised the project at Insight Guides' London editorial office, and wrote the essay on New York Food. Freelance travel editor **Zoë Ross** worked with her on the guide.

Writer and photographer **Mary Ann Lynch**, a Saratoga native, divides her time between New York City and upstate New York. She writes on popular culture, the arts, travel and indigenous peoples. For this book, she wrote the Capital-Saratoga chapter, the features on Artists and Writers and The Melting Pot, the picture stories on the Erie Canal and New York Festivals, and the various section introductions. Several of her photographs also appear in these pages.

Bill and Kay Scheller are a husband-and-wife travel writing team who have also written *Insight Pocket Guide: New England*. For this volume, Kay contributed the chapters on Long Island, the Hudson River Valley, the Catskills, the Adirondacks, and the Thousand Islands/ St Lawrence Seaway, and also compiled Travel Tips. Bill wrote the features on Flora and Fauna, Spectator Sports, and Architecture, The Great Outdoors and the chapters on New York History.

Christiane Bird, a former travel writer for the *New York Daily News*, is based in the city and has written several guides and travel books. For this book, she provided the chapters on Central-Leatherstocking, Finger Lakes, Greater Niagara and Chautauqua-Allegheny.

The chapters on New York City were taken from *Insight Guide: New York City*, edited by **Martha Ellen Zenfell**. **Louisa Campbell** wrote the essay on Man and Nature. Dropping Names was written by **Benjamin C. Swett**. Of Cows and Men was written by **Peter K. Mitchell**.

The book was proofread by **Lisa Cussans** and indexed by **Isobel McLean**.

Map Legend

—⸱⸱—	International Boundary
——	State Boundary
— — —	County Boundary
—⸱—	National Park/Reserve
— — —	Ferry Route
Ⓜ	Subway
✈ ✈	Airport: International/ Regional
🚌	Bus Station
ⓘ	Tourist Information
✉	Post Office
✝ † ⸸	Church/Ruins
†	Monastery
☾	Mosque .
✡	Synagogue
🏰	Castle/Ruins
∴	Archeological Site
∩	Cave
1	Statue/Monument
★	Place of Interest

The main places of interest in the Places section are coordinated by number with a full-color map (e.g. ❶), and a symbol at the top of every right-hand page tells you where to find the map.

CONTENTS

Autumn gold on
Gore Mountain

Travel Tips

Insight on ...

Information panels

Places

THE EMPIRE STATE

New York City may be the shiny Big Apple, but it's only a

small part of the orchard that calls itself the Empire State

New York State is an aggregate of American culture, from its largest metropolis to its rural roots. Like the nation itself, the city of New York has illuminated the hopes and dreams of countless millions. From all over the world they continue to come, entering the state at its southern tip. Universally known as the Gateway to America, the city is also the doorway into the 50,000 square miles (130,000 sq km) that lie beyond.

In the city, the code words are "speed" and "change." Expect everything to go fast and for little to be the way it was last month, last year, or even yesterday. Adrenalin flowing, some head for skyscraper views, the teeming streets of Chinatown, or the frenzied floor of the Stock Exchange. Others may savor bargaining with sidewalk vendors or indulging in a sumptuous meal in a Tribeca bistro or East Side hotel. For a slower pace, there is a surprising amount of acreage devoted to nature, from Staten Island's outdoor preserve to the Bronx's Wave Hill estate. You can also wander, in Greenwich Village's historic enclaves or through the latest exhibit at your museum of choice. Then, jammed shoulder-to-shoulder, you can enjoy the struggle to your seat at Yankee Stadium, Madison Square Garden, or Lincoln Center. The city exhilarates in its extremes. Created by Dutch merchants as a business venture, its defining elements are still its commercial matrices and their transformative nature. People move to New York to reinvent themselves. Others come for the spectacle.

Just as the city unfolds in neighborhoods, so, too, the state comprises distinctive regions. The geographic distance between places, and in particular, from big cities to remote outposts, determines much about the pace, quality, and appeal of everyday life. Away from the metropolitan furor, regional pockets are defined by distinctive character and local ways. Tales (some of them tall) of intrigue and idealism, of utopian reformers and industrial tycoons, of dairy farmers and madcap aviators, of lumberjacks of colossal strength and courageous Indian maidens, weave their spells in small towns like Greenfield Center and cities with literary and classical names, like Ithaca, Syracuse, and Troy. Historic architecture abounds, from Albany's Empire State Plaza, to pastel gingerbread cottages, to haunted Revolutionary-era homes.

Year-round there are sports, festivals, parades, and celebrations. You can also tour outstanding museums and institutions, climb an Adirondack peak, see Revolutionary War battles reenacted, or luxuriate in a mineral bath. Sample New York State's bounty in every season, and then return for more.   ❑

PRECEDING PAGES: a walk in the woods; minding the country store; wine-tasting in upstate New York; Radio City's world-famous Rockettes.
LEFT: autumn glory in the Empire State.

MAN AND NATURE

Geological activity has shaped New York State's whole outlook, from its natural borders to its naturally inspired industries

N ew York State's topography has always played a vital role in the area's destiny. The superb array of natural features has forged the lifestyles of the local inhabitants, from the Iroquois in the 14th century to the entrepreneurs who strut their 21st-century stuff. The Indians controlled the region by commanding its natural pathways, atop ridges, as well as beside streams and rivers. The white men soon exploited the same paths and made highways on top of the old, well-worn Indian trails. The natural borders of New York, formed by mountains, lakes and rivers, barricaded the area from Canada and neighboring states and gave New York a self-contained political identity. Today New York's borders embrace close to 50,000 sq miles (130,000 sq km) and as many as 18 million inhabitants.

Waterways

New York's waterways take much credit for the state's prosperity. Indeed, the splendor of the Hudson River's burnished palisades – 400 rocky feet (120 meters) in height – led the explorer Henry Hudson to hope that, at last, this was the passage to the Orient. On sailing upriver, he found a wide tidal way, which the Indians called "the river that flows both ways."

The Hudson River is navigable by ocean-going vessels as far as Albany, 155 miles (250 km) upstream. This remarkable penetration of the interior gave the Albany Dutch, perching on the edge of Iroquois fur country, imperious command of the trade. In later times the river made the town of Hudson, only 20 miles (30 km) downstream from Albany, one of New York's most important whaling centers.

Wars for the continent were won and lost on New York's waterways. Lake Ontario, the Mohawk River, lakes George and Champlain became the battlegrounds for the French-Indian War and, a few years after, the American

Revolution. On the eve of the Revolution in 1775, a citadel was commissioned by the Continental Congress. It was called West Point and still sits at the choke point of the Hudson, where the river is narrowest. Here rebels attempted to halt British warships by floating a monstrous chain across the river.

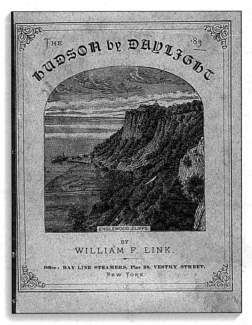

In 1815, the Hudson River was made to flow four ways, as Governor De Witt Clinton's dream was realized in the Erie Canal, a viable east-west waterway which linked the Great Lakes to the north-south flow of the Hudson. And so the heartland of America was linked to what was to become the commercial pacemaker of the modern world, New York City. New York City's many-piered harbor is the largest in North America.

Manhattan is in debt to geology for much of its prowess. The island's tough bedrock is an unusual triumvirate of rock, formed of Manhattan schist, layered above Inwoodmarble, atop a base of aged Fordham gneiss. This

---

LEFT: Indian Pass was once thought to be the source of the Hudson River.
RIGHT: Hudson River travel guide, 1883.

bedrock is extraordinarily sturdy and so can anchor Manhattan's many skyscrapers, the most prominent symbol of the city.

Glaciers and mountains

New York State owes much of its magnificent topography to the most recent of four glaciers that have blanketed North America in the last half a million years. As the ice crashed down from the north, it dragged with it greater and greater quantities of rock and other debris. The glacier worked like a giant scouring pad, gouging lakes and creating drumlins, the distinctive elongated hills of western New York.

summits bear witness to the glacier, which deposited the first spores for the subarctic plants, shrubs, and lichen which now grow. While the very stuff of the Adirondacks is some of the oldest on the continent – the crystalline anorthosite is more than 1 billion years old – the mountains themselves are remarkably young. The most recent theory holds that these mountains have existed for a mere 10 million years, a tenure in geologic time not much longer than man's. The Adirondacks were uplifted over a hot spot of molten rock, and they still continue to grow at a rate much faster than the erosion that wears them down.

Before the glacier carved its pass, Long Island Sound, the body of water which separates Long Island from the mainland, was a river valley. The ancient river ran between Connecticut and what then wasn't an island at all but merely an extension of the New England coastal shelf. The deep harbors of Long Island's north shore mark the pre-glacial valleys of the river's tributaries. The glacier lifted and pushed forward topsoil and soft bedrock, in turn creating moraines or ridges, such as the Huntington Hills in Long Island, as it subsided.

In the north of the state, the Adirondacks High Peaks reach heights of more than 4,000 ft (1,200 meters). Above the timber line, their

Other mountains of New York are far older. Consider the Taconics. Some 445 million years ago, the Taconics slipped away from their parent mountains, the Berkshires. (Accepted since the 1960s, the theory of plate tectonics holds that the earth's topography is formed by perpetual drift of subterranean plates. The plates move on molten fluid close to the core of the earth and act as rafts on which the continents and ocean float and occasionally collide.) The Taconics separated from the Berkshires at the same time as the African and North American plates clashed. So sounded the beginning of the great Appalachian upheaval, which formed a chain of mega-mountains.

Besides this giant mountain range, the Appalachian upheaval caused the upward thrust of the Appalachian Plateau, of which the Catskills form a part. These hills rise off the west of the Hudson for 30 miles (48 km). The Indians called the hills Onteora – "land in the sky."

Water-covered land

This upheaval transformed New York from a rolling plain, traversed by lazy rivers. At the time of this tremendous geological event, New York and

WATER WORSHIP

The Finger Lakes were holy to the Iroquois. Their unique form was evidence that the Six Nations were chosen people; Iroquois myth holds that the lakes were created by the handprint of the Great Spirit.

Appalachian Plateau, smashing 3,000 ft (900 meters) of moving ice into the river valleys and scooping out U-shaped grooves that became the Finger Lakes when the ice melted. The depths reached by these narrow lakes are amazing: the maximal sounding of the deepest, Seneca, is 634 ft (193 meters). Even this figure does not fully represent the depths of the impenetrable glacial debris on the seafloor.

As the glacier dug lakes in western New York, it left valleys hanging as high as 600 ft

much of the north-central United States were deep beneath the Paleozoic Sea. The fossil-laden sediments of this ancient sea, many miles thick, comprise much of New York's bedrock south of the Adirondacks. The sediment gives insight into New York's earliest life forms, from plants to fish, animals, reptiles, and insects.

The glacier left its signature in the Finger Lakes. Originally river valleys, the lakes were dug well below sea level by the relentless icy thrust. Here the glacier met the ridge of the

LEFT: the original inhabitants of the Upper Hudson.
ABOVE: the first picture of Niagara Falls, *circa* 1679, drawn by the French missionary Louis Hennepin.

(180 meters) above the lakes' level. The streams of the valley, too, were left hanging and had to wind down steep routes to find their level. So came about the fabulous waterfalls and gorges that texture western New York.

But the greatest waterfall of all, Niagara (Iroquois for "thunder of the waters"), is a product of more recent history, created as it was by a small river split from its parent. The rebel river became the American Falls, the original Horseshoe Falls. Around AD 1300, Indians stood in awe of this incredible parting of the waters. The birth of Niagara signified the beginnings of a struggle between man and land which would mold New York State. ❏

Decisive Dates

INDIANS AND COLONISTS: AD 1300–1776

AD **1300** Native American tribes known as the Iroquois Confederation occupy the region now known as New York State.

1524 The Italian navigator Giovanni da Verrazano - discovers New York harbor.

1609 Henry Hudson, an Englishman in the employ of the Dutch, sails his ship *Half Moon* into New York harbor and explores Hudson River; French explorer Samuel de Champlain, the first European to enter

New York from the north, travels on Lake Champlain.

1614 Hendrick Christiaensen builds a trading post he calls Fort Nassau, near site of present-day Albany.

1617 Dutch build Fort Orange, replacing Fort Nassau, on the west bank of the Hudson in the Albany vicinity.

1621 Dutch West Indies Company takes authority over the "New Netherland" colony along the Hudson River.

1624 Dutch colonists arrive at Fort Orange.

1625 Dutch first settle on Manhattan Island.

1626 Dutch governor Peter Minuit purchases Manhattan Island from the Iroquois in exchange for goods worth (according to legend) $24.

1629 The Dutch West Indies Company institutes the patroon system, offering large land grants to members who settle colonists on their estates.

1640 Dutch settlements on Long Island.

1643 English settlement at Hempstead, Long Island, as England presses claim to New Netherland.

1646 Jesuit missionary Father Isaac Jogues martyred by Mohawks near present-day Auriesville.

1647 Peter Stuyvesant appointed director general of New Netherland.

1653 New Amsterdam's "burgher" government is the first city government in the future United States.

1664 King Charles II of England includes New Netherland in grant to the Duke of York; Peter Stuyvesant surrenders New Netherland to the English; the colony becomes the Province of New York.

1673 A Dutch fleet briefly recaptures New York.

1674 The Treaty of Westminster secures English possession of New York and New Jersey.

1678 French build Fort Niagara, near Buffalo.

1679 Father Louis Hennepin, a French priest, is the first European to visit Niagara Falls.

1683 New York is formally established as a British colony; first provincial assembly elected.

1688 French Huguenot refugees settle New Rochelle.

1709 Palatine German emigrants begin settling in the Hudson Valley.

1755–63 French and Indian War leads to French defeat by the English.

1770–5 The Green Mountain Boys, under leadership of Ethan Allen, defy New York's claims to Vermont.

1775–83 The American Revolution results in English losing control of the American colonies.

INDEPENDENCE AND CONSTRUCTION: 1776–1900

1776 New York ratifies Declaration of Independence; New York City occupied by British forces.

1783 British evacuate New York City; Washington enters the city and delivers his farewell to his officers at Fraunces Tavern.

1788 New York ratifies the US Constitution.

1789 George Washington inaugurated as first US president in New York City, during city's brief period as the nation's capital.

1792 A group of 24 brokers form the New York Stock Exchange under a buttonwood tree on Wall Street.

1794 British withdraw from western New York under terms of the Jay Treaty.

1796 British evacuate Fort Niagara; first "salt well" dug near present-day Syracuse.

1797 New York State legislature appoints Albany the state's permanent capital.

1802 US Military Academy opens at West Point.

1807 Robert Fulton experiments with steamboat *Clermont* on the Hudson River.

1810 Township of Buffalo is established.

1812–4 Buffalo burned by the British; naval Battle of Lake Champlain; Americans defeat British fleet.

1817 Construction of the Erie Canal begins.

1823 Joseph Smith, a farm youth living near Palmyra, experiences the first of the visions that result in publication of the *Book of Mormon* and founding of the Church of Jesus Christ of Latter-Day Saints.

1825 Completion of the Erie Canal connects New York with the Great Lakes via the Hudson River.

1831 Mohawk and Hudson Railroad inaugurates rail service in New York State.

1848 First American Womens' Rights Convention held at Seneca Falls.

1863 Draft riots in New York City and Troy protest conscription into Union Army during the Civil War.

1867 "Commodore" Cornelius Vanderbilt acquires full control of the New York Central Railroad and forms a statewide rail colossus.

1871 William Marcy "Boss" Tweed, head of corrupt New York City politics for more than a decade, is arrested and removed from power.

1874 The Chautauqua program of adult education and wholesome entertainment is launched.

1880 George Eastman, a Rochester clerk, begins manufacturing photographic dry plates.

1883 The Brooklyn Bridge connects the municipalities of New York and Brooklyn.

1884 Grover Cleveland, governor of New York, elected president of the US.

1888 George Eastman introduces his Kodak camera.

1892 Adirondack State Park established.

1898 The City of New York merges with Brooklyn.

THE MODERN ERA: 1900 ONWARD

1901 President William McKinley shot dead by an anarchist while visiting Pan-American Exposition in Buffalo; Vice-President Theodore Roosevelt, former New York governor, is sworn in as president at Buffalo.

1911 Fire at the Triangle Shirtwaist Factory kills 150 workers in New York City's Greenwich Village, leading to reforms of sweatshop employment practices.

1920s "Harlem Renaissance" of African-American writers, composers, and artists in New York City.

1929 October crash of New York Stock Exchange foreshadows the Great Depression.

1932 New York Governor Franklin D. Roosevelt elected president of the US.

1933 Fiorello LaGuardia is elected mayor of New York City; the reformer serves three four-year terms.

PRECEDING PAGES: Fort George, mid-18th century.
LEFT: the New York State seal reflects its history.
RIGHT: making music at Woodstock.

1939–40 New York City hosts World's Fair at Flushing Meadows, Queens.

1954–9 Construction of St Lawrence Seaway.

1964–5 Second New York World's Fair.

Mid-1960s New York overtaken by California as most populous state.

1966 Demolition of Pennsylvania Station, New York City, galvanizes historic preservation movement.

1968 Students protesting local university policies and Vietnam War take control of Columbia University campus; rioting in Harlem follows assassination of Rev. Martin Luther King.

1969 "Stonewall riot" following a police raid on gay bar in New York City launches Gay Rights Movement;

Woodstock Festival draws an estimated 500,000 fans to three-day rock concert in Bethel.

Mid-1970s New York City reorganizes finances after approaching bankruptcy.

1980s Upturn in New York City real-estate market drives meteoric career of developer Donald Trump.

1987 Stock market crash tarnishes "Yuppie Decade."

1994 Election of George E. Pataki as governor ends 12-year incumbency of Democrat Mario Cuomo.

1990s Drop in New York City crime rate; Republican Mayor Rudolph Giuliani credits "get tough" policies.

2000 Record crowd in Times Square, New York City, peacefully welcomes new Millennium.

2001 Former First Lady Hillary Rodham Clinton sworn in as New York State Senator. ❏

NATIVES AND COLONISTS

After hundreds of years successfully trading in the region, the Native American Iroquois lost their homeland to the Dutch, and then the English

The history of human habitation in New York State begins with the penetration of hunting and gathering tribes into the region during the millennia that followed the retreat of the last Ice Age glaciers. Tracing a sophisticated succession of tools, weapons, and other artifacts, archeologists have documented the presence of Archaic, Laurentian, Mound Builder, and Algonquian peoples, of whom all except the Algonquian had disappeared before the arrival of European explorers and settlers. But the masters of New York at the time of the white man's initial appearance were the tribes affiliated with the Iroquois Confederation.

The Iroquois

Tribes belonging to the Iroquoian language group had come to dominate the future New York State region by AD 1300. Sometime during the late 16th century, five of these tribes – the Mohawks, Oneidas, Onondagas, Cayugas, and Senecas – organized what became known as the League of the Iroquois, or the Five Nations. Bound by an agreement not to wage war with other tribes of the confederation, each of the Five Nations sent chiefs, or *sachems*, to meet in council every summer. Although their unity of purpose and political sophistication have sometimes been exaggerated, the Iroquois were clever enough at the art of politics to keep peace among themselves as they overwhelmed their Algonquian rivals. They were fierce warriors, and by the middle of the 17th century they dominated the New York region. The Five Nations became Six in the 1720s as they were joined by the Tuscaroras, Iroquoian speakers who had migrated north.

The Iroquois penchant for organization extended to their village life. Calling themselves *Hodenosaune*, "people of the long houses," the Iroquois lived in palisaded communities made up of a number of these long,

rectangular, bark-sheathed structures. Each longhouse was inhabited by a group of families related through the female line. Iroquois society, despite the vaunted prowess of its male warriors, had a largely matriarchal structure. The oldest woman – and therefore leader – in each longhouse family group appointed male

representatives to tribal and League councils. Men fought and hunted, women farmed and managed their villages' day-to-day activities. Iroquois fields yielded 15 varieties of corn and more than 50 types of bean.

The Europeans arrive

The first documented European visitor to the territory that eventually became New York was the Italian navigator Giovanni da Verrazano, who in 1524 sailed through the Narrows between Long and Staten islands and entered one of the world's finest natural harbors. (The beautiful Verrazano-Narrows suspension bridge connecting the two islands commemorates his

---

LEFT: a warrior of the Iroquois Confederation, which dominated the area that became New York State.
RIGHT: Italian explorer Giovanni da Verrazano.

achievement.) Verrazano's voyage did not lead to land explorations or territorial claims, however, and the region remained unvisited by other Europeans for almost another century.

Then, within two months of each other in 1609, two intrepid explorers came to New York from different directions, under different flags. Henry Hudson was an English navigator sailing for the Dutch. Piloting his ship, the *Half Moon,* through the waters briefly visited by Verrazano, Hudson ventured farther into Upper New York Bay. At the tip of Manhattan Island he steered to the left and entered the broad river that emptied into the bay, attempting – like so many

Traveling on the Richelieu River, he made his way to a mountain-girt inland sea that reached for 125 miles (180 km) between the future states of New York and Vermont. He had discovered Lake Champlain.

New Netherland

The French were far too busy organizing their settlements along the St Lawrence to attempt to establish a permanent presence in New York during the years that followed Champlain's exploration. By contrast, the Netherlands was quick to react to the possibilities afforded by Hudson's discoveries.

explorers of his era – to find an easy Northwest Passage to the Orient and its riches. Disappointed as the waterway narrowed toward its distant source, Hudson turned the *Half Moon* around and returned to Holland. But the legacy of his voyage was a Dutch claim on the lands around that magnificent harbor, and the discovery of the Hudson River.

Meanwhile the "Father of New France" was pressing south from the St Lawrence River valley. Samuel de Champlain, the greatest of the French explorers of the New World, was, like Hudson, on an adventure that would result in his name being attached to one of North America's most storied bodies of water.

In 1621, the Dutch West Indies Company was established to exploit the resources of the territory they called "New Netherland" – in particular, the lucrative trade in beaver pelts throughout the Hudson River watershed. Like the French on the St Lawrence Seaway (and in contrast to the English settlers of New England), the Dutch were at first more interested in commerce than in colonization. They had already established trading posts in the vicinity of present-day Albany, in 1614 and 1617. The Dutch entrepreneurs would use these posts as bartering stations at which they could trade blankets, knives, kettles, and firearms for the furs brought to them by the Iroquois.

The West Indies Company did launch a program of colonization, although on a limited scale. In 1624, the company sent 30 families, mostly Walloons from present-day Belgium, to New Netherland. Eighteen of these families went to Fort Orange, the Albany outpost, thus founding the first permanent settlement in New York. (The other 12 families settled at a southern New Jersey location.) A year later, another contingent of Dutch settlers landed. The chosen spot was the southern tip of the narrow, wooded island which Henry Hudson had discovered at the mouth of his great river. Surrounded by the calm, protected waters of one of the world's

fledgling colony. Government was inept at best (Washington Irving's caricatures of early administrators in his *History of New York* had their basis in fact) and repressive at worst. Taxes were heavy, the laws on individual trading enterprises restrictive. The company's social policy was nonexistent; education and care of the needy were left to the Dutch Reformed Church.

Other European influences

Although well established throughout the Hudson Valley by the middle of the 17th century, the Dutch were not the only colonial power

great natural harbors, the little village, named New Amsterdam, was never inhabited by more than a few thousand people during the days of the Dutch colony. But it was destined to become the city of New York.

New Amsterdam showed very little of the dynamism for which the future metropolis would be renowned. The Dutch West Indies Company was interested in siphoning fur trade profits directly to old Amsterdam, and not in the social and economic development of the

LEFT: Henry Hudson (left) with his English compatriot and fellow explorer Sir Martin Frobisher.
ABOVE: a Dutch-Native American trade deal.

MANHATTAN PURCHASE

It was in 1626 that Peter Minuit, the director general of New Netherland, made his now famous purchase of Manhattan Island from the Iroquois, paying them with an assortment of goods said to be worth just $24. The Indians – many of whom lived in what is now New Jersey – were probably not sorry to lose the mosquito-infested rocky territory. Of course nobody can assign a modern-day value to the assortment of blankets, axes, kettles, and trinkets that Minuit handed over to the Indians. But whatever they were worth, the small sum has multiplied incalculably into one of the most fabulous real-estate deals in world history.

active in the region in that era. To the south, in what was to become New Jersey, they were harassed by a short-lived Swedish colony. To the north, French fur traders and missionaries followed in the footsteps of Champlain, hoping to extend their hegemony to the south of the St Lawrence Valley. This was not easy, as the French had incurred the wrath of the Iroquois Confederation when Champlain, eager to show solidarity with the Algonquin, had shot and killed two Iroquois chiefs.

The bravest of the 17th-century French adventurers were the Jesuit missionaries who risked their lives to bring Christianity to the Iroquois. The most celebrated of these "Black Robes," Father Isaac Jogues, was captured and tortured by the Indians at their village of Osser-nenon, near Auriesville, in 1642. Rescued by the Dutch at Fort Orange, Father Jogues returned to France but eventually made his way back to Ossernenon, where he and a companion were killed by tomahawks in October 1646. In 1930, Jogues and seven other Jesuits martyred by the Iroquois were canonized by the Roman Catholic Church *(see page 254).*

The most formidable threat to the Dutch colony of New Netherland, however, was the English presence in the northeast. The Dutch

AMERICAN FEUDALISM

To encourage cultivation of the Hudson Valley, the Dutch West Indies Company instituted the patroon (patron) system in 1629. This was a scheme by which any company stockholder agreeing to sponsor at least 50 settlers within four years would receive a large land grant in the valley.

The Dutch "patroonships" were vast beyond almost any landholdings the US has seen, short of a few southwestern ranches. They could extend for 16 miles (20 km) along one side of the river, or 8 miles (12 km) along both banks. And they could incorporate land 10 miles (16 km) east or west. Of six patroonships originally granted, only one remained viable by 1635 – Rensselaerwyck, so named by an Amsterdam jeweler, Kilaen van Rensselaer, who held his patent without ever crossing the Atlantic. He had his agents buy adjacent property and attach it to the original holding, so that his personal fiefdom soon exceeded the acreage nominally allowed. This private colony survived the American Revolution, and a large part of it became the possession of Robert Livingston – the same Livingston who helped draft the Declaration of Independence and backed Robert Fulton's experiments with the steamboat *Clermont* (which was named after Livingston's estate). Livingston was, in his way, a patroon of the new technology that changed the face of the Hudson River and valley.

had established their first settlement on Long Island in 1640, but three years later, emigrants from New England had established themselves at Hempstead. By 1650 the English presence was so strong that the Dutch East Indies Company's Peter Stuyvesant had to cede all of Long Island east of Oyster Bay to Connecticut.

England takes over

The noose around New Netherland was tightening, and its fate was sealed in 1664 when King Charles II of England granted all of the

RURAL TO RUNDOWN

Peter Stuyvesant's rural retreat in New York City is commemorated in the name of a far-from-bucolic street and district, the Bowery.

and he could not muster New Amsterdam's burghers to fight off the English invaders. The Dutch were ready to cast their lot with England, and Nicolls won the day.

So New Netherland became the English Province of New York. The terms of surrender were remarkably generous: Dutch land titles remained in effect, religious freedom was assured, and communities were permitted to elect governing boards and constables. Even Stuyvesant must have found England's terms amenable: he returned to New York in 1667 to

land between the Connecticut River and Delaware Bay to his brother James, Duke of York and Albany. Later that year, the king sent a fleet commanded by Colonel Richard Nicolls to take possession of the duke's new property, which included all of New Netherland. Nicolls entered what would thereafter be named New York harbor in September 1664.

Director General Peter Stuyvesant, who had run the Dutch colony since 1647, was an unpopular figure because of his dictatorial rule,

FAR LEFT: early Dutch colonists arrive in Manhattan.
LEFT: English settlers receive the keys to Manhattan.
ABOVE: New Amsterdam, 1650.

live out the remaining five years of his life at his farm, or *bouwerij*, on the northern fringes of a town which still clung to the southernmost tip of Manhattan Island. Other 17th-century place names also survive in the metropolis. Wall Street, for example, follows the outline of the old Dutch wall at New Amsterdam's northern limits.

The Dutch made one last attempt to regain their former colony, during a war with England in 1673. But the following year's Treaty of Westminster finally secured English rule. As part of the treaty's terms, the Dutch were given sovereignty over several Caribbean islands, which they possess to this day. ❑

THE AMERICAN REVOLUTION

The 18th century was a time of bitter conflict in the American colonies.

New York joined the struggles against the French and then the British

Despite the English takeover *(see page 29)*, Dutch customs, local institutions, and even the Dutch language survived throughout southeastern New York for many years. But the late 17th century saw the province fall in line with English patterns of colonial organization – and protest.

Like neighboring New England, New York chafed under the governorship of Sir Edmund Andros, who served as the representative of King Charles II from 1674 to 1681. Worse still, King James II (1685–8) revoked the colonies' independent charters and attempted to form a unified "Dominion of New England," including New York and New Jersey.

Dissatisfaction with such centralized administration led to a middle-class rebellion, which put power in the hands of one Jacob Leisler, a New York City merchant. After two years, Leisler was removed from power and hanged, but the tension between royal governors and elected assemblies remained a fact of life in New York, as it was in the other colonies.

Antagonism with New France

In the late 17th century and the first half of the 18th century, New York was caught up in the struggle for hegemony in North America between England (properly called Great Britain after the 1707 union with Scotland) and France. New York was crucial to this long and sporadic conflict, not only due to its central location and long border with French territory along the St Lawrence River and Great Lakes, but as a result of its strategic inland waterways.

Lake Champlain, which still forms the state's eastern border with Vermont, was a dagger thrust south from Canada into the very heart of the British colonies. In conjunction with Lake George and the Hudson River, it provided a very tempting avenue for invaders. So, too, did the Mohawk River, the traditional fur-trade

LEFT: volunteers stage a contemporary reenactment of the Revolutionary War.
RIGHT: George Washington, "father of the country."

waterway that slices across central New York. Whichever nation controlled these waterways would be well on its way to domination of the American northeast.

During the opening phase of British-French hostilities, the eight-year struggle (1689–97) known as King William's War, New Yorkers

were able to secure the loyalty of the Iroquois Confederacy, thanks to the long-smoldering animosity between the Iroquois and the French *(see page 28)*. Nevertheless, the French and their own Indian allies struck south to destroy Schenectady in 1690. In retaliation, New York joined with Connecticut and Maryland to launch what proved to be an unsuccessful expedition against Montréal.

The 1697 Treaty of Ryswyck not only ended King William's War, it ushered in an era of open cooperation between French and Anglo-Dutch merchants. The waterways that linked Albany and Montréal could, after all, serve as avenues of trade as well as invasion. Commerce in beaver pelts and other items moved along so briskly that when war between the two powers broke out again in 1702, New Englanders protested that their French-Indian enemies had been sold arms by Albany entrepreneurs loyal only to their ledger books. Many New Yorkers felt less threatened by New France than did the townspeople and farmers of New England.

But New York wasn't as secure as it liked to think, nor was it assured of the permanent loyalty of the Iroquois. Peace

> ### DUTCH LEGACY
>
> The Dutch influence can be seen in words common to the region – such as "stoop" (the front steps of a row house), "cruller" (a fried cake like a doughnut), and "cookie" – and hundreds of place names.

The French and Indian War

The French and Indian War of 1754–63 marked the final struggle for dominance in North America. By this time, the reliability of the Iroquois' anti-French position could not be taken for granted. French diplomacy had succeeded in securing the allegiance of the Senecas, and the remaining pro-British tribes were at best lukewarm in their support and at worst neutral.

The French and Indian War, much of which was fought within New York State, did not

came again with the Treaty of Utrecht in 1713, which ended Queen Anne's War. But over the next 30 years, the French entrenched themselves around the northern and western perimeters of New York with the construction of forts at Niagara, between Lakes Ontario and Erie, and at Crown Point on Lake Champlain. All through that era, New Yorkers traded with the French, often alienating the Indians by bypassing their traditional, fur-trading middlemen role. During King George's War (1744–8), New York leaned toward neutrality rather than outright solidarity with the New England colonies. New Yorkers did, however, contribute men to an abortive attack on Canada in 1746.

begin well for the British. In 1755, British forces failed in their attempts to take the French forts at Niagara and Crown Point. In the following year, the French seized Oswego on Lake Ontario, and the "Great Carrying Place," a key portage point on the Mohawk River at the future site of the city of Rome. With France thus firmly in control of New York's northern waterways, most of the Iroquois kept to a policy of strict neutrality. The exception was the Mohawks, who remained loyal to the British.

In summer 1758 the British failed to take the French Lake Champlain redoubt of Fort Ticonderoga, but by late August British forces had captured Fort Frontenac (today's Kingston on the Canadian shore of Lake Ontario), and soon after, Fort Stanwix at Rome. At this point, the wily Iroquois resumed support of the British.

Ticonderoga, Crown Point, Niagara, and Oswego all fell to the British in 1759. (The same year the French lost their fortress city of Quebec in the famous battle on the Plains of Abraham.) In 1760, following his victory at La Galette (later Ogdensburg, New York), British commander Lord Jeffrey Amherst accepted the surrender of New France. All Canada was now ceded to Great Britain and the menace of French colonials had vanished. The Indians, too, ceased to be a problem. Thirteen tribes,

Uncertainty over relations with the French and Indians kept the population from spreading far from the traditional areas of settlement along the Hudson Valley and in New York City, although there was some penetration of the Mohawk Valley by the mid-18th century. Some 10 years before the Revolution, frontier communities had been established no farther than 40 miles (65 km) north of Albany and 80 miles (130 km) to the west.

Today's Americans, accustomed as they are to New York's perennial rank among the most populous states in the US (it ranked first until the 1960s, when it was overtaken by California,

formerly allies of the French, signed a treaty with Britain at Detroit in 1761. Seven years later, the Treaty of Fort Stanwix provided for the handover of all Indian lands east of a line drawn south from Rome.

The progress of settlement

In the century that passed between the English takeover of New Netherland and the American Revolution, settlement in New York largely followed the pattern established under Dutch rule.

LEFT: a vicious battle in the French and Indian War.
ABOVE: New York colonists fight off British troops in the opening rounds of the Revolutionary War.

AN IMMIGRANT STATE

By the time of the American Revolution, New York State had already established a reputation as a haven in which immigrants from a number of different ethnic backgrounds had founded thriving farms, towns and the basis for a future metropolis. Aside from the original Dutch and English strains, there were Scottish and Scots-Irish settlers in the Hudson Valley; French Huguenots in New Paltz and New Rochelle; and a considerable number of Germans in New York City and throughout the Hudson, Mohawk, and Schoharie valleys. Even in these early colonial times, New York was beginning to display the ethnic diversity that would later become its hallmark.

then Texas), are often surprised to learn that it was by no means the most heavily populated colony. In 1670, there were approximately 5,800 New Yorkers; by 1770, that number had increased to 163,000. But over the same period, the population of the smaller Massachusetts colony rose from 35,000 to 235,000. As late as 1760, New York ranked seventh in population out of 13 colonies; and Boston and Philadelphia were more important ports than New York City.

Aside from the French and Indian threat, one of the brakes on population expansion was the survival of the old Dutch manorial system in the Hudson Valley. Most of the owners of these

vast manors, holdovers from the patroon system *(see page 28)*, leased their land to small farmers, and not to new settlers who wished to establish themselves as landowners.

Reluctant revolt

Like Great Britain's other American colonies, New York honed its revolutionary sensibilities in a series of struggles between crown-appointed governors and its locally elected provincial assembly. As elsewhere, these struggles centered upon what were perceived as unjust taxes. To the British, these levies attempted to recover some of the expense of the wars with France. But to the colonies, taxes such as those imposed under the Stamp Act, Sugar Act, and the Townshend Duties amounted to "taxation without representation." New York refused to comply.

When the port of Boston was closed by Britain under the "Intolerable Acts," colonial activists called for what became known as the First Continental Congress and agreed to suspend trade with Britain until their grievances were addressed. New York sent delegates to the congress but did not sign the agreement. Nor did it send delegates to the Second Continental Congress. The hesitation was due to its large number of conservatives, who were unsympathetic to the New England firebrands. When war broke out, New York had the most sizable contingent of Loyalists. Between 30,000 and 40,000 New Yorkers went into exile during and after the Revolution, predominantly to Canada, many leaving behind considerable fortunes.

New York could not help being drawn into the revolutionary vortex. In May 1775 a

WALTER BUTLER: BUTCHER OF THE REVOLUTION

One of the most reviled figures in the lore of the American Revolution was Walter Butler (*circa* 1752–81), scion of one of the largest landowning families in the Mohawk Valley prior to the war. Though Butler was a Loyalist, his reputation stems not from his political persuasion but from his participation in several notorious guerrilla raids along the Mohawk. In 1778, Loyalist and Mohawk Indian bands laid waste to several valley settlements. The most lethal was led by Butler and the Mohawk chief Joseph Brant who, with a force of 700 Tories and Indians, razed the village of Cherry Valley on November 11, 1778, killing 32 men, women, and children along with 16 soldiers.

Butler was held accountable for the raid, and for attacks in which he was not even present: it was anathema for a white man to join with the Indians and turn on his own kind. Some evidence suggests that Butler tried to restrain the Mohawks from butchering civilians. After the Cherry Valley massacre, he supposedly swore to desist from participating in another raid. In October 1781 he died covering the retreat of a Loyalist contingent after a battle in Mohawk Valley. Butler's reputation was secure. When Stephen Vincent Benet wrote his short story *The Devil and Daniel Webster* more than 150 years later, he had Satan place Butler on the jury summoned from the fires of hell.

minority group within the assembly organized its own convention and appointed delegates to the Second Continental Congress. This breakaway faction, the Provincial Congress of New York, ratified the Declaration of Independence on July 9, 1776. They then framed a new state constitution, usurping power from the old assembly and bringing New York into the war.

A major battleground

Nearly a third of the Revolutionary War's 308 battles were fought in New York, and nowhere else – with the possible exception of New Jersey – did the advantage seesaw so precariously from one side to the other. The war in New York opened promisingly for the Americans, as Ethan Allen seized Fort Ticonderoga in May 1775, followed soon after by Seth Warner's capture of Crown Point. The following year, Benedict Arnold lost the Battle of Valcour Island *(see page 234)*, but managed to forestall a British naval attack on Ticonderoga.

But 1776 saw a sharp reversal of fortunes. British forces under Sir William Howe defeated General George Washington at the Battle of Long Island, opening the way for Howe's capture of New York City – a prize the British did not yield until the end of the war. Howe delivered a second blow to Washington at the Battle of White Plains in Westchester County. Washington saved his army by crossing the Hudson River from Fort Washington to Fort Lee around the site of the present George Washington Bridge. This move set the stage for his westward withdrawal across New Jersey – one of history's greatest strategic retreats.

The British plan to separate New England from the rest of the colonies by a three-pronged campaign in New York came unglued in 1777. After taking Ticonderoga, General John Burgoyne was halted in his southward march along Lake Champlain and the Hudson Valley by the defeat of two detachments at Walloomsac, New York, in the misnamed Battle of Bennington (a nearby Vermont town). Burgoyne suffered a conclusive defeat at the second Battle of Saratoga on October 7. Saratoga was a crucial turning point, as news of the American victory brought the French into the war against the

British. Two months earlier, the western thrust of the British attack was cut off in the Mohawk Valley; General Nicholas Herkimer's victory at the Battle of Oriskany was one of the bloodiest of the war *(see page 257)*. After the defeat at Saratoga, Britain's Sir Henry Clinton abandoned the southern thrust, venturing no farther north than Kingston, which he burnt down.

The remainder of the war in New York was largely a story of guerrilla-style fighting, involving Indians and Loyalists, along the western frontiers. New York was the setting for one of the war's darkest chapters. Colonel Benedict Arnold, commander of the American defenses

at West Point, planned to deliver West Point to the British, but he was foiled in 1780 when correspondence implicating him in a conspiracy with Clinton was found in the possession of Britain's Major John André. The British officer was hung as a spy at Tappan; Arnold lives on as a byword for traitor; and West Point remained in American hands *(see page 186)*.

The war was effectively ended with Lord Cornwallis's defeat at Yorktown, Virginia, in 1781, but the British evacuation of New York City did not take place until 1783. The post-Revolutionary history of New York properly begins with Washington's triumphal march into the city on November 25 of that year. ❑

LEFT: a drum roll in the course of a modern-day reenactment at Fort Ticonderoga.
RIGHT: the infamous traitor Benedict Arnold.

THE FLEISCHMANN CO.
COMPRESSED YEAST

THE AGE OF INDUSTRY

In the 19th century New York was the undoubted center of the nation in terms of industry, innovation, and style

Strategically located on the Atlantic seaboard at the heart of the new nation, the state of New York was primed to take a leading role in America's post-revolutionary economic development. Its prestige was temporarily enhanced by the choice of New York City as the nation's capital, although the capital was transferred to Philadelphia in 1790, the year after George Washington was inaugurated in New York as the first US president. (The capital moved once again, to Washington DC, in 1800.) New York's great promise, though, was centered not upon political advantage but on the geographical good fortune of its excellent harbor, connected via the Hudson River to the state's heartland.

The final elimination of the Native American threat along the state's northern and western frontiers helped to accelerate settlement of the virgin territory that lay beyond the Hudson and Mohawk river outposts. (The power of the mainly pro-British Iroquois Confederacy had been crushed after the Revolutionary War.) Rich farmland attracted immigrants, primarily from parts of New England in which arable land was already becoming scarce.

The Federal age

New York did not become the colossal metropolis familiar to Americans and visitors alike since the late 19th century for quite some time. During the years before the War of 1812, New England ports still dominated the young country's mercantile life. For New York to achieve preeminence, it had to exploit to the full not only its magnificent harbor, but also the great opportunities its geographical position offered for communication and trade with the American interior – particularly the Great Lakes.

There were also political difficulties to be ironed out. The most important question after the Revolution was whether to ratify the

Federal Constitution, a document which gave more power to the new central government than many New Yorkers felt appropriate. The farmers and small tradesmen who supported the state's first post-Revolutionary governor, George Clinton, were suspicious of a strong central power. But business interests eager for

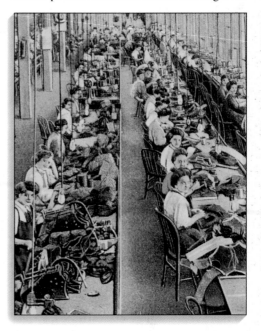

the sound trade and currency policies which they felt a central government could promote won the day. This early lobby group was led by John Jay, who became the first Chief Justice of the US Supreme Court and state governor, and Alexander Hamilton, who became George Washington's treasury secretary. New York ratified the Constitution on July 26, 1788.

As a result of its long border with Canada, New York State was a major player in the War of 1812. None of the invasions launched from the state against Canada were successful, although the Americans did cross Lake Ontario to burn York, later renamed Toronto. The British, in turn, burned Lewiston, Black Rock,

LEFT: the Fleischmann factory at Peekskill claimed to be the largest yeast factory in the world in 1916.
RIGHT: Endicott Johnson leather works, 1920.

and Buffalo. In 1814, an attack on Plattsburgh was repulsed by New Yorkers and Vermonters at the Battle of Lake Champlain.

The Erie Canal

The War of 1812 underscored the need for a more efficient means of moving goods within New York, and gave impetus to an idea which the state's most dynamic politician had long promoted. DeWitt Clinton, George Clinton's nephew, was mayor of New York City at the war's end. In this and other capacities he worked tirelessly for construction of a water link between Lake Erie and the Hudson River.

In 1817, the year he was elected governor, work finally commenced on the Erie Canal.

Completed in 1825, the Erie Canal was the first great engineering feat of the young republic *(see page 200)*, and untold numbers of ships lined up in New York City's harbor to celebrate the grand opening. The canal spanned a distance of 275 miles (442 km) – the way the crow flies, although its real mileage is greater – and enabled barges drawn by draft animals to travel a level route, with the assistance of locks. In financial terms alone, freight charges between Buffalo and New York City ranged from $14 to $120 a ton.

SOCIAL AND RELIGIOUS FERVOR

New York in the 19th century was fertile ground for new social and spiritual thought. The staunch abolitionist and temperance societies that took root in the central and western parts of the state reflected the tradition of moral zeal that characterized the New Englanders who had settled the region. Another movement that achieved early prominence in New York was both truly radical and ahead of its time. Women's rights pioneers Amelia Jenks Bloomer and Elizabeth Cady Stanton began their alliance in Seneca Falls. Together with Susan B. Anthony, they convened the first groundbreaking American women's suffrage convention at Seneca Falls in July 1848.

Religious fervor also ran strong. At Palmyra in 1823, Joseph Smith claimed to have been visited by the angel Moroni, who revealed to him the location of golden tablets that told of Christ's ministry among a race of Native Americans. Smith translated the tablets in the *Book of Mormon*, the founding document of the Church of Jesus Christ of Latter-Day Saints. William Miller, an émigré from Vermont, began preaching the second coming of Christ in Washington County in 1831. He predicted that the end would come in 1843 and again in 1844. Millerites refused to be discouraged when these dates passed; they met at Albany in 1845 to form the Seventh-Day Adventists.

It was the establishment of the Erie Canal more than anything else that set New York City on its way to becoming a world metropolis. As farms and cities began to thrive around the Great Lakes, the raw materials and produce of the interior poured into New York; goods manufactured in urban mills and factories flowed in the opposite direction. In 1800 the entire population of New York State amounted to fewer than 600,000. By 1850 – with a major boost from a new influx of Irish and German immigrants – the city alone was

CITY FAIR

The international significance of New York, the nation's largest city, was confirmed in 1853 by the decision to hold the first World's Fair in the borough of Queens.

Rise of the railroad

No sooner had the Erie Canal and its feeder system of smaller waterways become the lifelines of New York, than the emergence of a competitor presaged even greater economic opportunities. On August 9, 1831, the *DeWitt Clinton* steam locomotive chugged out of Albany and, hauling half a dozen open coaches, made its way to Schenectady. The rail tracks along which the little train traveled belonged to the Mohawk and Hudson, the third steam railroad

home to nearly 700,000 people, and was the nation's preeminent seaport.

The Erie Canal was also directly responsible for the rapid growth of Buffalo, Rochester, Syracuse, Utica, Rome, Albany, Troy, and a score of smaller cities and towns around the state. Buffalo became a flour-milling center that processed grain from the Midwest; Syracuse constructed an enormous salt-mining industry *(see page 263)*; and Albany became a center of the lumber industry.

LEFT: Uncle Sam greets Europe's dispossessed at the port of New York with the promise of a better life.
ABOVE: an early journey through the Mohawk Valley.

in America and the first in New York State. The trip between the two upstate cities, which covered 40 miles (65 km) by canal, would now be reduced to 17 miles (27 km).

New York became the linchpin of the Atlantic seaboard's rail system, with connections to the burgeoning Midwest provided by companies such as the New York Central and Erie. As the railroads began to flourish, so all of the biggest cities in the state developed to such an extent that they were soon among the largest and most industrially important in the nation. In 1850, New York State accounted for one-seventh of the property valuation of the entire United States.

Civil War discord

New York's economic development – the centralization of financial power on Wall Street in particular – was, like that of all the industrial northeast, given enormous impetus by the outbreak of the American Civil War in 1861. Paradoxically, the war, which was bitterly fought for four years on distant southern battlefields, also brought severe civil discord to New York.

In 1863, the policy of conscription to fill the ranks of the Union Army was met with violent

resistance in the form of four-day Draft Riots in Troy and New York City. Recent immigrants were particularly opposed to compulsory military service, not least because they were generally unable to pay the $300 that would buy exemption. In addition they feared that newly liberated slaves would compete with them for employment. During the course of the riots, numerous African-American New Yorkers were terrorized and killed, and the homes of slavery abolitionists were gutted by rioters who held them responsible for the war.

Ultimately, New York contributed 500,000 men to the Union cause, the vast majority volunteers. Some 50,000 never returned.

The Gilded Age

The three decades that followed the Civil War constituted America's fabled "Gilded Age," and nowhere were the country's restlessness and excesses better exemplified than in New York. If capitalism is a key component of the spectacle that is 21st-century life, in the Gilded Age it was baseball, football, and basketball combined – with a saltier array of characters than that found in any major league.

New York was the venue in which rascals and visionaries alike played for the highest stakes. Men such as Jim Fisk, Jay Gould, and Daniel Drew manipulated railroad stocks with an abandon that sent Wall Street reeling. More importantly, financiers and industry consolidators, such as banker J.P. Morgan, oilman John D. Rockefeller, and railroader E.H. Harriman set American business on firmer (if sometimes monopolistic) ground. Corruption was rife: William "Boss" Tweed controlled the city government of New York City and stole thousands of dollars of city funds.

But it was a glorious era, comparable to the *fin-de-siècle* transition in Europe. Ornate buildings were constructed *(see page 93)*, New York City became the fashion capital of the world, and the arts were boosted by institutions such as the Metropolitan Museum of Art *(see page 146)*, which are still revered today.

By the end of the 19th century, New York led the nation in one other vital category, one inexorably linked with the vigor of its industries: the city and state had become the most important entry point for immigrants, who were now arriving principally from southern and eastern Europe. Many were bound for points no farther than the city's teeming boroughs, but many more fanned out to the foundries and knitting mills of Troy, the shoe factories of Rochester, and the locomotive works of Schenectady. Though it was George Washington who coined the sobriquet "Empire State," it was this rich cast – eager immigrants, hardworking New Yorkers of old Dutch and Yankee stock, and the new titans of Wall Street – who gave the title credibility as the industrial age reached its zenith. ❏

LEFT: "Boss" Tweed personified the political corruption that scandalized 19th-century New York.

Cornelius Vanderbilt

Before the name "Rockefeller" became a synonym for American riches, one of the old Dutch surnames of New Amsterdam had come to symbolize the wealth that awaited a man who could turn the opportunities of the Industrial Revolution to his advantage. Cornelius Vanderbilt saw those opportunities and he took them. Even today, his name denotes the summit of New York's Gilded Age and its moneyed aristocracy.

Cornelius Vanderbilt was born in 1794 on his family's farm in Staten Island. As a boy, he helped his father ferry produce to Manhattan markets. Realizing that tmore money could be made on the water than on the farm, he invested $100 in a two-masted boat and began taking commuters into the city. Still in his teens and an up-and-coming figure around the harbor, "Cornele the Boatman" was known for his low fares and regular sailings.

After profiting from contracts to supply ships to local military bases during the War of 1812, Vanderbilt branched out further still. By 1837, when the press gave him the unofficial title "Commodore," he was well on his way to owning the country's largest steamboat fleet. During the 1849 Gold Rush, Vanderbilt took passengers to California by way of Nicaragua; in 1855 he began a regular service to Europe. His 1857 steamship *Vanderbilt* was the largest, fastest Atlantic liner of its era.

But Vanderbilt isn't known today for his success on the high seas. In one of the 19th century's greatest career shifts, he dropped his disdain for land travel and by 1864 had sold his fleet of ships, and invested $20 million in the railroads. He bought the New York and Harlem Railroad, which had access rights into downtown Manhattan, then acquired the Hudson River Railroad, which had connections to Albany. In the winter, Vanderbilt's railroad received freight from the New York Central, which ran between Buffalo and Albany via the Mohawk Valley; but in summer Central shipped goods to New York City. In retaliation, Vanderbilt moved his Albany terminal across the Hudson, denying Central a winter connection. Central's management submitted – then found themselves out in the cold when, during a business downturn, their stockholders asked Vanderbilt to take over as president and name his board of directors. The

New York Central system now spanned the state – and it all belonged to Vanderbilt.

But the Commodore – a big, profane man who ate lamb chops and eggs for breakfast until the end of his 83 years – wasn't finished yet. He knew that, with the completion of the transcontinental railroad in 1869, anyone with ambitions to be a major player in US railroads had to have access to Chicago. He bought the connecting railroads from Buffalo through Chicago via Cleveland and thereby created a rail colossus that survived until the 1960s, when a merger of the New York Central and Pennsylvania railroads resulted in the short-lived Penn Central.

Cornelius Vanderbilt died in 1877, leaving his son William in command of the Central and the largest fortune yet amassed by an American – $100 million. The money supported generations of Vanderbilts in spectacular style, and built mansions that stand to this day in Hyde Park, New York *(see page 177)*, Newport, Rhode Island and – grandest of all – Asheville, North Carolina, where the 1895 250-room Biltmore House remains the largest private home ever built in the US. But the old boatman's greatest monument is New York City's Grand Central Terminal. Facing Park Avenue in front of the station, looking as if he might be asking for a fare, is the Commodore himself, cast in larger-than-life bronze. ❏

RIGHT: Cornelius Vanderbilt caricatured as a "Colossus of Roads" monopolizing the train routes.

THE WHEEL OF FORTUNE

The 20th century was a time of both boom and bust in New York. The state was the nation's economic center, but it struggled to survive its own excesses

Two significant events heralded the advent of the 20th century in New York. The first was the 1898 merger of New York City and the city of Brooklyn into one municipal entity, the City of New York. The union of the cities had been more or less inevitable since John and Washington Roebling's Brooklyn Bridge had linked the two cities physically 15 years earlier. Now the stage was set for New York's dominance of US cultural and economic life in the century to come.

The second event was the September 1901 assassination of President William McKinley while he was visiting the Pan-American Exposition in Buffalo *(see page 283)*. Although this was a great blow to the nation, McKinley was succeeded in the White House by Theodore Roosevelt, the most dynamic New York politician of the age. Roosevelt, a former New York City police commissioner and governor of the state, was the first of eight 20th-century New York governors to be nominated for, elected to, or at least seriously considered for the presidency. For most of the 20th century, New York was a proving ground for the men and issues that drive US politics.

An economic giant

Although farming, particularly dairy farming, still looms large in the counties west of Albany *(see page 59)*, the story of New York's economy throughout much of the 20th century has been the story of manufacturing. Having lost ground in the processing of raw materials as enterprises such as steel mills gradually moved closer to their resources, New York State moved ahead in industries that required advanced technologies.

Rochester native George Eastman made his city the camera capital with his Kodak company *(see page 278)*; in Schenectady, General Electric became the dominant employer after

Thomas Edison set up an electric motor plant there. Carrier, the pioneer in air-conditioning, made Syracuse its home. New York City produced just about everything, but was – and still is – especially prominent in the garment industry *(see page 134)*.

The Roaring Twenties was a time of high

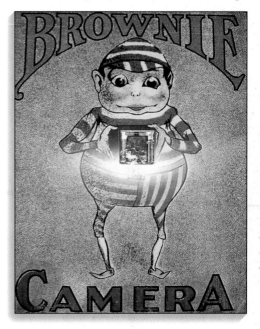

living, particularly in New York City, where gangsters and Hollywood stars rubbed shoulders in Harlem joints such as the Cotton Club, speakeasies defied Prohibition, and Broadway enjoyed its musical heyday.

New York's economy was hard hit by the 1929 Wall Street crash and the ensuing Great Depression. As if in response to the economic doldrums of the 1930s, the state produced an unusually farsighted crop of political leaders, whose programs to tackle unemployment and poverty were among the most progressive in the country. These included Governor Herbert Lehman, New York City Mayor Fiorello La Guardia *(see page 44)*, and of course Franklin

LEFT: a view across Lower Manhattan in 1911.
RIGHT: George Eastman's Brownie camera made photography a popular pastime for all.

D. Roosevelt, who served for four years as governor before his landslide presidential election victory in 1932. FDR's mentor, Governor Alfred E. Smith, was a progressive Democrat who in 1928 became the first Roman Catholic to run for president. During the 1930s, however, Smith took an increasingly conservative view of Roosevelt's New Deal programs. The colorful, self-educated Smith is remembered for his comment that he received an "FFM" degree – referring to Fulton Fish Market, where he worked as a boy.

In 1940, New York State produced 14 percent, by value, of the nation's manufactured goods. The state, and particularly New York City, was already providing a glimpse of what the US economy would look like at the century's end: more than any place else, New York was responsible for the conception of the "Information Society." By the 1920s, Madison Avenue was the country's advertising headquarters. And during the two decades following the introduction of radio, two individuals based their airwave empires in New York City. David Sarnoff, with his National Broadcasting Company (NBC), and William Paley, lord of the Columbia Broadcasting Company (CBS), made New York City America's most important radio

FIORELLO LA GUARDIA: MAYOR OF THE PEOPLE

New York City's best-loved mayor was a short, round dynamo of a man who typified the city's boundless energy. Fiorello H. La Guardia was the son of an Italian immigrant father and a Jewish mother, though he worshipped as an Episcopalian. Thus he embodied the "melting pot" ideal.

La Guardia was born in New York in 1882. He worked his way through law school as an interpreter at Ellis Island, and entered politics soon after admission to the bar. Most of his early career was spent in the US Congress. A Republican who also supported the anti-big business programs of the Progressive Party, La Guardia was elected mayor in 1933, after the corrupt James J. Walker was

forced from office. La Guardia fought the city's Democratic machine, yet identified himself with Democratic President Franklin Roosevelt's "New Deal." As mayor, he dismantled the old patronage system, reorganized the police, fought organized crime, built parks and housing, and restored the city's credit. For all these achievements, to the average New Yorker he was the man who read out the comic pages over the radio during a newspaper strike and smashed illegal gambling machines while cameras rolled. Seldom have substance and showmanship been combined so effectively in an American politician. La Guardia died in 1947, a year after leaving office.

address. Their companies, along with the rival American Broadcasting Company (ABC), and a host of smaller independent companies, also ushered in the age of television in the years immediately following World War II.

Truly an Empire State

World War II brought New York out of the Great Depression: in the 1940s the state stood on the threshhold of its most prosperous era. New York City was especially poised for great things. As Jan Morris wrote in her fine book *Manhattan '45*: "Few cities in the history of the world can have stood so consciously at a

(see page 239). In New York City, the Verrazano-Narrows Bridge, the longest suspension bridge in the world at the time of its completion in 1964, joined Brooklyn and Staten Island. The Governor Thomas E. Dewey Thruway joined other components of a new interstate highway system, and master planner Robert Moses – who filled several state and municipal positions – laced the metropolitan area with highways, bridges, and parks conceived on a superhuman scale. Even the field of private housing developed a case of enormity, as developer William Levitt built the first of his Levittowns on Long Island: tens of thousands

moment of fulfillment, looking into a future that seemed so full of reward."

Indeed, New York was embarking on a 25-year boom, the longest in the state's history. It was an era marked by heroic achievements in engineering. On the state's northern border with Canada, the St Lawrence Seaway opened the way to the Great Lakes for the largest ocean-going vessels, while hydroelectric projects planned in conjunction with the Seaway vastly increased the region's electric power supply

of new homes, all built to a handful of patterns, were offered to returning veterans for little or no down payment.

Decline and rebirth

As is so often the case, the boom years sowed the seeds of a reversal . By the 1960s, American manufacturing jobs were starting to head west and south, as companies realized that the labor, tax, and infrastructure costs of what would soon be called the "Rust Belt" of northeastern industrial states were more than they cared to bear. Companies remaining in the region tended to move to the suburbs, so the onset of hard times hit urban areas first.

LEFT: two exceptionally popular New York City mayors, Fiorella La Guardia (far left) and Ed Koch.
ABOVE: jitterbugging in Harlem.

In the late 1960s, the erosion of both the employment market and the tax base began to translate into strikes, burgeoning welfare rolls, increased crime and crumbling public facilities. In the state's smaller towns and cities, the most dramatic evidence of a downturn appeared in the form of a plummeting population: Buffalo, which had 580,000 inhabitants in 1950, today has only slightly more than half that number.

BOOM TIME

The yuppie era of the 1980s was symbolized by wealthy tycoons such as Donald Trump, and was parodied in Tom Wolfe's novel *The Bonfire of the Vanities.*

In New York City, the population figure stayed more or less stable, but a crisis was just

around the corner. In the mid-1970s, the city's revenues fell so far short of expenditures that bankruptcy seemed a very real possibility. Federal aid wasn't in the offing – President Gerald Ford's refusal to even consider a relief plan resulted in the era's most famous New York City newspaper headline: "Ford to City: Drop Dead." It took the formation of a state-organized public-private entity called the Municipal Assistance Program to haul the city back from the brink of disaster.

In the 1980s and 1990s, an upsurge in the financial markets, accompanied by a boom in Manhattan real estate, put New York City back on track. The recovery was, appropriately

enough, led by the mayor, Ed Koch, who helped mastermind the return to solvency. Suburban areas thrived with the burgeoning high-technology and service industries – Armonk, in Westchester County, is the home of mighty IBM. However, Koch was undone, as were many New Yorkers, by the bust that followed the boom. He also failed to address racial tensions and, following various corruption scandals, he was succeeded in 1989 by the city's first African-American mayor, David Dinkins.

Meanwhile Mario Cuomo had been elected state governor in 1982. During his 12-year term, more than 500,000 jobs were created in the state, and the "New York, New York" development plan was the largest in its history. In 1994 however George E. Pataki became the state's first Republican governor; four years later he was reelected by a huge majority.

Dinkins was less fortunate. In 1993 he was voted out of office and replaced by the Republican Rudolph Giuliani, whose controversial tough policies on crime were successful in cleaning up the city (though urban crime declined elsewhere in the state, too). The city's economy grew under his stewardship, but the smaller upstate cities have been slow to reap the benefits. The rivalry between upstate and downstate New York, often focusing on the conflict between urban and rural interests, thus goes on. During a 1980s campaign, Koch declared rural life "a joke"; he lost the subsequent election.

The 1990s ended with a revival of the stock markets, and a third great wave of immigration, mainly from Asia, Latin America, Africa, the former Soviet Union, and the Middle East.

Whether this is again a city and a state "at a moment of fulfillment, looking into a future... full of reward" remains to be seen, but the new immigrants, like the émigrés of old, certainly see their own lives that way when they arrive in New York. In 1990 Ellis Island was turned into a museum of immigration, a fitting tribute to all the people who have made the state what it is today *(see page 113).* ❑

LEFT: New York Yankee Babe Ruth, perhaps the greatest baseball player in the sport's history.
RIGHT: a man and his wheels.

THE MELTING POT

New York's absorption of numerous nationalities and races

has not been at the expense of the immigrants' original cultures

The great New York melting pot began with Dutch settlements that were taken over by the British. After the country gained its freedom from the British, the matter of a United States national seal arose. It is interesting to note that Founding Fathers Franklin, Jefferson, and Adams proposed that the seal include the emblems of Holland, England, Scotland, Ireland, France, and Germany – hardly a symbol of the "melting pot" ethos that became a byword for immigrant integration in New York.

The melting-pot metaphor may first have been broached by St John de Crevecoeur. This French-born American proclaimed in his 1782 book *Letters from An American Farmer*: "Here individuals of all nations are melted into a new race of men." In 1908 the writer Israel Zangwill coined the term "melting pot" and spoke of "the coming superman" who would be created from "the fusion of all the races."

The truth is, cultural traditions have not been boiled away in a melting pot, though some historians fear their continued dilution. It is often a parade or festival that announces the vitality of a group: a Saint Patrick's Day Parade for the Irish; the Italian Feast of San Gennaro; the Caribbean Day Celebration; a Native American pow wow. There are also, throughout the state, enclaves, subcultures, and diverse communities, some long-established (though perhaps in need of reviving), and others just starting up among the country's more recent immigrants, such as the Haitians or Cubans.

The fascinating immigration museum at Ellis Island in New York City has ignited a resurgence in interest in the preservation of New York's pluralistic heritage. There you can research an individual immigrant's journey from his country of origin to the new world. Tourists from all over the globe visit the Wall of Honor, which is inscribed with the names of thousands of immigrants *(see page 113)*.

PRECEDING PAGES: sailing on the Staten Island ferry.
LEFT: dressed in their Sunday best in Harlem.
RIGHT: taking pride in the old country.

The spread of populations

On May 18, 1840, Hans Brandt, a physician, left Norway and departed from Hamburg for New York, a voyage that lasted 67 days. In a letter to friends in Norway he declared that his fellow passengers "seemed to be under the impression that New York's roofs, streets, and

alleys were covered with these precious and rare metals [silver and gold] and that they were even easily accessible in the rivers... But soon, of course, they were disillusioned... most of them had to get work at canal digging, the coal mines, the railroad, and so on."

Between 1830 and 1840, about 600,000 immigrants – largely from Britain, Ireland, Germany, and Scandinavia – landed on the shores of America. About 150,000 of these opted to stay in New York City while the rest fanned out, either upstate or to other states. Large numbers of Germans settled in Rochester and Buffalo, sometimes working as gardeners on estates or cultivating vegetables.

From 1840 to 1850, over 1.7 million further immigrants arrived in New York. By 1849, the Irish made up nearly half of the total number of new arrivals. Scandinavians for the most part headed up the Hudson toward the Midwest, but some found employment in New York's shipping industry. German Jews came from 1820 to 1880, many becoming highly successful. The next, impoverished, Jewish immigration, from East Europe and Russia, involved the arrival of 2 million people between 1870 and 1914. In the 1880s millions of Slavs and Italians also made for the New World. Exclusion policies restricted Asians for a time but eventually they

too joined the ranks of newcomers in New York. The impact of the Italians and Chinese can be seen in the number of restaurants opened throughout the country by these ethnic groups.

"No Irish Need Apply"

Not surprisingly, immigrants created their own social and political groups. The Slovaks built their Sokol halls, the Italians their social clubs. As immigrants began to outnumber what had been a WASP majority, the attitude toward immigrants became hostile. "No Irish Need Apply" is the title of a song from this period, when a number of anti-Irish and anti-Catholic

IMMIGRANT FARMERS: BACK TO THE LAND

"Luring Immigrant Farmers" read the headline in the *New York Times* in July 2000. Though this sounds sinister, the topic is ingenious: helping skilled farmers find their way back to the land. There are 29 thriving Greenmarkets around the city and a demand for more – but farmers are in short supply. Small farms in New York have been declining for years. Greenmarket director Tony Mannetta turned to *El Diario*, the city's leading Spanish newspaper. There a call for experienced farmers interested in managing or owning farms brought more than 500 replies.

After a series of workshops, 37 people with dreams of farming boarded a bus for a farm tour in Orange County's

"black-dirt country," northwest of the city. Included were a banana farmer, a cattleman from the Dominican Republic, an Ecuadorian cane farmer, and a Colombian agronomist who was an organic farming expert. Their occupations in New York City included construction worker, guard, waiter, cleaner, and salad chef. After their tour, Greenmarket would help those who wanted to move forward into farming.

Immigrants come to contribute and succeed, but often wind up in employment beneath their abilities. This Greenmarket program has laid groundwork for matching up skills with jobs, that can benefit both the people and the economy. The American dream, where everybody wins.

groups were formed. "Nativism" was the name given to the anti-foreign movement. To defend themselves from the xenophobic nativists, immigrants formed still more organizations, such as the Irish Ancient Order of Hibernians. Thus the pendulum swung.

The European Jews, and their Yiddish subculture, were very visible. Most settled in New York City in the Lower East Side, many initially working in garment-trade sweatshops *(see page 134)*. In spite of various policies of social exclusion and anti-Semitism, Jewish culture endured. The Borscht Belt, a vacation resort that was popular with Jewish families,

1940. But the agricultural sector remained a steady employer of immigrants. By 1920 the state's foreign-born farm population was about 71,000. Of these, 25 percent – mainly Irish, Italians, and Poles – were employers rather than employees. Other farm workers came from Canada, Germany, Finland, and Wales.

Caribbean islanders, drawn by the prospect of wartime jobs, began to complement the state's population in the 1940s. The area known as Spanish Harlem on the city's Upper East Side became the focal point of their community. During the early 1950s, more than 1,000 Puerto Ricans a week arrived in New

developed in the Catskills. The spa baths in Saratoga Springs were particulary attractive. As more and more members of the Jewish community became regular summer visitors to the baths, a number of kosher boarding houses were established *(see page 212)*.

Later waves of immigration

Immigration restrictions, World War I, and the Great Depression contributed to a reduction in the state's population growth from 1910 to

LEFT: when it comes to clothes, anything goes.
ABOVE: immigrants and their descendants constitute the lifeblood of New York City.

York. The numbers were constantly shifting but in the 1960s, Italians formed the largest immigrant group resident in the city.

As a manufacturing center, Buffalo was popular with Poles, Germans, and Italians *(see page 283)*. "Cluster" populations also developed: a real estate agent from a particular country might buy up a lot of upstate land. Then he would advertise it to his compatriots in one of the foreign-language papers published by nearly every ethnic group that came to the country. In this way, what had been exclusively Anglo-Saxon neighborhoods could suddenly find themselves hosting a small settlement of, say, Greeks or Scandinavians.

New York's native peoples

The state's area once formed half the domain of the Iroquois Confederation, but the arrival of the white man did not bode well for the native peoples. The climate following the American Revolution, when the Iroquois had sided with the British, left the Indians a scorned people. The Native Americans were often dispossessed of their land by the encroaching white population, or on the frequent occasions that the government reneged on assorted treaties. (Even in the early 20th century, bounties were still paid for Indian scalps in the Wild West.)

French-Canadians who emigrated into New

labor built much of early New Amsterdam. Much later, in the 1910 migration, blacks from the southern states traveled north in search of work. Harlem, once exclusively white, became an African-American community and before long "the Negro capital of the world" *(see page 147)*. Large numbers of blacks also settled in Brooklyn, Rochester, and Syracuse.

Preserving cultural pluralism

The image of impoverished immigrants is now largely outdated. Many individuals realized their dreams by making their fortunes in America. Today many of the Asians who own stores

York State as lumbermen or guides were often of mixed Indian ancestry, even if they did not admit to it. When skyscrapers started to fill the city landscape, a group of Mohawk Indians from Akwesasne near Plattsburgh proved to be adept "sky walkers" and a Mohawk community of construction workers grew up in Brooklyn.

Southern blacks

The hatred and intolerance directed by some toward the Native Americans was equalled only by that directed toward the black population. Many immigrants of West Indian origin entered New York as "involuntary immigrants" – that is, brought in by the Dutch as slave labor. Their

in New York City are saving money so that they can leave the city – not to return to their original countries but to settle in quiet upstate communities. At the other end of the spectrum, third and fourth generations of families descended from immigrants thrive in pleasant Long Island communities or upstate, or else make their mark in the metropolis where the immigrant experience began. Obviously there are as many tales of frustration as there are success stories: such is the excitement of cultural pluralism. ❏

ABOVE LEFT: a Native American ceremony.
ABOVE RIGHT: a young actress portrays her heritage in the role of the freedom fighter Sojourner Truth.

The Way to New York's Heart

When it comes to cuisine, New York is not so much a melting pot as a giant Mulligan stew. Just as the hobos during the Great Depression used to add whatever meager morsels they had to the communal cooking pot, so has each immigrant group brought its own spices and specialties to New York's shores.

New York City, of course, is famous for its ethnic cuisine: Chinatown with its dim sum houses and duck-draped restaurant windows, Little Italy with its pukka restaurants and the best pizza this side of Napoli (they claim the secret is in the water!), the Lower East Side with its kosher delicatessens and old-fashioned pickle barrels. New York has more delis than any other city. And while bagels the world over are now laced with everything from sunflower seeds to sun-dried tomatoes, the best ones are the simple, New York originals – sweet water bagels that are boiled, then baked to produce a chewy center beneath the crust.

In the Big Apple, you can dine on elegant cuisine from the chef-of-the-moment, feast on Middle Eastern falafel, Caribbean roti or Mexican burritos, or grab a hot dog with "the works" (mustard, ketchup, onions, relish) from a street corner vendor and eat it on the run, New York-style. In fact, America's favorite fast food originated here, at Coney Island in Brooklyn. And Manhattan clam chowder, unlike its creamy New England cousin, is made with tomatoes, green pepper, carrots, and celery.

This international flavor doesn't stop at the edges of the city, for immigrants spread throughout the state, taking their recipes with them. In upstate towns and cities and especially at local fairs, you'll find German, Swedish, Polish, and countless other food specialties handed down the generations. And over the decades, the multifaceted cuisine of New York evolved into dishes as American as, well, apple pie. It is said that the nation's first apple pie was served in the Capitol-region town of Cambridge, at the Cambridge Hotel on Main Street.

Meanwhile, at Moon's Lake House at Saratoga Lake, George Crum, an Indian cook, accidentally burned some fried potatoes and invented the

RIGHT: hot dog vendors cater for the fast-food, eat-on-the-run generation in New York City.

original potato chip. The Anchor Bar, in Buffalo's Allentown district, is a bustling Italian restaurant that gave birth to spicy Buffalo wings – chicken wings dipped in blue cheese. And the Thousand Islands Inn in Clayton is home to the salad dressing of the same name.

The first chocolate-drenched ice-cream sundae was concocted in Ithaca in 1891. In New York, custard is not a gloppy yellow pudding, but a thick, rich ice cream which was also first sold at Coney Island. One of the best places to try it is Abbott's Frozen Custard, whose homemade, hand-dipped flavors are sold at Charlotte Beach and other outlets around Rochester.

The Culinary Institute of America in Hyde Park is the training ground for the nation's top chefs. It has three restaurants where students serve creative menus, and diners have the opportunity to discover the up-and-coming star chef of tomorrow.

And a drink to accompany the food? New York's Finger Lakes is the country's largest wine-producing region after California. Most of the wine is sold locally before it ever reaches export, so the chance to try the excellent Reisling, Merlot, ice wine, and sparkling wine produced here is not to be missed. The vineyards have produced another Finger Lakes specialty: the delicious grape pies made during the autumn harvest at Naples. ❑

HOW FESTIVALS REFLECT THE ETHNIC HERITAGE

From food to music to history and ethnic heritage, something is being celebrated somewhere in the Empire State almost every day of the year

 New York's diverse landscape and cultural heritage has generated a vast array of festivals matched by few other US states. There are festivals that take place along city streets or in huge open spaces in the country; others are held on water, underground, and even in the air, such as the hot-air balloon festivals in the Adirondacks and the Catskills.

Many events highlight a particular ethnic heritage. New York City has some of the most famous celebrations, from Chinese New Year in Chinatown (February) to Little Italy's Feast of San Gennaro (September). But you don't have to visit the city to enjoy major merry-making. There's Dyngus Day, a Polish event in Buffalo (April), the East Durham Irish Festival in the Catskills (May), Albany's Latin Fest (August), and the Capital District Scottish Games in Altamont (September). Thirty-five tribes from across the nation take part in the Native American Festival at Hunter Mountain in the Catskills (September), one of many celebrating Indian culture with crafts and ceremonial dancing.

A FESTIVAL FOR ALL SEASONS

Food is at the heart of many festivals. You can munch on delectable homemade pies and frothy spun-sugar cotton candy; sample American Indian fry bread, Caribbean jerk chicken, Middle Eastern falafel, and Cuban pulled-pork; or sip the wines of the Hudson Valley and Finger Lakes. Festivals honor apples, corn, strawberries, and tulips; falcons, whales, and teddy bears; saints and even sinners. Some events mark momentous historic achievements, such as women getting the vote, or tongue-in-cheek local high points, like the official end of the black fly season.

To find out what happens when, contact the New York State Division of Tourism, which cross-references festivals by region down to the day and hour *(see page 311)*.

▷ **BLOOMING GOOD TIMES**
Albany celebrates its Dutch heritage with the Tulip Festival in May. Rochester's Lilac Festival and Rose Festival are other flowery events.

▽ **MAKING MUSIC**
The Corinth Bluegrass Festival draws musicians from miles around, including this mandolin player from the Appalachian country.

▷ **PRIDE IN THE PAST**
The Mexican Independence Day Celebration in New York City is one of many events in which New Yorkers honor their roots in the old country.

◁ HIGH-FLYING FUN

The midway amusement section of the New York State Fair in Syracuse features both old-time rides like the ever-popular Ferris wheel and new state-of-the-art thrill rides.

△ NATIVE HERITAGE

From the Sunrise Ceremony in Central Park to the Genundowa Iroquois festival, Native American gatherings are held in nearly every region of New York State.

OLD-TIME FAIRS AND FESTIVITIES

The very first festivals in New York involved agriculture. Many of the state's celebrations today spring from that tradition, county fairs in particular. Smaller fairs offer regional charm, such as Hemlock Little World's Fair in Conesus (July). Listed on the registry of historic places, it dates from the 1850s and features such events as truck and tractor pulls and horse shows.

Syracuse has the fair with a Capital "F." For 12 days, from the end of August through Labor Day, the official New York State Fair takes center stage. Nearly 1 million people come from across the northeast for hundreds of activities, from agricultural and livestock competitions, to demolition derbies and celebrity entertainment.

For other glimpses into the past, the Macedon Center Lumberjack Festival (September) features log rolling, log chopping, and the essential back-woodsman cuisine: a pancake breakfast. The Sterling Renaissance Festival (July) presents the pageantry and crafts of medieval England.

△ CASTLES IN THE AIR

A sandcastle-building competition is part of the fun at the Erie County Fair and Expo in Hamburg, Greater Niagara, in August.

▷ AUTUMN GLORY

Halloween is part of a long tradition of autumn festivals that dates back to ancient times. In upstate New York, harvest festivals abound, from the Pumpkin Fiesta to the Apple Fest to the Festival of Grapes.

OF COWS AND MEN

*From the earliest days of settlement, dairy farming has been a mainstay of
New York's economy, a tradition that shows no signs of dying out*

It is often said that the lives of dairy farmers in upstate New York are ones of endless toil – milking, plowing, planting, spreading, lifting, and sowing the soil they depend on – from sunrise to sunset. In fact, farmers usually begin work at 4.30am, before the sun rises.

It is not, farmers quickly admit, an easy life, but it is for many the only life they have ever considered. They were born farmers, the way some people are born with red hair. Chances are their fathers and grandfathers were farmers as well. And while they could cash in the thousands, sometimes millions, of dollars invested in machinery and land, and go and live the rest of their lives as successful real estate dealers, they know they would do so only as a last resort. They want to continue to do as generations of farmers have done before them.

A rural routine

Tradition has sculpted New York's rural landscape. One does not have to venture far from cities such as Syracuse, Albany, and Buffalo to be surrounded by a world where the air is filled with the scent of freshly cut hay and the sound of a brisk breeze.

The hills are alive with the sound of dairy farms. From a hilltop, one can command a view of farm after farm surrounded by checkered countryside, each with a red barn at its center flanked by silos reaching like steeples into the sky. During spring, a tractor may be rounding the corners of an endless field, dragging a grader through fertile black dirt and slowly taming one farmer's great expanse of land. Soon, he will be filling the field with seeds and fertilizer. Then he will wait, until a tiny sprout appears out of what was once bare ground.

Life centers on the barn, where cows are herded as the first chore of the morning and later again in the afternoon. When a farmer walks out into the cool air before sunrise, his

animals will be waiting, like passengers for a train, outside the barn doors.

The sun is just rising as the farmer leaves the main part of the barn to feed the young calves and heifers. The morning's chores are done automatically and almost effortlessly day after day. But a farmer will also notice any change in

his stock, almost by the moment. He knows which cows are in heat, which are not feeling well, and which feel ill at ease with visitors. In the field, a farmer can pick out any cow by name. Some chores are dictated by the weather. In the cold of winter, a farmer may be found inside the machine shed repairing a hay bailer or tractor. On a clear summer's day a farmer will almost surely be in the field, and sometimes, during planting season, he will plow well into the night.

By noon, it is lunchtime on the farm. For many farmers, lunch is still a time to return home for a midday break and prepare for the afternoon's labor. The farmer, his family and

---

LEFT: the dairy cow has been one of New York's most valued inhabitants since the early days of settlement.
RIGHT: the farmer's lot is a busy one.

his hired help sit around the kitchen table and talk about their afternoon plans. The conversation may wander into the troubles encountered that morning in the field or about a piece of machinery that is not working properly. Someone might mention a piece of nearby land that is for sale, and if times are good and the farmer feels he can afford it, the acquisition of more land may be hard to resist.

The business of agriculture

More than 12,000 sq miles (31,000 sq km) of the 48,000 sq miles (125,000 sq km) that make up New York State is agricultural land. The landscape, formed primarily by glaciers centuries ago, is today full of moraines and drumlins, valleys and ridges *(see page 18)*. Where the land is clear of trees and deep swamp, it is almost always suitable for farming. New York's soil has long been some of the most fertile in the country.

All this may be changing, however. When the first settlers came to New York, they found the land so fertile there was no need to stimulate growth artificially. Today, most farmers use fertilizers and, in areas such as the "mucklands" of central New York, the soil may be eroding beyond repair – it loses half an inch (1cm) of

MILKING PRACTICE

Most dairy farms in upstate New York use some sort of mechanical milking equipment, such as milking parlors. In these parlors, cows are milked six or eight at a time, standing three or four in a row on each side of a pit that holds a farmer and his equipment. The cows enter at one end and exit at the other. The average cow produces about 5.3 gallons (20 liters) of milk a day; the average dairy farm in New York has approximately 80 cows, producing over 428 or so gallons (1,620 liters) of milk a day. A farmer feeds the milk to a holding tank using either a pipe which runs the length of the barn or a machine that looks like a vacuum cleaner connected to a tank.

fertile soil a year. There are some farmers who believe the soil that supports them today may be unusable in as little as 20 years time, and many are being forced to leave the soil they have spent their whole lives cultivating.

Decisions involving profit and investment, buying and selling, are the stuff of a businessman's daily routine; a farmer must be as familiar with these concepts as he is with his animals. He must be an analyst of trends in property and in produce. He must know what to plant and how much land to use. He will work with loans and figures that can reach into thousands, perhaps millions of dollars. When interest rates are high and the prices for milk low, a farmer may grumble at the business aspect of farming and long for the following day's escape to the fields and animals. Conversely, many farmers also enjoy business planning, which makes the culture of farming complete.

A farmer wears many hats. Should a member of the herd fall sick, he immediately becomes a physician. Another regular task on the farm is that of bovine midwife, delivering calves. There are medicines to administer, and there is the planning of a cow's diet. A good farmer will feed each cow exactly what she needs to give a sufficient amount of milk – nothing more, nothing less.

Family life

As the chores that follow the afternoon's milking end and sunset approaches, the entire family is expected to gather at the homestead for dinner. This is the time when every adventure is shared, when a farmer's children take center stage, describing their latest tales of school or of a hot summer day's activities. The meal is usually early, around 6.30pm, and as it ends a farmer may return to the fields in a busy season. But if he has the time, the energy and the inclination, he may tackle some bookwork, sitting in an old chair in his clapboard country home, and then slowly drift off to sleep. ❏

A farmer may find himself acting as a mechanic, his back on a dolly and covered with lubricant. Their are no tow trucks in the fields, only a farmer's resourcefulness. If a tractor needs a new tire or a cable as it stalls during planting, a muddy field becomes the farmer's workshop, his arms and legs his only source of power. Sometimes a farmer becomes an inventor, remaking his old equipment, putting a motor from an unused machine onto one he cannot continue without.

LEFT: a dairy farm might have several silos in which to store feed for the herd.
ABOVE: resting cows take fall's fine colors for granted.

THE COUNTRY AUCTION

A regular social event for the farmer is the country auction, the place where old equipment is traded and old rumors are joked about. These country auctions hold much of the romance of rural life. An auctioneer will scream prices at the huddled farmers in front of him. These are neighbors who have watched each other across a fence for as long as they can remember. These events are appreciated as a chance to get together, away from the fields and, as the farmers stand and bid for the day's lots, there is an air of both camaraderie and mystery. The farmers radiate either a welcoming warmth or, on lesser days, a cool aloofness.

ARTISTS AND WRITERS

Americans may have struggled against European traditions in the early days but, by the 20th century, New York had found its artistic voice

In the first decade of the 20th century a group of young Greenwich Village painters calling itself "the Eight" adopted the rallying cry: "Don't imitate; be yourself!" The group's artwork featured realistic studies of tenements, bars, shops, and streets, along with the people who populated them, from pushcart peddlers to prostitutes. John Sloan and the rest of the Eight thus boldly proclaimed their break with a tradition represented by formal portraits, such as the works of John Singleton Copley (New York's and indeed the country's first well-known painter), and grand evocations of nature, such as those by Thomas Cole and others in the Hudson River School of landscape painting *(see page 199)*. As is their wont, the critics responded with equal boldness, derisively labeling these modernists "the Ashcan School."

A new spirit in art

Americans had won their political freedom with the American Revolution, but developing the confidence to establish a national aesthetic took longer. There were a number of artistic alignments and manifestoes before the Armory Show of 1913 raised art's profile in New York to hitherto unimagined heights. Galvanizing the conflict between modernists and traditionalists, the show included 1,600 works of modern American and European painting and sculpture. Few of the exhibition's visitors, or even critics, had ever seen anything like French Post-Impressionism, let alone Cubism. The people were, to put it mildly, taken aback.

Cézanne was denounced by one critic as being "absolutely without talent"; Duchamps was surely a hoax on the public. Van Gogh, Picasso, Kandinsky, Leger – none fared much better. Theodore Roosevelt reviewed the show as "noteworthy," but also warned, "probably we err in treating most of these pictures seriously." Potential buyers of Cubist works were, he suggested, like the "thousands of people who will pay small sums to look at a fake mermaid" in a P.T. Barnum show.

The sponsors, including the Ashcan School, were vindicated in their view of the exhibition as "a great chance to make the Americans think." Beyond the controversy it generated,

the show announced New York as a center of art. Existing museums began to collect American works and new museums opened – the Museum of Modern Art in 1929, the Whitney Museum, devoted to American art, the following year, after Gertrude Whitney's offer to donate her modern art was rejected by the Met.

Themes and directions

As the 20th century progressed, traditional approaches to art coexisted with the new. In the 1930s and 1940s, Ben Shahn gravitated to social themes, Andrew Wyeth and Edward Hopper produced modern representational work. Artists such as Mary Cassatt, James

LEFT: New York inspired many paintings, such as *The Hudson River from Hoboken* (1878) by Robert Weir.
RIGHT: illustration in Irving's *Rip van Winkle*.

Edward Whistler, and Brooklyn-born Man Ray sought inspiration in Europe.

In the mid-1950s, Jackson Pollock and Willem de Kooning broke away in another new direction, toward what was called Abstract Expressionism. A style known as "action painting" emerged, based on the idea of the blank canvas as an area to be acted upon by the artist. The idea was not to copy, redesign, or express an object or even an idea in art; it was to make the very act of painting itself an event.

> **RIVER VIEWS**
>
> The Brooklyn Bridge has inspired hundreds of New York artists and writers, from painter Joseph Stella to poets Walt Whitman, Hart Crane, and Marianne Moore.

chauvinism. The US government lauded Robert Rauschenberg's prize at the 1964 Venice Biennale to the point of embarrassment. But the event was a landmark in the history of American art.

Today's art market

The current New York art scene constitutes a mixture of the old and new, with an occasional controversy raised when works feature an unwholesome ingredient such as dung, or are exhibited in non-chronological order. Some artists invite audience involvement

The young Robert Rauschenberg and Jasper Johns, original innovators influenced by Dada and Duchamp, dominated the late 1950s and early 1960s. Color field painters like Helen Frankenthaler also were on the scene.

In the 1960s, Andy Warhol and Roy Lichtenstein made their presence felt through the use of a graphic style borrowed from comics and advertising. Thus did Pop Art erupt in primary colors. In the 1980s, Keith Haring's graffiti-inspired drawings brought back the street life that had seized both the Ashcan School and Weegee, the photographic chronicler of New York City's nocturnal life. But to many art remained alien, unless coupled with American

in conceptual art, performance, and installations that utilize everything from film, video, sound, and light to virtual reality. In photography, conceptual concerns and size align Cindy Sherman's work with postmodernist art.

Digital processes often elevate technique over content. A resurgence in alternative processes has reintroduced hand- (as opposed to computer-) crafting. The beautiful print as object, created by Robert Mapplethorpe and Tom Baril, is in demand, and the collectors' market is booming. Works by photographers such as Sally Mann can fetch prices of $20,000 to $30,000 at auction. Authentic masterpieces can change hands for millions of dollars.

The first writers

For decades, uncertainty plagued American writers just as it had the country's artists. This inferiority complex was very much at odds with the confidence that was fuelling the nation-building activities in other fields. The English could be quite scathing about the colonists' inability to create an indigenous aesthetic movement, or even a single notable work. In 1820, an acerbic English critic asked rhetorically: "In the four quarters of the globe, who reads an American book? Or goes to an American play? Or looks at an American picture or statue?" The answer, of course, was "nobody."

for American letters. Moreover, he adapted German tales he collected along the Rhine to a Hudson River setting in stories such as *The Legend of Sleepy Hollow*. When he returned to New York he was heralded as the country's first great writer. He was also the first American to make his living from writing.

Works by Irving, James Fenimore Cooper, and William Cullen Bryant, all from the 1820s and 1830s, constitute the first flowering of American literature. Cooper's Leatherstocking saga told tales of Indians and frontiersmen. Humorist Mark Twain, who worked summers in Elmira, let his characters Tom Sawyer and

New Yorker Washington Irving was the first author to leave the US and tour Europe, from 1815 to 1832. Irving essentially invented the artist's Grand Tour, and he met Keats, Wordsworth, and others on his travels. Irving's *The Sketch Book* (1819) developed stories based on the differences between the Old World of Europe, with its antiquities and history, and the New World of America, which was full of promise but short on traditions. His articulation of this idea was important as a starting point

Huck Finn speak in the ungainly vernacular. Herman Melville, Albany-born, went to sea, lived at times in New York City, and drew upon his experiences to create the timeless classic *Moby Dick* (1851). Walt Whitman was born in Long Island. He lived in Brooklyn and Manhattan in the 1840s, during which time he edited *The Brooklyn Eagle* newspaper. *Leaves of Grass* (1855), with its new American idiom, established him as a leading contemporary poet.

In the 1930s, upstate authors turned to Empire State history and lore. Boonville's Walter Emonds, most remembered for *Drums Along the Mohawk* (1936), about the revolutionary war, also wrote about the Erie Canal.

LEFT: a SoHo portrait artist. **ABOVE LEFT:** Edith Wharton wrote about genteel New Yorkers. **ABOVE RIGHT:** Mark Twain spent summers writing in Elmira.

In folklore, Carl Carmer's books, including *Listen for a Lonesome Drum* (1936), revealed storied regions with a poetic flair. Edna Ferber's novel *Saratoga Trunk* (1941), was set in the heyday of Saratoga Springs as a resort.

Writing into the 20th century

After the Civil War, Henry James and Edith Wharton established the American novel of manners, starring genteel New Yorkers. Important writers, including both Charles Dickens and Oscar Wilde in the 1880s, thronged to New York City. In the 1920s, F. Scott Fitzgerald turned to the lives of the wealthy on Long

Island's Gold Coast for material for *The Great Gatsby*. Ernest Hemingway, another stylistic radical, introduced staccato, simple sentences, and exalted stoic manhood. Eugene O'Neill was at the fore of a group of playwrights, the Provincetown Players, in Greenwich Village.

Writers emerged from ethnic neighborhoods, from Chinatown and the Lower East Side to Harlem and the boroughs. Alfred Kazin, who came from a Russian immigrant background, took New York as his co-subject in his 1978 autobiography, *New York Jew*. Piri Thomas, author of *Down These Mean Streets* (1967), wrote about life in Spanish Harlem. Richard Wright and James Baldwin, living in Greenwich Village, worked with African-American themes in numerous groundbreaking novels and articles. Toni Morrison won a Pulitzer Prize for fiction in 1988 for *Beloved* and the Nobel Prize for Literature in 1993.

In the 1990s, Tom Wolfe, Norman Mailer, Gloria Steinem, Erica Jong, and Anne Rice were among the city's leading literary lights. Meanwhile a hard-edged sensibility depicting modern hedonistic lifestyles characterized works by Brett Easton Ellis and Jay McInerney. In contrast, Paul Auster's Brooklyn-related works, some written for the screen, sang with a broader authenticity of quirky characters and locales. The publishing industry responded to the new wave of multiculturalism with imprints for topics ranging from Native American to Lesbian and Gay Writers.

Places to gather and retreat

Although New York's literati have never had a focal point such as London's Bloomsbury of the 1930s or Paris's Left Bank of the 1960s, they have benefited from a number of meeting places. Edgar Allen Poe found his milieu in a private salon in Greenwich Village in the 1820s, and in the 1920s writers Langston Hughes, Zora Neale Hurston, and other members of the "Harlem Renaissance" met regularly at a Harlem branch library *(see page 147)*.

In Saratoga Springs, in 1900, the Trask family left their estate to be endowed as an artist's retreat. Yaddo received its first guest in 1926 and remains one of the foremost of such venues in the country *(see page 212)*. Similarly, Millay Colony in Austerlitz was founded in 1973 at Steepletop, where poet Edna St Vincent Millay lived and wrote.

PUBLISHING CHANGES

By the 1930s, New York had become the world headquarters of the books industry. This is where Scribner, Macmillan, Henry Holt, and others published the works of literary giants. In the 1990s the industry was transformed as conglomerates started to buy publishing houses, and the rise of mega bookstores resulted in the closure of many independent booksellers. Paradoxically, innovations in publishing now seem to depend on small startups. Stephen King tried to bypass agents, publishers, and bookstores by releasing a novel in installments to prepaid subscribers over the Internet. The initial sales results were disappointing, but the potential is there.

Frances Stelloff's Gotham Book Mart on 47th Street (founded 1920) carried works by important writers, and scores of journals and small press books found nowhere else. Novelist William Kennedy used money he received from a MacArthur grant to found the New York State Writers Institute in Albany in 1983. Kennedy's novel *Ironweed*, set in the Albany area – to which he returned after living in Puerto Rico for many years – earned him a Pulitzer Prize and National Book Award in the same year.

> ### LITERARY TALKS
>
> Libraries, the Y, the National Arts Club, St Mark's Poetry Project, the Nyorican Cafe, and bookstores are all places in which you can hear writers in New York City.

a number of literary and theatrical lights who figured in the Algonquin Round Table group amused each other with their repartee in the course of meetings at the Algonquin Hotel *(see page 318)*. The author O. Henry frequented Pete's Tavern near Irving Place, which still sports its original tin roof. Ohio's Hart Crane found poetry in the Brooklyn Bridge.

When the poet e.e. cummings returned from Europe in 1923, he moved to a small court off 10th Street. In 1940 a new neighbor arrived. Djuna Barnes, celebrated for

New York City literary haunts

Some writers are associated with particular hotels and bars. A plaque outside the Chelsea Hotel features a list of the eminent writers and artists who have lived there since 1905, from Mark Twain to Arthur Miller. Among the works that were actually written at the Chelsea Hotel are Arthur C. Clarke's *2001: A Space Odyssey*, William Burroughs's *Naked Lunch*, and Bob Dylan's song "Sad-Eye Lady of the Lowlands." In the 1920s Dorothy Parker, Harpo Marx and

---

LEFT: Henry James wrote about Americans abroad.
ABOVE: like a number of foreign writers, Quentin Crisp found that New York City suited his lifestyle.

her 1936 novel *Nightwood*, had just returned from 20 years in Paris and before long the two writers were regularly engaged in shouting battles conducted through their windows. Cummings died in 1962, Barnes 20 years later.

Chumley's bar and restaurant in the West Village, a former speakeasy, is still a writers' haunt – its walls are covered with vintage book jackets *(see page 347)*. Dylan Thomas, the Welsh poet and notorious drinker, was a regular at the White Horse Tavern on Hudson Street until his death in 1953. The Cedar Tavern on University Avenue, and Village coffeehouses, provided inspirational venues for Beat writers Jack Kerouac and Allen Ginsberg. ❑

SPORTS

No other state in the country has such a plethora of top sports teams in every arena – a fact New Yorkers celebrate with their unswerving support

New Yorkers are among the most fervent sports fans in the country. In terms of professional teams, the state enjoys an embarrassment of riches, and it's a rare year when at least one of these mighty institutions, whether it's baseball, football or hockey, isn't in contention for supremacy in its league.

Baseball

There was a time when New York City was a three-team baseball town, with loyalty to the New York Yankees matched by the equally unswerving affection heaped upon Manhattan's National League team, the New York Giants, and especially upon the Brooklyn Dodgers, also a National League outfit. Both of the latter teams, however, moved to the West Coast at the beginning of the 1958 season, and there are sports fans who still maintain that the departure of the Dodgers tore the heart out of Brooklyn.

New York became a National League town again in 1962, when the Metropolitans – which have never been called anything but the Mets – took to the field at the Giants' old Polo Grounds. In their first few seasons, the Mets seemed like nothing more than comic relief, intended as a counterbalance to the peerless Yankees. But the team soon settled into their new quarters at Shea Stadium, next to the 1964–65 World's Fair grounds in Queens *(see page 150)*, and started playing serious baseball. In 1969 the Mets astounded the sports world – their own supporters included – by winning the World Series. The shock was underscored by the simultaneous, and uncharacteristic, loss of form suffered by the Yankees. The Mets went on to repeat their championship performance in 1986, and in recent years they have made regular appearances in the post-season playoffs.

Baseball fans don't have to head to the Bronx or Queens – or even into New York City – to catch a game. Minor league teams, which serve as farm clubs developing and training younger players for future careers in the major leagues, are distributed throughout the state. Numerous connoisseurs of the grand old game's finer points are more than delighted to watch the Jamestown Jammers battle it out against the Hudson Valley Renegades, or to take in a match

between the Staten Island Yankees and the Batavia Muckdogs.

The first organized New York baseball team was the Knickerbocker Ball Club, which took to the field in the early 1840s. The team's name was borrowed from Washington Irving's fictional chronicler of old Dutch New York, Diedrich Knickerbocker *(see page 65)*. Indeed, thanks to that influential man of letters, "Knickerbocker" was for a long time the nickname applied to any New Yorker, or in fact to anything pertaining to New York. Nowadays, though, the word conjures up just the one institution – the National Basketball Association team known as the New York Knicks.

LEFT: the New York Knicks go for the long shot in the NBA finals against the San Antonio Spurs .
RIGHT: the Mets' Dennis Cook.

Basketball

The Knicks are heirs to a New York basketball tradition almost as old as the game, which dates from its invention by a Massachusetts Young Men's Christian Association (YMCA) instructor named James Naismith in 1891. The New York City 23rd Street YMCA team won the first national amateur basketball tournament in 1897 before reinventing itself as a successful professional outfit known as the New York Wanderers. New York has been basketball-mad ever since – just take a look at any public playground. In 1949 the Knicks were one of the original members of the National Basketball Association. The team, which plays its home games in Madison Square Garden in midtown Manhattan, honed the competitive skills of its onetime star Bill Bradley, later a US senator for New Jersey and presidential candidate.

Madison Square Garden is also the home of New York's professional Women's National Basketball Association team, the Liberty. The women take to the court during late spring and summer, which just about makes the Garden a year-round basketball venue.

College basketball is also popular throughout the state. The most constantly formidable team belongs to Syracuse University, a frequent

MADISON SQUARE GARDEN

Madison Square Garden, the fourth sports palace to bear the name, isn't a garden and it isn't in Madison Square, although the first two Gardens did stand at Madison Avenue and East 26th Street. The original Garden was a former railroad depot, replaced in 1890 by a splendid structure designed by Stanford White. The third, a 1925 building at Eighth Avenue and West 49th Street, was succeeded in 1968 by the present Garden, which is above Pennsylvania Station at West 31st Street *(see page 135)*. The colonnaded 1910 Pennsylvania Station was destroyed to make room for the new station and Garden, which, according to some, now needs to be replaced.

contender among the national Collegiate Athletic Association's annual "March Madness" winnowing of teams down to the "Final Four" and the eventual championship game. Another yearly college basketball event is the National Invitational Tournament (NIT), in which select teams play down to a concluding championship match. The NIT games are held at Madison Square Garden in late winter.

American football

New York State has three professional football teams – but only one plays its games within the state's borders. The Buffalo Bills' home field is Ralph Wilson Stadium, in the Buffalo suburb of Orchard Park *(see page 288)*. The Bills, who during the early 1990s won four consecutive conference championships – and then lost four consecutive Super Bowls – also have a political connection. One of their star quarterbacks was Jack Kemp, who ran for vice-president of the US in 1996 after a congressional career.

The New York Giants and New York Jets, both of which have loyal followings in the New York City metropolitan area, actually play on the other side of the Hudson River at Giants Stadium, in East Rutherford, New Jersey. Regardless of their current address, the Giants have a particularly long pedigree: in 1925, one

years, New York hosts the match between two of college football's most legendary rivals, Army and Navy, when the service academy teams play at the US Military Academy in West Point *(see page 185)*.

Hockey

There are three National Hockey League (NHL) teams in New York State – the Buffalo Sabres, New York Islanders and New York Rangers. The Sabres and Islanders are among the league's newer teams, although the Islanders – formerly the Québec Nordiques – won a remarkable four consecutive Stanley Cup championships in the

Tim Mara bought the franchise for $500. The Jets didn't come along until 1960, when they were known as the New York Titans; under their present guise, they achieved a moment of glory in 1969, when they won Super Bowl III under the leadership of quarterback "Broadway Joe" Namath. The Giants won again in 1991.

Colleges and universities large and small field football teams throughout New York State, and there are those who say that the college sport is a purer version of the game. In alternate

early 1990s. The Islanders play at the Nassau Coliseum in Uniondale, on Long Island. The Rangers, who play home games in Madison Square Garden, were among the NHL's original six teams; they won the cup in 1994, and in recent years counted among team members the now-retired "Great One," Wayne Gretzky, considered the finest hockey player of all time.

Soccer

The newest major league sport to arrive in New York is soccer, which has been making increasingly confident inroads into the American sporting scene during the past two decades. New York City's team is the New York/New

---

LEFT: Madison Square Garden hosts sports and entertainment events.
ABOVE: Tiki Barber leads the Giants to victory.

Jersey Metro Stars, who play home games at Meadowlands Stadium in East Rutherford. Major League Soccer, the professional organization, was established in 1996 with 10 teams. There has been talk of expansion, with New York and New Jersey each fielding teams of their own. In the meantime, the trip out to Meadowlands is a quick one, with buses from midtown Manhattan (connections are the same for Giants and Jets football games).

Other sports

New York has one of the most active horse-racing scenes in the United States, with inter-est sustained not only by track patrons but by participants in state-sponsored off-track betting. The state's major racetracks are Aqueduct, in New York City's borough of Queens; Belmont, site of the Belmont Stakes race (with the Preakness and Kentucky Derby, it's one jewel in the "Triple Crown"); in Elmont on Long Island; Saratoga, in Saratoga Springs north of Albany; and Yonkers Raceway in Yonkers, just north of New York City. Each of these tracks, with the exception of Yonkers, is operated under the authority of the New York Racing Association.

The place to watch auto racing in New York is Watkins Glen, in the Finger Lakes region at the southern end of Seneca Lake *(see page 274)*. For more than 50 years, The Glen has been home to numerous Sports Car Club of America-sanctioned events, as well as Formula One, Indy Car and NASCAR circuits.

New York State's premier tennis event, the US Open, is the richest of the world's four Grand Slam titles. It is held at the US Tennis Association's Arthur Ashe Stadium in Flushing, Queens (New York City) in late August and early September of each year.

New York also hosts the oldest invitational track meet staged in the United States – the Millrose Games; events are held at Madison Square Garden every February.

Long-distance runners compete in the New York Marathon in October. ❑

LEFT: racegoers have a choice of five major tracks in New York State.
RIGHT: New York Rangers hockey star Peter Nedved.

THE HOUSE THAT RUTH BUILT

One New York sports organization towers above all others. It has earned a reputation so august that its home ground is known throughout the United States as The Stadium. This refers to Yankee Stadium, also affectionately known to Yankees devotees as "The House that Ruth Built."

The stadium was completed by the Yankees' owner Jacob Ruppert in 1923. Since the 1920s heyday of Babe Ruth, perhaps the greatest baseball player in the game's history, the New York Yankees (American League) have dominated baseball, winning no fewer than 25 World Series championships – far more than any other team. Their two greatest modern eras have been in the 1950s, heyday of that other great baseball hero, Joe DiMaggio, and in the late 1990s. The 1998 players formed what many described as baseball's greatest team ever. (The only serious challenger to this title are the 1927 Yankees.)

The Yankee Stadium was modernized in the 1970s and is also used to stage concerts and other sports championships. Despite the occasional blusterings of owner George Steinbrenner about moving to New Jersey if the city doesn't help him build a new stadium in Manhattan, the team is likely to be suiting up in its home-game pinstripes at its Bronx headquarters for many years to come. After all – it's The Stadium.

DROPPING NAMES

The state's history is reflected in the variety of place names in New York, from
Native American and Dutch translations to those honoring American heroes

The great French novelist Marcel Proust compared the lure of place names to the attraction of unknown women passed in the street. Always mysterious, always different, their beauty lay in the fact that you could never possess them. (If you did come to possess, know, and understand them, your curiosity diminished and your sense of them as uncharted wildernesses waiting to be conquered changed into something more akin to mere affection.) There are always unknown place names on the map, just as there are always new women on the street: the traveler, like the lover, is ever hopeful, and is always likely to find himself surrounded by new possibilities.

New York, like many of the country's early colonies, is a land made up of strange place names. Its first European settlers, the Dutch, called it, with no undue modesty, Nieu Nederlandt (New Netherland). Before that, to all intents and purposes it was a nameless place populated by a loose confederation of Indian tribes *(see page 25)*. Since then, New York has collected a myriad of oddly juxtaposed and unexpected place names that recall different periods of the state's history.

These include Native American names such as Mannahatta, Niagara, and Montauk, and European names that survived the changing sovereignty of early colonial times – Cortlandt and Yonkers from the Dutch; Champlain and Versailles from the French; Bedford, Rochester, Albany from the English. Mixed in with these is an unexpected series of classical names: Utica, Troy, Syracuse, and Rome.

The dynamism of the New World is not merely a historical matter but rather an ongoing aspect of an ever-growing society. Thus place names in New York reflect recent as well as centuries-old immigrations. Canton and Delhi have a place here, as do Ghent, Peru, Smyrna, Amsterdam and, returning to Greece, Delphi.

LEFT: the name of New York's capital, Albany, reveals its English origins.
RIGHT: map of New Amsterdam.

Native influence

Historians differ on the proper translation of "Mannahatta." Probably the most accurate is that of the early 20th-century Indian expert William Beauchamp, who said the name means "hilly island." Another chronicler, inspired no doubt by reports of the Dutch influence on the

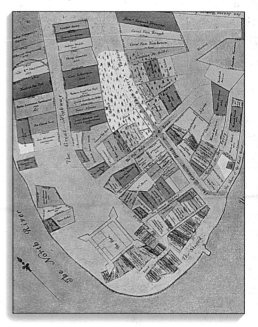

Indians, said the name means "place of general intoxication." Washington Irving, with no little sarcasm, proclaimed "Mannahatta" to mean an "Island of Manna, in other words – a land flowing with milk and honey."

Taken literally, the Indian names usually did no more than describe a particular place or scene. The word "Niagara" for example may not refer to the awesome impression of the famous waterfall as some believe *(see page 289)*, but means merely "neck" in the Seneca language, and referred to the strip of water that connects Lake Ontario to Lake Erie. Oswego, at the mouth of the river flowing into Lake Ontario, means "small water flowing into large." To the Native Americans, these names were often charged with some religious or tribal significance, but they were nearly always tied to the particularities of landscapes.

It was the descriptiveness of the Indian names that gave them their charm and, for many American writers, their moral superiority. To Walt Whitman and, to an even greater degree, James Fenimore Cooper, the Indian words had a naive quality that symbolized an innocent imagination unburdened by the traditions of European civilization. Theirs were the most truly "American" names available, and anything else was a hypocritical intrusion.

Names of victory

It might seem as though the European settlers displayed a marked lack of imagination in naming places after locations at home. When not bestowing names that reminded them of people and regions back home, they would simply use an appropriate description of a particular landscape. Today's travelers can only imagine the excitement felt by European explorers as they came up with new names for freshly discovered territories.

The greatest contribution of the Dutch to New York's toponymy was the suffix "kil" ("creek" in Dutch). As a result of Dutch-led

explorations up and down the Hudson River, most of the major streams and rivers in that valley bear names along the lines of Wynants Kill, Peekskill, and Quackenkill. Other suffixes introduced by the Dutch include "clove" ("gap" or "ravine"), as in Katerskill Clove, and "wyck." The most lasting German legacy is "burg" ("town"), as in "Staatsburg."

The honor of renaming a conquered place is, historically, a right of military victors; if few French names remain in New York, it is largely because it was the English forces that emerged triumphant from the French and Indian War (*see page 32*). Notable exceptions, such as Lake Champlain in the east, Versailles in the far west, and New Rochelle in Westchester notwithstanding, most French names south of Québec have been usurped by English names.

Some two-thirds of the place names in New York State today are of English derivation. Many of them commemorate either English nobility (Earlsville) or a wide range of towns, cities and counties back in the old country (New York, Albany, Rochester, Liverpool, Essex, Bedford). A number of names refer to the otherwise forgotten men and women who first eked a living out

PRESIDENTIAL NAMES

Political influence is evident in the numerous place names that honor acclaimed presidents such as George Washington, Abraham Lincoln, and John F. Kennedy.

now stands was renamed "Liberty Island." A Rhode Island senator had decided that the new name would be more appropriate than its earlier appellation of Bedloe's Island, a name it had borne on and off since 1670.

Route to nowhere

The origins of many of New York's place names have been forgotten. Good examples can be found along Route 22, which forms a tertiary black line on the map. It begins just above Manhattan and meanders up the length of the

of the wilderness. A good example is the pre-Revolutionary village of Wadhams Mills, now called Wadhams, in Essex County.

Communities often engaged in internecine struggles over what to name themselves, with political considerations often being paramount. The village of Delhi (pronounced "Dell-High" in New York) was apparently named after the Indian city as a result of the influence wielded by one Judge Ebenezer Foote. Similarly, in 1956 the island on which the Statue of Liberty

state, passing Connecticut, Massachusetts and Vermont before coming to an abrupt end on the other side of the Canadian border. One of the oldest roads in the state, it passes through once-prosperous villages with names such as Pawling, Amenia, Truthville, Comstock, West Chazy, Ticonderoga, and Mooers.

The road and its villages now seem somehow frozen in another time. The road is punctuated by a series of peeling billboards, motels whose hopeful "Vacancy" lights never stop flashing, trailer parks forgotten by all except their residents, and abandoned gas stations. These dilapidated reminders of the past are now as mysterious as the the villages' names. ❏

LEFT: in New York, every postmark tells a story.
ABOVE: the back roads of New York pass through places whose origins are long forgotten.

THE GREAT OUTDOORS

Visitors to New York need never feel trapped in the urban jungle – the state

utilizes some of the nation's finest scenery for a multitude of outdoor activities

New York State's tremendous diversity of climate and topography *(see page 17)* creates an array of opportunities for outdoor recreation unparalleled in the northeastern United States. Millions of acres of rugged backcountry feature salt- and freshwater lakes, daunting mountains and gentle hills. This hinterland, and tamer suburban territory, provide the venues for wilderness challenges and casual family weekends alike.

On the trail

New York State's most famous hiking trail is the Maine-to-Georgia Appalachian National Scenic Trail. Heading north out of New Jersey, the trail cuts across the state's southeastern corner, taking in parts of Bear Mountain State Park before crossing the Hudson River on the Bear Mountain Bridge and meandering through the scenic uplands of Putnam and Duchess counties toward the Connecticut border.

Also taking in much of southern New York State is the Long Path trail, which follows the Hudson from the palisades cliffs west of the George Washington Bridge in New Jersey all the way to Thacher State Park outside Albany. Both the Appalachian Trail and Long Path connect with dozens of shorter trails en route.

The Catskill and Adirondack Mountains contain much of the most picturesque – and most challenging – hiking terrain in the state. The Catskills offer trails threading through the rugged landscape that inspired the Hudson River School, most notably in the vicinity of Katterskill Falls and among the deep cloves (valleys) of Greene County Route 16. In the Adirondacks, the hiker's challenge is famously vertical: more than 40 of the region's peaks exceed 4,000 ft (1,220 meters) in height. The Adirondacks offer an extensive network of trails, along with rustic overnight lodging at the facilities of the Adirondack Mountain Club *(see*

page 359). Throughout New York, camping with a broader range of amenities is available at state parks and private campgrounds.

Rock climbing is popular in the Whiteface Mountain area of the Adirondacks, but the true mecca of the sport in New York – and one of the leading attractions for rock climbers

throughout the northeast – is the Shawangunk Mountains (popularly known as the 'Gunks), which range west and south of New Paltz *(see page 182)*. Scores of named technical routes in the 'Gunks have sharpened the skills of climbers who have gone on to challenge far greater cliffs and crags around the world.

Trail sports aren't exclusive to foot travelers. In recent decades there has been an upsurge in interest in mountain biking, which has led to the designation of many miles of trails specifically for cyclists. Furthermore, every year more alpine ski areas are opening their trails to mountain bikers in the summer. Touring cyclists can take advantage of a wonderful

LEFT: rock-climbers find plenty of challenges to test their skill and courage in the Catskills.
RIGHT: ready to hit the trail.

system of attractive secondary roads set amid the gently rolling wine country of the Finger Lakes. Snowmobilers also benefit from the private-public cooperation that has resulted in the creation of hundreds of miles of groomed trails, primarily in the Adirondacks.

On the water

Inland New York's signature watercraft is the canoe, along with its sleeker cousin the kayak, and its specialized offspring the Adirondack Guide Boat. The state's finest canoeing waters, in the Adirondacks, offer an incomparable combination of lake and stream paddling, as well as a system of portages and connecting waterways so extensive that it's possible to canoe for weeks without retracing a route. The Raquette River system is only one of the region's most popular routes; others center upon Saranac Lake or the state-designated St Regis Canoe Area. For whitewater rafting, enthusiasts take their kayaks to the Class III and IV rapids of the Mad River, or the Class V waters of the Hudson River Gorge.

Farther south, the headwaters of the Delaware River are another popular canoeing destination, as are the flat blue waters of Long Island's Peconic, Carmans, and Connetquot rivers. Long

ADIRONDACK GUIDE BOATS

The Adirondack Guide Boat is as much a symbol of the outdoor heritage of New York's North Country as the Great Camp and those Winslow Homer watercolors in which the tug of a trout on the fishing line is almost palpable.

The birchbark canoe, the original watercraft of the Native Americans, was light, easily portaged and simple to repair. By the 1830s, white settlers in the Adirondacks had begun to develop a vessel more suited to their needs – a work boat for hunting, fishing, and transporting heavy bundles of beaver pelts. The Adirondack Guide Boat, canoe-based in design, was broader, round-bottomed, built of cedar planking, and rowed rather than paddled.

They are called "guide boats" because, by the end of the 19th century, these light, sturdy craft were used by local guides for transporting visitors though the region's network of lakes and streams. A typical guide boat could carry three people, slip across 30 miles (48 km) of water in a day and flip easily onto a guide's shoulders for portage. In contrast with canoes, the boats were constructed without crosspieces known as thwarts, so that an angler working on board need not feel thwarted in his movements.

Refined by generations of guides into an efficient craft capable of cutting through wind and waves, guide boats are still custom-made by a few North Country artisans.

Island also offers sea kayaking, with favored spots at Montauk Point and on the sheltered waters between the north and south forks. At the other end of the state, kayakers and canoeists alike appreciate the challenge of navigating their way through the Thousand Islands in the St Lawrence River – well away, of course, from seaway traffic.

Other watersports in New York State include rafting on the Black and Salmon rivers in the Thousand Islands and St Lawrence Seaway region and on Moose River

best for rolling surf. (The north shore, with fewer beaches, faces the calmer Long Island Sound.) The surf begins at legendary Coney Island, right in Brooklyn *(see page 150)*, and extends east through public facilities at Jones Beach and Robert Moses state parks, Fire Island National Seashore, and the town beaches of the Hamptons.

Upstate, there are ample opportunities for sun-worshipers, with state park beaches on Lakes Ontario and Erie, the two Great Lakes that border New York; in the

MASS EXODUS

Long Island is an easy day-trip from New York City, so be prepared to jostle with crowds of city dwellers escaping the urban heat during the summer months.

in the Adirondacks; tubing – floating on truck inner tubes – on Esopus Creek, near Phoenicia in the Catskills; and canal boating on the peaceful waters of the old Erie Canal, Oswego River and auxiliary waterways. Houseboats are often available to rent on the Thousand Islands.

At the beach

Virtually all of New York's saltwater exposure is found on Long Island, where the Atlantic Ocean beaches facing the south shore are the

LEFT: a girls' day out on the sparkling waters of Otsego Lake, near Cooperstown.
ABOVE: a game of volleyball on a Long Island beach.

Thousand Islands area; and along the Finger Lakes. The cool waters of Lake George and Lake Champlain also invite swimmers – think of pine instead of salt as the prevailing scent.

Fishing and hunting

Ringed by enormous lakes, and with a saltwater threshold at Long Island, New York has long been known as prime fishing territory. Fly fishing in the Adirondacks and Catskills – where the east branch of the Delaware is a legend unto itself – offers brook, rainbow, and brown trout *(see page 361)*. Lake trout and landlocked salmon can be found in the big, deep lakes of the Adirondacks, in Lake

Champlain, and in the Finger Lakes, and Coho salmon have been successfully bred in lakes Erie and Ontario. Anglers on the St Lawrence River and other northern waters pursue pickerel, pike and their big, feisty relative, the muskellunge. Large- and small-mouth bass inhabit warmer waters, and the shad has recently made a comeback in the Hudson River. In winter, ice fishing is a popular method of catching perch and walleye.

Saltwater fishing centers on Long Island. Here any number of surfcasters wait patiently

HERMIT'S HAVEN

Almost half of the state's population live in New York City, leaving some 47,000 sq miles (122,000 sq km) of tranquil landscape to explore.

firearms regulations, and with laws pertaining to local municipalities, as well as with statewide hunting regulations.

Winter activities

New York State played an early role in the popularization of skiing in the United States. It was in the Lake Placid area that the legendary Norwegian outdoorsman Herman "Jackrabbit" Smith-Johanssen laid out some of the nation's first cross-country ski routes. The former New York governor W. Averell Harriman was an enthusiastic downhill skier who helped develop the state-run Belleayre ski area near Phoenicia *(see page 196)*. Belleayre and privately owned Hunter are the preeminent downhill resorts in the Catskills, where a lot of the snow is often machine-made. The Adirondacks, which hosted both the 1932 and 1980 Winter Olympics at Lake Placid, offer, among smaller areas, Whiteface, Gore, Big Tupper, Titus and McCauley, and are renowned for providing European-style ski hospitality *(see page 362)*. There is even a scattering of smaller ski areas among the gentler hills of the Finger Lakes and in the far western parts of the state.

for the summer runs of striped bass and bluefish; the charter boats that set off from Montauk and neighboring ports go after these as well as larger prey such as bluefin tuna.

New York State maintains hunting seasons for deer, bear, wild turkey, small game (grouse, pheasant, rabbit, hare, squirrel), ducks, geese and several other species. Deer and bear (both of which can be hunted with firearms or by archery, depending on the season) in particular have made inroads even into suburban areas, although prime hunting grounds are necessarily far away from heavily populated regions. Hunters planning a visit to New York should familiarize themselves with both state and local

Cross-country skiers enjoy their sport in winter everywhere from New York City's Central Park to the wilds of the Adirondacks. Generally, cross-country ski trails fall into two categories, aside from the opportunities afforded by urban parks and bikeways. First are the groomed public and private areas, such as those maintained by many downhill ski resorts and at the sport's most famous New York venue, the Olympic course at Lake Placid's Mount Van Hoevenberg. But there are also the backcountry trails, which are generally ungroomed except for the tracks of the last skiers to pass by. The Adirondacks are laced with these serene but often challenging forest byways, including the one named after the great man himself – the Jackrabbit Trail covers some 34 miles (55 km) from Keene to Paul Smiths.

Head outdoors in New York, and it's easy to follow in the footsteps of giants, while taking in the state's dramatic, unspoiled scenery. ❑

LEFT: striped bass at Montauk Harbor.
RIGHT: after the snowfall, New York State is a winter sports playground.

FLORA AND FAUNA

Although no longer the forested landscape it once was, New York has managed to preserve a range of vegetation, mammals, and birdlife

For a state with a population density of approximately 400 people per square mile (2.6 sq km), New York possesses a very broad variety of plant and animal species. In part this diversity is due to the fact that New York's population is largely concentrated in the vast conurbation at its southern extreme and in a string of cities along the river valleys and Great Lakes. Human demography notwithstanding, quite a range of animals inhabit the border between city and country habitats. Many species thrive in just this type of environment – ask any suburban gardener whose precious shrubs have been devoured by wild deer.

Trees and forests

New York's location – at the point where the typical hardwood forests of the southern and central Appalachians meet the coniferous zone popularly known as the North Woods – is another reason for the presence of an extensive range of species here. Within the state's boundaries is a broad swath of the Allegheny Plateau, along with Appalachian sub-ranges such as the Catskills and Taconics. In the Adirondacks, which are not part of the Appalachians, but of the Laurentian Plateau, individual peaks rise high enough to constitute a genuinely alpine environment at their summits. Long Island has the sandy soils, barrier beaches, and relatively moderate temperatures that are more often associated with places such as Cape Cod and the coast of New Jersey.

The extensive logging and clearing of farmland in the 19th century left little of the virgin forest that once flourished in New York. What remains can be found in remote parts of the Adirondacks. A glimpse into how the New York City area probably looked in its primeval state can be had at Riverdale's Wave Hill Preserve in the Bronx, where a 10-acre (4-hectare) tract of land has been returned to its virgin state.

LEFT: the red fox is primarily nocturnal, but during the day it can sometimes be seen looking for food.
RIGHT: the ailanthus, the "tree of heaven."

New York has about 150 tree species. These include the hardwoods maple, beech, walnut, birch, oak, tulip, hazelnut, alder, sweetgum and sycamore (birch, maple and oak are represented by a number of species). Elm, once a staple of small towns and residential neighborhoods due to the graceful way its branches arch over streets,

has been devastated by Dutch Elm disease since the 1960s. Shrubs and smaller trees include witch hazel, rhododendron, mountain laurel, dogwood, elderberry, and sumac (staghorn and poison). Conifers predominate at higher elevations in the Catskills and Adirondacks, and include red, white and black spruce and balsam fir. White pine, long a lumberman's staple, thrives in the northern forests although seldom at the 100–200-ft (30–70-meter) heights once favored for naval ship masts.

One of the most remarkable success stories among tree species introduced from abroad is the ailanthus, known as the "tree of heaven" as a result of the considerable heights it can attain.

It can grow as much as 8 ft (2.5 meters) in a year and may reach a height of 100 ft (30 meters). It can thrive under conditions – smog, dust, exhaust fumes – that would kill many other species and is the fastest-growing woody plant in the region. Of the numerous ailanthus trees that can be found throughout New York City, many sprouted from the debris of vacant lots or from cracks in the sidewalks.

New York's mammals

The largest animal resident of New York State – and the largest member of the deer family in the world – is the moose. The revival of the moose is one of the great comeback stories of the northeast. Killed or driven out of its North Woods haunts (northern Maine excepted) by the end of the 19th century, this fine creature has returned over the past decades and now numbers well into the thousands in the northern tier of the New England states and New York.

A moose can grow to 7 ft (2 meters) in height at the shoulder, and can weigh as much as 1,400 lbs (640 kg). Mature males shed their distinctive antlers, which frequently reach lengths of 4 ft (1.2 meters) or more, every year. Semi-aquatic in summer, moose feed on vegetation in lakes, streams, and marshes; in winter, they

THE CHESTNUT TREE

Of all the species of hardwood tree that made up the primeval New York forests, one of the most beautiful, and useful, was *Castanea dentata*, the chestnut. Growing to heights of 100 ft (30 meters), with a trunk diameter of 2–4 ft (0.5–1.5 meters), the chestnut spread its canopy of leaves throughout the New York uplands and neighboring states. Its wood was light and strong – 17th-century chestnut-framed houses stand to this day – and it provided the tasty nuts sold by vendors on the streets of Manhattan.

However, the chestnuts sold by today's vendors have to be imported from Europe. In the early years of the 20th century, a fungus that attacks chestnut bark arrived in the United States, most likely from Asia. Within a generation, the state's entire chestnut population had been lost.

The chestnut and its blight survive, in a weird symbiosis. New chestnut saplings can sprout from the roots of dead parent trees and may reach a height of 15 ft (4.6 meters). The same fate nearly always awaits them, though: once a chestnut is mature enough for its bark to begin forming furrows, the blight lodges in the furrows, girdles the tree and kills it. Some day, silviculturalists hope, a blight-resistant variety of chestnut might appear, or an inoculation may be derived from a strain of the fungus. Until then, New York's chestnut tree will survive only in its stunted form.

browse on woody plants. Drivers in rural regions of upstate New York should be careful of moose crossing roads, especially during fall mating periods. In the wild, moose should not be approached. Although generally shy, they can charge when they feeling threatened or when defending their calves.

The whitetail deer, a far smaller relative of the moose, is plentiful throughout New York State and is actually becoming a nuisance in suburban areas where its numbers are not kept in check by hunting. Only half as tall as a moose – males weigh 200–300 lbs (90–135 kg) – and sporting a multipointed annual growth of

to be lethal (except to the deer) than moose-car encounters.

Another emblem of the northern forest is the black bear. This is an extremely reclusive creature and yet, like the deer, it has made inroads into the fringes of civilization as suburbs encroach on woodlands. As many humans have discovered, bears are attracted to bird feeders and garbage alike. A male black bear can easily measure 3 ft (1 meter) at the shoulder when on all fours, and weigh over 400 lbs (180 kg). Females are considerably smaller. Solitary except when mating or raising cubs, bears emerge from a deep winter sleep (as opposed to

antlers, the whitetail is a denizen of woodlands and fringe areas along meadows, particularly old farmland returning to forest growth. Green plants, twigs and buds, nuts, apples, and corn crops are their favored diet, and they often dine in suburban gardens, much to the disgruntlement of human inhabitants. Especially in spring and early fall, it's not uncommon to see deer browsing in groups in open areas along roadsides. Collisions with cars are not infrequent but, given the deer's lesser size, are less likely

LEFT: the moose has made a remarkable comeback.
ABOVE LEFT: black bears shy away from humans.
ABOVE RIGHT: coyotes have something to howl about.

an authentic hibernation) to forage for the feasts of spring – green shoots, insects, grubs, fish, and rodents. In the fall, before "denning up," they add nuts, fruits, and berries to their diet. Bears are mainly nocturnal and, even when out and about in daylight, they are so shy of human contact that they are rarely seen. They would rather run away than confront a potential threat, but are unpredictable and especially dangerous when cornered – or, in the case of a female, when a threat to cubs is perceived. Never come between a mother bear and her cubs.

Several species of canine and feline predators play a role in New York's fields and forests. The primarily nocturnal red fox, similar in size to a small dog, patrols the fringes of farmland in pursuit of small rodents or of insects and vegetation when hunting is unsuccessful. The fox's larger cousin, the Eastern coyote, is about the size of a German Shepherd dog but is less full-bodied. The coyote, also largely nocturnal, hunts either alone or in packs; rodents are its preferred food. Even in neighborhoods with relatively large human populations, the coyote's trademark yelps and howls have increasingly become a part of the nightime soundscape.

It's a rare observer who comes across the elusive bobcat or lynx in New York's forests. Solitary and nocturnal, these tawny cats prey primarily on snowshoe hare, cottontail rabbit, and other small creatures. The bobcat, the larger of the two species, measures 2–4 ft (about 1 meter) in length and weighs from 15–65 lbs (7–30 kg). The lynx, identified by its distinctive ear tufts, is the rarer of the two.

New York shares a considerable variety of smaller mammals with the other Appalachian states – skunks, porcupines, raccoons, rabbits and hares, opossums (a fairly recent arrival from more southerly regions), and red and gray squirrels. Gray squirrels predominate in the cities, but they are not always gray. In Inwood Hill Park in Manhattan for example, an isolated

ACID RAIN AND THE ADIRONDACK LAKES

The web of life in the lakes of the Adirondacks depends upon a delicate balance of many factors, not least of which is the acidity level of the water, measured in pH balance. The pH scale of acidity and alkalinity runs from 1 (most acidic) to 13 (most alkaline), with pure, neutral water registering a pH of 7. Unfortunately, the precipitation called "acid rain" can have a significantly lower pH level and when it begins to influence the acidity level of lakes and ponds, aquatic life is threatened.

Acid rain is a serious problem in the Adirondacks for two reasons. First, the mountains lie in the path of prevailing winds that carry pollution – particularly sulfur dioxide – from coal-burning power and industrial plants in the Midwest. Second, the soil is generally incapable of buffering the effects of precipitation that has been acidified by pollutants. When acidity in the region's water begins to build, there is little alkalinity in surrounding soils or lake bottoms to ward off the damage.

There are roughly 2,800 lakes within the boundaries of the 6-million-acre (2.4-million hectare) Adirondack Park and researchers say that as many as 500 of them are too acidified to support plant or animal life. If acid rain isn't quickly and significantly reduced, they warn, half of all Adirondack lakes and ponds may be lifeless by 2040.

population carries a gene that determines the surprising black color of local squirrels.

Less frequently encountered, but fairly common in undeveloped areas, are the mustelid species mink and muskrat, which live around wetland areas, and weasel, ermine, marten and fisher in drier habitats. Somehow the beaver managed to survive the onslaught of the fur trade that first brought the Dutch West Indies Company into the hinterlands of New York. Today's populations of these industrious creatures are busy building lodges and dams on streams and ponds across the north country.

Snakes

There are only two poisonous species of snake in New York and neither are particularly common. The timber rattlesnake is identified by the sound of its rattle and by its coloring – dark brown or black V-shaped cross-bands on a yellow or brown background. The timber rattler primarily inhabits extremely rocky areas such as slate or limestone outcrops. It averages about 3½ ft (1 meter) in length, and is quite shy, but don't be fooled into cornering it.

The Northern copperhead is more heavy-bodied. It is generally less than 3 ft (1 meter) in length, and has a coppery red head with chestnut-brown cross-bands (wider toward the middle) on a lighter background. Partial to rocky or wooded areas, they also tend to avoid encounters with humans if at all possible.

Bites from either species are severe enough to require medical attention, following the usual recommended first aid practices.

Birdlife

In large measure, New York owes its abundance of birdlife to its location on the Atlantic flyways frequented by songbirds, waterfowl, and shorebirds. The state features numerous fine sites from which to see both year-round and migratory species, but there are two particularly good locations for watching waterfowl migrations in spring and fall. Between early March and mid-May, the wetlands of the Iroquois National Wildlife Refuge, 40 miles (65 km) northeast of Buffalo, are a prime spot for viewing northbound black, pintail, ring-necked

and mallard ducks, northern shovelers, teal, American wigeo, and Canada geese *(see page 294)*. Farther east, the Montezuma National Wildlife Refuge, north of Cayuga Lake near Seneca Falls, offers similar waterfowl viewing opportunities *(see page 269)*.

Shorebirds – plovers, sandpipers, red knots, willets, yellowlegs, and other related species dependent on foraging along tidal areas during migration stopovers – are most common in New York on Long Island, during the spring migration. Viewing spots include Fire Island National Seashore and nearby Wertheim National Wildlife Refuge *(see page 166)*.

In the Adirondacks, two species of bird bear the special stamp of this vast wilderness, and both impart their own differing brands of majesty to this remote terrain. The bald eagle, which has long been a rare presence, if not altogether absent from the northeast, can still occasionally been seen circling the skies above New York's northern counties. And on many Adirondack lakes, there is at least one breeding pair of common loons. These birds are remarkable divers whose tessellated black-and-white backs barely ride above the water. Nothing represents the North Woods so much as the maniacal laughter of a loon, or its high-pitched wail drifting across a still inlet at dusk. ❏

LEFT: skunks feature among the many mammals to be found in the Appalachian states.
ABOVE: New York is an ornithologist's heaven.

ARCHITECTURE

From the classically inspired mansions around the state to Manhattan's trademark
skyscrapers, New York's architecture has always been both ambitious and striking

Long before the arrival of the first European settlers, the area we now know as New York State was clustered with communal longhouses built by the Iroquois tribes. New York's earliest architects were practitioners of a "form follows function" regime that might have impressed that dictum's famous originator, Louis Sullivan. These rectangular structures with barrel-shaped roofs and walls sheathed in bark were set within wooden stockades and were especially practical during winter, when the body heat of the inhabitants and their dogs was augmented by fires vented via smokeholes in the roofs. A replica of a small longhouse (some were over 200 ft/60 meters long) is on view at the Fenimore House Museum in Cooperstown *(see page 250)*, and there is a large one at Ganondagan State Historic Site in the Finger Lakes *(see page 276)*.

Early European architecture

If a landmarks preservation commission had existed during the 18th and 19th centuries, we might have a better idea today of the architecture of Dutch New Amsterdam. But since historic preservation was an all but unheard-of concept until relatively recently, we can only surmise what Peter Stuyvesant's 17th-century town looked like by turning to examples of architecture of the period that have survived in The Netherlands. Early Manhattan had similar step-gabled brick buildings, although wood construction and simple sloping roofs would have been far more common than in the Dutch homeland.

Although the last of Manhattan's 17th-century structures disappeared long ago, there are several survivors in the outer boroughs, all modest farmhouses and one-time village residences. The oldest is the Pieter Claesen Wyckoff house, a modest, one-and-a-half-story cottage in the Flatlands section of Brooklyn

LEFT: a country church in upstate New York.
RIGHT: the bark longhouse at Ganondagan State Historic Site is an authentic reconstruction.

dating from 1652, possibly earlier. Rural areas of southern New York State offer a number of examples of what has become known as "Dutch Colonial" architecture, characterized by stout brownstone construction and gambrel roofs.

New York architecture of the 18th century followed the Georgian pattern. Always more

formal in its urban manifestations, Georgian is a classically inspired style often executed in brick, with simple, elegant proportions dependent on the basic rectangle, ornate treatment of doorways (often with flanking columns), and steep hipped or gable-ended roofs. Although it is essentially a 1907 reconstruction of a 1719 building, Manhattan's Fraunces Tavern, site of Washington's farewell to his officers in 1783, is a good example of the style *(see page 114)*.

The Federal style, essentially a lightening and simplification of Georgian elements, predominated from the 1790s to 1820s. In the city, Federal architecture came to be associated with the new vogue for row houses, and Greenwich

Village retains several fine examples. Upstate, the 1807 mansion at Lorenzo State Historic Site, Cazenovia, typifies this graceful style as applied to a country home *(see page 259)*.

Revival styles

During the early 19th century, US architects began to seek inspiration from Greece and Rome. Greek Revival architecture – highlighted by stately columns capped with Parthenon-style pediments, corner pilasters, and broad triangular gables – projected dignity and practicality. With its noble proportions and cool, reasonable façades, Greek Revival seemed the perfect

stylistic expression for the new republic. Wall Street's 1842 Federal Hall is an outstanding example *(see page 116)*; so is the 1840 St Peter's Church at Barclay and Church streets. As with Federal, the style was applied to Greenwich Village row houses. The style also caught on in small cities and towns across the New York hinterlands – not surprisingly, in a state peppered with place names out of classical antiquity.

As the 19th century advanced, other revival styles followed. Two of the most important were Gothic and Italianate. The former had its most notable New York City exponent in Richard Upjohn, architect of the 1846 Trinity

THE FASHION FOR CAST IRON

A corner of Manhattan contains dozens of remnants of one of New York's most interesting, if short-lived, architectural periods: the Soho Cast-Iron Historic District *(see page 125)*.

In 1850s New York, a premium was placed on new buildings that could be cheaply and quickly constructed but that would exhibit the rich detailing then in vogue. This latter requisite was especially important for new retail outlets in the fashionable Broadway blocks north of Canal Street. These requirements were met by an iron-foundry owner, James Bogardus, who began casting façades in iron and assembling them on site. The façades could be extensively and repetitively ornate since only a single mold

needed to be fashioned and, since the cast-iron façades bore none of the building's load – taken by traditional wood framing and brick side and rear walls – there was room for spacious windows. The buildings erected by Bogardus and his competitors were precursors of the curtain-wall structures that dominate the modern city skyline.

By the 1870s, enthusiasm for cast iron had waned as the buildings were prone to collapse in fires. After decades of neglect, Soho's cast-iron structures were discovered in the 1960s by artists seeking inexpensive loft space. Recognition of their historical importance followed, and this 26-block area was designated an official historic district.

Church *(see page 117)*; and James Renwick, Jr, who followed his 1845 Grace Church (Broadway at 10th Street) with his 1858–79 masterpiece St Patrick's Cathedral, with spires completed in 1888 *(see page 141)*.

One of the most influential Gothic Revival architects practicing in New York State was Alexander Jackson Davis. Davis's grandest structure is Lyndhurst in Tarrytown *(see page 173)*. Davis designed this stone mansion in 1838, expanding it and adding a tower in the 1860s. Later, it became famous as the residence of railroad robber baron Jay Gould. On a less pretentious level, Andrew Jackson Downing

York City dwellings, the brownstone row house. Look for flat roofs, roundheaded windows, and projecting cornices supported by ornate brackets. In small towns and rural areas, freestanding Italianate houses have similar features, and are often topped by an ornamental cupola or "lantern."

Residential and public styles

The late 19th century served up a welter of residential styles. Among the most popular was French Second Empire, easily identifiable in the mansard-roofed "haunted house" style of architecture. Although this expansive style

helped spread the popularity of "Carpenter Gothic" country cottages with his Cottage Residences and the Architecture of Country Houses. Find a gingerbread-style farm or village home and you're looking at Downing's legacy.

While neo-Gothic architecture represented the romantic stylistic impulse, the mode that carried the classical tradition through the mid-19th century was Italianate. Italianate is the prevailing style of that most typical of New

---

LEFT: the Haughwout Building, Soho's cast-iron queen.
ABOVE LEFT: a Greek Revival mansion.
ABOVE RIGHT: Second Empire mansard-roofed house of the 1870s.

turns up less frequently in space-conscious New York City, there are several examples along Buffalo's Delaware Avenue.

Among other residential architectural trends popular in New York during the late 19th and early 20th centuries was the Queen Anne style. Asymmetrical façades and floor plans, wrap-around porches, dormers, bay windows, stained glass, and a reliance on contrasting textures characterizes Queen Anne, as in Theodore Roosevelt's 1885 Long Island mansion, Sagamore Hill *(see page 158)*.

The Georgian Revival offered a return to the formal, symmetrical approach of the 18th century. President Franklin D. Roosevelt's

Hyde Park home, Springwood, was given its current Georgian appearance in 1915 *(see page 177)*. Another grandly proportioned example is the 1909 Rochester mansion of Kodak founder George Eastman, now the International Museum of Photography *(see page 278)*.

Architects of public and commercial buildings of the *fin de siècle* were much enamored of the Beaux Arts style, a French import that drew heavily on classical and Renaissance traditions to create a formal, monumental look. New York City's greatest examples are Richard Morris Hunt's 1902 Metropolitan Museum of Art *(see page 146)*, Carrére and Hastings' 1911 New

York Public Library *(see page 139)*, and Warren and Wetmore's 1913 Grand Central Terminal *(see page 139)*.

Modern architecture

In their 1896 Guaranty Building (now the Prudential Building) Dankmar Adler and Louis Sullivan gave the Buffalo skyline one of the first truly modern skyscrapers, a 13-story gem that combines unabashed modern verticality with a formal base-and-capital design and lush ornamentation in terra cotta.

This organic integration of ornament and surface, a Sullivan trademark, was carried much farther by his disciple Frank Lloyd Wright, for whom surface texture became ornament. Wright did much fine residential work in Buffalo, including the 1906 Darwin Martin House, an exercise in his Prairie Style characterized by horizontal massings, low overhanging roofs and flowing, open interior spaces.

Wright's most famous New York building is in Manhattan – the 1959 Guggenheim Museum *(see page 146)*. Working at the end of his 70-year career, Wright designed the flowerpot-shaped Guggenheim to provide an upwardly spiraling exhibition gallery with no formal division of stories. It is one of New York's most personal and stylistically unclassifiable architectural statements, equaled in that regard only by Eero Saarinen's swooping TWA terminal at Kennedy International Airport (1959).

Prior to their near-universal embrace of the International and successive Post Modern styles, government and corporate architectural clients helped popularize the Art Deco trend of the early 20th century. Outside of New York City, two of the state's most distinctive essays in Art Deco are Buffalo's City Hall (Dietel and Wade, 1931), a bluff, massive building whose central tower is capped by a low dome and observatory deck and with striking mosaics in the lobbies *(see page 283)*; and Rochester's 1929 Genesee Valley Trust Building (now the Times Square Building), designed by Voorhees, Gmelin and Walker *(see page 277)*. This is easily the most unusual office tower in New York State. It's topped by four 42-ft (13-meter) aluminum wings, each pointing upward, and practically shouts the idea of Art Deco as an architecture soaring into tomorrow.

Modern architecture reached its New York apotheosis in Albany's Empire State Plaza (Wallace K. Harrison, 1973–9), Governor Nelson Rockefeller's city-within-a-city of government offices. One 44-story and four 22-story towers rise in stark white marble from a 98-acre (40-hectare) mall, which also supports an egg-shaped meeting center. It is the farthest any buildings in New York have come from the idea of human scale and amount to a gargantuan display of Rockefeller's great passion: abstract modernist sculpture. Long after the days of the Iroquois longhouse, form was now following form. ❏

LEFT: many wooden houses in upstate New York sport Grecian-style pediments above the entrance.

The Manhattan Skyscraper

Although Chicago architects invented the skyscraper, it was in New York City that the steel frame, curtain wall, and elevator – the three elements that made tall buildings possible – were employed to the most dramatic effect. The term "skyscraper" properly applies to a tall building freed from the constraints of all-masonry construction and allowed to rise unfettered by the requirements of load-bearing walls. Its support derives from its steel skeleton, and the term "curtain wall" refers to walls that are mere coverings for the frame.

Throughout the 1890s, a great many steel-framed buildings were constructed in New York City. People called them skyscrapers – but the first real attempt to break from the eight- and 10-story pack was Daniel Burnham's 1902 Flatiron Building *(see page 133)*. Rising 22 stories in the shape of its triangular lot (its form suggests an old-fashioned clothes iron), the Flatiron owes its aesthetic appeal not only to its freestanding height but to the appearance it gives of sailing up Broadway.

A trio of new towers soon proved that steel framing and electric elevators were capable of soaring far higher than 22 stories, although their architects remained committed to historical styles. Ernest Flagg capped the tower of his 600-ft (182-meter) 1908 Singer Building (since demolished) with a mansard roof. A year later, Napoleon LeBrun gave the Metropolitan Life Insurance Company a 700-ft (213-meter) tower that replicated the campanile of St Mark's in Venice – at more than twice the campanile's height. Finally, Cass Gilbert handed the tallest building title to retail tycoon F.W. Woolworth, also with a historical twist. The 1913 Woolworth Building soars 792 ft (241 meters) and is so unabashedly Gothic that it has been called a "cathedral of commerce."

But the great era of New York skyscrapers began during the economic boom of the 1920s. The Art Deco style and the skyscraper were made for each other – and nowhere are they better paired than in the Chrysler Building, William Van Alen's 1930 masterpiece in stone and steel *(see page 140)*. The 1,048-ft (320-meter) structure, which employs automotive motifs such as enormous gargoyles

RIGHT: the Woolworth Building, completed in 1913, was for a time the world's tallest building.

inspired by radiator caps, reaches a pinnacle of successive narrowing crowns topped with a rapier-like spire – an immense piece of Art-Deco jewelry.

The 1,250-ft (380-meter) Empire State Building by Shreve, Lamb and Harmon, took the "world's tallest" title from the Chrysler in 1931 *(see page 134)*. It toned down the Art-Deco vocabulary but its sleek capstone tower and soaring lobby still incorporate the geometry that is a hallmark of the style. Raymond Hood's 1934 RCA Building, centerpiece of Rockefeller Center, was a more muted version, presaging the slablike skyscrapers to come.

During the post-World War II era, the International style ruled in monuments such as the 1952

Lever House by Skidmore, Owings and Merrell, and Mies van der Rohe's 1958 Seagram Building, both illustrating the grace with which glass curtain walls can rise from an open plaza. However, much of the 1950–60s gave the city scores of anonymous glass boxes, setting the stage for the inarticulate twin towers of the World Trade Center (1973).

Since the late 1970s, skyscraper architects have returned to historical references – such as Philip Johnson's AT&T Building with a broken-pediment top said to resemble a piece of Chippendale furniture – and midtown and financial district towers that seem to fight each other for predominance. They will have to fight harder, most critics agree, to fend off the Flatiron and Chrysler buildings. ❑

PLACES

*A detailed guide to the entire state, with principal sites
clearly cross-referenced by number to the maps*

New York State is one of the easiest states in which to chart a journey, whether it be a day's jaunt or an extended vacation. Each of its 11 regions has a character all its own, often revealed in its name. New York City needs little introduction. The world's capital of finance and entertainment, it offers a range of incomparable attractions and the richest architecture in the country. Long Island, at the southern tip, is the Atlantic seaboard's largest island and is known for its historic fishing villages and whaling museums; the Hamptons' dunes and surf are especially popular with celebrities and wealthy New Yorkers escaping the city's heat.

The beauty of the Hudson Valley, just to the north, inspired an entire school of landscape painting. Its mansions, historic sites, and grand estates speak of the age of gentility and grace. The Catskills encompass 3,000 miles (5,000 km) of mountains, forests, trails, and outdoor attractions. Known for the Borscht Belt vacation area, it offers a variety of charming places to stay. Midway up the northern route to Canada is the Capital-Saratoga region, a populated nexus of canal towns and watering places grown into venerable cities. Politics and history at Albany quicken the pace before it slows down again to embrace the tranquility of the Adirondacks. Here is nature at its most sublime: 6 million acres (2.4 million hectares) of lakes, rivers, and wilderness peaks.

Curving along the state's northwestern edge, nearly 2,000 islands make up the Thousand Islands Seaway. Water is the key to attractions here, from boat cruises to fishing, with 22 state parks lining the Seaway Trail. The predominantly rural Central-Leatherstocking region takes its name from the literary saga penned by James Fenimore Cooper, whose family virtually settled this area after the Indian peoples. Now it has several important museums, plus Glimmerglass Lake with a wonderful summer opera season.

The Finger Lakes, named for the configuration of its six major lakes, is a region of farms, apple orchards, and vineyards as well as spectacular glens and gorges. Rochester and Syracuse, two of the state's major cities, are replete with museums, technology centers, and events. In Greater Niagara, most head for the Falls, or for a quick trip into Canada. Metropolitan Buffalo's attractions include Artpark and the nation's third-oldest zoo. The grand natural feature of this region is Letchworth State Park, "The Grand Canyon of the East."

Indian reservations and the famed Chautauqua Institution, still operative, are in the Chautauqua-Allegheny region, named for a lake and a mountain range. Lake Erie here is great for fishing, while Allegany State Park is New York's largest four-season park. ❑

PRECEDING PAGES: cruising through the Thousand Islands; cottages at Conesus Lake in the Finger Lakes; view of Manhattan from the Empire State Building. **LEFT:** Lake Placid in the Adirondacks lives up to its name.

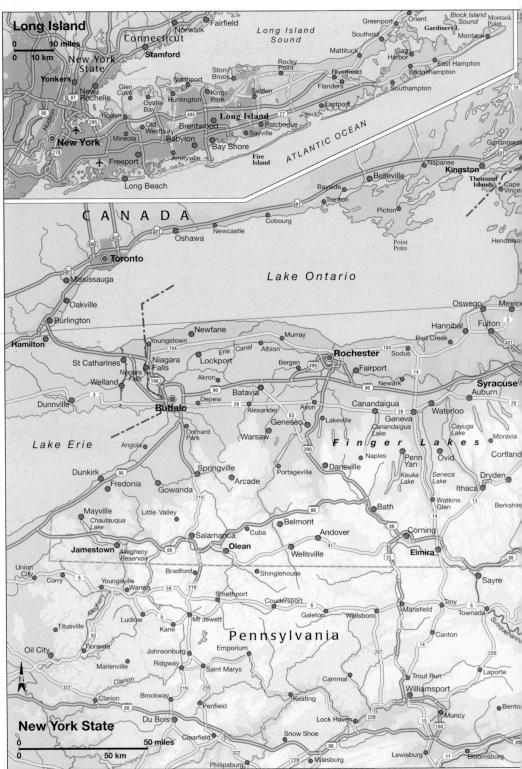

Long Island

0   10 miles
0   10 km

New York State

Connecticut

Fairfield
Norwalk
Stamford

Long Island Sound

Greenport   Orient
Southold
Mattituck
Sag Harbor

Block Island Sound   Montauk Point

Gardiners I.

Montauk

Yonkers
New Rochelle
Glen Cove
Oyster Bay
Roslyn
Old Westbury
Mineola
Freeport
Long Beach

Northport
Stony Brook
Kings Park
Huntington
Brentwood
Babylon
Amityville

Selden
Long Island
Patchogue
Sayville
Bay Shore

Rocky Point
Riverhead
Flanders
Eastport
Fire Island

Bridgehampton
Southampton
East Hampton

ATLANTIC OCEAN

New York

Gananoque

Napanee
Kingston

Thousand Islands
Cape Vince

Bayside
Trenton

Belleville

Picton

Point Petre

Henderso

CANADA

Cobourg
Newcastle

Oshawa

Toronto
Mississauga

Oakville

Burlington

Hamilton

Lake Ontario

Oswego
Mexic

Hannibal
Red Creek
Fulton

3

481

Newfane
Youngstown
Niagara Falls
St Catharines
Welland

Murray
Albion
Erie Canal
Bergen

Rochester
Sodus

Fairport

104

Lockport
Akron
Depew
Buffalo

Batavia
Alexander
Avon

490

Newark

14

90

Syracuse
Auburn

Dunnville

Lake Erie

Angola

Orchard Park

Warsaw
Geneseo

Canandaigua

Lakeville

Waterloo

Canandaigua Lake

Geneva

Cayuga Lake

20

Moravia

Finger Lakes

Cortland

Dunkirk
Fredonia

Springville
Arcade
Gowanda

Portageville

Dansville

Naples

Penn Yan

Keuka Lake

Seneca Lake

Ovid

Watkins Glen

Dryden
Ithaca

Berkshire

13

Mayville
Chautauqua Lake

Little Valley

Salamanca
Cuba

Belmont
Andover

Bath

Corning

14

Elmira

86

Jamestown
Allegheny Reservoir

Olean
Wellsville

417

15

Sayre

Union City
Corry

6

Youngsville
Warren

59

219

Bradford

Smethport

Shinglehouse

Coudersport

6

Galeton
Wellsboro

Mansfield

Troy

6

Townada

Titusville

62

Ludlow
Kane

6

Mt Jewett

Pennsylvania

Canton

14

220

Susquehanna

Oil City
Tionesta

Johnsonburg
Marienville
Ridgway
Clarion

Saint Marys

219   255

Emporium

Cammal

Keating

287

Trout Run

Williamsport

Laporte

Bento

New York State

0   50 miles
0   50 km

Clarion
Brockway
Penfield

80

Du Bois
Clearfield

322

Snow Shoe

Lock Haven

220

80

Philipsburg

220

Milesburg

180

Muncy

15

Lewisburg

11

Bloomsburg

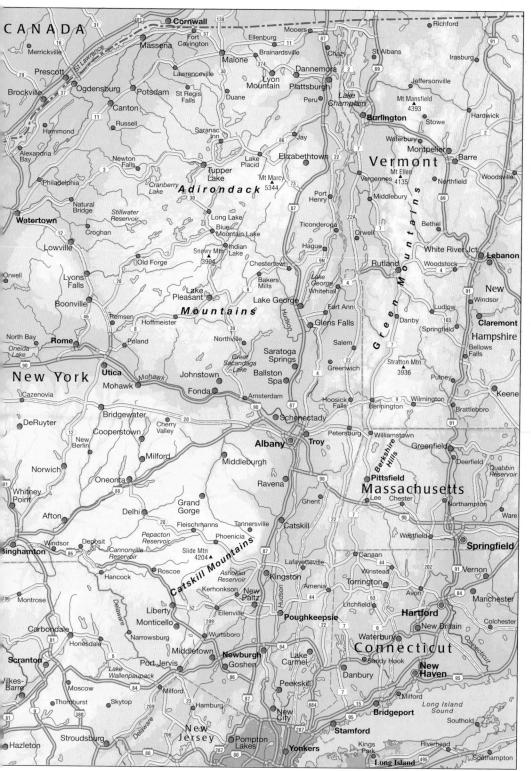

CANADA

Merrickville
Prescott
Brockville
Alexandria Bay
Philadelphia
Watertown
Lowville
Orwell
Lyons Falls
Boonville
Rome
North Bay
Oneida Lake
Utica
New York
Mohawk
DeRuyter
Whitney Point
Afton
Cazenovia
Norwich
New Berlin
Cooperstown
Bridgewater
Oneonta
Delhi
Grand Gorge
Binghamton
Windsor
Deposit
Hancock
Montrose
Carbondale
Honesdale
Scranton
Wilkes-Barre
Moscow
Skytop
Hazleton
Stroudsburg

Cornwall
Fort Covington
Massena
Malone
Lawrenceville
Ogdensburg
Potsdam
Canton
Hammond
Russell
Croghan
Old Forge
Remsen
Hoffmeister
Poland
Johnstown
Fonda
Milford
Roscoe
Liberty
Monticello
Narrowsburg
Port Jervis
Middletown
Goshen
Milford
Hamburg

Mooers
Ellenburg
Brainardsville
Lyon Mountain
Duane
St Regis Falls
Saranac Inn
Jay
Tupper Lake
Cranberry Lake
Adirondack
Mt Marcy 5344
Long Lake
Blue Mountain Lake
Snowy Mtn 3904
Indian Lake
Chestertown
Bakers Mills
Lake George
Lake Pleasant
Mountains
Northville
Great Sacandaga Lake
Ballston Spa
Saratoga Springs
Amsterdam
Schenectady
Albany
Middleburgh
Ravena
Ghent
Catskill
Tannersville
Phoenicia
Fleischmanns
Pepacton Reservoir
Cannonville Reservoir
Slide Mtn 4204
Ashokan Reservoir
Catskill Mountains
Lafayetteville
Kingston
Kerhonkson
New Paltz
Ellenville
Wurtsboro
Poughkeepsie
Newburgh
Lake Carmel
Peekskill
New City
New Jersey
Pompton Lakes
Yonkers

Richford
St Albans
Irasburg
Chazy
Plattsburgh
Peru
Lake Champlain
Burlington
Waterbury
Stowe
Hardwick
Mt Mansfield 4393
Vermont
Montpelier
Barre
Northfield
Woodsville
Mt Ellen 4135
Vergennes
Middlebury
Bethel
Elizabethtown
Port Henry
Ticonderoga
Orwell
White River Jct
Woodstock
Lebanon
Rutland
Hague
Whitehall
Lake George
Fort Ann
Glens Falls
Salem
Greenwich
Hoosick Falls
Bennington
Williamstown
Petersburg
Troy
Danby
Springfield
Ludlow
Claremont
Hampshire
Bellows Falls
Putney
Stratton Mtn 3936
Wilmington
Brattleboro
New Windsor
Keene
Greenfield
Deerfield
Quabbin Reservoir
Berkshire Hills
Pittsfield
Massachusetts
Lee
Chester
Northampton
Ware
Westfield
Springfield
Canaan
Winsted
Torrington
Litchfield
Amenia
Avon
Vernon
Manchester
Colchester
Hartford
New Britain
Waterbury
Connecticut
Sandy Hook
Danbury
New Haven
Milford
Long Island Sound
Bridgeport
Stamford
Southold
Kings Park
Riverhead
Southampton
Long Island

Jeffersonville
Woodstock

St Lawrence
Natural Bridge
Stillwater Reservoir
Newton Falls
Delaware

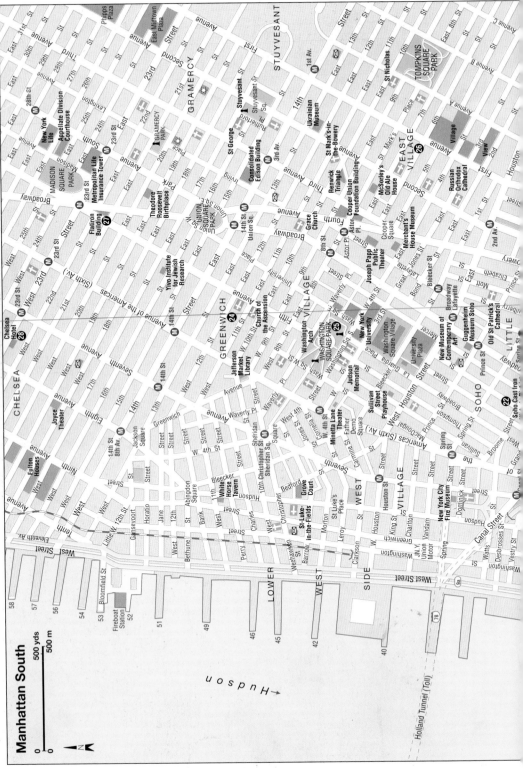

Manhattan South

0 ——— 500 yds
0 ——— 500 m

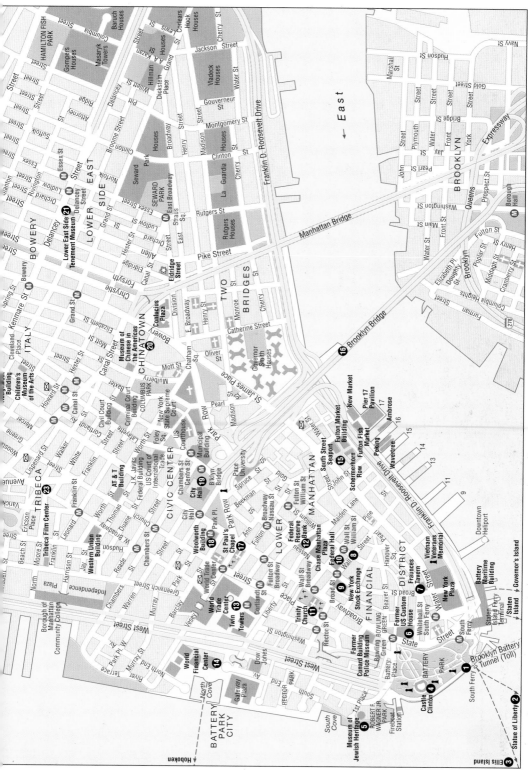

Manhattan North

500 yds

500 m

N

NEW YORK CITY

From Broadway to the Statue of Liberty, Central Park to the most famous skyline in the world, the city that never sleeps never ceases to amaze and enthrall

Map on pages 106–7

If you are traveling to New York for the first time, expect anything to happen, except boredom. The only emotion that the place does not arouse is indifference. Since its founding by the Dutch in 1626, through its growth as a maritime hub, fueled by cheap immigrant labor, to its contemporary position as, arguably, the cultural and financial center of the world, New York has become a city that can't be ignored.

The entire city covers a surface area of 300 sq miles (780 sq km). Of its five boroughs, only the Bronx lies on the mainland; Manhattan and Staten Island are islands, while Brooklyn and Queens form the westernmost point of Long Island. Manhattan, the smallest borough, has a surface area of just over 22 sq miles (57 sq km), but is the most densely populated part of the city, with approximately 1.5 million of the city's total 7.4 million inhabitants. The city lies at the mouth of the Hudson River. The East River, which borders Manhattan to the east, is not actually a river at all, but a narrow strip of water connecting Long Island Sound and Upper New York Bay. Manhattan is laid out primarily in a rectangular system of numbered streets and avenues. An exception is the island's oldest section, from Greenwich Village south to Battery Park, an area that can be confusing without the assistance of a map.

Culturally, New York City has more than 150 museums, including the third largest in the world (the Metropolitan Museum of Art), around 400 art galleries, more than 240 theaters and more than 17,000 restaurants. Amid all the bustle, there are quiet places, too: the city has over 26,000 acres (10,500 hectares) of parks, the most famous of which is Central Park.

New Yorkers may have a reputation for being hurried, even rude, but under their frequent brusqueness is a sense of humor. Just remember that normality is said to bore them, while spontaneity delights them.

Lower Manhattan

Lower Manhattan is the original New York, where winding streets once led to bustling docks and clipper ships. Today these narrow byways, with names such as Pine Street, Pearl Street, and Wall Street, are lined by towering temples of finance.

Perhaps the best place to start a tour of the city is the point at which so many of its immigrant communities first caught sight of their new home. **South Ferry ❶** is where the ferries to both Ellis Island and Liberty Island dock. Tickets for both ferries are sold inside Castle Clinton *(see page 113)*, and the ferry to the latter runs daily between 8.30am and 4.30pm in summer (departures every 20 minutes) and between 9am and 3.45pm in winter (departures every 45 minutes); the trip lasts 20 minutes.

LEFT: Lady Liberty, a beacon to all.
BELOW: taxi driver.

BELOW: seeing the
sights of New York.

The **Statue of Liberty ❷** is 151 ft (46 meters) high, but its pedestal is nearly
the same height; indeed, the history of the pedestal is perhaps even more inter-
esting than that of the statue. *Liberty Enlightening the World* was donated to
America by the French as an expression of their admiration for the American
Revolution, which they termed "the completion of the French Revolution across
the Atlantic." The original proposal was made by the historian Edouard de
Laboulaye; the sculptor responsible was Frédéric-Auguste Bartholdi; and
Gustave Eiffel constructed the scaffolding inside.

Ms Liberty crossed the Atlantic in 200 packing cases and arrived in New
York Harbor in 1885. But the French had made it a condition that New York
build a suitable pedestal for their gift. The fact that this was almost as expensive
as the statue dampened the enthusiasm of New Yorkers, who saw no point in
paying for a present that had been forced on them. This explains why $100,000
for the pedestal were still missing when the crates containing the famous lady
arrived in New York Harbor – until a prominent publisher, Joseph Pulitzer (for
whom the Pulitzer Prize is named), organized a campaign for donations in his
newspaper *The World*, promising that all benefactors would be mentioned. It was
a clever move: within six months he had not only collected the required sum, but
also significantly increased the circulation of his newspaper.

Liberty was unveiled with much pomp on October 28, 1886. But, perhaps
because of the site chosen for the statue, so exposed out in the harbor, or perhaps because of the pose, with the arm outstretched as if in greeting, within a
few years her original significance was forgotten and what the French saw as a
symbol of Franco-American brotherhood was soon regarded as the incarnation
of American freedom. Liberty became the "Mother of Exiles," greeting over 16

million immigrants between 1892 and 1954. The Statue of Liberty Museum, situated on the first floor of the pedestal, is dedicated to them.

The route taken by 12 million of the new arrivals first led them to **Ellis Island ❸**, a small dot in the harbor where immigrants were asked embarrassing questions and searched. The reality of immigration was very different from the poetic promise. Laws, which were changed according to the current political situation and the number of immigrants arriving, barred the sick, the weak, the politically undesirable, the penniless, and even unmarried women from entering the land of the free. Those who failed the test were detained on the island and sent back on the next available ship – a cruel end to all those dreams of a bright new future. Two thousand immigrants a day was no rarity in the record years of 1907 and 1914, and conditions in the Great Hall were appalling. Ellis Island is now a national monument; the restored buildings contain an immigration museum with exhibits as heart-wrenching as they are fascinating.

Apart from the ferries to Liberty and Ellis islands, visitors should consider taking the **Staten Island Ferry**, which docks at the Whitehall Ferry Terminal at the eastern end of Battery Park. On its way to the borough of Staten Island *(see page 151)* it crosses New York Harbor, providing superb views of the Statue of Liberty and the Manhattan skyline.

A modern Lady Liberty carries the torch in Battery Park.

Just across State Street from the Staten Island Ferry Terminal is **Battery Park** and the fortress of **Castle Clinton ❹**, originally called the West Battery. In 1824, the original fort – which then stood a few yards offshore – was converted to a place of entertainment known as Castle Garden. In the first half of the 19th century concerts and festivals of all kinds were held here, but from 1885 Castle Garden was used as an immigrant processing center. However, in 1896 the popular New York Aquarium (now located in Brooklyn) moved in. The old walls of the Castle were saved from demolition in the 1940s, and in 1950 the semi-circular fortress became a national monument.

BELOW: the squarerigger *Pioneer* passes Lower Manhattan.

Farther north, just off Battery Place, is the **Museum of Jewish Heritage – A Living Memorial to the Holocaust ❺** (18 First Place; tel: 212/978-1800; open Sun–Fri; entrance fee), which contains poignant letters, photographs and videotaped testimonies (some donated by Stephen Spielberg after he directed the film *Schindler's List*) from victims of the Holocaust.

Early New York City

Where Broadway crosses Exchange Place is the presumed site of the camp of Dutch explorer Captain Adriaen Block and his crew, who arrived here in 1614, six years before the Pilgrims landed on Plymouth Rock. They didn't intend to stay, but their ship burned, forcing them to remain on Manhattan Island for the winter while they built a new seagoing vessel, appropriately named *Restless*.

The next Europeans to arrive were eager to stay. Dutch colonists settled on the island of *Mannahatta* – as the Indians called it – in 1624, and in 1626 Peter Minuit, director general of the Dutch Province of New Netherland, "purchased" Manhattan from the Indians for 60 guilders ($24) worth of trinkets *(see page 27)*. This transaction is said to have taken place in the

Map on pages 106–7

Sculptures adorn the outside of the US Custom House.

BELOW:
Bowling Green, an oasis amid the concrete canyons.

fenced pocket park now known as **Bowling Green**. In the early days of the city, Bowling Green was a marketplace and used for troop exercises; later, during the struggle for independence from Britain, it developed into a center of resistance. Tensions were so high in the 1770s that a statue of the English king, George III, had to be protected from the angry crowds by a fence. In 1776, after the adoption of the Declaration of Independence, the statue and parts of the fence fell victim to popular sentiment.

To the north of Bowling Green is the **Cunard Building** (25 Broadway), with its fine lobby. Built in 1921 to house the headquarters of the Cunard shipping line, it now contains a post office and the New York City Police Museum.

The southern side of the green is dominated by the **US Custom House ❻**, a Beaux Arts building designed by the architect Cass Gilbert and completed in 1907. The sculptures representing Asia, America, Europe, and Africa are by Daniel Chester French. Twelve statues along the sixth-floor cornice symbolize historical trading centers: Greece, Rome, Phoenicia, Genoa, Venice, Spain, Holland, Portugal, Denmark, Germany, England, and France. (Anti-German sentiment in 1917 caused the statue for Germany to be renamed "Belgium.") Today the building is home to the **George Gustav Heye Center of the National Museum of the American Indian** (tel: 212/668-6624; open daily; entrance free), housing a selection of Native American artwork and crafts with religious or social significance. Exhibits range from a symbolic circle of beaded moccasins to interactive "discovery boxes" with mini-histories of tribal artifacts.

Take Bridge Street to the intersection of Pearl and Broad streets, and you'll find **Fraunces Tavern ❼**, named after Samuel Fraunces who ran it from 1762. In 1776 Fraunces became George Washington's steward, and on December 4,

Map on pages 106–7

1783 the general returned here to bid farewell to his troops. The present structure dates from 1907 and is an approximation of the original tavern, built in 1719. On the upper stories the museum contains historical documents and period furniture, as well as items such as a lock of Washington's hair, a fragment of one of his teeth, and a shoe that belonged to his wife Martha. The ground floor is still a restaurant, frequented these days by bankers and stockbrokers.

Take a short detour east to the harbor and to Coenties Slip. A slip was an old docking bay for merchant ships, and several street names still contain the word. The **Vietnam Veterans Memorial**, a 14-ft (4-meter) high monument erected in 1985, now stands here. Its wall of green glass is etched with excerpts from soldiers' letters; the senselessness of war and the desperation of those forced to take part has rarely been more eloquently conveyed.

America's financial heart

Following Water Street northward, bear left to attractive **Hanover Square**, which derives its name from the time of the monarchy. Hanover Square was a fine address and in the course of the 18th century developed into the center of New York business. However, due to the Great Fire of 1835, which broke out on the corner of Hanover Square and Pearl Street and destroyed most of the area flanked by South, Broad, and Wall streets, no original structures survive. Over 600 buildings burned down during those three winter days; the cold made it almost impossible to extinguish the flames because the water froze in the hoses.

The finest building in Hanover Square is **India House**, which dates from the period of reconstruction. Built in Italianate style between 1851–4, it originally served as a bank building and today houses a private club, but anyone can drop

Wall Street is named after an earthen wall built to protect the Dutch settlement. When the English arrived in 1664 they pulled the wall down and the city spread northward. A slave market was held at the center of today's Financial District; it later became a grain market.

BELOW: the floor of the New York Stock Exchange.

A statue of George Washington stands outside Federal Hall.

BELOW: Dubuffet's *Group of Four Trees* sculpture at Chase Manhattan Plaza.

into the restaurant, as well as Harry's on the ground floor. The latter is something of an institution in banking circles: long before their minions have arrived at the office in the morning, Wall Street tycoons are making decisions over "power breakfasts" – if you can get a table here or at nearby Delmonico's (56 Beaver Street) it's a good way of soaking up the legendary Wall Street atmosphere.

Wall Street ❽ is best observed at its most hectic time of day – shortly before 9am on weekdays. Limousines with tinted glass and smart young brokers talking on cell phones are everywhere. Thousands of them pour out of subways and vanish through the revolving doors of banks and office buildings – and then suddenly everything is still, and Wall Street seems almost deserted.

The seeds of Wall Street's fame were sown in 1792. Newly formed New York State was in financial difficulties as a result of the struggle for independence, and decided to issue bonds. To discuss conditions of trade, 24 brokers met beneath a buttonwood tree on Wall Street and founded the New York Stock Exchange. Wall Street remains a locale for deal-clinching, and the sign language used by today's brokers is supposed to date back to when partners in adjoining buildings had to be informed about buying and selling from the sidewalk below. By the end of the 19th century the industrial revolution and the American Civil War had made some people very rich. Small businesses were passé and huge corporations began to form, most with a need for more money than they had at their disposal. The banks found the capital and trade in securities reached record levels. But on October 29, 1929, the day that came to be known as "Black Friday," the bubble burst. The stock market collapsed, ushering in a global slump. Stories of bankrupt shareholders committing suicide by jumping out of skyscrapers went round the world.

Viewed from the outside, the **New York Stock Exchange ❾** looks like a temple, with its huge pillars and elaborate frieze on the portico. It was built in 1903 and enlarged in 1923, although it could move to larger quarters yet again. At the Visitor Center entrance (20 Broad Street; open Mon–Fri 9.15am–4pm; entrance free) guards direct visitors to elevators that take them up to a gallery overlooking the main floor. Here, a number of interactive machines and displays shed some light on the feverish activities of the folks downstairs.

Opposite the New York Stock Exchange is **Federal Hall ❿** (26 Wall Street; tel: 212/825 6888; open Mon–Fri; entrance free), a magnificent neo-classical building. The site was previously occupied by New York's old city hall, built around 1701 and the scene of a trial that became a milestone in the history of press freedom. In 1735, John Peter Zenger, publisher of the *New York Weekly Journal*, was arrested for libel after printing several articles accusing colonial governor William Cosby of corruption. To the delight of the general public, the colonial jury acquitted Zenger on the grounds that his charges were based on fact – a key consideration in libel cases since that time.

Another announcement, made on this site 41 years later, was just as unwelcome to the colonial government: the opening words of the Declaration of Independence that was approved and signed on July 4, 1776 in Philadelphia by the Second Continental Congress. The only colony that did not sign was New

York, but this didn't prevent the rebels from reading out the document outside the old city hall 14 days later. A statue of George Washington stands outside Federal Hall. It was in his honor that the city hall was renovated and changed its name: for just over a year it served as the Capitol.

After New York had ceased to be the nation's capital, the old city hall fell into disrepair and was pulled down. Today's structure dates from 1842 and was originally the City Custom House. The museum inside serves as a reminder of the momentous events that took place here in the past.

On the other side of Federal Hall is Pine Street, which leads to **Chase Manhattan Plaza**, with its notable *Four Trees* sculpture by Jean Dubuffet. At Liberty Street and Broadway is the **Equitable Building**. This huge structure caused such a stir when built in 1915 that new zoning ordinances, designed to prevent city streets from becoming sunless canyons and leading to the introduction of stepped skyscrapers, were introduced a year later.

Nestling between the many temples of wealth around it is the red-sandstone **Trinity Church** ⓫ (Broadway and Wall Street; open Mon–Fri 9–11.45am, Sat 10am–3.45pm, Sun 11am–3.45pm; entrance free). The first church on this site was built in 1697 but burned down in 1776. A second structure, built in 1790, was torn down in 1839 and replaced with the current neo-Gothic example. The church interior is simple and unpretentious; the bronze doors were added in the 20th century. The churchyard dates from 1681, and contains the pyramid-shaped tomb of Alexander Hamilton, first secretary of the US Treasury.

The building that takes up the block between Maiden Lane, Nassau, and Liberty is the **Federal Reserve Bank** ⓬ (33 Liberty Street; tours Mon–Fri; tel: 212/720-6130 for bookings). Designed by architects York & Sawyer, it was completed in 1924, and its fortress-like appearance has a purpose: the vaults are said to contain more gold than Fort Knox. The entrance lobby is impressive.

The World Trade Center

The plaza of the **World Trade Center** ⓭ measures 24,000 sq yds (20,000 sq meters), the largest enclosed shopping area in New York, with some 208 elevators, 50,000 workers, around 200,000 visitors daily, and two 1,377-ft (420-meter) high towers – even for this city of superlatives, it's utterly gigantic. It was the world's tallest building for just a few months in 1973, until Chicago set new standards with its Sears Tower (1,453 ft/443 meters). Today both are outranked by Kuala Lumpur's Petronas Towers. The construction of the twin towers was a magnificent technical achievement. Because of the height involved, the building had to be assembled from the inside out. Cranes installed in the elevator shafts hoisted tons of steel, and gradually built the outer walls. The building's aesthetic value remains controversial, however, and critics accused architect Minoru Yamasaki of creating too bare and massive a structure.

The Windows on the World restaurant is at the top of Tower 1 (North Tower), where the prices are nearly as high as the establishment itself. The view of New York is stunning from here, though it's far cheaper to take the 58-second elevator to the observation deck of

Map
on pages
106–7

For theater lovers, a TKTS office is located on the mezzanine level of Tower 2 of the World Trade Center.

BELOW: palms grace the Winter Garden of the World Financial Center.

TIP

The Museum Visitors Center at South Street Seaport sells maps and tickets for exhibitions and boat tours (as well as tours of the nearby Fulton Fish Market) and is located at 12 Fulton Street. There is also a ticket office at Pier 16.

the Top of the World on the 107th floor of Tower 2 (South Tower). Those with heads for heights could even try the rooftop promenade on the 110th floor (only open on clear, calm days). Although the attractions up top include a simulated helicopter ride, on gloomy days you might want to check whether it's worth making an ascent: a display in the foyer provides information on visibility.

The complex known as **Battery Park City**, overlooking the Hudson River, owes its existence to the World Trade Center – it was built on top of the land-fill that remained after its construction. The new land became state property and construction work was carried out according to a harmonious urban plan.

The commercial center of the complex is the **World Financial Center ⑭**, which is reached from the World Trade Center via a glass bridge (North Bridge). The four towers containing offices have a cozy air to them in contrast to the World Trade Center, and the design of the squares and arcades is attractive. The atmosphere is pleasant, with music, palm trees, and people strolling and dining. Creating space accessible to everyone was one of the main objectives of the city planners; 30 percent of the area covered by Battery Park City fulfills this stipulation. The Esplanade along the river's edge is one of the most popular features; it leads north to Rockefeller Park and south to Battery Park.

South Street Seaport

On the eastern edge of Lower Manhattan is the **South Street Seaport ⑮**. This area of the city is a real mixture: it's a museum (with exhibitions on New York's maritime history), a shopping center (with boutiques, gift shops, galleries, the **Fulton Market Building**, and the Pier 17 Pavilion), a starting point for harbor trips, a fine place to eat, and a center of entertainment.

BELOW:
fish for sale at
the Fulton Market.

New York owes its rise to prominence as a world capital to this port. It was here that overseas trade first began, and where the large sailing ships from all over the world used to dock. However, the arrival of the steamship in the mid-19th century ushered in a period of steady decline, for there was more room for piers along the Hudson River, and the area fell into disrepair. It was eventually awoken from its long sleep by a revitalization program, begun in 1967. An alliance was formed with commercial interests to underwrite restoration of the old harbor buildings and a growing collection of antique sailing vessels.

South Street Seaport is made up of 12 blocks of early 19th-century buildings and three piers. **Schermerhorn Row**, situated on the south side of Fulton Street, consists of commercial buildings in the Georgian-Federal and Greek Revival styles. The main attractions are the historic ships at piers 15 and 16, including the classic square-rigger *Wavertree* (1885), the four-masted *Peking* (1911), and the lightship *Ambrose* (1906). Harbor trips organized by Circle Line Seaport cruises (tel: 212/630-8888) go around the southern tip of Manhattan, with views of the Statue of Liberty, Ellis Island, and Battery Park.

From Pier 17, peppered with shops and restaurants, you can obtain an excellent view of the **Brooklyn Bridge** ⑯. This masterpiece of 19th-century bridge design was by John Roebling. After his death during the first year of construction (he contracted tetanus after his foot was crushed by a docking ferry), his son Washington took over. Rising too fast from an underwater chamber, Washington suffered an attack of the bends and was wheelchair-bound from then on. Nevertheless, he oversaw the project to its conclusion, and the bridge opened in May 1883. The best way to experience it is on foot; the entrance to the pedestrian walkway is located at the ends of Frankfort Street and Park Row.

Map
on pages
106–7

Some tourists get into the spirit of New York with Statue of Liberty souvenirs.

BELOW: the
Brooklyn Bridge.

A statue of Justice tops the marble dome at City Hall.

Civic landmarks

Taking Fulton Street north back to the junction with Broadway, you will come to **St Paul's Chapel** ⑰. St Paul's is quintessentially European. Its architect, Thomas McBean, was probably a pupil of James Gibbs, who built St-Martin-in-the-Fields in London. The chapel was completed in 1766, and is authentic Georgian apart from the steeple, which was added 30 years later. It has two claims to fame: it is both the oldest church as well as the oldest civic building in Manhattan. George Washington worshipped here – his roped-off private pew in the north aisle is marked with a "G."

At 233 Broadway is the "Cathedral of Commerce," the **Woolworth Building** ⑱, which made architect Cass Gilbert world famous and was considered by many in its day to be the finest commercial building in the world. Frank Winfield Woolworth, the farm worker turned retail entrepreneur, had this neo-Gothic temple built in honor of his success story. By the time he died in 1919, his company controlled over 1,000 stores from its New York headquarters. The entrance hall with its mosaic ceiling contains statues of Gilbert and Woolworth, the former holding a model of the building, the latter counting coins. The building cost $13 million and was officially opened by President Woodrow Wilson. With its 60 stories, it had the additional distinction of being the tallest in the world (not counting the Eiffel Tower) for 18 years, from its construction in 1912 to 1930, until its 790 ft (241 meters) were superseded first by the Chrysler Building and then the Empire State Building.

In the 18th century, when only the southern tip of Manhattan island was inhabited, the area between Broadway, Park Row, and Chambers Street, known today as City Hall Park, was a common. When New York began to expand

northward in the early 19th century, and its inhabitants needed a new town hall – the third in just 170 years – they chose the common as a construction site. The architects' competition for the new **City Hall ⓲** (Broadway and Park Row) was won by Joseph F. Mangin and John McComb, a Frenchman and a Scotsman, and the building is a mixture of French Renaissance and English Georgian. It was opened in 1812, with a fine marble façade to the south and brownstone to the north. In 1956 it was restored and preserved as one of the finest historic structures in the US. The marble façade was refaced with Alabama sandstone. Behind it stands the former **New York County Courthouse**.

Between Chambers and Reade streets is the **Hall of Records**, completed in 1911 and one of the finest Beaux Arts buildings in New York. The façade, dominated by eight Corinthian columns and several sculpture groups and statues, hides a rather sober interior. The building also contains the Surrogate's Court.

Chinatown to Little Italy

A few blocks north of the city's government district, and you're in another world. Telephone booths have pagoda roofs, shop signs are written in Chinese, shopkeepers can be seen carrying crates of exotic vegetables, and red ducks dangle from shop windows. This is **Chinatown ⓴**, one of Manhattan's most vibrant neighborhoods, begun in the 1870s and now the largest Chinese-American community in the US. It has been estimated that this section of the city is home to about 150,000 people, and the population is increasing all the time, with most residents coming from Taiwan and Hong Kong. Chinatown has now spread well beyond its original borders of Bowery, Baxter, Canal, and Worth streets and made inroads into neighboring Little Italy and the Lower East Side.

Map on pages 106–7

In mid-September, when Mulberry Street is decked out in honor of the Feast of San Gennaro, Little Italy turns into a huge party, with food stalls and religious processions.

LEFT: Peking ducks and chickens on Canal Street.
BELOW: there are lots of good places to eat in Chinatown.

A caricature cook entices the customers into a pizzeria in Little Italy.

Life in Chinatown is a rule unto itself – the towers of the World Trade Center in the distance are the only reminders that that this is actually still New York. A good way to learn more about this neighborhood is to stop by the **Museum of Chinese in the Americas** (70 Mulberry Street, 2nd floor; tel: 212/619-4785; open Tues–Sat; entrance fee). Founded in 1970, when the area's population began to explode, the museum features a permanent exhibit on the Chinese-American experience, as well as walking tours and lectures. It also has a research library and a small gift shop. From here, walk past sidewalks thick with stands selling fruit, vegetables, fish, and leaf-wrapped packets of sticky rice, and turn right on **Canal Street**, crowded with vendors hawking Taiwanese tapes, old men and women reading fortunes, and shops stocked to the brim with imported goods. Turn right down Mott Street and you'll see the Eastern States Buddhist Temple, with a multi-armed statue of the Goddess Kuan-Yui. The air is thick with the scent of sickly sweet incense.

Assuming there isn't a festival on – Chinese New Year, for instance, held in February – New Yorkers generally visit Chinatown to eat. There are hundreds of unpretentious restaurants here, all serving up magnificent delicacies. More often than not they are cramped, noisy, and shabby, and tables can't usually be reserved. Lines form outside the most popular establishments on Saturdays and Sunday mornings, when New Yorkers make their weekend pilgrimages here for a delicious *dim sum* brunch *(see Restaurant Listings, page 331)*.

For coffee or dessert take a short walk across Canal Street back to Europe: **Little Italy** has a fine selection of typical Italian food and *espresso*. Mulberry Street is lined with restaurants, cafés, delicatessens, and small houses with zigzag fire escapes, which give the neighborhood a certain European flair.

BELOW: catching up on the news.

The Lower East Side

A few blocks farther east is the **Bowery**, one of New York's most notorious byways, associated for decades with social deprivation. The street was famous for vagrants, bars, and cheap boarding houses as recently as the 1950s. Today, it's still pretty seedy, with a few notable cultural exceptions, including CBGB (315 Bowery), the club where punk started in the US. Other local landmarks include the tiny, family-run Amato Opera House and the Bouwerie Lane Theater, a relic of the era when this was a thriving theater center.

Before it went into decline at the end of the 19th century, the Bowery was a very fine street. Dutch governor Peter Stuyvesant used it as an approach road for his country estate of Bouwerij, and anyone headed north toward Boston would gallop its length. In the second half of the 19th century the street developed notoriety as an entertainment district, with German beer halls and theaters.

Starting in the mid-19th century, waves of immigrants came to the New World, and many of them lived in the Lower East Side between the Bowery and the East River. They included Irish and Germans, but it was the massive influx of European Jews, spurred by the *pogroms* in Russia, that shaped the character of the neighborhood. Of more than 2 million Jewish immigrants who eventually came to the US, over 500,000 settled here. Grand Street, between Broadway and Essex Street, was the main shopping street at that time, and textile wholesalers and suppliers had their warehouses along Canal Street. The area filled with garment sweatshops, kosher restaurants, and synagogues, and by 1900 the Lower East Side had become the most densely populated urban area in the world – a new-world ghetto. As the people of the Lower East Side painfully ground out a living, the area's substandard living conditions spawned various immigrant and labor rights movements. Emma Goldman preached her gentle anarchism here, socialist newspapers such as the *Jewish Daily Forward* flourished, and settlement houses offering immigrants help with health and education were formed.

Today, the landmark building at 173 East Broadway where the *Daily Forward* was published has been converted into exclusive apartments (although the faces of Karl Marx and Friedrich Engels still peer from a frieze over the entrance). Other signs of change can be seen in stores with Jewish names but Chinese or Hispanic owners. But the neighborhood retains the flavor of its early immigrant roots in Jewish restaurants such as Katz's Delicatessen (205 East Houston Street) and Ratner's (138 Delancey Street), as well as Guss's (35 Essex Street), where fresh pickles are still sold out of a barrel. **Orchard Street** still gives an impression of those early days, with tiny cramped shops heaped with clothes and amazing discounts that become even more attractive after a bit of haggling.

You can also experience the neighborhood the way it used to be at the **Lower East Side Tenement Museum** ㉑ (90 Orchard Street; tel: 212/431-0233; open Sun–Fri; entrance fee), centered around a preserved 1863 tenement building. Cramped apartments from different eras of immigration have been re-created in all their bleakness, and there's a gallery with changing exhibits as well as walking tours. ❑

Map on pages 106–7

TIP

Note that many shop-owners along Orchard Street are Orthodox Jews and close their businesses on Friday afternoon and all day Saturday.

BELOW: a Lower East Side tenement on Orchard Street.

SOHO TO TIMES SQUARE

Map on pages 106–7

From the artists' lofts and art galleries of Soho, to the trendy cafés of Greenwich Village to the Broadway theater district, these famous neighborhoods are some of the most stimulating in Manhattan

When Abraham Lincoln made his first campaign speech at Cooper Union, Soho was the center of New York City's most fashionable shopping and hotel district. By the end of the 19th century, however, the narrow streets were filled by factories whose imaginative cast-iron façades masked sweatshop conditions so horrific that the city fire department dubbed the region "Hell's Hundred Acres." The entire area might have been razed in the 1960s if local artists hadn't started moving into the old lofts and the city hadn't changed zoning laws so they could do so legitimately. Around the same time, conservationists established the **Soho Cast Iron Historic District ㉒** to protect these elaborate "temples of industry."

Now too expensive for all but the most successful New Yorkers (or those who got in when prices were still cheap), Soho, an acronym for South of Houston (pronounced HOUSE-ton), is bordered by Canal Street to the south, Lafayette Street to the east, and the Avenue of the Americas (Sixth Avenue) to the west. Once home to the city's most elegant shops and later to textile outlets, discount stores, and delis, the stately cast-iron buildings on Broadway below Canal Street reacquired cachet in the 1980s as museums, later as galleries, and finally as stores like Pottery Barn and Eddie Bauer.

LEFT: the distinctive Flatiron Building in Midtown.
BELOW: girls just want to have fun.

The **Guggenheim Museum Soho** (575 Broadway; tel: 212/423-3500; open Wed–Sun; entrance fee) opened in 1992 in a building that was originally constructed in the late 1880s for John Jacob Astor III. Now transformed into a minimalist exhibition space, even the entranceway feels auspicious: you pass across a blackened raw-steel bridge hung by stainless steel cable railings. On the next block down is Dean & Deluca (560 Broadway), a cornucopia of fruits, vegetables, and gourmet specialties. Several art galleries are located on the upper floors of these buildings along Broadway *(see page 135)*. The Palazzo-style **Haughwout Building** at the corner of Broome Street is one of Soho's oldest and most striking cast-iron edifices. Designed by John Gaynor, it was constructed in 1857 as one of the country's first retail stores, complete with America's first elevator.

Greene Street, like Mercer and Wooster streets, runs parallel to West Broadway and Broadway. In the late 19th century it was the center of New York's most notorious red-light district, but today it's known for the rich concentration of this uniquely American architecture at its best, including (at the Canal Street end) the city's longest continuous row of cast-iron buildings. Before continuing on, stop and admire the cream-colored "king" (architecturally speaking) of cast-iron splendor at 72–6 Greene Street, designed by Isaac Duckworth and built in 1873.

Soho shops sell almost anything your heart desires.

For art lovers, the PaceWildenstein Gallery (142 Greene Street) shows contemporary painting, drawing, and sculpture. Turn onto stone-cobbled Wooster Street for the Tony Shafrazi Gallery (119 Wooster) and the Howard Greenberg Gallery (upstairs at 120 Wooster) which, like many galleries, seems to hop from street to street. At the Dia Center for the Arts' second-floor space at 141 Wooster Street, *New York Earth Room* by Walter De Maria is on display.

Soho comes to a halt at Canal Street, a bedlam of cheap stores, hot dog carts, and street vendors. To end a tour of Soho in grander fashion, stop in at the Soho Grand Hotel (310 West Broadway, between Grand and Canal streets), with its cozy lobby bar and lounge that's become a popular meeting place for fashion and entertainment-industry types.

In the late 1970s, artists in search of cheaper rents migrated south from Soho to **Tribeca** ㉓ – the Triangle Below Canal – which lies south of Canal Street to Chambers Street, and west from Broadway to the Hudson River. Called Washington Market in the days when the city's major produce businesses operated here (before they moved to Hunt's Point in the Bronx), this part of the Lower West Side is one of Manhattan's fastest-growing neighborhoods. An eclectic blend of renovated warehouses sporting Corinthian columns, condominium towers, and celebrity restaurants, Tribeca was where artists like David Salle and Laurie Anderson showed their early works at the Alternative Museum (now in Soho) and Franklin Furnace (now closed). Today, its largely residential atmosphere is a pleasant change of pace from Soho's tourist-packed streets.

BELOW: brightening up the Village.

Greenwich Street is where much of Tribeca's new development is centered, although you can still find some authentic early remnants, like the 19th-century lantern factory between Laight and Vestry streets that has now been converted

to million-dollar lofts. At the corner of Greenwich and Franklin streets, where actor Robert de Niro transformed the old Martinson Coffee Factory into the Tribeca Film Center, the ground-floor Tribeca Grill attracts bicoastal movie-makers and shakers.

The late 18th- and early 19th-century brick houses on Harrison Street look like a stage set plonked down in the shadow of adjacent Independence Plaza's gargantuan 1970s apartment towers, survivors of Tribeca's residential beginnings. A block down is Bazzini's (339 Greenwich Street), a fruit and nut wholesaler since 1886, where you can buy bags of pistachios and other delicacies.

Map on pages 106–7

Greenwich Village

The free-wheeling atmosphere of **Greenwich Village** ❷ was epitomized by the poets and musicians of the 1950s and 1960s, but today, as other neighborhoods set the scene, some New Yorkers consider "The Village" just one big tourist attraction. Though a commercial element exists, many of the streets are as residential as they were in the late 18th and early 19th centuries, when the village was first settled by New Yorkers fleeing a series of epidemics at the tip of the island. As in other Manhattan areas, real estate prices have forced out all but the most successful, but the Village is still where many people would prefer to live – and barring that possibility, it's where they go to walk and shop and enjoy the variety of street life.

Here you can find cobblestone alleys, graceful architecture, Italian bakeries, gourmet markets, theaters, and the oldest gay community in New York. In addition, there's a remarkable array of restaurants, bars, and jazz clubs. Bordered by 14th Street to the north, the Hudson River to the west, and Broadway to the east, it's where the offbeat is the norm, and where the annual Halloween Parade has to be one of the world's most fascinating spectacles.

Walk south down Fifth Avenue and you'll see Washington Arch rising in the distance. First designed in wood by Stanford White to memorialize the 1889 centennial of the first president's inauguration, this imposing marble version, completed in 1918, stands at the entrance to Washington Square, the geographic and spiritual heart of Greenwich Village.

Before continuing, walk east to Broadway and Grace Church, one of the city's loveliest ecclesiastical structures. Built in 1846, its exterior white marble, now a muted gray, was mined by convicts at the infamous Sing Sing prison in upstate New York. Take a stroll west along 9th and 10th streets, two of the most picturesque in the city. Lined by stately brick and brownstone houses, these desirable residential byways have been home to numerous artists and writers (including Mark Twain, who lived for a time at 14 West 10th).

Washington Square Park ❷ was originally a potter's field, where the poor and unknown were buried; it later became a parade ground, then a residential park. Although it's lost the cachet it knew in the days of Henry James – who was inspired to write his novel by the same name while living nearby – on weekend afternoons the park is filled with musicians,

BELOW: Greenwich Village fire escapes.

The gay community struts its stuff on Christopher Street.

BELOW: kicking around in Washington Square Park.

mime artists, jugglers, and street performers playing to appreciative crowds.

With its two blocks of Greek Revival townhouses, Washington Square North retains a 19th-century elegance at odds with the monolithic New York University buildings that adjoin the park. The enormous gray building on Washington Square East is NYU's main building. Inside you'll find the Grey Art Gallery (tel: 212/998-6780; open Tues–Sat; entrance fee), showcasing some of the savviest contemporary and historical art exhibits in town.

Turn left off Washington Square South onto MacDougal Street, and you're in the heart of what was once beatnik heaven, where world-weary poets sipped coffee and discussed the meaning of life late into the night. These days, it's a mecca for out-of-towners, drawn by the bevy of ersatz crafts shops and "authentic" ethnic restaurants. Stop in at the Minetta Tavern where Ernest Hemingway hoisted a beer or two, or Caffé Reggio (119 MacDougal), one of the old-time coffee houses made famous in the 1940 and '50s. Another is Le Figaro on Bleecker Street, which offers maximum sidewalk people-watching opportunities, along with first-rate espresso and cappuccino. Nearby entertainment options include performances by the world's jazz greats at the Blue Note (West 3rd Street between MacDougal Street and Avenue of the Americas); contemporary theater at the Minetta Lane Theater; and the production of *The Fantasticks*, which has been entertaining audiences at the Sullivan Street Playhouse (118 Sullivan Street) since 1959.

The area west of the Avenue of the Americas (Sixth Avenue) and a few blocks north is the area that hosts the annual Halloween Parade and has pretty streets that wind confusingly between the major avenues. **Christopher Street** is the symbolic center of the gay community and a main cross-street that slants across

Map
on pages
106–7

the heart of the West Village. Just past Waverly Place is the Stonewall Inn (51 Christopher Street), where the gay rights movement got its spontaneous start one night in 1969 when the bar's gay habitués got tired of being rousted by police. Today, there's a bar with the same name operating next door. Just across the street is the small, fenced-in Christopher Park.

On the other side of Seventh Avenue South, Sweet Basil (88 Seventh Avenue South) is one of the most established Village jazz venues. Greenwich Avenue angles past Jackson Square to the heart of Manhattan's wholesale meat district, an area populated by galleries, gay clubs, and transsexual hookers. Hudson Street runs south from 14th Street and includes the White Horse Tavern, serving drinks from the corner of 11th Street since 1880. This is where the poet Dylan Thomas had one too many before expiring at nearby St Vincent's Hospital.

Above the White Horse, Abingdon Square leads to the start of **Bleecker Street**, which at this end is lined by pleasant stores like Susan Parrish Antiques (No. 390), a good source of American folk art. It is also bisected by some of the village's prettiest thoroughfares. Bank Street is particularly scenic, with its cobblestones and pastel houses, and lies in the center of the **Greenwich Village Historic District**'s finest 19th-century architecture.

East Village

Bordered by 14th Street to the north and Houston Street to the south, roughly centered between Third Avenue and Avenue B, the **East Village** ㉖ is a place that stays up late, where fashions and politics are more radical than elsewhere in the city, and residents have included Beat icons like Allen Ginsberg, Yippies, and Hell's Angels. The East Village is also a neighborhood of immigrants,

BELOW: making all the right moves.

The brown Italianate Cooper Union Building between Third and Fourth avenues opened in 1859 as one of the country's earliest centers of free education. Famous as an art school, it's also where Abraham Lincoln gave the speech said to have launched his presidential campaign.

with Ukrainian and Puerto Rican social clubs next-door to offbeat boutiques.

St Mark's-in-the-Bowery, at Second Avenue and 10th Street, is the second-oldest church building in Manhattan. Built in 1799 on a *bouwerie* (farm) belonging to Dutch governor Peter Stuyvesant, St Mark's has a long history of liberal religious thought, a reflection of the neighborhood that manifests itself in such community programs as the Poetry Project. The red-brick Anglo-Italianate houses across from the church on East 10th Street, and on Stuyvesant Street, form the heart of the St Mark's Historic District.

It's a short walk from here to **Astor Place**, named for John Jacob Astor, who arrived in New York in 1784 as a penniless immigrant and was the richest man in town by the time he died 36 years later. Today the area's most notable landmark is the giant rotating black cube by Tony Rosenthal called *The Alamo*. One of the first abstract sculptures installed on city property, it has stood at the intersection of Astor Place, St Mark's Place, and Lafayette Street since 1967.

Colonnade Row on Lafayette Street, which runs south from Astor Place, was originally a group of nine columned homes built in 1833, when this was one of the city's most elegant neighborhoods. Only four of the original houses still stand, with current occupants including the stylish Indochine restaurant (No. 430) and the Astor Place Theater (No. 434).

Across the street, the **Joseph Papp Public Theater** (actually a complex of five theaters) was originally the Astor Library. This was Astor's only public legacy, which he envisioned as a center of learning for the common man. Since 1967, the building has been home to the city's Shakespeare Festival as well as many productions that have gone on to Broadway.

A block farther down you can drop in and see the city as it used to be at the

BELOW:
Japanese teens in the East Village.

Merchant's House Museum (29 East 4th Street; tel: 212/777-1089; open Sun–Thur afternoons; entrance fee), a small Greek Revival-style brick town-house built in 1832. The same family lived here for generations and their furnishings and personal effects are on display.

St Mark's Place, a continuation of 8th Street between Third Avenue and Avenue A, was the East Coast's counter-culture center in the 1960s. The Dom (a former Polish social club where Andy Warhol presented Velvet Underground "happenings" and, later, barefoot freaks tripped out at the Electric Circus) is now a community crafts center. The Fillmore East, which presented rock concerts, is also long gone. But this is still one of the city's liveliest thoroughfares. Sidewalk cafés and restaurants are usually heaving with customers, and the bazaar-like atmosphere is enhanced by street vendors selling T-shirts, jewelry, and bootleg CDs. Take a detour down Third Avenue to East 7th Street for a true drinking man's pub. **McSorley's Old Ale House** has been in business since the 1850s, although women weren't allowed inside until more than a century later. This was one of Irish writer Brendan Behan's favorite New York hangouts.

As befits a neighborhood that's a typical melting pot, you can find just about any cuisine here, from trendy to traditional. If cheap and exotic is your preference, you can't do much better than "**Little India**" on 6th Street between First and Second Avenues. All restaurants here are inexpensive, most stay open pretty late, and some even feature live Indian music on weekend evenings.

At 10th Street and Avenue A is the top of **Tompkins Square Park**, a patch of reclaimed swamp used as a drill ground and recruiting camp during the Civil War. It was later the center of the *Kleine Deutschland* (Little Germany) community that thrived here more than a hundred years ago. A gathering place for

Map on pages 106–7

Buskers play everything from rock to classical music on New York streets.

BELOW: a favorite old watering hole in the East Village.

*New York's finest
keep the peace on the
streets of New York.*

hippies and runaways in the late 1960s, the park was a focal point for conflicts between homeless activists and police in the 1980s. Today, however, it's a generally peaceful place frequented by young mothers with kids and folks walking their dogs. Many of the homes have been renovated by young professionals (the 19th-century rowhouses on 10th Street at the park's northern border are a good example), fueling a hike in rents that's led to further gentrification.

Along avenues A and B, drug dealers and graffiti have been usurped by bars and restaurants with a young, hip clientele. Nevertheless, strolling farther into Alphabet City (avenues C and D) is not recommended, especially late at night.

Gramercy Park and Chelsea

On the East Side between 20th and 21st streets, **Gramercy Park** is a 2-acre (1-hectare) square that punctuates Lexington Avenue and Irving Place with welcome greenery. This is Manhattan's only private park, established in the 1830s by a wealthy lawyer named Samuel Ruggles. Only residents of the surrounding townhouses have keys, although guests at the Gramercy Park Hotel, a hostelry at 2 Lexington Avenue, are allowed in, too. On the park's southern perimeter, note the elaborate 19th-century façades of the National Arts Club, home to the Poetry Society of America, and the next-door Players Club, where members have included Mark Twain, Winston Churchill, and Frank Sinatra.

Drifting northward, the often overlooked green space positioned between Madison Avenue and Broadway from 23rd to 26th streets is **Madison Square Park**. A century ago, this was one of the city's cultural hearts and, until 1925, home to the original Madison Square Garden. Opposite the park, on Madison Avenue, the 54-story **Metropolitan Life Insurance Tower**,

BELOW: ornate cast-iron grillwork adorns the homes of Gramercy Park.

completed in 1909, was briefly considered to be the world's tallest building.

The triangular **Flatiron Building** ㉗, which rises 285 ft (87 meters) from the corner where Broadway crosses Fifth Avenue, just below 23rd Street, raised both eyebrows and hopes for a bright future when it was erected in 1902. Originally called the Fuller Building, it soon became known as the Flatiron because of its distinctive shape.

From here, Broadway follows the old "Ladies Mile," along Broadway and Sixth Avenue, from 23rd Street down to 9th Street. Among the emporiums were Lord & Taylor, which began as a small shop on Catherine Street and opened on the southwest corner of Broadway and 20th Street in 1872 (10,000 customers used its elevator in the first three days). The store eventually moved uptown in 1914 *(see page 139).*

At the **Theodore Roosevelt Birthplace** (28 East 20th Street; tel: 212/260-1616; open Wed–Sun; entrance fee), the late president's toys and collection of mounted lion heads are on display, along with various other memorabilia.

Named for the convergence of Broadway and Fourth Avenue, **Union Square** sits between 17th and 14th streets. A stylish prospect in the mid-1850s, by the turn of the 20th century it was more or less deserted by residents and became a thriving theater center. Eventually the theaters moved north and the square became known for political meetings. In the years preceding World War I, anarchists and socialists regularly addressed sympathizers here. Rallies continued to draw crowds throughout the 1930s, but finally the area went into a decline that lasted until the 1980s.

Today, Union Square bustles with life, a resurgence that might be attributed to the Greenmarket, which brings farmers and their produce to the northern edge of the square four days a week. It's a great place to wander around on a Saturday morning. An outdoor café operates on the nearby plaza in warm weather, and there are a number of adjacent restaurants, including the fashionable Union Square Café *(see page 332).*

In 1750, a large piece of land along the Hudson was acquired by Captain Thomas Clarke and inherited in 1813 by his grandson, Clement Clark Moore. Faced with the onslaught of the northward-creeping city, Moore divided it into lots that were sold off with certain restrictions: "undesirable" uses, like stables, were prohibited, and all houses had to be set back from the street. Today, these make up the **Chelsea Historic District,** in the gentrified blocks between Eighth and Tenth avenues from 19th to 23rd streets.

A walk west on busy 23rd Street takes you past the Gothic-looking **Chelsea Hotel** ㉘, which rises almost halfway between Seventh and Eighth avenues. One of the city's most famous residential hotels, since 1909 it has been home to writers such as Thomas Wolfe, Arthur Miller, Jack Kerouac, and Brendan Behan. This hotel is where Andy Warhol filmed *Chelsea Girls* in 1967 and also where punk-rocker Sid Vicious murdered his girlfriend before dying of a drug overdose several weeks later. If you can appreciate the weirdness, it's a reasonable place to stay. By all means have a look at the unusual artwork in the lobby (done by guests and changed at a whim).

Maps:
106–7
108–9

BELOW:
Union Square
on market day.

Chelsea's gallery scene flourishes nearby, particularly along 22nd Street between Tenth and Eleventh avenues. In 1987, the Dia Center for the Arts opened at 548 West 22nd Street, eventually followed by the Matthew Marks Gallery (No.522) and other refugees from Soho's congested art scene, including Pat Hearn (No.530) and Paula Cooper (No.534). Designer stores and restaurants have also opened in the converted garages and warehouses of this quiet area. There are still a few original pioneers, too, including the Empire Diner (Tenth Avenue and 22nd Street). It looks like an old-time aluminum-sided diner on the outside, but inside it's an Art-Deco fantasy. And as you'd expect, the clientele is hip and the prices inflated, but it's open 24 hours and therefore popular with diehards after a night of partying.

Before heading elsewhere, stop in at Chelsea Market (75 Ninth Avenue between 15th and 16th streets). An ambitious renovation in 1996 transformed what were 18 individual buildings erected between 1883 and 1930 into a single wholesale food market, with a waterfall, sculpture, and more than 20 outlets selling meats, vegetables, farm-fresh milk, and baked goods.

Around Fifth Avenue

When the film *King Kong* was shot in 1933, the **Empire State Building** ㉙ (Fifth Ave and 33rd Street; tel: 212/279-9777; open daily; entrance fee) was the obvious building to choose for its grand finale. The building was just two years old and considered to be the eighth wonder of the world. At 1,250 ft (381 meters) it was the tallest building on earth, and was only outdone by the World Trade Center in 1973. No less wondrous was the speed at which the Empire State was constructed – the whole thing took about a year and a half. Its 6,500

windows need to be washed twice every month, and there are 73 elevators.

The lobby is superb: three stories high, faced with marble and decorated with bas-relief. There's more than enough time to admire it because the lines for the elevators tend to be very long. The view from the top is worth the wait, however. The 86th floor has a glass-enclosed area and an outdoor promenade, while the observatory on the 102nd floor is completely enclosed (the viewing terraces are open till midnight; tickets are on sale until 11.25pm). Manhattan by night – or at dusk, when the lights start coming on – is particularly memorable. The New York Skyride is also a popular attraction, a simulated flight through and above the city, but not recommended for those prone to motion sickness.

Still turning out a lion's share of American fashion, the **Garment District** extends roughly from 30th Street to 40th Street, and from Sixth to Eighth avenues. The garment trade, originally located on the Lower East Side (*see page 123*), shifted north at the beginning of the 20th century, bringing an improvement in work conditions, less because of the new location than because the first trade unions had recently been formed. Many buildings here are being converted for use, mostly by new-media companies, but the weekday atmosphere in the streets around Seventh Avenue, known locally as "Fashion Avenue," is still hectic. Trucks block the streets, and clothing rails laden with skirts, coats, and blouses clutter the sidewalks.

In the southern part of the Garment District, the uninspiring **Pennsylvania Station**, which replaced a grand, early 20th-century railway station in 1968, is currently being transformed. **Madison Square Garden**, world famous as a venue for sporting events and concerts, remains on the building's flat roof, but a renovation project encompassing the **General Post Office**, across Eighth Avenue at 33rd Street, provides a majestic new portal for visitors arriving by train. Like Penn Station, the 1913 post office building was designed by McKim, Mead & White. The **Jacob K. Javits Convention Center**, opened in 1986 and designed by I.M. Pei & Partners, sprawls along Twelfth Avenue from 38th to 34th streets. This is the country's largest exhibition space, with the impressive Crystal Palace lobby that rises 165 ft (50 meters) high.

From here it's back to Broadway and Sixth Avenue, and into the world of consumption. At Herald Square stands **Macy's** ㉚, which claims to be the biggest department store in the world. Stroll across the ground floor just to take in the huge selection of goods. Macy's was built on the site of the former Metropolitan Opera House.

A cigarette seller plies her wares in the Theater District.

The Great White Way

At 40th Street is Broadway "proper," the street famous throughout the world. The name **Broadway** ㉛ is synonymous with theaters, entertainment, and the glitzy world of the Great White Way, as this section between 40th and 53rd streets was referred to after electric light made its appearance for the first time. Its heyday was in the 1920–30s, when there were over 80 theaters on and around Broadway. The most famous section was 42nd Street – so famous that theater owners whose properties were actually on 41st or 43rd Street had passageways constructed through entire buildings just to be able to boast a 42nd Street address.

But in the late 1920s the cinema learned to talk, and Broadway theater began to decline. The Great Depression added to Broadway's woes, turning many of the theaters along 42nd Street into burlesque houses and then cinema palaces. As it fell into decay, the street developed a very different kind of fame – as a red-light district, becoming synonymous with drugs and prostitution.

Nearby **Times Square** ㉜ is named after the *New York Times* newspaper, which moved into offices here in 1904. At the junction of Broadway and Seventh Avenue, this is the traditional center of the Theater District; it is also the site of the city's boisterous annual New Year's Eve celebration. In the immediate vicinity, more than 35 Broadway theaters attract audiences to over 30 new theatrical productions a year. Several vintage theaters in the area have been renovated and reopened after a long period of decline, and Times Square is again one of the city's most popular tourist destinations *(see page 136)*.

For a bird's-eye view, step into one of the glass elevators at the Marriott Marquis Hotel, which go up to a revolving restaurant. ❑

BELOW: spreading the word in Times Square.

TIMES SQUARE THEN AND NOW

How long does it take for a Times Square light bulb to burn out? 2½ years. For more about the "Crossroads of the World," read on...

Times Square 42 Street Station

Ⓐ Ⓒ Ⓔ Ⓝ Ⓡ Ⓢ
① ② ③ ⑨ ⑦

In the late 1800s, the harness shops and stables around 42nd and Broadway began to give way to an entertainment district that came to be known as Times Square. Theaters sprouted up all around the area, and hotels and restaurants soon followed. During the Golden Age of the Theater District in the 1920s, big-name producers like the Shubert Brothers and song-and-dance man George M. Cohan staged as many as 250 shows a year. That same decade, Prohibition brought speakeasies, gangsters, and Damon Runyon stories to the square.

The 1930s saw the premier of such classic plays as *Our Town*, although many of the old vaudeville theaters were by this time being replaced by burlesque or movie emporiums. In 1945, more than 2 million people crowded into the square to celebrated VJ Day. Twenty years later, Times Square was in the midst of a decline that lasted another couple of decades, its image indelibly linked with sleaze, crime, and porn.

In one of the great revival stories of the 20th century, in the 1990s a combined public and nonprofit private sector effort transformed the area into a tourist mecca once again, with hotels, restaurants, and entertainment offerings that attract more than 20 million visitors a year. The big draw continues to be the plays and musicals presented in the theaters; while ticket prices can be high, the TKTS Booth at Broadway and 47th Street offers half-price relief. *For more about tickets, see Travel Tips.*

◁ **BROADWAY BABE**
1942's Miss Greenwich Village, Lauren Bacall, 21 years later at Loew's State Theatre for the world premiere of the film *How to Marry a Millionaire.*

◁ THE GREAT WHITE WAY
Free walking tours of the area depart from the Times Square Visitors Center at 1560 Broadway between 46th and 47th streets. The center, in the historic Embassy Theater, is open daily 8am–8pm.

△ **CRIME AND PUNISHMENT**
Times Square may have been cleaned up, but pickpockets still operate on the side streets. Be alert!

THE NEW YORK TIMES

Times Square takes its name from *The New York Times*, which used to be headquartered at the Times Tower at the intersection of 42nd Street and Seventh Avenue, now called One Times Square. Founded in 1851 as *The New-York Daily Times*, in 1896 the paper was purchased by Tennessee newspaperman Adolph S. Ochs, who in 1904 moved its offices from downtown Manhattan to what was then known as Longacre Square. (The poster detail above is *circa* 1900.) The first New Year's Eve celebration was held that year. In 1913 it relocated around the corner to 229 West 43rd Street where today, headed by publisher Arthur Sulzberger, Jr, Ochs' great-grandson, the paper continues to follow its mandate as "an independent newspaper... devoted to the public welfare" under the slogan: "All the News That's Fit to Print." *The New York Times* currently has a weekday circulation of around 1.1 million (around 1.6 million on weekends), and it has received the most awards for journalistic excellence of any other newspaper in the world, including almost 80 Pulitzer Prizes.

△ **BREADLINES ON BROADWAY**
During the Great Depression in the 1930s, a city newspaper opened a relief kitchen in the square to feed the poor.

△ **MANHATTAN VICE**
Times Square reached a low point in the 1980s, when 256 people in NY were robbed every 24 hours. Now officials claim it is the safest of the 25 largest US cities.

▷ **21ST CENTURY**
To celebrate the "new" Times Square and the new millennium, the New Year's Eve ball from 1907 was replaced by a Waterford Crystal-designed ball.

NORTH FROM MIDTOWN

Map
on pages
108–9

Farther uptown, Manhattan becomes increasingly upscale, with famous hotels and department stores, Rockefeller Center, Museum Mile, and the chic residential areas either side of Central Park

R eturning to Fifth Avenue, walking north from the Empire State Building, you will come across **Lord & Taylor** (Fifth Avenue and 39th Street), one of New York's most enduring department stores, and famous for its extravagant holiday displays. People have been known to line up on cold winter days just to peer into the windows.

On the next block up, office workers and tourists can usually be found lounging in front of the main branch of the **New York Public Library** ㉝, under the watchful gaze of two stone lions who flank the marble steps. Stretching between 40th and 42nd streets, this 1911 Beaux Arts monument is one of the world's finest research facilities, with some 88 miles (140 km) of bookshelves and a vast archive collection that includes the first book printed in the United States, the *Bay Psalm Book* from 1640, and the original diaries of Virginia Woolf. In addition to a fine permanent collection of paintings, the library has a third floor space for exhibits. The biggest treasure of all, however, may be the restored Reading Room, a vast gilded gem whose windows overlook adjacent **Bryant Park**. Ask inside about joining one of the twice-daily tours of the building.

Two blocks east, there's a Midtown branch of the **Whitney Museum of American Art** ㉞ (120 Park Avenue; tel: 212/878-2550; open Mon–Fri; entrance free), with a gallery and sculpture court, in the lobby of the Philip Morris Building.

LEFT: the much-loved Art-Deco Chrysler Building.
BELOW: Jules Coutan's statue and clock at Grand Central Terminal.

Grand Central

Historically, Madison Avenue has been a metaphor for the advertising industry, especially the blocks between 42nd and 57th streets. This is one of the city's commercial hearts, where attaché-cased men and women stop off for cocktails at the Yale Club one block east on Vanderbilt Avenue, before running to catch their trains home to the suburbs from **Grand Central Terminal** ㉟. With entrances at Vanderbilt and 42nd Street, as well as Park and Lexington avenues, Grand Central is the hub in a spoke of Metro-North commuter lines reaching deep into the suburbs of Westchester County and Connecticut, and is used by almost half a million passengers each day.

Unlike the old Penn Station, Grand Central was saved from demolition by the city's Landmarks Preservation Commission, and thus this 1913 Beaux Arts beauty remains almost intact, with a $200 million restoration to renew its former glory. Advertising signs were removed, new restaurants and stores have been opened, and the illuminated zodiac on the vaulted ceiling of the main concourse – one of the world's largest rooms – gleams like new. Tours are available on Wednesdays (inquire at the main information booth or call the Municipal Art Society at 212/935-3960).

GRAND CENTRAL TERMINAL

Don't miss the lower-level Oyster Bar, a culinary landmark in its own right.

Around the corner on Lexington Avenue, the famed **Chrysler Building** ㊱ is one of the jewels of the Manhattan skyline. Erected by auto czar Walter Chrysler in 1930, its Art-Deco spire rises 1,000 ft (300 meters) into the city air like a stainless-steel rocket ship. Stop in and admire the lobby's marble-and-bronze decor, enhanced by epic murals depicting transportation and human endeavor. Farther west on 42nd Street, the lobby garden of the **Ford Foundation,** glass-enclosed with lush trees and flowers, is considered one of the city's most beautiful institutions.

It's worth stopping at the **United Nations** ㊲ (46th Street and First Avenue; tel: 212/963-7713; tours every half hour) for a fascinating look at the workings of international diplomacy. Free tickets are available for meetings of the General Assembly when it's in session. Be sure not to miss the moon rock display just inside the entrance, the superb Chagall stained-glass windows, or the excellent gift shop, which sells handicrafts originating from all over the world. On weekdays, you can have lunch in the Delegates' Dining Room, where the view of the river is almost as interesting as the many opportunities for multilingual eavesdropping.

Back on **Fifth Avenue**, historically one of the city's most famous shopping streets, is **Rockefeller Center** ㊳. This huge compound of office towers is a "city within the city," and extends from Fifth to beyond Sixth Avenue and from 48th Street to north of 51st Street. It was designed to integrate several functions within a single complex: accommodation, work, shops, restaurants, and entertainment. The centerpiece of the complex is the **Sunken Plaza**, which serves as a skating rink in winter and an outdoor café in summer. Colorful flags flap quietly, and a golden *Prometheus* hovers in front of the waterfall. This work by Paul Manship is the most well known but not the only artwork in Rockefeller Center: there are over 100 paintings and sculptures here by more than 30 artists. Outside the International Building on Fifth Avenue is Lee Lawrie's *Atlas*; another work by the same artist, *Wisdom,* can be seen above the entrance portal of the General Electric (formerly RCA) Building. The entire compound was financed by just one man: John D. Rockefeller, Jr. The Rockefeller name spells wealth, but the surprising thing about the Center is that John D. managed to come up with the $125 million needed for its construction during the Great Depression. The first 14 buildings were constructed between 1931 and 1940. Thousands of people who would otherwise have remained unemployed found work here.

Radio City Music Hall

The entrance to one of the highlights of the Rockefeller Center, the Art-Deco **Radio City Music Hall** ㊴, is on Sixth Avenue. This theater, too, was built during the Great Depression – it was opened in 1932 – which makes the sheer amount of pomp and splendor inside all the more surprising. The six-story foyer contains a magnificent staircase, the seats are all upholstered in velvet, and the stage is as wide as a city block. The satin curtain weighs 3 tons and is raised and lowered by 13 motors. The sun, moon, and stars appear at the touch of a button; likewise lightning and storm effects.

BELOW: *Prometheus* glitters at Rockefeller Center.

Map on pages 108–9

The enormous 6,200-seat auditorium was always sold out, even during the Depression, when the theater either presented the famous Rockettes revue group, or the very latest movies on the huge screen. It was only with the arrival of television that the theater suffered. Rumors of demolition were rife, but New Yorkers amassed a small fortune to save their last great entertainment center, and Radio City underwent restoration. Today it is a landmark building, and hosts extravagant shows as well as popular-music concerts on a year-round basis. A guided tour is worthwhile (tel: 212/247-4777).

Opposite Rockefeller Plaza on Fifth Avenue is **St Patrick's Cathedral ⓐ**, the largest Catholic church in the country. Opened in 1879, when the city didn't extend beyond 42nd Street, the church is now one of Midtown's most formidable landmarks, its ornate Gothic façade working an intriguing counterpoint against the skyscrapers around it. And yet St Pat's is unmistakably New York: where else would one need tickets to attend Christmas midnight Mass? Take some time for a look around the cathedral's magnificent interior. The bronze doors and stained-glass windows are particularly striking.

St Patrick's is the focal point of New York's sizeable Catholic community.

Farther east, on Park Avenue between 49th and 50th, the **Waldorf-Astoria ⓐ** is one of the city's grandest hotels, and has attracted royalty and presidents since it opened in 1931. The Duke and Duchess of Windsor and Cole Porter were some of the "permanent residents" who lived in the hotel. The original Waldorf Hotel, on Fifth Avenue, was torn down to make way for the Empire State Building.

The Four Seasons restaurant, on East 52nd Street between Park and Lexington, is so important that its interior has been declared a historic landmark. The world's largest Picasso can be found inside, as can notable figures from the worlds of politics and publishing. The restaurant is located inside the **Seagram**

BELOW: New York's fleet of Yellow Cabs.

*Mannequins model
the current fashion
trends at Bloomies.*

BELOW: the
sculpture garden
at the Museum
of Modern Art.

Building. The tycoon Samuel Bronfman, head of Seagram Distillers, had planned to erect an ordinary office block until his architect daughter introduced him to Mies van der Rohe. The result is one of the best of the Modernist constructions of the 1950s.

The **Museum of Modern Art** ⓫ (11 West 53rd Street; tel: 212/708-9400; open Thur–Tues; entrance fee) was founded by Abby Rockefeller, the wife of John D. Rockefeller, Jr. She was a passionate collector of modern art, including works by Georgia O'Keefe, Picasso, and Georges Braque. The museum opened in 1929, and 10 years later the collection was shifted to its present home on 53rd Street. The building has undergone quite a few alterations since that time. In 1951, architect Philip Johnson added two wings; during the 1960s several neighboring buildings were acquired; and in 1983 the western part of the building was provided with a controversial 42-story apartment tower that doubled the museum's exhibition space, providing room for Cubists, Expressionists, Pop Artists, and Dadaists. Exhibition space is currently being doubled again, thanks to another major expansion that will absorb an adjacent hotel and provide an additional entrance on 54th Street. Due for completion by 2004, this latest renovation is designed by Yoshio Taniguchi.

MoMA is considered by many to be the most important museum of modern art in the world, starting with the Impressionists in the 1880s. Van Gogh, Monet, Chagall, Matisse, Toulouse-Lautrec, Picasso, Miró, Pollock, and Warhol are just a few of the artists represented. There is also an architecture and design section, with works by Tiffany, Thonet and Marcel Breuer, and a photography section. In the midst of it all is a Sculpture Garden, designed by Philip Johnson.

At 57th Street, the super-rich (and those who like to pretend) can be seen

bouncing between Bulgari, Tiffany and Co., and the shops inside soaring **Trump Tower** . You've got to hand it to realtor Donald Trump: the design, with its marble and a five-story waterfall, may be a little plush but it's effective.

Farther west at 57th Street and Seventh Avenue, is **Carnegie Hall** ⓙ. As every New Yorker knows, there's only one way to get to Carnegie Hall – practice. The joke is about as old as the hall itself, which was built in 1891 by super-industrialist Andrew Carnegie. Ever since Tchaikovsky conducted at the opening gala, Carnegie Hall has attracted the world's finest performers, including Rachmaninov, Toscanini, and Sinatra.

Grand Army Plaza on 59th Street punctuates Fifth Avenue and marks the boundary between Midtown and the **Upper East Side**. Usually jammed with taxis, limousines, and hansom cabs, it borders the **Plaza Hotel** ⓚ, a grand, 19th-century home-away-from-home in days past for people like Mark Twain, Frank Lloyd Wright, and Eleanor Roosevelt. It's still popular with celebrities today. Stop in for a drink at the Plaza's Oak Bar, a wood-paneled salon where prices are high but worth it for the views.

Serious shoppers may want to head straight for one of the city's retail queens, **Bloomingdale's** ⓛ, at 59th Street (entrances on both Third and Lexington avenues.). It's a minor institution that many New Yorkers could not live without. Style and quality are keynotes at Bloomies. The shop is almost always crowded (it can be oppressively so during holidays and sale times), but if you only go to one department store in New York City, this should probably be it.

Central Park

If the plans of those who designed Manhattan had been followed to the letter, there wouldn't have been any **Central Park** ⓜ. The members of the commission that decided Manhattan's architectural future in 1811 only allowed enough room for four squares of green; they wanted the rest of the land to be developed.

New Yorkers soon experienced the consequences of this way of thinking. Between 1820 and 1840 the city's population swelled from 124,000 to 313,000, and Manhattan's riverside spaces were covered with warehouses, dockyards, and other installations. Voices were soon raised in protest. William Cullen Bryant, publisher of the *New York Evening Post*, the author Washington Irving, painters, architects, and many others all insisted that an area of land at the center of the island be kept free of development and turned into parkland. In 1856 the decision was made: the city purchased a 2.5-mile (4-km) long, narrow strip of land between Eighth and Fifth avenues and 59th and 110th streets for a hefty $5.5 million.

Frederick Law Olmsted and Calvert Vaux, the two architects who had won the Central Park design competition in 1857, made the dream a reality. Trans-forming this former swamp, Vaux contributed a formal mall, fountain, and ornamental bridges, while Olmsted was determined to make the new park as natural as possible, keeping intact the rocky outcrops that once characterized the rest of the island, design-ing sunken crossroads to keep traffic from intruding,

Olmsted's aim for Central Park was to "supply hundreds of thousands of tired workers, who have no opportunity to spend summers in the country, with a specimen of God's handiwork."

BELOW: chic shopping at the Trump Tower.

Map on pages 108–9

You can hire a carriage from the Tavern on the Green, at Fifth Avenue and 59th Street. Each ride lasts half an hour. Although there's a fixed price, you could always try negotiating, especially if trade isn't particularly brisk.

and creating meandering pathways to draw pedestrians deeper into his engineered wilderness. It took them some 16 years, more than $14 million, 21,000 barrels of dynamite, and the planting of 17,000 trees and shrubs to turn this wilderness into the world's first major public park.

Roughly divided into a north and south end – with the **Reservoir** (around which the city's fleet of joggers make their rounds) in the middle – the park has entrances at regular intervals around the periphery. At the northern end is the **Conservatory Garden**, the park's only formal horticultural showcase, where in spring more than 20,000 tulips burst into bloom. To get here, walk through the elegant Vanderbilt Gate at Fifth Avenue and 105th Street.

Most visitors tend to stick to the park's southern end, entering through the Maine Memorial at Columbus Circle or Grand Army Plaza. Go past the statue of General Sherman and follow the path to get to the **Central Park Wildlife Center** (tel: 212/861-6030; open daily; entrance fee), known to locals as the Central Park Zoo. Exhibits include re-creations of Temperate, Tropic, and Polar Zone environments, and the emphasis is on education.

Farther into the park, **The Dairy** (also reached via the 65th Street Transverse or up the East Drive from Grand Army Plaza) used to be where milkmaids served fresh milk to city kids. It now serves as Central Park's Visitor Center (tel: 212/794-6564), and is the place to go for maps and directions to places like **Strawberry Fields**, Yoko Ono's memorial to the murdered John Lennon. There are also special exhibits on the park's history as well as information about daily walking tours, led by the Urban Park Rangers, and other events.

To the west, **Sheep Meadow** is a 22-acre (9-hectare) zone popular with picnickers and sunbathers. The sheep that grazed here in the 1800s are long gone,

BELOW: rest and recreation on the Sheep's Meadow.

but nearby is the upscale Tavern on the Green restaurant. There's a **carousel** with over 50 handcarved horses and the **Wollman Rink** for ice skating in the winter. (You can rent skates, too.) From here, follow paths north to **The Mall**, Central Park's only formal promenade. This leafy expanse is lined by the country's finest stand of elm trees, one of which was planted by the Prince of Wales in 1919. From Bethesda Fountain there's a wonderful view of **The Lake**; the Loeb Boathouse has rowboats and bikes for rent. There's also an outdoor restaurant.

Northeast of the Lake, the **Ramble** is the wild heart of the park. Its 38 acres (15 hectares) of twisting paths and rocky cliffs are a favorite with birdwatchers in search of the more than 250 migratory species that stop off here; it's also popular with gay couples and the occasional mugger. Despite its reputation, Central Park has one of the city's lowest crime rates, but it is advisable to explore the more secluded areas with a friend or two.

Above the 79th Street Transverse, **Belvedere Castle** sits like a Gothic folly atop Vista Rock and serves as a US weather bureau station. Today, it is also a children's environmental education facility and information center – and the best place to go for that quintessential view of the park and surrounding city.

The **Shakespeare Garden** is planted with various trees and flowers mentioned in the playwright's work. The Bard's plays are presented free of charge during the New York Shakespeare Festival, held every June through August at the open-air **Delacorte Theatre**. Not far away, the **Great Lawn** is where music lovers spread their blankets for free evening performances by the Metropolitan Opera and the New York Philharmonic Orchestra in June and July.

The best day of the week to appreciate Central Park is on summer Sundays, when New Yorkers come to stroll, play, cycle, canoe, drink coffee, or just to see and be seen. But no matter what day of the week, or time of the year, New Yorkers come to Central Park to find a brief respite from the stress of city living.

Museum Mile

The beginning of Manhattan's museum stretch is the **Frick Collection** ㊽ (1 East 70th Street; tel: 212/288-0700; open Tues–Sat, Sun afternoon; entrance fee), a collection of art treasures assembled by steel manufacturer Henry Clay Frick, and housed in his former palazzo, built in French neo-classical style in 1913. The Frick is enchanting, and feels more like a beautifully decorated house than a museum. Goya, Titian, El Greco, Vermeer, and Renoir are just a few of the artists represented here.

The **Whitney Museum of American Art** ㊾ (945 Madison Ave; tel: 212/570-3676; open Wed–Sun; entrance fee) was the idea of Gertrude Vanderbilt Whitney, a wealthy sculptor who helped young artists to exhibit their work in Greenwich Village as early as the 1930s. The Whitney exclusively exhibits 20th-century American art. The latest paintings and sculptures are always presented each autumn. "Classics" include Lichtenstein, Pollock, Rauschenberg, and Shan. One highlight here must not be missed: the 2,000 or so works by Edward Hopper. The museum has a midtown branch, too (*see page 139*).

One of New York's most famous cultural institu-

Map on pages 108–9

Get your bearings at the Central Park Visitor Information Center.

BELOW: a summertime concert in the park.

Visitors gain new perspectives on art at the Guggenheim.

tions, parts of which overflow into Central Park, is the **Metropolitan Museum of Art** ❺⓿ (82nd Street; tel: 212/535-7710; open Tues–Sun; entrance fee). Calvert Vaux had a hand in its design and the original carriage entrance, dating from 1880, is still intact, though on view in the museum's sculpture court. Sections have been added continually to cope with the massive amount of art, but the present building still holds less than half the museum's permanent collection of over 3 million objects. The most recent addition is the Lila Acheson Wallace Wing (1987), including a roof-garden with a superb view of Central Park.

In order to avoid spending several weeks inside the Metropolitan Museum one has to concentrate on just a few rooms. There is an information desk in the museum's Great Hall (just inside the main entrance). Among the highlights are the Robert Lehman Collection (European art including works by Rembrandt, Goya, Van Gogh and Matisse); Egyptian Art; Greek and Roman Art; Michael C. Rockefeller Wing (pre-Columbian art, tribal art and artifacts from Africa, Oceania and the Americas); American Wing (four floors containing every possible manifestation of American art); European Paintings (including a number of Rembrandts); Islamic Art; South and Southeast Asian Art; Drawings, Prints, and Photographs (artists represented include Leonardo da Vinci, Titian, Michelangelo, Turner, and Degas) and Greek and Roman Art (including new galleries added in 2000). This great treasure trove of art, along with a regular series of spectacular special exhibitions, has made the Metropolitan Museum of Art one of the world's most impressive centers of culture.

Four blocks away, the **Solomon R. Guggenheim Museum** ❺❶ (1071 Fifth Avenue; tel: 212/423-3500; open Fri–Wed; entrance fee) is worth visiting for its wonderful architecture alone, designed by Frank Lloyd Wright. From the outside it resembles an upturned snail-shell; inside, the spiral ramp affords continually new perspectives on the artworks displayed. The museum was opened in 1959, 16 years later than planned, due to bureaucracy and protests from local residents. Guggenheim and Frank Lloyd Wright were both dead by this time. When it was finally ready it was an architectural sensation, but still had far too little room for Guggenheim's mammoth collection – the copper magnate owned over 4,000 paintings, sculptures, and drawings. A new building, which rather dominates the original, was opened in 1992 to provide more space. Highlights include the largest collection of Kandinskys in the world, plus works by Picasso, Chagall, Mondrian, Miró, Renoir, Manet, and many others.

Many of Fifth Avenue's 19th-century mansions are now museums. The **Cooper-Hewitt National Design Museum** ❺❷ is in the former villa of millionaire Andrew Carnegie (2 East 91st Street; tel: 212/849-8300; open Tues–Sun; entrance fee). New York's so-called Museum Mile extends more than a mile (from 82nd to 104th streets) and includes the **International Center of Photography** ❺❸ (1130 Fifth Avenue; tel: 212/860-1777; open Tues–Sun; entrance fee); the **Museum of the City of New York** (103rd Street; tel: 212/534-1672; open Wed–Sun; entrance fee); and **El Museo del Barrio** (1230 Fifth Avenue; tel: 212/831-7272; open Wed–Sun; entrance fee).

Harlem

Originally the home of Native Americans, **Harlem** was settled by the Dutch in 1658 as Nieuw Haarlem, after the city in the Netherlands. In 1664, it fell to the British and the name was anglicized by dropping one "a." Still farmland in the early 1800s, Harlem became New York City's first upscale suburb when Alexander Hamilton, the Secretary of the Treasury, built a country home called Hamilton Grange. This exclusivity changed in 1837 with the opening of the Harlem River Railroad, followed by Harlem's 1873 annexation to New York City, the extension of the rapid transit lines in 1880, and in 1904 by the building of the IRT Lenox Avenue subway.

All of this made Harlem more accessible, which in turn led to an influx of immigrants. In the early 1900s, African-Americans began moving to 135th Street, west of Lenox Avenue. From then on, Harlem became an African-American enclave. Poet Langston Hughes and writer Zora Neale Hurston, along with musicians Duke Ellington, Louis Armstrong, and Bessie Smith, all launched their careers here in the 1920s and '30s, during what was termed the Harlem Renaissance, gaining the area a reputation as a playground for thrill-seekers.

Harlem's late 20th-century reputation as an area rife with drugs and crime is changing. Today it is a diverse community where Irish, Italian, Dominican, Haitian, Puerto Rican, West African, and other residents sometimes live side by side, and where ongoing renovations are attracting increasing numbers of the middle-classes. Nevertheless, there are some areas tourists should avoid. To best experience this part of the city, take a tour or contact the Harlem Visitors and Convention Association (tel: 212/862-8497).

Upper West Side

The spicy bits of the Upper West Side are Broadway, Columbus, and Amsterdam Avenues, a sort of 24-hour circus squeezed between the dignified calm of Riverside Drive and Central Park West. The entrance to all this is **Columbus Circle**, a tangle of cars and pedestrians zipping around a statue of Christopher Columbus, who looks a bit frazzled by all the commotion. Central Park West branches off Columbus Circle and heads up into the area's most affluent residential section. The apartment houses overlooking the park are among the most lavish in the city, and the cross streets, especially 74th, 75th, and 76th, are lined with splendid brownstones.

The most famous apartment building on this stretch is **The Dakota** (1 West 72nd Street), built in 1884 by Henry Hardenbergh, who also designed the Plaza Hotel. It has attracted tenants like Boris Karloff, Leonard Bernstein, Lauren Bacall, and John Lennon, who was shot outside the building in 1980.

Returning to Columbus Circle, Broadway swerves west toward Columbus Avenue and just nicks the corner of the Lincoln Center, flanked by the prestigious Juilliard School of Music and Fordham University. The **Lincoln Center for the Performing Arts** began construction in 1959 as part of a massive redevelopment plan intended to clean up the slum that used to occupy the site. More than 180 buildings were demolished and 1,600 families relocated in order

Map on pages 108–9

Harlem's Apollo Theater (253 West 125th Street; tel: 212/749-5838) has long been a showcase for top African-American entertainers, such as Billie Holiday, Charlie Parker, James Brown, and Aretha Franklin. It opened in 1913 as a burlesque house and still hosts top acts.

BELOW: towering above Columbus Circle.

to make room for the complex, inflaming social critics who saw it as nothing more than a playground for the élite. Architectural critics gave it a beating, too, citing a lack of gravity and an overdose of ornamentation. Despite all this, Lincoln Center has become one of the city's most vital outlets for the performing arts. And with yearly attendance now running at about 5 million people, it is obviously meeting a popular need.

Standing at the black marble fountain in the middle of the plaza, you are surrounded by the glass and white-marble façades of the center's three main structures. The Metropolitan Opera is directly in front with two large murals by Marc Chagall hanging behind the glass wall – *Le Triomphe de la Musique* to the left, *Les Sources de la Musique* to the right. The Met is home to the Metropolitan Opera Company from September to April and the American Ballet Theater from May to July. To the left of the central fountain, the New York State Theater is shared by the New York City Opera and the New York City Ballet. If the doors are open, look at the Jasper Johns painting on the ground floor and the two controversial marble statues by Elie Nadelman in the upstairs foyer.

The third side of the main plaza is occupied by **Avery Fisher Hall**, home of the New York Philharmonic and the Mostly Mozart series held in the summer. Peek in for a look at Richard Lippold's *Orpheus and Apollo*, a hanging metal sculpture that dominates the foyer.

When you've finished gazing around Lincoln Center, cross Columbus Avenue for a quick look at the **Museum of American Folk Art** (2 Lincoln Square; tel: 212/595-9533; open daily; entrance free), which has a great little gift shop.

The **American Museum of Natural History** ⑤ (79th Street; tel: 212/769-5100; open daily; suggested fee) sprawls over four city blocks. Guarded by an

Sherman's Barbeque on 151st Street and Amsterdam Avenue, is where the all-girl singing group the Ronettes brought the Beatles in 1964. Sneaking out of the Plaza Hotel, the Beatles were able to breathe easy, play the jukebox, and relax with like-minded musicians.

BELOW: lighting up at Lincoln Center.

equestrian statue of Theodore Roosevelt, the museum's main entrance is actually one of the many additions built around the original structure. The old façade, a stately Romanesque arcade with two ornate towers, was built in 1892 and is visible from 77th Street. There are 40 exhibition halls housed in 23 buildings. Highlights include a 34-ton meteorite, the largest blue sapphire in the world, a full-scale model of a blue whale, and a renowned anthropological collection. The dinosaur exhibits, installed in six renovated halls, offer an astounding look at life on earth over many millennia. The world's tallest dinosaur – the 50-ft (15-meter) high Barosaurus – can be found in the Theodore Roosevelt Rotunda, off of which a Hall of Biodiversity includes a stunning re-creation of an African rainforest. The Center for Earth and Space includes a planetarium.

West Harlem extends from around Amsterdam Avenue to Riverside Drive, taking in the Convent Avenue and Sugar Hill areas, along with Hamilton and Morningside Heights. Many of Harlem's white residents live in this district, which includes **Columbia University** ❺, alma mater of several Pulitzer Prize winners, on upper Broadway.

At 122nd Street, **Grant's Tomb** ❺ is the final resting place of former president and Civil War general Ulysses S. Grant and his wife, Julia. It was dedicated in 1897 as a national park site and is said to be inspired by Napoleon's final resting place. At 112th Street and Amsterdam Avenue, the impressive **Cathedral of St John the Divine** ❺ is home to the city's largest Episcopal congregation; it's also the world's second-largest Gothic cathedral (and still under construction). Not far away, at Riverside Drive and 120th Street, the nondenominational Riverside Church has the world's largest bell carillon atop its 22-story tower. Both churches feature special cultural events throughout the year. ❏

Imposing statuary graces the American Museum of Natural History.

BELOW: The Dakota, last home of John Lennon.

The Outer Boroughs

Although most people say "New York" when they actually mean "Manhattan," the city has four other boroughs. New York City's population of 7½ million is distributed across all five of them: Manhattan, Brooklyn, the Bronx, Queens, and Staten Island. Only around 1½ million people live in Manhattan itself. Its population doubles on weekdays because of commuters from the other boroughs, and also from New Jersey and Connecticut.

But there is plenty to see in the other boroughs. Manhattan's great competitor on the other side of the East River, Brooklyn, is rich with cultural highlights. You can reach Brooklyn on foot, across the famous Brooklyn Bridge *(see page 119)*, which was considered the eighth wonder of the world on its completion in 1883. The view of the Manhattan skyline it affords is breathtaking.

Those eager to see Manhattan from another dramatic perspective should take a stroll along the Promenade in Brooklyn Heights, one of Brooklyn's most attractive neighborhoods. Although the 19th-century brownstone mansions here have long been popular with artists and writers, today the rents are as high as in Manhattan.

Brooklyn's population has more African-Americans than Harlem, a substantial Jewish community and enclaves of Italians, Arabs and Chinese. There's a large contingent from the Caribbean, and some sections, such as Brighton Beach, are home to Russian and other East European immigrants. Famous Brooklynites include Norman Mailer, Arthur Miller, Barbra Streisand, and Woody Allen.

Brooklyn lies on the westernmost tip of Long Island, so it's possible to go swimming here. Although these days not the most savory of prospects, Coney Island Beach, the "poor man's Riviera," is packed on hot summer days. Coney Island itself, formerly the site of one of the world's largest amusement parks, was laid out in the 1880s and thrived until the 1960s. Today the area is a jumble of apartment blocks and empty lots, but you can still ride on the Cyclone, a 1927 roller coaster, and watch the weird acts presented by Sideshows by the Seashore (Surf Avenue and west 12th Street). You can also savor Nathan's famous hot dogs and admire the sea lions at the New York Aquarium (Surf Avenue and 8th Street).

Another popular Brooklyn destination is Prospect Park, which, like Central Park, was laid out by Frederick Law Olmsted and Calvert Vaux. To the northeast of the park is the Brooklyn Botanic Garden; across the street is the Brooklyn Museum. Alongside its impressive Egyptian collection, the museum also has a vast collection of art from all over the world. In another part of the borough, the Brooklyn Academy of Music (30 Lafayette Avenue) is best known for its annual autumn "Next Wave Festival," which features avant-garde theatrical and musical performances.

To the north of Brooklyn is Queens, the largest of New York's boroughs. About 2

LEFT: the Enid A. Haupt Conservatory at the Bronx Botanical Gardens.
RIGHT: Staten Island ferry ready to dock.

million people live here although it is often referred to as the "bedroom" of Manhattan. Not that it's necessarily a quiet place: broad highways cut through monotonous rows of terraced houses, and La Guardia and John F. Kennedy airports keep the noise level high.

Every visitor who lands at JFK International Airport and takes a taxi to Manhattan goes through Queens. Tennis fans watching TV coverage of the US Open at the National Tennis Center are actually looking at Queens, too. During the silent movie era, Queens was the equivalent of today's Hollywood and movies and TV shows are still produced at the Kaufman-Astoria studios here. The American Museum of the Moving Image (35th Avenue and 36th Street, Astoria) celebrates this early movie history. Worth visiting is the Queens Museum of Art, in Flushing Meadows-Corona Park (site of the National Tennis Center), which features a model of all five boroughs created for the 1964 World's Fair.

Many associate the Bronx with a rough, tough image. However, not all its population of 1.2 million live behind burned-out façades.

Only the southern part of New York's only mainland borough corresponds with the notorious image – and even parts there are experiencing a rebirth; the northern part, with its leafy enclaves along the Hudson River, contains magnificent villas and mansions. The main attraction is the Bronx Zoo/Wildlife Conservation Park (Bronx River Parkway and Fordham Road), the largest municipal zoo in the US. Next to it is the New York Botanical Garden, laid out in 1891 and modeled after Kew Gardens in London.

With a population of just 413,000, Staten Island is the most thinly populated of New York's boroughs and its bucolic atmosphere can be a refreshing contrast to the bustle of Manhattan. The Staten Island Ferry has been in operation since 1840. The trip provides a fine view of the southern tip of Manhattan and its skyline. One of Staten Island's most interesting sites is the reconstructed Historic Richmond Town (441 Clarke Avenue), an open-air museum documenting life in Richmond (Staten Island's former name) between the 17th and 19th centuries. ❏

LONG ISLAND

Although often mistaken as a suburban extension of New York City, Long Island is much more, with fine beaches, historic mansions, fishing villages, traditional farms, and new vineyards

Map on pages 156–7

New York

I n his novel *The Great Gatsby*, F. Scott Fitzgerald called Long Island "that slender riotous island" extending east of New York City. He was referring to the Jazz Age shenanigans of the idle rich on what was, in the 1920s, still essentially an island of farms and villages. Today, although things can no doubt get frisky on summer weekends in the Hamptons, "riotous" is not a word many people would use to describe Long Island. It has become instead a microcosm of the rest of New York State, a place where burgeoning cities and suburbs, surviving small towns, dwindling farmlands and expansive parks coexist on a forked strip of land 118 miles (at its widest point) by some 20 miles (190 by 32 km).

All this, along with vivid reminders of many layers of history and the state's only ocean beaches, makes for an eclectic destination. Walk across the Brooklyn Bridge from lower Manhattan, and you are on Long Island. It's easy to forget that New York City's boroughs of Brooklyn and Queens are in fact part of the island, as are Kennedy and LaGuardia airports, Shea Stadium, and the urban beaches of Coney Island. But when New Yorkers refer to Long Island, they almost always mean the territory that stretches east beyond the city limits.

PRECEDING PAGES: a Long Island sand dune. **LEFT:** Montauk Point Lighthouse. **BELOW:** freshly dug clams.

The island's beginnings

Long Island is largely a creature of Ice Age glaciers, which at various times terminated along the island's east-west axis, depositing heaps of gravel called moraines. Glacial moraines define Long Island's ridges of insignificant hills, none of which reach more than 400 ft (120 meters) above sea level. The glaciers' meltwater drowned an ancient river valley to create Long Island Sound.

Indians reached the gentle terrain and rich fishing grounds of Long Island some 10,000 years ago, and European settlement dates from 1636 when Dutch Manhattanites, feeling the need for elbow room that has ever since driven migrants from the city, crossed the East River to establish Brooklyn. In the 17th century New Englanders from the British colonies also settled in Long Island, and the fishing villages they established still retain a flavor reminiscent of seaside towns in Massachusetts and Connecticut.

Although fishing and whaling drove the economy of the towns along the Sound and the Atlantic coast (Long Island Sound still supports a healthy lobster fishery), colonial and post-Revolutionary Long Island developed primarily as a back garden for the tables of New York City, with agriculture creating the main income well into the 20th century. Its two principal products, potatoes and ducks, were so well established that "Long Island potatoes" and "Long Island duckling" were terms regularly used in markets and restaurants.

Today, potato and duck farms are both endangered species on Long Island, owing to the island's value as an enormous piece of residential real estate. The boom began at the high end of the market, when 19th-century financial barons established enormous estates easily accessible from New York City via rail (the Long Island Railroad, still an essential commuter conduit, dates from the 1840s). It continued with the post-World War I heyday of "Gatsby-esque" summer mansions along the "Gold Coast" of the North Shore. Today, the well-heeled crowd is centered farther east and south, among the Hamptons on the South Fork.

After World War II, middle-class suburban expansion swelled small towns until their borders became indistinguishable, filling fields with strip malls and subdivisions. Relocation of industry to Long Island and the improvement of commuter highways led to the creation of instant communities such as Levittown, where tens of thousands of houses were built for returning soldiers and their new families. Still, Long Island is not one vast housing development. Many small, traditional communities have survived, and among them are a wealth of museums and period restorations that reveal centuries of regional history.

Since Long Island developed largely as a rural and suburban adjunct to New York City, it is easily accessible. Long Island Railroad trains run frequently from Manhattan's Pennsylvania Station (see page 135), on lines extending all the way to Greenport on the North Fork and Montauk on the South Fork. The Long Island Railroad also offers a variety of escorted rail/bus tours throughout the island during spring, summer and fall (tel: 516/822-LIRR for information). For travelers desiring more leeway in schedules and destinations, though, a car is the best way to get around. There are four major east-west routes: the Northern State Parkway and Long Island Expressway (Interstate 495) in the north, and

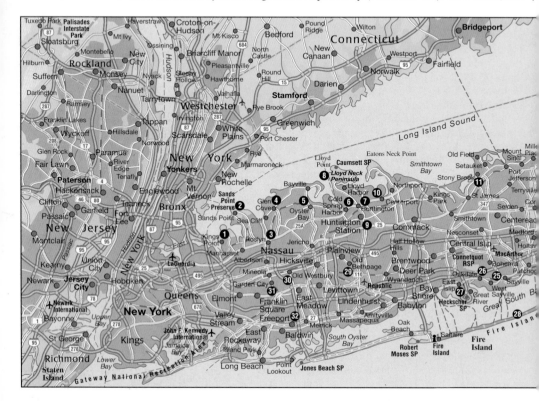

the Southern State Parkway and Sunrise Highway (Route 27) in the south. (The two state parkways prohibit recreational vehicles and commercial trucks.)

Many Long Island attractions are only open during the May to September season. Parks, beaches, and other outdoor sites are, however, often open all year.

Map on pages 156–7

The North Shore

Turn off Route 25A, which parallels the Long Island Expressway, onto Great Neck Peninsula and begin your tour of the island at **Kings Point ❶** overlooking Long Island Sound. Here you will find the American Merchant Marine Museum (Steamboat Road; tel: 516/773-5515; open Tues–Sun, closed July and Federal and Academy holidays; entrance free), on the grounds of the US Merchant Marine Academy. "Ships made in America" is the theme, and exhibits include models, documents, paintings, and maritime artifacts. The academy is on the grounds of the former Chrysler Estate; the Beaux Arts Wiley Hall Mansion is surrounded by manicured lawns with reflecting pools and fountains.

Back on Route 25A, continue through **Manhasset**, one of the oldest communities on the North Shore and the site of the county's first school for African-Americans. Today, it's home to Miracle Mile, a large upscale shopping mall.

Off the highway through Port Washington, overlooking Manhasset Bay, continue to **Sands Point Preserve ❷** (95 Middleneck Road; tel: 516/571-7900; open May–Oct; entrance fee), the former property of railroad heir Howard Gould. He built two mansions here: the 1912, 40-room Tudor-style Hempstead House, and the 1920 Castlegould, built to resemble Ireland's Kilkenny Castle. The former exhibits the Buten Collection of Wedgwood; the latter is a natural history museum. Also on the property is Falaise (French for "cliff"), built by

Yachting is one of the most popular sports on Long Island.

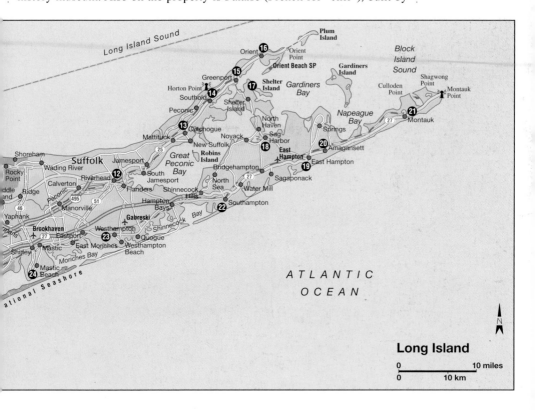

Long Island

Offshore activities bear closer scrutiny at the beach.

Harry F. Guggenheim on the bluffs overlooking the Sound. The mansion, one of the few remaining from the "Gold Coast" era, is based on a 13th-century Norman manor house and furnished with 16th- and 17th-century antiques.

Cedarmere (Bryant Avenue; tel: 516/571-8130; open Apr–Nov Sat–Sun and holidays; entrance free), on the harbor in **Roslyn ❸**, was the home of editor and poet William Cullen Bryant for more than 50 years from the mid-1800s. The neo-classical mansion on the 145-acre (59-hectare) former estate of Childs Frick, son of US Steel cofounder Henry Clay Frick, houses the Nassau County Museum of Art (1 Museum Drive; tel: 516/484-9338; open Tues–Sun; entrance fee to buildings). Outdoor sculptures include works by some of the country's leading artists. Inside are special exhibits and a permanent collection of miniature rooms.

Many of the restored homes that line Main Street of the Roslyn Historic Shopping District were built between 1690 and 1865. Just south of town, in Roslyn Heights, is Christopher Morley Park, named for the essayist, poet, and novelist who built his rustic retreat, Knothole, here (tel: 516/571-8131; open Jun–Oct Sun; entrance free), which provided him with seclusion in the 1930s while he compiled the 11th edition of *Bartlett's Familiar Quotations.*

Head back toward the Sound to Garvies Point Museum (Barry Drive; tel: 516/571-8010; grounds open daily, museum open Wed–Sun; entrance fee to museum) in **Glen Cove ❹**. The museum, on 62 acres (25 hectares) of woodlands and meadows, has exhibits of prehistoric Indian culture, and geology.

Oyster Bay ❺ is home to Sagamore Hill National Historic Site (20 Sagamore Hill; tel: 516/922-4788; open Oct–Apr Wed–Sun; entrance fee), the 23-room Victorian mansion built by Theodore Roosevelt in 1884–5 and used as his "Summer White House" from 1901–9. It is packed with his personal possessions, including

BELOW: building a sand castle at Jones Beach.

Map on pages 156–7

hunting trophies. Across the street, the 12-acre (5-hectare) Theodore Roosevelt Sanctuary (134 Cove Road; tel: 516/922-3200; open daily; entrance free) profiles the former president's conservation efforts. He is buried in the adjoining Young's Cemetery. At the 409-acre (165-hectare) Planting Fields Arboretum (Planting Field Road; tel: 516/922-9210; open daily; entrance fee), gardens and woodlands are the setting for two greenhouse complexes of native, tropical and subtropical plants. Tours are offered of the 1918 Tudor Revival-style Coe Hall.

In the one-time whaling port of **Cold Spring Harbor** ❻, the Cold Spring Harbor Whaling Museum (Route 25A; tel: 631/367-3418; open daily in summer, off season Tues–Sun; entrance fee) documents the village's prosperous past. Exhibits include a scrimshaw collection, a 19th-century whaleboat, and ship models. The DNA Learning Center (334 Main Street; tel: 631/367-7240; open Tues–Sun; entrance free), "the world's first biotechnology museum," teaches about genes, while a multimedia presentation explores the history of Long Island. The Cold Spring Harbor Fish Hatchery and Aquarium (Route 25A Southside; tel: 631/692-6768; open daily; entrance fee), opened in 1883 to hold the first brown trout imported into the country, now also houses the state's largest collection of native freshwater fish, reptiles, and amphibians. The Society for the Preservation of Long Island Antiquities Gallery (1 Shore Road; tel: 631/692-4664; open daily; entrance fee) hosts changing exhibits on the area's history.

In **Huntington** ❼, the Heckscher Museum of Art (2 Prime Avenue; tel: 631/351-3250; open Tues–Sun; entrance fee) has a small but worthwhile European and US collection. The local Historical Society (tel: 631/427-7045) also maintains three sites: Kissam House (*circa* 1795), David Conklin Farmhouse (*circa* 1750), and Huntington Sewing and Trade School (*circa* 1905).

Long Island is the largest island adjoining the continental United States. If it were a city, its population of 2.7 million would make it the fourth largest in the nation.

BELOW: spring flower show at the Planting Fields Arboretum greenhouse.

PLANTING BIG AT PLANTING FIELDS

In 1913, when William Robertson Coe began horticultural work at the Long Island estate that later became Planting Fields Arboretum, he was primarily concerned with camellias, rhododendrons, azaleas, and saplings. But he had one project in mind that required a bit more than a few men with shovels. When Coe's wife was growing up in Fairhaven, Massachusetts, she used to play beneath two old copper beech trees. Coe thought she might like to have the trees around again, so in late 1914 he decided to move them. The fact that they were 60 ft (18 meters) high, with branches spreading 40 ft (12 meters) and a trunk diameter of 30 inches (76 cm) was but an inconvenience – one overcome at an expense of $4,000 and two months' work. First the trees were dug up and their massive roots placed in timber boxes. The 56-ton load was then hauled to a Fairhaven wharf and loaded onto a barge for the two-and-a-half day trip across Long Island Sound. Finally, a team of 72 horses pulled the beeches from Oyster Bay to Planting Fields – after Coe paid the local electric company to remove and replace wires that were in the way.

One of the copper beeches has since died, but its mate still thrives on the north lawn of the Coe mansion. Presumably, it is finished with its travels.

Continue north to **Lloyd Neck Peninsula**  and the undeveloped, 1,500-acre (607-hectare) Caumsett State Park (tel: 631/423-1770; open daily; entrance fee). No vehicles are allowed: this is a haven for fishermen, hikers, and those who don't mind walking 2 miles (4 km) to the secluded beach on the north shore. The park was once the estate of the grandson of department store tycoon Marshall Field, and many of his buildings (closed to the public) still stand.

Head south on Route 110 to **Huntington Station**  and the Walt Whitman Birthplace State Historic Site and Interpretive Center (246 Old Walt Whitman Road; tel: 631/427-5240; open Wed–Sun; entrance free). The poet's father built the house; Walt lived here until he was five and returned in later years. The museum exhibits period furnishings and biographical material. If you're a Whitman aficionado, ask for a map of Whitman-related area sites.

In **Centerport** , the 43-acre (17-hectare) former estate of William Kissam Vanderbilt II, great-grandson of railroad king Commodore Cornelius Vanderbilt, is now the Vanderbilt Museum, Mansion, Marine Museum, and Planetarium Park (180 Little Neck Road; tel: 631/854-5555; open Tues–Sun; entrance fee). The ornate, Spanish-Moroccan-style, 24-room mansion, Eagle's Nest, is filled with Vanderbilt's collection of decorative pieces. The marine museum houses his specimens as well as sundry objects such as shrunken heads. The planetarium is one of the country's largest.

Before continuing east, detour north a short distance to **Northport**, which over the years has been a shipbuilding center and resort. Today it's a quiet spot with a well-preserved Main Street, marina, and bandstand.

The National Landmark St James General Store (516 Moriches Road; tel: 631/862-8333; open daily; entrance free) in **St James** opened for business in 1857, and today – looking just as it did in 1890 – it is the oldest operating general store in the country.

BELOW: the Vanderbilt Mansion.

In 1939 Ward Melville, owner of the Thom McAn shoe company, helped **Stony Brook**  metamorphose from a rural 18th-century village into a well-planned and attractive town that has become one of Long Island's major tourist attractions. Folks come to shop at the upscale Stony Brook Village Center, sleep and eat at the 1751 Three Village Inn (Village Green; tel: 516/751-0555), the former home to Long Island's first millionaire sea captain, and visit The Museums (Main Street; tel: 631/751-0066; open July–Aug daily, Sept–Jun Wed–Mon; entrance fee). This complex of several museums includes the Margaret Melville Blackwell History Museum, with 15 period rooms and one of the country's finest collections of antique decoys; the Dorothy and Ward Melville Carriage House, with horse-drawn carriages; and the Art Museum, with US art from the 18th century to the present and works by US genre painter William Sidney Mount (1807–68). All Souls' Episcopal Church, behind the post office, was built in 1889 by renowned architect Stanford White. On the Wetlands Discovery Cruise (tel: 516/751-2244; open May–Oct; entrance fee), a naturalist conducts a boat tour of the wetlands. Mr Melville also renovated the town's 1751 Gristmill (Harbor Road; tel: 631/751-2244; open June–Aug Wed–Sun, Apr–May, Sept–Nov

Sat–Sun; entrance fee), Long Island's most completely equipped working mill.

Continue east to the picturesque waterfront village of **Port Jefferson** and the 1840 Mather House Museum (Prospect and High streets; tel: 631/473-2665; open May–Labor Day Sat–Sun, July–Aug Tues–Wed, Sat–Sun; entrance fee), which has maritime exhibits, gardens, and a country store. The Port Jefferson–Bridgeport Ferry (tel: 631/473-0286) crosses the Sound to Connecticut.

The North Fork

Riverhead ⓬, on the Peconic Bay at the head of North and South Forks, has been the Suffolk County seat since 1727. Once a commercial center, it is somewhat tired looking now, but still has an attractive downtown center. It also has the newly opened Atlantis Marine World (469 East Main Street; tel: 631/369-9840; open daily; entrance fee), one of New York State's largest aquariums. Among more than 80 displays are a 120,000-gallon (450,000-liter) shark tank within the "Lost City of Atlantis" ruins, and America's largest coral reef display. The aquarium is also home to the Riverhead Foundation for Marine Research and Preservation, which offers an educational 2½-hour boat cruise of the Peconic River from April to October. The Suffolk County Historical Society (300 West Main Street; tel: 631/727-2881; open Thur–Sat; entrance free) houses a hodgepodge of local artifacts, including local Indian implements and early crafts spanning more than three centuries.

Head east on Route 25 (the Main Road) through Aquebogue and Jamesport to **Cutchogue** ⓭, home to nine wineries and the state's oldest house, appropriately named the Old House. The handsomely restored National Historic Site, built down the road in 1649 and moved to the spacious Village Green in 1660,

Map on pages 156–7

Flags fly along the beach for the Fourth of July holiday.

BELOW: riding along the South Shore.

A young surfer rides the waves on a Long Island beach.

sits amid a number of other historic buildings including the 1840 Old School-house Museum and the 1740 Wickham Farmhouse. The complex is run by the Cutchogue-New Suffolk Historical Council (tel: 631/734-6977; open late June–early Sept Sat–Mon; entrance free). Many of the town's earliest settlers are buried in the Old Burying Ground just down the road.

Detour south on New Suffolk Road a few miles to First Street in **New Suffolk** if you want to see the marker designating the spot where, in 1899, John Philip Holland, inventor of the modern submarine, tested the SS *Holland VI*. The US Navy purchased it a year later to inaugurate its submarine fleet.

Southold ⓮, one of the state's oldest communities, is home to the Southold Historical Society Museums complex (54325 Main Road; tel: 631/765-5500; open July 4–Labor Day Sat–Sun; entrance free), which encompasses several period houses including the 1750 Thomas Moore House, a working blacksmith shop, a carriage house, and an 18th-century barn with early farming equipment. The Southold Indian Museum (1080 Main Bayview Road; tel: 631/765-5577; open July–Aug Sat–Sun; entrance free) has an extensive collection of Algonquin artifacts, including Native American pottery. The Custer Institute (Main Bayview Road; tel: 631/765-2626; entrance free), a small astronomy museum with the world's largest pair of refracting binoculars, opens its observatory to the public on Saturday evenings after 8pm. Head north a few miles to the Historical Society's Horton Point Lighthouse/Nautical Museum (tel: 631/765-5500; open Memorial Day–Columbus Day Sat–Sun; donation), perched on a 110-ft (33-meter) bluff overlooking the Sound's Dead Man's Cove (many a ship encountered the area's submerged glacial boulders). Built in 1847, the working lighthouse (now automated) replaced one built here in 1790 on George Washington's recommendation.

BELOW: exciting discoveries on Shelter Island.

In the 1700s ships from the West Indies sailed into the harbor at **Greenport** to unload their cargoes of rum and molasses. Today the North Fork's largest town is home port for several cruise ships and a number of interesting shops and restaurants. The East End Seaport Maritime Museum (3rd Street at Ferry Dock; tel: 631/477-0004; open May–Dec; donation), in a former railroad terminal, displays maritime artifacts and exhibits of local history. Next door, in the old freight station, the Railroad Museum of Long Island (tel: 631/477-0004; open May–Dec Sat–Sun; entrance fee) exhibits old railroad artifacts.

Continue east to **Orient** and the Oysterponds Historical Society Museum (1555 Village Lane; tel: 631/323-2480; open June–Sept; entrance fee), a complex of buildings portraying life here in the 18th and early19th centuries (it was a popular summer resort in the 1900s). Among the buildings are Webb House, a pre-Revolutionary inn and the 19th-century Village House. One exhibit highlights the Tuthills, a family of midgets who lived in Orient in the early 1800s.

One of the finest beaches on the island is the 357-acre (144-hectare) Orient Beach State Park (North County Road; tel: 631/323-2440; open year-round; entrance fee) at **Orient Point**. A ferry and high-speed boat to New London, Connecticut (with connecting bus service to Foxwoods Casino in Ledyard) leave from the dock (for information tel: 860/443-5281).

Hop aboard the 7-minute Shelter Island North Ferry (tel: 631/749-0139; entrance fee) in Greenport to reach **Shelter Island** . (Another ferry transports passengers to North Haven on the South Fork.) Nestled between the two forks, this is an unspoiled paradise reminiscent of New England seaside villages of the 1950s. It's a hilly outcrop of land with white, sandy beaches, lovely inns and a small downtown shopping area. Nearly one-third of the 8,000-acre (3,240-hectare)

Map on pages 156–7

TIP

More than 20 of Long Island's wineries are on the 28-mile-long (45-km) North Fork. *The Wine Press*, available in liquor stores and Chambers of Commerce, has a listing of the island's vineyards, and tells which have tasting rooms.

BELOW: maritime pursuits at Greenport.

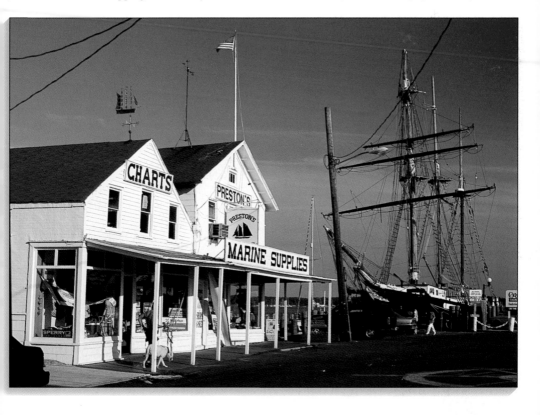

Long Island has more than 150 beaches. Its largest is 2,400-acre (970-hectare) Jones Beach, developed in 1929 by master planner Robert Moses.

island is owned by the Nature Conservancy, whose Mashomack Preserve (79 South Ferry Road; tel: 631/749-1001; open Wed–Mon; donation) is a delightful spot for a hike. Shelter Island Heights Historic District, with its assortment of Victorian architecture, was begun in the 1870s by a group of Methodists from Brooklyn who established a summer campground for revival meetings here.

The South Fork

Follow Route 114 into **Sag Harbor** . Founded in 1707 and a major whaling port in the 1800s, it relies today on a tourist economy. The streets of Sag Harbor's historic district are lined with 19th-century homes, shops, and restaurants, but its whaling history has been preserved in the Sag Harbor Whaling Museum (200 Main Street; tel: 631/725-0770; open May–Sept; entrance fee), housed in an 1845 mansion whose entryway incorporates the jawbones of a right whale. Some of the original furnishings of Henry Packer Dering, the town's one-time customs inspector, are on display at the late-1700s Old Custom House (Main Street; tel: 631/725-0250; open July–Aug Tues–Sun, May–June, Sept–Oct Sat –Sun; entrance fee), where he worked and lived for 30 years.

Turn east onto Route 27 to fashionable **East Hampton** . Some of the most elaborate homes are along Ocean Avenue. Many writers and artists have had retreats here, a trend begun by John Howard Payne, composer of the song "Home Sweet Home," who lived in a 1650 saltbox during the early 1800s. His house (14 James Lane; tel: 631/324-0713; open July–Aug; entrance fee) is filled with 17th- and 18th-century furniture and antiques. Next door, at Mulford Farm (10 James Lane; tel: 631/324-6869; open July–Labor Day; entrance fee), costumed guides lead visitors around a 4-acre (1½-hectare) farm and home-

BELOW:
the Montauk Point Lighthouse stands on the eastern tip of New York.

Map on pages 156–7

stead that was in the same family from 1712 to 1944. The farm is one of six historic sites and museums overseen by the East Hampton Historical Society (tel:
516/324-6850). The 1931 Guild Hall Museum (158 Main Street; tel: 631/324-
0806; open year round, schedule varies; entrance fee for some events) exhibits
works by contemporary artists including Jackson Pollack and Willem de Kooning. Live performances are presented at the museum's John Drew Theater.

Continue east through **Amagansett** ❷⓿, where the Amagansett Historical
Society (Route 27 at Watermill Lane; tel: 631/267-3020; open July–Aug;
entrance fee) oversees both the 1725 Miss Amelia's Cottage, built by town
founders and furnished with finely crafted Dominy furniture, and the Roy K.
Lester Carriage Museum, with 28 horse-drawn vehicles.

Montauk ❷❶, one of the South Fork's major tourist destinations, is also a
thriving commercial and recreational fishing port. The Second House Museum
(Second House Road; tel: 631/668-5340; open July–Columbus Day Thur–Tues;
entrance fee), the oldest building in town, was built in 1746, rebuilt in 1797, and
is filled with historical memorabilia. At the tip of the island, Montauk Point
Lighthouse Museum (open Memorial Day–Columbus Day; tel: 631/668-2544;
entrance fee), the state's oldest operating lighthouse, was commissioned by
George Washington in 1796. There are 137 steps to the beacon.

Head back toward the mainland on Route 27. The Water Mill Museum (Old
Mill Road; tel: 631/726-4625; open Memorial Day–mid-Sept; donation), in the
appropriately named village of **Water Mill**, grinds wheat and corn just as it
did when built in 1800.

Take Route 80 west to chic **Southampton** ❷❷, the oldest and one of the
wealthiest of the Hamptons. The village's oldest building, the 1648 Old Halsey

This mini-lighthouse is really a shop in Montauk Harbour.

BELOW:
Georgia Beach,
East Hampton.

House (South Main Street; tel: 631/283-3527; open mid-June–mid-Sept Tues–Sun; entrance fee) is filled with 17th- and 18th-century furnishings. The Southampton Historical Museum (17 Meetinghouse Lane; tel. 631/283-2494/ 1612; open mid-June–mid-Sept Tues–Sun; entrance fee), a complex of historic buildings including an apothecary and one-room schoolhouse, is built around a handsomely furnished 1843 whaling captain's Greek Revival-style home. American art from the 19th and 20th centuries, including an extensive collection of works by William Merritt Chase and Fairfield Porter, is on display at the Parrish Art Museum (25 Job's Lane; tel: 631/283-2494; open Apr–Dec Tues–Sun; entrance fee). There is also a sculpture garden and arboretum.

Continue west on Route 80, through the Shinnecock Indian Reservation and Hampton Bays. The road into **Westhampton ㉓**, lined with mansions, is a perfect introduction to the rarefied air of this resort town, which is made up of several exclusive communities, including Quogue, home to the Quogue Wildlife Refuge (Old County Road; tel: 631/653-4771; open daily; entrance free). The 300-acre (120-hectare) sanctuary has 7 miles (11 km) of self-guided tours.

In Mastic, jog south to **Mastic Beach ㉔** and the William Floyd Estate (245 Park Drive; tel. 631/399-2030; open June–Sept Sat–Sun; entrance free). Now part of the Fire Island National Seashore, it was the ancestral home of William Floyd, a signer of the Declaration of Independence. The 613-acre (248-hectare) estate has a 25-room mansion built in stages from 1724 to 1930.

The ferry from **Sayville ㉕** (River Road; tel: 631/589-8980; open May–Nov; entrance fee) transports passengers to Sailors Haven (tel: 631/597-6183; entrance fee), a beach with bathhouses and interpretive center; and Sunken Forest, where a boardwalk winds through a 300-year-old, 40-acre (16-hectare) forest below sea level. Back on Route 80, continue to West Sayville, home to the Long Island Maritime Museum (86 West Avenue; tel. 631/854-4974; open Wed–Sun; donation) overlooking Great South Bay. Among its exhibits are the island's largest collection of small craft and an 1890s bayman's cottage. Ferries leave from here to the National Seashore.

In **Oakdale ㉖**, the former 690-acre (280-hectare) estate of financier and railroad magnate William Bayard Cutting is now the Bayard Cutting Arboretum (466 Montauk Highway; tel. 631/581-1002; open Tues–Sun; entrance fee). Cutting's 68-room Tudor mansion and manicured grounds, with its many species of trees and plantings, is adjacent to the 3,400-acre (1,375-hectare) Connetquot River State Park Preserve (off SR 27; tel: 516/581-1005; open Tues–Sun; entrance fee), where rangers give guided nature walks and interpretive tours (reservations required). Due west, in **East Islip ㉗**, the 1,657-acre (670-hectare) Heckscher State Park (Great South Bay; tel: 631/581-2100; open daily; entrance fee in summer) has a protected beach, pool, and nature trails.

Continue south to Route 46 and the eastern end of 32-mile (50-km) barrier island **Fire Island National Seashore ㉘** (tel: 631/289-4810), a "forever preserved wilderness area" that separates the Atlantic Ocean from Great South Bay and stretches from Smith Point West to the east to Robert Moses State Park to the

BELOW: the windmill at East Hampton.

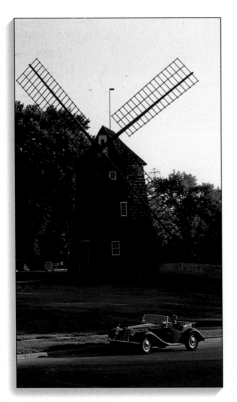

west. There are 17 separate resort communities between the two parks, but only those at each end are accessible by car; the other communities are accessible only by public ferry, private boat, or by foot along the shore. The Robert Moses Causeway goes to the 1,000-acre (400-hectare) Robert Moses State Park (tel: 631/669-0449; open Memorial Day–Labor Day; entrance fee), with swimming, a fishing pier, bathhouses, and a pitch-and-putt golf course. The Fire Island Lighthouse (tel: 631/661-4876; open Apr–June, Labor Day–Dec Sat–Sun, and July–Labor Day Wed–Sun) has a museum and tours up the 192-step tower.

Head inland for the next two attractions. Old Bethpage Village (Round Swamp Road; tel: 516/572-8400; open Mar–Dec Wed–Sun; entrance fee) in **Old Bethpage** ㉙ is a reconstructed pre-Civil War village and now a living history museum where costumed guides explain the buildings, including a church, blacksmith shops and a tavern. The 150-acre (60-hectare) Old Westbury Gardens (71 Old Westbury Road; tel: 631/333-0048; open Apr–Oct; entrance fee) in **Old Westbury** ㉚ is home to one of Long Island's most elegant mansions and one of the country's finest English gardens. The 1906 Charles II-style mansion is furnished with antiques and displays works by artists including John Singer Sargent and Sir Joshua Reynolds.

One of the island's newest attractions, the Cradle of Aviation Museum (Mitchell Field; tel: 516/572-0411), is in **Garden City** ㉛. Highlights include 65 air and spacecraft, an IMAX Dome Theater, a "Mission to the Moon" immersive experience, and a virtual reality ride to Mars.

Back toward the ocean, **Freeport** ㉜, gateway to the 2,413-acre (976-hectare) Jones Beach State Park and the self-proclaimed "Boating and Fishing Capital of the East," has a Nautical Mile lined with shops, pubs, and restaurants. ❑

Map on pages 156–7

BELOW: mansion on the dunes at South Hampton.

Map on pages 170–1

New York

THE HUDSON VALLEY

This river valley has long been a site of historic events, from its early Dutch settlers to Revolutionary battles, and the chosen residence of some of America's most prestigious dynasties

It has been nearly 400 years since Henry Hudson, an English navigator in the employ of the Dutch East India Company, nosed his ship *Half Moon* up the river that now bears his name, looking for the Northwest Passage to Asia which tantalized so many early adventurers in the New World. American rivers far longer than the Hudson would later be discovered and explored – none filled the bill as a Northwest Passage – but few are grander or more storied than the Hudson. The Hudson was America's first river highway into the continent's mysterious interior and its first pathway of colonial empire and private ambition, much like the St Lawrence was for Canada during the same distant era.

As the short-lived Dutch colony of New Amsterdam took root around what is now New York Harbor, the Hudson served as an avenue of transportation to The Netherlands' fur-trading outpost at Fort Orange, now Albany. However, the river valley was recognized as a valuable property in its own right, as Dutch "patroons" (holders of land grants) took charge of tracts along both shores.

America's Rhine

If the patroon system was feudal *(see page 28)*, its locale looked like just the place for it. The Hudson has been called "America's Rhine," and, given a few castles, the resemblance would be complete. Actually, the Hudson Valley did come to have its own sort of castles. They were built by 19th-century magnificoes, and include showplaces such as the Rockefellers' Kykuit, railroad baron Jay Gould's Lyndhurst, Hyde Park's Vanderbilt estate, and, in that same community, the more modest but ultimately far more famous Springwood, a riverside property inherited by James Roosevelt's son Franklin. The most fanciful Hudson River castle of all, perhaps, is Olana, home of the artist Frederic Edwin Church *(see page 179)*.

The Hudson River Valley unfolds magnificently to a traveler heading north from New York City. Just beyond the metropolitan area and the steep cliffs of the Palisades, the river widens into a lake-like expanse still known by the old Dutch name, Tappan Zee. Beyond are the Hudson Highlands, where the river narrows between the brooding heights of High Tor, Bear Mountain, Anthony's Nose, and Storm King. The sharp bend and stark promontory at West Point leave no doubt as to why this was such a vital point of defense for the Americans during the Revolution, and a commanding site for the establishment of the United States Military Academy. Farther north still, the river flows through rich farmlands and serene hills, amid landscapes that so charmed the dynasties of the Rockefellers, the Roosevelts, the Vanderbilts, and Frederic Edwin Church.

LEFT: speeding along the banks of the Hudson River.
BELOW: the flamboyant façade of Olana.

There are several main highways that parallel the Hudson River Valley. The fastest north-south route is the New York State Thruway, also known as the Governor Thomas E. Dewey Thruway and Interstate 87; this toll road runs west of the river and affords frequent exits to valley points of interest. The slower and more scenic Route 9W follows the river more closely. Heading west from the valley, take routes 17, 44, and Interstate 84 into the Catskills foothills.

On the east shore of the Hudson, Route 9 and, farther north, Route 9G run closest to the water. Farther east, the Taconic State Parkway is a scenic, truck-free route. Easternmost of the main north-south roads is Route 22, which meanders through small towns and countryside reminiscent of New England – no surprise, since the Connecticut and Massachusetts borders are right nearby.

It is a good idea to avoid the Tappan Zee Bridge and its approaches during rush hour. If you're heading north, crossing at the Bear Mountain Bridge is a scenic and less busy alternative.

Spectacular mansions

The Hudson River Museum of Westchester (511 Warburton Avenue; tel: 914/963-4550; open Wed–Sun; planetarium open Fri–Sun; entrance fee, except Fri in planetarium) in **Yonkers** ❶ is a good place to begin a tour of the Hudson Valley. Exhibits of 19th- and 20th-century American art include works by Andy Warhol, George Segal, and Robert Rauschenberg, while a tour of the 1877 Glenview Mansion gives a feel for what life in the valley was like at the turn of the 20th century. Star shows are presented at the museum's Andrus Planetarium. The oldest Hudson River estate and one of the northeast's finest Georgian buildings is preserved as Phillipse Manor Hall State Historic Site (29 Warburton Avenue; tel. 914/965-4027; open Apr–Oct Wed–Thur, Sat; entrance free). The building, built in 1682 and enlarged in 1716, displays works by US painters including Gilbert Stuart, and has a superb rococo ceiling.

The Tappan Zee Bridge spans the river at one of its widest points at **Tarrytown** ❷, home to three of the valley's most visited

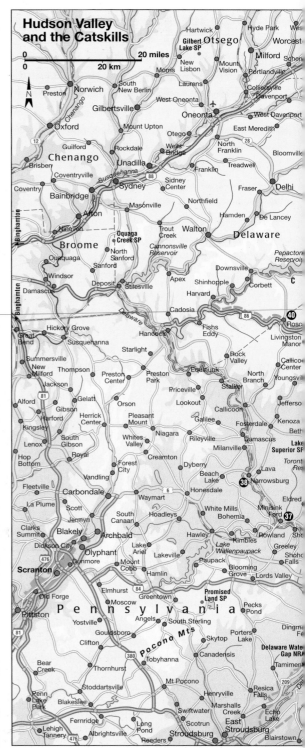

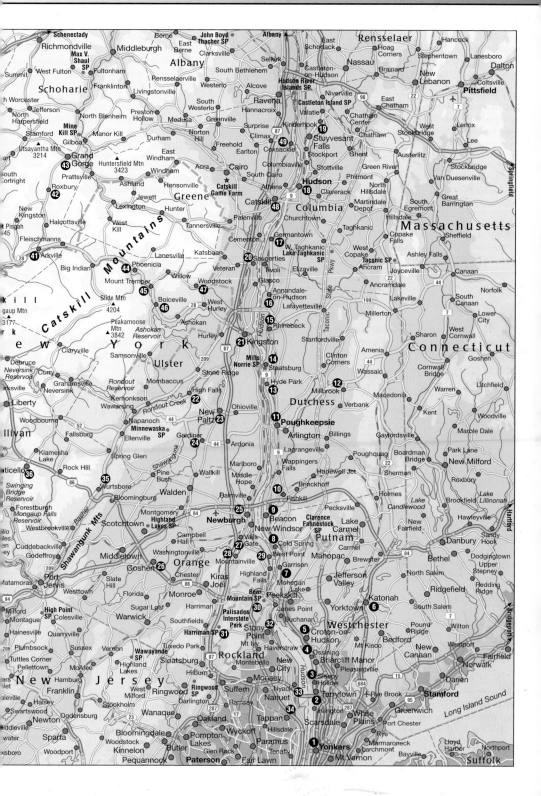

tourist sites. One of the newest has also quickly become the most popular: Kykuit, Rockefeller House and Gardens (150 White Plains Road; tel: 914/631-8200; open Apr–Nov Wed–Mon; tours leave from Phillipsburg Manor in Sleepy Hollow, reservations required; entrance fee), has been home to four generations of the Rockefeller family. The Beaux Arts estate, in the village of Pocantico Hills, was built in 1908 by John D. Rockefeller, Sr, and highlights include the landscaped grounds with works by some of the world's great sculptors. A later addition was Nelson Rockefeller's underground art gallery, with work by artists such as Picasso and Léger. The 1838 Gothic Revival mansion Lyndhurst (635 South Broadway; tel: 914/631-4481; open May–Oct Tues–Sun, Nov–Apr Sat–Sun; entrance fee), overlooking the Tappan Zee, was purchased in 1880 by railroad robber baron Jay Gould, and his furnishings and art are still on exhibit.

Just down the road, Washington Irving described his 19th-century home Sunnyside (West Sunnyside Lane; tel: 914/591-8763; open Mar–Dec Wed–Mon; entrance fee) as "a little old-fashioned stone mansion, all made up of gable ends, and as full of angles and corners as an old cocked hat." The Union Church of Pocantico Hills (Bedford Road, Route 448; tel: 914/631-8200; open Wed–Mon; entrance fee) has nine stained-glass windows by Marc Chagall and a rose window by Henri Matisse.

At the reconstructed 17th- and 18th-century Philipsburg Manor (381 North Broadway; tel. 914/631-8200; open Mar–Dec Wed–Mon; entrance fee) in **Sleepy Hollow ❸**, costumed guides take visitors through the manor and outbuildings, which include a working gristmill. Several luminaries are buried in Sleepy Hollow Cemetery (Route 9), including Washington Irving and Andrew Carnegie. Adjacent to the cemetery, the 1685 Old Dutch Church of Sleepy

BELOW: old-time domestic chores at Philipsburg manor.

THE PALISADES

The Indians called them *wee-awk-en*, "the rocks that look like trees." They are the Palisades, one of the most dramatic natural features of the Hudson River Valley. Beginning in New Jersey just south of the George Washington Bridge, crossing the New York border and extending northward along the river's west shore for a more than 40 miles (70 km), the towering black cliffs seem to be made of separate columns of stone. The appearance suggested trees to the natives, while the area's first European visitors were reminded of the military fortification made up of a wall of sharpened stakes called a "palisade."

The Palisades are nearly 200 million years old. They were formed when magma oozed into vertical fissures in the compacted sediment of the Newark Basin. The magma cooled and solidified beneath the sediment, forming a basalt-like substance called diabase. As it cooled, the diabase contracted and splintered vertically to create rows of huge columned crystals. Over millions of years, erosion reduced the sediments encasing the columns, exposing them as the cliffs we see today.

Impregnable as they seem, the Palisades were once almost lost to quarrying. They were saved a century ago, by the formation of Palisades Interstate Park.

Hollow (Route 9; tel: 914/631-1123; tours Memorial Day–Oct Sun–Thur; services Sun at 10am; donation) is the state's oldest church in continuous use.

Ossining ❹ is home to the infamous Sing Sing prison, built in 1826 by prisoners. Exhibits at the Ossining Heritage Area Park Visitors Center (Joseph G. Caputo Community Center, 95 Broadway; open Mon–Sat; entrance free) document the history of the prison as well as the building of the Old Croton Aqueduct, part of a system built in 1840 to transport water 32 miles (52 km) from manmade Lake Croton to Manhattan.

George Washington and Benjamin Franklin were among the visitors to Van Cortlandt Manor (South Riverside Avenue; tel: 914/631-8200; open Mar–Dec Wed–Sun; entrance fee) in **Croton-on-Hudson ❺**, a restored, 18th-century Dutch-English manor house once owned by a prominent local family. The home is filled with family heirlooms; the grounds encompass flower gardens and the restored Ferry House inn and tavern.

Art and industry

Jog east past the New Croton Reservoir to the historic village of **Katonah ❻**. The 55 houses that line the National Register of Historic Places Bedford Street were moved here between 1895 and 1897 when the original village was flooded to create the reservoir. Just out of town, the Italianate-style mansion Caramoor Center for Music and the Arts (149 Girdle Ridge Road; tel: 914/232-5035; open May–Oct Wed–Sun; entrance fee) was built in the 1930s by financier Walter Tower Rosen to house his art collection. Today his House Museum exhibits European and Asian art. A highly regarded outdoor summer music festival is held here annually. Just down the road, the John Jay Homestead State Historic

Costumed guides at historic sites portray life in the 17th and 18th centuries.

BELOW: the historic gristmill and house at Philipsburg.

Site (400 Route 22; tel: 914/232-5651; open Wed–Sun; entrance fee) was the home of the US Supreme Court's first Chief Justice, state governor, and co-author of the Federalist Papers. Visitors to the 700-acre (283-hectare) Muscoot Farm (Route 100; tel: 914/232-7118; open Memorial Day–Labor Day; entrance free) get a feel for what life was like on a "modern" 19th-century farm.

Detour east a short distance to **North Salem** and the New Hammond Museum and Japanese Stroll Gardens (Deveau Road; tel: 914/669-5033; open Apr–Oct Wed–Sat; call for off-season hours; entrance fee), a 3½-acre (1½-hectare) Japanese garden and art museum designed to serve as a "cross-cultural center" for Eastern and Western arts. It was begun in 1957 by Natalie Hays Hammond, daughter of the discoverer of South Africa's King Solomon Mines.

The mammoth, 24,000-sq-foot (2,230-sq-meter) "Great Buddha Hall" at Chuang Yen Monastery in **Carmel** (Route 301; tel: 845/225-1819; open daily; entrance free), the largest Buddhist monastery in the eastern United States, houses a 37-ft (11-meter) statue of the Buddha Vairocana, the largest Buddha statue in the Western hemisphere. The building and nearby Kuan-Yin Hall are both in the style of architecture of the Tang Dynasty.

In **Garrison** ❼, designer Russell Wright opened the grounds of his home to the public a year before his death, and visitors can hike through the living theater of native trees, ferns, mosses, and wildflowers that he created at Manitoga (Route 9D; tel: 845/424-3812; open Apr–Oct daily, Nov–Mar Mon–Fri; entrance fee). Tours of his home, Dragon Rock, are given the third Saturday of the month between April and Oct. There's a spectacular view across the river to West Point from Garrison Landing, just off Route 9D. Boscobel Restoration (Route 9D; tel: 845/265-3638; open Wed–Sun; entrance fee), perched high

BELOW:
the Tappan Zee
Bridge at sunset.

above the Hudson River overlooking West Point, is one of the jewels of the Hudson Valley. Period rooms in the beautifully preserved early 19th-century mansion are filled with locally made, Federal-period decorative arts, and furniture by Duncan Phyfe and other leading New York artisans of the day. Rose and herb gardens, an orangery, and houses dot the lovely grounds.

The fascinating story of West Point Foundry, founded in **Cold Spring ❽** in the 1800s, is brought to life at the Putnam Historical Society Museum (63 Chestnut Street; tel: 845/265-4010; open Mar–Dec Tues–Thur, Sat–Sun; entrance free), which also exhibits 19th-century furnishings and several Hudson River School paintings. Ask for directions to the remaining foundry building, now being restored. The bandstand by the river, across from the historic Hudson House (2 Main Street; tel: 845/265-9355), has a model of the Parrott Gun invented at the foundry. Cold Spring's West Point Foundry was famous for producing ordnance for the 19th-century US Army, but along with the famed Parrott Gun, the first rifled cannon, the foundry built America's first steam locomotive, *The Best Friend*. The Greek Revival Chapel of Our Lady overlooking the river, a popular subject for Hudson River School painters *(see page 199)*, was built in 1834 for Catholic foundry workers.

Beacon ❾ was once a thriving manufacturing center. Today its prime attraction is the 1709 Madame Brett Homestead (50 Van Nydeck Avenue; tel: 845/831-6533; open May–Dec, first Sun of the month; entrance fee), Dutchess County's oldest homestead. The 17-room stone house, which once sat amid a 28,000-acre (11,300-hectare) estate, is now in the heart of the city.

Civilization also overtook the 1732 Dutch Colonial Van Wyck Homestead (1 Snook Road; tel: 845/896-9560; open Sat–Sun; entrance fee), at the junction

TIP

Near the Vanderbilt mansion, at the Culinary Institute of America (Route 9; tel: 845/452-9600), the oldest culinary college in the US, student chefs prepare meals at four restaurants with varying cuisines and prices.

BELOW:
the view from Garrison's Landing.

Colonial flags fly from many historic houses around New York State.

of Route 9 and Interstate 84 in **Fishkill** ❿. The National Historic Site served as Revolutionary War headquarters from 1776 to 1783 and is believed to have been James Fenimore Cooper's inspiration for the locale in his book *The Spy.* Tours of the building include displays of artifacts from the Revolutionary War.

In the Dutchess County seat of **Poughkeepsie** ⓫, the restored 1869 National Historic Landmark Bardovan Opera House (35 Market Street; tel: 845/471-5313; open for tours by appointment Oct–June; donation) is the state's oldest operating theater and the country's 12th-oldest theater. The dock at the Main Street pier is home port for the *Clearwater* (112 Market Street; tel: 845/454-7673), whose crew sails the Hudson River to promote conservation and clean water. The octagonal, Tuscan-style riverfront estate of the inventor of the telegraph is now the Samuel F.B. Morse Historic Site-Locust Grove (370 South Road; tel: 845/454-4500; open May–Nov daily Dec, Mar–Apr by appointment; entrance fee). Designed by architect Alexander Jackson Davis, the eccentric home has a skylit billiard room, tower, and an extensive collection of furniture, china, and art, including paintings by John James Audubon, George Catlin, and Mr Morse himself. The 150-acre (60-hectare) estate also has formal gardens and an interesting nature walk.

Vassar College's Frances Lehman Loeb Art Center (124 Raymond Avenue; tel. 845/437-5237; open Tues–Sun; entrance free) exhibits more than 14,000 works of art, including Hudson River School landscapes, and prints by Rembrandt and James McNeill Whistler. The 1,000-acre (405-hectare) campus, with 200 species of trees, lakes, and an ecological preserve, is itself a work of art. The Norman Chapel has five windows designed by Louis Comfort Tiffany.

Northeast on Route 44 in **Millbrook** ⓬, overlooking the Hudson Valley, is the

BELOW: the Vanderbilt mansion near Hyde Park.

eccentric Wing's Castle (Bangall Road; tel: 845/677-9085; open Wed–Sun; entrance fee), complete with a tower and moat, which Peter Wing and his wife have been building since the 1970s with materials salvaged from antique buildings. At the 200-acre (81-hectare) Innisfree Garden (Tyrrel Road; tel: 845/677-8000; open May–mid-Oct Wed–Sun; entrance fee) another husband and wife team, Walter and Marion Beck, have also been working for more than 60 years to develop a series of "cup gardens" designed according to Eastern principles.

Map on pages 170–1

Famous residents

Springwood, a neo-Georgian house in **Hyde Park** ⓭, was the childhood home of Franklin Delano Roosevelt, who later lived here with his wife Eleanor and their children. Today the Franklin D. Roosevelt National Historic Site (Route 9; tel: 800/967-2283; open daily mid-Mar–early Jan; entrance fee) encompasses the ancestral home, graveyard, and rose garden. Val-Kill, Eleanor's Dutch-style stone cottage a few miles east of the family home, is now the Eleanor Roosevelt National Historic Site (Route 9G; tel: 800/967-2283; open May–Oct daily, Nov–Apr Sat–Sun; entrance fee). The Franklin D. Roosevelt Library and Museum (Route 9: tel: 800/967-2283; open daily mid-Mar–early Jan; entrance fee) highlights the lives and careers of President and Mrs Roosevelt.

The 1899 Italian Renaissance-style, Gilded Age Vanderbilt Mansion National Historic Site (Route 9; tel: 800/967-2283; open daily; entrance fee), with its Flemish tapestries, gold-leaf ceilings, vast living room, and exquisite formal gardens, is a marked contrast from the relatively simple homes of the Roosevelts. Hudson Valley squire James Roosevelt, father of Franklin, once declined an invitation to the Vanderbilt mansion because he didn't want to have to invite the *nouveau riche* Vanderbilts to his home.

BELOW: memorabilia from the Franklin D. Roosevelt archives.

Author Edith Wharton lived in **Staatsburg** ⓮ at the neo-classical Gilded Age estate on Mills Mansion State Historic Site (Old Post Road; tel: 845/889-8851; open mid-Apr–Oct Wed–Sun; entrance fee), and used it as a model for the estate in *The House of Mirth*. Financier Ogden Mills' 1896 addition to the 1832 mansion was designed by McKim, Mead and White, making the Beaux Arts structure the Hudson Valley's answer to England's Blenheim Palace.

The handsome village of **Rhinebeck** ⓯, with its restored Victorian downtown, is home to the 1766 Beekman Arms, the oldest inn in continuous operation in the US. It has been a meeting place for everyone from American Revolutionary War generals to Franklin D. Roosevelt and his cronies. The interiors and windows of the 1896 Queen Ann mansion at the National Historic Landmark Wilderstein Preservation (Morton Road; tel: 845/876-4818; open May–Oct Thur–Sun, Thanksgiving–Dec Sat–Sun; entrance fee), were designed by J.B. Tiffany. Landscape architect Calvert Vaux, who helped plan New York City's Central Park, laid out the grounds overlooking the Hudson. Three miles (5 km) upriver at the Old Rhinebeck Aerodrome (44 Stone Church Road; tel: 845/758-8610; open mid-May–Oct; entrance fee), visitors can take a ride in a 1929 open-cockpit plane and view a vast collection of aircraft, automobiles, and other

vehicles made between 1900 and 1937. Air shows are performed on weekends from mid-June through to mid-October.

In **Annandale-on-Hudson** ⑯, the 23-room Federal-style Montgomery Place (River Road; tel: 845/758-5461; open Apr–Oct Wed–Mon, Nov–mid-Dec Sat–Sun; entrance fee) overlooks the Hudson. Built in 1802, it was remodeled in the 1860s by architect Alexander Jackson Davis. The interior, a confection of Czechoslovakian chandeliers, Persian tile chairs, and portraits by masters such as Gilbert Stuart, is a perfect foil for the richly textured grounds, which include gardens, waterfalls, and walking trails.

Dance aficionados will want to stop in **Tivoli** at Kaatsbaan International Dance Center (33 Kaatsbaan Road; tel: 845/757-5106; fee for performances), a 153-acre (62-hectare) center for the growth, advancement, and preservation of professional dance. The American Ballet Theatre, among others, perform here throughout the year. The center is on the grounds of the former Livingston estate, and the Visitors Center is in a historic barn designed by Stanford White.

After the British burned down his mansion in **Germantown** ⑰ in 1777, Robert R. Livingston, one of the authors of the Declaration of Independence, rebuilt his estate; it has since been home to seven generations of the family. Today the 485-acre (196-hectare) estate, with a 35-room mansion and extensive and varied gardens (including the Lilac Walk planted in the 1820s), make up the Clermont State Historic Site (1 Clermont Avenue; tel: 518/537-4240; open Apr–Oct Tues–Sun, Nov–mid-Dec Sat–Sun; visitor center open all year; entrance fee). A plaque near the river marks the spot where Robert Fulton landed his steamboat on its maiden voyage up the Hudson from New York City.

Just south of the city limits of **Hudson** ⑱, high on a hill overlooking the

BELOW: a late summer afternoon on the Hudson River, near Olana.

river, is the fabulously eccentric, Persian Gothic castle that Hudson River School master Frederic Edwin Church built over six years beginning in1870. Church's home at Olana State Historic Site (Route 9G; tel: 518/828-0135; open Apr–mid-Oct Wed–Sun; entrance fee) draws heavily upon Islamic and Byzantine motifs, with Persian arches, Oriental carpets, brasswork, and inlaid furniture. Each room is filled with possessions that the artist accumulated over a lifetime of travel. Several of his works are on display, but Olana itself is considered to be one of his greatest masterpieces. In town, Warren Street is lined with antiques shops and buildings of various periods and architectural styles, including Greek Revival, Queen Anne, and the 1811 Federal-style Robert Jenkins House (113 Warren Street; tel: 518/828-9674; open Jul–Aug Sun–Mon; entrance fee), now maintained as a museum of local history. Retired firemen from the rest home next door conduct tours at the American Museum of Firefighting (Harry Howard Avenue; tel: 518/828-7695; open daily except major holidays; entrance free), which documents nearly 300 years of firefighting history with one of the country's largest collections of firefighting apparatus and memorabilia.

Continue north on Route 9 to **Kinderhook** ⑲ (Dutch for "children's corner") and Lindenwald, the birthplace of the country's eighth President, Martin Van Buren, and his home in later life. The ornately finished and opulently furnished 1797 Italianate-style home at the Martin Van Buren National Historic Site (1013 Old Post Road; tel: 518/758-9689; open mid-May–Oct daily, Nov–mid-Dec Sat–Sun; entrance fee) has been restored to the time he lived here – a time, he wrote, when he "drank the pure pleasure of a rural life." Film buffs may recognize the 1737 Dutch Luykas Van Allen House (Route 9H; tel: 914/758-9265; open Memorial Day–Labor Day Thur–Sun; entrance fee); it was the setting for

Map
on pages
170–1

The Jam and Jelly Jazz Band plays music for a summer afternoon.

BELOW: Warren Street in Hudson.

Martin Scorsese's *The Age of Innocence*. The National Historic Landmark property, with its parapet gables, Dutch doors, and other traditional Dutch features, is representative of 18th-century rural Dutch architecture. Also on the property is the restored, one-room Ichabod Crane School House, built around 1820. It's said that Washington Irving based his *Legend of Sleepy Hollow* character on a teacher who lived here.

West of the Hudson

In **Castleton-on-Hudson**, cross over to the western side of the Hudson River and head south on Route 144 to **Saugerties ⑳**. At the mouth of Esopus Creek, the Saugerties Lighthouse Conservancy (tel: 845/247-0656 or 246-4380; open Apr–Nov Sat–Sun and holidays; entrance fee) maintains a more than 130-year-old stone lighthouse as a museum and two-bedroom bed-and-breakfast. Deactivated in 1954 and reactivated in 1990, it can be reached by private boat from the south side of the Creek or by a nature trail on Lighthouse Drive. At Opus 40 & Quarryman's Museum (7480 Fite Road, High Woods; tel: 845/246-3400; open Memorial Day–Oct Fri, Sun, Mon, holidays, and some Saturdays; entrance fee) Harvey Fite has spent the past 40 years using quarrymen's tools to carve a 6-acre (2½-hectare) bluestone sculpture out of an abandoned quarry.

Historic **Kingston ㉑**, established in 1614 by the Dutch as a trading post, became a permanent settlement just 38 years later, and the first capital of New York in 1777. Either of the Kingston Urban Cultural Park visitor centers (the Stockade, 308 Clinton Avenue, and Rondout Landing, 20 Broadway; tel: 845/331-7517; open May–Oct daily, Nov–Apr Sat–Sun; entrance free) provides a walking map of the historic Stockade Area where many of the city's most

historic buildings are clustered, including the steepled 1700s Old Dutch Church (272 Wall Street; tel: 845/337-6759; open for self-guided tours Mon–Fri; entrance free). The church's museum is open by appointment only (tel: 845/334-9355). In 1777 the state's first senate met in a home that is now the Senate House and Museum (312 Fair Street; tel: 914/338-2786; open mid-Apr–Oct Wed–Sun; free). Restored to the way it looked that year, the museum contains historical exhibits and paintings. The Hudson River Maritime Museum (1 Rondout Landing: tel: 845/338-0071; open May–Oct Wed–Mon; entrance fee) preserves the Hudson's maritime heritage. The museum operates a boat tour to the 1913 Rondout Lighthouse (open May–June Sat–Sun, July–mid-Oct daily), where memorabilia documents the history of the lighthouses and their keepers. A trolley at the Trolley Museum at Rondout Landing (89 East Strand; tel: 845/331-3399; open Memorial Day–Columbus Day Sat–Sun and holidays; entrance fee) rides along the waterfront to Kingston Point Park.

Head south on Route 209 through **Hurley**. The more than two dozen restored stone cottages were built in 1669 after Esopus Indians burned the wooden houses of French Huguenots who had settled here. The private residences are open to the public the second Saturday in July.

At the D & H Canal Museum (Mohonk Road; tel:

845/687-9311; open Memorial Day–Labor Day Thur–Mon and May, Sept–Oct, weekends; entrance fee) in **High Falls** ❷ visitors learn about the 108-mile (174-km) canal, built in the 1820s to help transport coal from Pennsylvania to New York, and can take the self-guided Five Locks Walk alongside the locks and past the remains of a suspension aqueduct built by John Roebling who, with his son Washington, designed and built the Brooklyn Bridge *(see page 119)*. Nearby is the 57-acre (23-hectare) National Historic Register Minisink Battleground Park (County Road; tel: 845/794-3000 ext. 5002; open May–Oct; entrance free), site of one of the bloodiest battles of the Revolutionary War.

Detour south a bit farther toward the 90,000-acre (36,400-hectare) Northern Shawangunk mountain range, which has been designated a "Last Great Place on Earth" by the Nature Conservancy. In **Ellenville**, at the base of the mountains, ice caves were formed more than 330 million years ago at the National Natural Landmark Ice Caves Mountain (Sam's Point Road off Route 52; tel: 845/647-7989; open Apr–Nov; entrance fee). A road climbs into the mountains to Sam's Point, almost half a mile (1 km) above sea level. This area is a popular spot for paragliders. The 685-room Nevele Grande (tel: 845/647-6000 or 800/647-6000), one of the region's mega-resorts, commands a lovely lakeside location.

Back toward the river, in the Shawangunks just outside New Paltz, is the Minnewaska State Park Preserve (off Route 44/55; tel: 845/255-0752; open year round; entrance fee mid-June–Labor Day and weekends), an outdoor paradise of waterfalls, scenic vistas, and hiking trails. There's also fine swimming here at Lake Minnewaska.

In **New Paltz** ❷, the National Historic Landmark Huguenot Street is the oldest street in the US that still has its original houses. Most of the six stone houses

Map on pages 170-1

TIP

In Central Valley, Woodbury Common Premium Outlets (Route 32; tel: 845/928-4000; open daily), bills itself as "the world's largest outlet center" with 220 stores including Donna Karan, Armani, Wedgwood, and Brooks Brothers.

BELOW: cruising up the Hudson River.

A lifeguard keeps a watchful eye on swimmers at Mohonk Mountain House.

here were built between1692 and 1712 by members of a Protestant sect who came from France in search of religious freedom. The houses and a French Church and burying ground are maintained by the Huguenot Historical Society (PO Box 339; tel: 845/255-1889; open late May–Oct Wed–Sun; entrance fee). The Jean Hasbrouck House, which once served as a tavern, remains open on weekends from November to April. The early 19th-century National Historic Landmark Mohonk Mountain House (Mountain Rest Road, Lake Mohonk; tel: 845/255-1000; open daily; entrance fee for grounds and facilities), nestled in the heart of a 22,000-acre (8,900-hectare) natural area in the Shawangunks, is a sprawling Victorian castle overlooking a 60-ft deep (18-meter) glacier-carved lake. Both overnight guests and day-pass users can use the many recreational facilities, which include boating and horseback riding. But the highlights here are the mountain views and the landscaped grounds, including a Victorian maze.

Historic farmlands

In 1814 Josiah Hasbrouk, a Revolutionary War veteran, member of the House of Representatives and one of the county's wealthiest men, built a handsome Federal-style mansion just south of New Paltz, in **Gardiner** ㉔. Locust Lawn (Route 32; tel: 845/255-1660/1189; open late May–Sept Wed–Sun; entrance fee) still has many of its original furnishings as well as an excellent collection of 18th- and 19th-century furniture and decorative arts.

The property, along with the fine Dutch-Huguenot 1738 Terwilliger House just down the road, is administered by the Huguenot Historical Society and tours depart from their New Paltz Visitor Center. The gristmill at Tuthilltown Gristmill & Country Store (1020 Albany Post Road; tel: 845/255-5695; open

BELOW: Mohonk Mountain House, near New Paltz.

Wed–Sun; entrance fee to mill) has been grinding flour and meal since 1788.

Back on Route 9W, in **Marlboro**, the Gomez Mill House (Mill House Road; tel: 845/236-3126; open mid-Apr–Oct Wed–Sun, Nov–Mar Mon–Fri; entrance fee), the earliest surviving Jewish residence in North America, was built in the early 1700s by Louis Moses Gomez, a refugee from the Spanish Inquisition. The house, inhabited for more than 280 years, was at one time home to Arts and Crafts-era designer Dard Hunter, who converted the gristmill into a paper mill.

General George Washington spent the last months of the Revolutionary War in **Newburgh** ㉕, and it was here that he issued the command that ended the hostilities. Washington's Headquarters State Historic Site (Liberty and Washington streets; tel: 856/562-1195; open Apr–mid-Oct Wed–Sun; entrance fee) appears much as it did when he and his staff lived here. There's also a museum, and a Tower of Victory built 100 years after the war. Just a few blocks away, the 1830 David Crawford House and Historical Society Museum (189 Montgomery Street; tel: 845/561-2585; open Jun–Oct Sun or by appointment; entrance fee) houses a fine collection of antiques, Hudson Valley paintings, and historical memorabilia relating to Newburgh's history as a whaling and seafaring port.

On its river cruise, Hudson River Adventures (Newburgh Landing Shipyard; tel: 845/782-0685; open May–Oct; entrance fee) passes by Pollepel Island – also known as Bannerman's Island – and the remains of a turreted castle and warehouses built by Scottish-born Frank Bannerman VI to store military surplus until it was sold; at one point Bannerman's inventory included 90 percent of the surplus equipment from the Spanish-American War.

Detour west on Route 416 to **Campbell Hall** and Hill-Hold Museum (Route 416; tel: 845/457-4905; open May–Oct Wed–Sun; entrance fee), an 1830s work-

Map on pages 170–1

TIP

Visitors who dine in one of the three dining rooms at the Mohonk Mountain House receive complimentary day passes.

BELOW: a scenic ride along Lake Mohonk.

ing farm with several barnyard animals in residence. Continue southwest to **Goshen**  and the Harness Racing Museum and Hall of Fame (240 Main Street; tel: 845/294-6330; open daily except major holidays; entrance fee), which immortalizes standardbred horses and the sport of harness racing. Among the exhibits is the state-of-the-art "Thrill of Harness Racing 3-D Simulator," where visitors get to experience the excitement of being in a race. Just across the way is Goshen Historic Track (44 Park Place; tel: 845/294-5357/3; entrance fee), the oldest active harness track in the country and the first sporting site to be designated a National Registered Historic Landmark.

True harness racing fans may want to make a pilgrimage 6 miles (10 km) southeast to **Chester** to the grave of Hambletonian (Hambletonian Avenue off Route 94), whose bloodline extends down to virtually all of today's trotters. The nearby hamlet of Sugar Loaf has thrived as a crafts community for more than 250 years. More than 60 craftspeople have studios in buildings dating back to the 1700s and 1800s at **Sugar Loaf Village** (Kings Highway; tel: 845/469-9181; open Tues–Sun, shops open Wed–Sun; entrance free).

Military sites, past and present

Back on Route 9w, in **Vails Gate** ㉗, there are two more Revolutionary War sites. Colonial generals Henry Knox, Horatio Gates, and Nathanael Greene made their headquarters at a handsome stone house now known as Knox Headquarters Historic Site (Route 94, Forge Hill Road; tel: 845/561-5498; open Memorial Day–Labor Day Wed and Sun; entrance fee). The house has been restored to appear as it did in the Revolutionary era. The Jane Colden Native Plant Sanctuary at the back of the house honors the country's first female

BELOW: trotting along Goshen's Historic Track.

botanist. Just northwest is New Windsor Cantonment State Historic Site (374 Temple Hill Road, Route 300; tel: 845/561-1765; open mid-Apr–Oct Wed–Sun; entrance free), a living history museum which re-creates the last encampment of the Revolutionary War army, where more than 7,000 troops and their families waited for the war to end. The original Purple Heart, the US decoration for wounded soldiers, is here. At the Last Encampment of the Continental Army (Route 300; tel: 845/561-5073; open mid-Apr–Oct Thur–Sun, entrance free) a section of the actual campground used by soldiers from 1782 to 1783 has been preserved, along with two new enlisted men's huts.

Detour west on Route 94 to Brotherhood, America's Oldest Winery (100 Brotherhood Plaza; tel: 914/496-3661; open May–Dec daily, Jan–Apr Sat–Sun; entrance fee for tour) in **Washingtonville**. Folks at the vineyard have been making wine here since 1839, and the facility is open for tours and tasting.

Off Route 9w, on a hill in **Mountainville** ㉘ overlooking the Shawangunks, is one of the country's finest outdoor sculpture museums. More than 120 masterworks by sculptors including Alexander Calder, Louise Nevelson, Richard Serra, and Isamu Noguchi are on exhibit at the 500-acre (202-hectare) Storm King Art Center (Old Pleasant Hill Road; tel: 845/534-3115; open Apr–Nov daily; entrance fee). Temporary exhibits are displayed at the mansion.

The museum at the US Military Academy at **West Point** ㉙ (off Route 9W; tel: 845/938-2638; open daily except major holidays; entrance fee for bus tour) is the oldest and largest army museum in the nation. Among its 45,000-piece collection are Napoleon's sword, George Washington's pistols, and a Stone Age axe. But the museum is just one of the many fascinating places to visit on the campus. Among others are the Cadet Chapel, with the

Map on pages 170–1

West Point's Victory Monument is a symbol of its ideals.

BELOW: West Point Military Academy rises out of the mist.

Map on pages 170–1

world's largest church organ, and the Revolutionary War Fort Putnam, high on a hill overlooking the Hudson. Some links of iron chain on display at the Military Academy's Trophy Point are part of a 150-ton chain stretched across the river from West Point to Constitution Island by Colonials during the Revolutionary War to prevent the British from sailing up the Hudson. The island was also the site of Fort Constitution, begun in 1775 and left unfinished when the British captured the island two years later. A visit to the fort's remains are included in a Constitution Island tour (Constitution Island Association, PO Box 41, West Point 10996; tel: 845/446-8676; open June–Sept Wed–Thur; entrance fee).

At Bear Mountain, Seven Lakes Parkway runs between **Bear Mountain State Park** ㉚ and **Harriman State Park** ㉛ (off Route 17; tel: 845/786-2701; open daily; entrance fee May–Sept), passing by several lakes with excellent beaches, including lakes Tiorati and Sebago.

Eight miles (12 km) south of Bear Mountain Bridge, in **Stony Point** ㉜, is the Stony Point Battlefield State Historic Site (Park Road; tel: 845/786-2521; open Apr–Oct Wed–Sun; entrance free) where, in 1779, the American Corps of Light Infantry under the command of Brigadier General "Mad" Anthony Wayne captured British troops who were planning an assault on West Point. Costumed guides re-create daily camp life, and visitors can tour the 1826 lighthouse.

The river front town of **Nyack** ㉝, a pretty little village with a restored Victorian downtown, was settled in the mid-1600s by Dutch farmers and was a thriving transportation and manufacturing center until the late 1800s. After the depression it was reborn as an antiques and arts center, and has been home to numerous luminaries, including its most famous son, artist Edward Hopper, whose boyhood home has been preserved as the Edward Hopper House Art Center (82 North Broadway; tel: 914/358-0774; open Jan–Nov Thur–Sun; entrance fee). The artist was born in 1882 in the two-story clapboard house his grandfather built in 1858, and lived here until he moved to New York City in the early 1900s. Today it serves as a community arts center, with the Edward Hopper Room devoted to the artist's life and works.

It was at his headquarters in **Tappan** ㉞ that General Washington turned over the command of West Point to Benedict Arnold, who then conspired with Sir Henry Clinton to hand the garrison over to the English. The plot was uncovered when British Major John Andre was captured; he was later tried and hung. The story is recounted at the George Washington Masonic Historic Site (20 Livingston Avenue; tel: 914/359-1359; open daily; entrance free), and the DeWint House, built around 1700, where General Washington made his headquarters, has been restored to reflect that period. Andre Monument on Andre Hill marks the spot where the major was hung in October 1780. Although he requested that he be shot as a soldier, not hung as a spy, his wish was denied, thus prompting his final words: "All I request of you gentlemen is that you bear witness to the world that I die like a brave man." ❑

BELOW: tasty gems at the Brotherhood Winery.

Master of Arden

An immense portion of the Palisades Interstate Park that spans the southern Hudson Valley is the legacy of railroad titan Edward Henry Harriman. E.H. Harriman was a minister's son who began his career as a Wall Street clerk, and finished it as master of more miles of American rail track than any other man. His first major acquisition was the Illinois Central; by the turn of the 20th century, he also controlled the Union Pacific and Southern Pacific, as well as a slew of smaller roads. At his zenith, he told a congressional committee that, were he allowed to proceed without interference, he would buy up railroads until every mile of track in the country was in his hands. He dreamed, in fact, of controlling a worldwide network of railroads and steamships.

On Harriman's behalf, it should be said that he ran his railroads well, making necessary capital improvements and not running them merely as "cash cows" in the style of so many of his robber baron contemporaries. He was also interested in the well-being of the regions he served. Among Harriman's contributions was leadership in launching flood control programs to benefit farmers in southern California's Imperial Valley. He also organized a Manhattan boy's club, as well as a scientific expedition to Alaska. But in New York State, Harriman is mainly remembered as perhaps the greatest benefactor of the state's park system.

Although not by nature an extravagant man – he never showed any interest in making the social scene at Newport, Rhode Island or other Gilded Age resorts – Harriman pieced together a 20,000-acre (8,100-hectare) property in the Ramapo Mountains of New York's Orange County with the same determination that he brought to his railroad dealings. His purpose in this enterprise was not merely acquisitive, as he was keenly interested in preserving southern New York's forest lands from logging. He called his estate "Arden," and crowned it with a 150-room French Renaissance chateau surrounded by formal gardens. The house was finished in 1906, at a cost of 2 million uninflated, pre-income tax, gold-standard dollars.

It was just about his last major accomplishment. Harriman died in 1909, aged 61, leaving his wife the house, the land, and $100 million. In accordance with his wishes, she deeded the eastern portion of the estate – some 11,000 acres (4,450 hectares) – to the state of New York. The bequest became the nucleus of Harriman State Park, which, combined with adjacent Bear Mountain State Park, forms the largest component of Palisades Interstate Park.

That wasn't all E.H. Harriman gave New York and the nation. His son, W. Averill Harriman, enjoyed a career as one of postwar America's most distinguished diplomats. He served as ambassador to the Soviet Union and Great Britain, and was US representative at peace talks with North Vietnam. Between 1954 and 1958 he was governor of New York and, in this official capacity, became steward of a vast parkland that had once been his family's private domain. ❏

RIGHT: the"Railway King" E.H. Harriman was the greatest benefactor of New York's park system.

THE CATSKILLS

*The rugged landscape of the Catskill Mountains has long
attracted artists and writers; today it is equally popular with
sports lovers, from anglers to hikers and skiers*

Map
on pages
170–1

New York

Daunting to New York's early Dutch settlers, the mountainous region known as the Catskills remains mysterious even to this day, at least in terms of its definite boundaries, the origin of its name and, most of all, the character conveyed by its rugged, brooding landscape.

The Catskills are part of the Allegheny Plateau of the Appalachian Mountains, and although nowadays the region is popularly assumed to include nearly the entire wedge of land between the Delaware and Hudson rivers, from the New Jersey border almost to Albany, the term "Catskills" was applied in colonial times and as recently as the late 19th century only to the high country which today occupies the eastern portion of Catskill State Park. (The 650,000-acre/263,000-hectare park is not a completely sequestered wilderness preserve, but a designation that wraps around many long-settled villages and towns, much like far larger Adirondack State Park to the north.) This is where the most impressive peaks are, including the Catskills' highest, 4,204-ft (1,281-meter) Slide Mountain. As for the name, "kill" is Dutch for "stream," but the meaning of "Cats," either with a "c" or in its forms beginning with "k," remains unclear.

The Catskills landscape has been suggestive of mystery since the arrival of the first Dutch explorers – so much so that author Washington Irving used Palenville in the foothills of the region's highest mountains *(see page 197)* as the home of Rip Van Winkle, and the surrounding countryside as the locale of his 20-year sleep. The Catskills are old, rounded mountains, like the entire Appalachian chain, but these peaks tumble together wildly, with steep sides descending into deep cloves – that's another Dutch word, signifying a sharply defined ravine. There is an eerily atmospheric play of light and shadow in this sort of terrain; follow a winding Catskills road, and it might dip down into a pass so shaded from daylight that the effect is almost melancholy, or downright spooky at dusk.

But the Catskills aren't just a brooding dreamscape. They are, in fact, the country's oldest established summer resort region. The tradition dates to 1824, when a hotel called the Catskill Mountain House was built; it was followed a few years later by the Laurel House, which stood at the top of Kaaterskill Falls, New York State's highest waterfall, near Palenville. Both are long gone, but in their heyday, they and other resorts lured countless seekers of fresh air and sublime scenery, including important painters of the Hudson River School *(see page 199)*, which could just as easily have been called the Catskill Mountain School.

The Catskills' place in American vacation history, though, has been secured not by those long-ago retreats, but by the big 20th-century resorts of what became known as the Borscht Belt, southwest of the

LEFT: the pretty town of Liberty.
BELOW: the Catskills are for climbers.

old Catskills proper and closer to Route 17. Originating as boarding houses favored by immigrant Jewish families eager to escape sweltering New York City (*borscht* is a beet soup dear to Russian Jewish palates), these modest establishments grew to become enormous country hotels, several of which thrive to this day. The Borscht Belt resorts built their reputations on sumptuous buffets and outdoor sports, but became famous to the world at large for lavish, big-name entertainment. Several generations of singers and comedians honed their acts in the Catskills and returned in later years to perform as stars.

Somewhere between Rip Van Winkle and savvy nightclub comedy lies the rest of the Catskills experience – hiking on hundreds of miles of trails, skiing on mountains such as Hunter and Belleayre, fly-fishing for trout on Esopus Creek or the East Branch of the Delaware River, or perhaps just meandering along the back roads, watching the play of light and shadow on kill and clove.

The southern Catskills

In **Wurtsboro** ㉟, named after the Wurts brothers who built the Delaware and Hudson Canal, even visitors with no experience can soar like eagles in gliders above the Catskill Mountains from Wurtsboro Airport (Route 209; tel: 845/888-2791; open daily except major holidays; entrance fee), the country's oldest soaring site. Canal Towne Emporium in Wurtsboro (Sullivan and Hudson streets; tel: 845/888-2100; open daily; entrance free) is a classic 1840s country store.

Head west on Route 70 to **Monticello** ㊱, where pacers and trotters strut their stuff at Monticello Raceway (Exit 104 off Route 17B; tel: 845/794-4100; open daily; entrance free), one of the world's fastest half-mile (1-km) harness

BELOW:
hitching a ride.

tracks. Two of the Borscht Belt's most famous resorts are nearby: the sprawling Kutscher's Country Club (Kutscher Road; 845/794-6000 or 800/431-1273) and, just a few miles north on Route 42 in Kiamesha Lake, the 1,200-room, 300-acre (121-hectare) Concord Hotel (Concord Road; tel: 800/431-3850).

Map on pages 170-1

Everybody remembers the Woodstock Festival of August 1969, but not everybody remembers that it was held not in Woodstock but in tiny **Bethel**. Detour on Route 17B to Hurd Road where a marker designates the spot on Max Yasgur's farm where the festival was held. The Bethel Woodstock Museum (Route 55; tel: 845/583-4300; open daily; entrance free), "the first and only museum of its kind in Bethel," displays pictures and articles documenting events around the world over the past 30 years.

From Monticello, head south on Route 42 through **Forestburgh**, and turn west onto Route 43 to Mongaup Falls Reservoir (for information contact the Eagle Institute; tel: 914/557-6162), where bald eagles are often spotted. Back on Route 42, continue south and then turn west onto Route 97, a magnificent stretch of highway that follows the Delaware River and a part of the Upper Delaware National Scenic and Recreation Area. This is prime canoe, kayak, and rafting country, and concessions alongside the road rent equipment.

Racing is the name of the game in Monticello.

Along the Delaware

A few miles west, in **Minisink Ford** ❸❼, the Minisink Battleground Park (Route 97; tel: 845/794-3000; open mid-May–mid-Oct; entrance free) commemorates the spot where Revolutionary troops were defeated by Iroquois and Tory forces led by Mohawk Chief Joseph Brant in July 1779. There are an interpretive center and hiking trails on the 57-acre (23-hectare) site. Just across the way, John

BELOW: a spin around the track.

Stained-glass windows adorn small country churches.

Roebling's wire suspension bridge, the oldest in the country, spans the Delaware River to Pennsylvania. A half-mile (1 km) across the bridge is the Zane Grey Museum (Scenic Drive, Lackawaxen, PA; tel: 717/685-4871; open Memorial Day–Labor Day daily, rest of year Sat–Sun; entrance free), filled with the Western novelist's personal possessions and mementos.

Continue northwest alongside the Delaware to **Narrowsburg** ㊳. The 1840 Narrowsburg Inn (176 North Bridge Street; tel: 845/252-3998) is Sullivan County's oldest hostelry. The Delaware Valley Arts Alliance (170 Main Street; tel: 845/252-7576; open Mon–Sat; entrance free) has a gallery in The Arlington, a former hotel on the National Historic Register. At the log stockade Fort Delaware Museum of Colonial History (Route 97; tel: 845/252-6660; open Memorial Day–June Sat–Sun, July–Labor Day daily; entrance fee) guides in period costume interpret what life was like along the river in the 1750s. Among the buildings are blockhouses, log cabins, a blacksmith's, and an armory. Colonial activities such as candlemaking and cannon-firing are demonstrated.

Head east then north on Route 52 to **Kenoza Lake** and Stone Arch Bridge Historical Park (Route 52; open daily; entrance free), where a three-arched stone bridge built of hand-cut local stone without an outer framework spans Callicoon Creek. Plaques tell about a grizzly murder involving witchcraft that occurred here in 1882. The 9-acre (3½-hectare) park has a lovely picnic area.

Continue north to the historic, working North Branch Cider Mill (Route 121, North Branch; open Apr–Christmas; entrance free), then to **Callicoon Center**. Advance reservations are required to visit the organic, horse-powered Apple Pond Farming Center (Hahn Road; tel: 845/482-4764; open daily; entrance fee), a working farm since 1865. Guests can relax and enjoy the mountain views

or help in daily chores, which may include making goat's cheese or spinning wool. There are horse-drawn hay and sleigh rides in summer and winter, respectively, and overnight accommodations are available.

Fishing center

This area of the Catskills is known for its excellent fly-fishing, and Catskill Fly-Fishing Center and Museum (Old Route 17; tel: 845/439-4810; open Apr–Oct daily, Nov–Mar Tues–Sat; entrance fee), between **Livingston Manor ㊴** and **Roscoe ㊵**, set on 53 acres (21 hectares) bordering Willowemoc Creek, recounts the history of the sport in the US. Visitors can learn how to tie their own flies before testing their skill in the creek.

To see where all those stocked trout come from, detour north a short distance via routes 81 and 82 to the New York State Fish Hatchery (402 Mongaup Road; tel: 914/439-4328; open daily; entrance free) in **Debruce**, where more than 1 million trout are raised annually.

The Willowemoc and Beaverkill rivers meet just to the west of Roscoe, in Junction Pool, and it's here that US fly-fishing began. Many fishermen arrived in "Trout Town USA" by train, and exhibits at the Roscoe O&W Railway Museum (Railroad Avenue; tel. 607/498-5500; open June–Oct Fri–Sun; entrance free) highlight the impact of the railroad on the area's tourism, fishing, and hunting industries. The complex houses a refurbished caboose, watchmen's shanties, the Beaverkill Trout Car Museum, and an HO model railroad.

The 1854, single-span, 174-ft-long (53-meter) bridge at the western end of Pepacton Reservoir in **Downsville** (great for trout and bass fishing) is the world's second-longest bridge of its kind.

**Map
on pages
170–1**

 TIP

The Delaware County Fair (Route 10, Walton) is an old-fashioned event with farm animal exhibits; prizes for produce, baked goods and handicrafts; and rides for the kids. It's usually held the second week in August. Arrive hungry!

BELOW: a golf course near Liberty.

The Mountain Top region

Another trip for rail fans is east on Route 30, in **Arkville** , where the Delaware & Ulster Rail Ride (Route 28; tel: 800/225-4132; open late May–Oct Sat–Sun and holidays, late June–early Sept Wed–Sun; entrance fee) offers 1- and 2-hour scenic trips through the Catskills to Lake Wawaka in Halcottsville, and to Roxbury, on cars pulled by vintage steam engines.

Fleischmanns is named after distilling titan Charles F. Fleischmann, who created one of the Catskill's first Jewish settlements here. The Museum of Memories (Main Street; tel: 800/724-7910; open July–Aug, call for hours; entrance free) relates the town's fascinating history. Folks from miles around flock to Roberts' Auction (820 Main Street; tel: 845/254-4490; open all year; entrance free) for Saturday night auctions beginning at 7pm.

Head north on Route 30, past **Halcottsville** and the reconstructed 1899 Kelly Brothers Round Barn (open for the Round Barn Festival in July; tel: 845/586-2611), to **Roxbury** ⊕, whose most famous son, railroad baron Jay Gould, contributed to the town's stately appearance. The Tiffany-windowed, English Gothic Revival Jay Gould Memorial Reformed Church (North Main Street; open Sun and Mon–Fri morning by appointment; entrance free) was built in his memory by his six children in 1893–4. Another native son was writer and naturalist John Burroughs, who said of the Catskills: "Those hills comfort me as no other place in the world does – it is home there." Woodchuck Lodge, built around 1864, was Burroughs' summer home for the last 10 years of his life (closed to the public); his hilltop grave and the "boyhood rock" he loved are at the John Burroughs Memorial State Historic Site (Route 30; tel: 607/326-7641; open daily; entrance free). In 1895 Burroughs also built a rustic log hideaway

BELOW: skiing in the Catskills.

Map on pages 170–1

in the woods outside the village of West Park, just a few miles from the west bank of the Hudson. Today this cabin, Slabsides, is within the 191-acre (77-hectare) John Burroughs Sanctuary, which is open daily. In May and October, the John Burroughs Association also holds an open house (tel: 914/384-6320 or 212/769-5169 for information). The Catskill Mountain Heritage Trail, which forms a "loop" between Roxbury and the Thomas Cole House in Catskill *(see page 199)*, begins here and follows two of the state's most scenic and historic routes: the Rip Van Winkle Trail and the Mohican Trail. Much of the route below follows these trails.

Continue north through scenic **Grand Gorge ㊽**, the headwaters of the east branch of the Delaware River, and turn east on Route 23 to **Prattsville** and Pratt Rock Park, named for Zadock Pratt, the industrialist and US Congressman who sponsored the bill creating the Smithsonian Institution. The cliffs of the park, donated to the town by Pratt in 1843, have been dubbed "New York's Mount Rushmore" and have numerous carvings pertaining to his life, including a relief of a son killed in the Civil War. His restored homestead is now the Zadock Pratt Museum (Main Street; tel: 518/299-3395; open Memorial Day–Columbus Day Wed–Sun; entrance fee). Eagles nest in the cliffs beyond Benham Cemetery, where Revolutionary and Civil War soldiers are buried.

Veer south on Route 23A through **Jewett Center** to the St John the Baptist Ukrainian Catholic Church (tel: 518/263-3862), built in 1962 without the use of nails as a memorial to Ukrainians killed in World War II by Communist forces. The hand-carved interior is magnificent. Continue on Route 23A approximately 10 miles (16 km) to Route 23C in **Tannersville** to visit the Mountain Top Arboretum (tel: 518/589-3903; open daily, guided tours June–Sept; entrance

Prohibition-era gangster Jack "Legs" Diamond holed up in the little Catskills town of Acra, near Tannersville, toward the end of his career. He was shot and wounded by locals who resented his attempts to organize their illegal applejack business.

BELOW: a Catskill farm.

free), where a multitude of flowering trees, evergreens, and shrubs flourish.

Continue south on Route 214 to the junction of Route 28 into **Phoenicia ⓮**. This is tubing country: several companies in town rent equipment (and provide transportation) for a 5-mile (8-km) float down Esopus Creek as it winds through the Catskills. In town, the Empire State Railway Museum (Main Street; tel: 518/688-7501; open Memorial Day–Columbus Day Sat–Sun; donation), in the historic 1899 Delaware & Ulster Railroad Station, chronicles the history of railroading in the region. There's a 2-8-0 steam locomotive, a 1913 Pullman dining car, and lots of photographs and films. Visitors who want to actually ride the rails can hop aboard the Catskill Mountain Railroad (tel: 518/688-7400; operates late May–July 4 Sat–Sun, July 5–early Sept daily, early Sept–early Oct Sat–Sun; entrance fee) for a scenic ride along Esopus Creek.

Worth a detour is the Hanford Mills Museum, at routes 10 and 12 in East Meredith (tel: 607/278-5744), a working, water-powered mill dating from 1846. Visitors can see woodenware being crafted on antique machines.

A few miles south in **Mount Tremper ⓯**, the Catskill Corners Festival Marketplace (5340 Route 28 at Mount Pleasant Road; tel: 888/303-3936 or 845/688-2451; open Wed–Mon; entrance fee to attractions) is home to the world's largest kaleidoscope, reaching 60 ft (18 meters), housed in the silo of a 19th-century barn. It's part of Kaleidoworld, a collection of giant interactive kaleidoscopes that visitors can look through, ride on and, on the Amazing Don Doakahedron, take on an excursion through the universe. There are also shops, galleries, restaurants, and exhibits about the region in the Longyear House, home of the founder of the Delaware & Ulster Railroad. John Burroughs' (see page 194) papers and writings are on exhibit in the 1841 Riseley Barn.

BELOW: tubing on
a Catskill creek.

Artists' enclave

In **Boiceville** ⑯, Emil Brunel, founder of the New York Institute of Photography and the man who perfected the 1-hour film developing process 70 years before it became popular, built several megalithic sculptures dedicated to the memory of travelers to the "Happy Hunting Grounds." They're at the back of Sacred Ground (Route 28; tel: 914/657-2531; open Fri–Sun; entrance free), Ulster County's oldest Indian trading post. Brunel's ashes are interred in one of his works. Turn south onto Route 28A, a scenic route which follows the 12-mile-long (19-km) Ashokan Reservoir, set like a jewel amid the mountains.

At the junction of Route 28A and Route 28, backtrack west on Route 28 for a few miles and take Route 375 north to **Woodstock** ⑰, the town the famous concert of 1969 was erroneously named for *(see page 191)*. Woodstock has been an artists' retreat since 1902 when Ralph Radcliffe Whitehead, a disciple of John Ruskin, came here to establish the art colony he called Byrdcliffe. The buildings are preserved as Byrdcliffe Historic District (Upper Byrdcliffe Road, 34 Tinker Street; tel: 845/679-2079; open mid-Apr–Sept; entrance free), where many artists now have studios and exhibition space. The Tibetan Buddhist Monastery, Karma Triyana Dharmachakra (352 Meads Mountain Road; tel: 914/679-5906; open Sat–Sun; entrance free), has one of the country's largest statues of Shakyamuni Buddha. Just across from the monastery is the trailhead for Overlook Mountain. It follows an old railbed for 2 miles (4.5 km) to the top, where there's a lookout tower, picnic area, and views of the valley.

Take Route 212 east from Woodstock to Route 32 and head north to Route 32A, which will take you into **Palenville**. The "Village of Falling Waters" was the reputed home of the legendary Rip Van Winkle. A thriving artists' colony

Map on pages 170–1

This peace wreath carries on the spirit of Woodstock.

BELOW: a quaint country store.

Map on pages 170–1

grew up in the late 1840s around Hudson River School artist Asher B. Durand, who lived here for a number of years. Three miles (5 km) west of town is the path (a relatively easy 1-hour round trip) to Kaaterskill Falls (Route 23A; tel: 518/589-5058). The falls plummet 230 ft (70 meters) to the floor of Kaaterskill Clove. The winding road from here to Haines Falls offers magnificent views of the Catskill mountains.

From Palenville, head east on Route 23A toward Route 32, then head north 2 miles (3.5 km) to one of the area's oldest and most-touted tourist attractions, the Catskill Game Farm (400 Game Farm Road; tel: 518/678-9595; open May–Oct; entrance fee). More than 2,000 animals representing 150 species from around the world, including elephants, bears, and giraffes, live here, and some of the tamer species are in a petting area. There are animals shows at weekends, and amusement rides. Continue north a bit farther to Ted Martin's Reptile Land (formerly Clyde Peeling's Reptileland, 5464 Route 32; tel: 518/678-3557; open daily except major holidays; entrance fee), another venerable Catskills attraction, with more than 50 exhibits featuring snakes, lizards, turtles, and crocodiles from around the world. The live animal shows are very popular.

Continue north to the village of **Catskill** ㊽, a thriving commercial hub until the Erie Canal *(see page 200)* channeled traffic north to Albany. The Hudson River School artist Thomas Cole lived here for many years, and it was at the Thomas Cole House (218 Spring Street; tel: 518/943-6533; open July–Labor Day Wed–Sun; donation) that he did much of his painting and tutored his only pupil, Frederic Edwin Church. The house, newly renovated and on the National Historic Register, is known locally as Cedar Grove. Cole and his wife are buried at the Thompson Street Cemetery, overlooking the eastern escarpment of the Catskills.

From Dutchman's Landing, a riverside park and artists' interpretive walking path, there are fine views across the river to Church's home, Olana *(see page 179)*.

North on Route 385 in **Athens**, the Second Empire-style Athens Lighthouse (tel: 518/828-3828; entrance fee for tour) has been aiding mariners since 1874. Tours launch from Riverfront Park and Hudson Marina on selected dates between June and October.

Coxsackie ㊾ (pronounced "Cook-sackie") was first settled by the Dutch in the 1600s, and the home of its original founder, Pieter Bronck, is today the Bronck Museum (Route 9W at Pieter Bronck Road; tel: 518/731-6490; open Memorial Day–mid-Oct Tues–Sun and Mon holidays; entrance fee). The 1663 Dutch Colonial stone farmstead, home to eight generations of the Bronck family, traces not only the history of the Broncks, but also of the Upper Hudson Valley itself. Now the property of the Greene County Historical Society, the farmstead with its barns, outbuildings and furnishings serves as a visual document of two centuries of changes in style, taste, and sophistication. Textiles, spinning wheels, and looms are displayed, along with 18th- and 19th-century paintings by artists such as Thomas Cole, Ammi Phillips, and Frederic Church. The three barns include a 13-sided Liberty Barn and the Victorian house barn, with an exhibit of wagons and carriages. The family and slave cemeteries complete the picture of early life here. ❑

BELOW: a day out at Haines Falls.

The Hudson River School

The first great movement in American painting was born here in the Catskill Mountains and Hudson River Valley. The Hudson River School was the first to appreciate the glories of landscape, after centuries of painterly concern with manmade environments and the human condition.

Englishman Thomas Cole is recognized as the founder of the Hudson River School. He came to the US aged 17 in 1818 and worked as an art teacher and portrait painter before becoming intrigued by the possibilities of the natural environment. In 1825, he took his first sketching trip up the Hudson River, past the Palisades and the Highlands and into the Mountain Top region of the Catskills. Here he saw peaks which he described as heaving "from the valley of the Hudson like the subsiding billows of the ocean after a storm."

The paintings resulting from this excursion were discovered later that same year by influential artists and collectors in New York City, launching not only Cole's career but a new vogue for raw nature. Cole didn't live long – he died in 1848 aged 47 – and he did his best work in his early years, but paintings such as *Catskill Mountain House* and *Kaaterskill Falls* set the standard for the use of drama and an accentuated beauty in the depiction of natural scenes.

The next major figure in the Hudson River School was Asher Durand, who carried naturalism to the point of painting in oils on location, rather than working in his studio from preliminary outdoor sketches. Durand created canvases rich in browns, deep greens, and the gold of diffused sunlight. His location work also enabled him to capture a tremendous amount of detail in the near and middle distance.

As the Hudson River School matured, younger painters such as John Frederick Kensett and Jasper Cropsey explored the effects of atmospheric light. Paintings such as Cropsey's *Upper Hudson* and Kensett's

Lakes and Mountains employed a light whose source is at once nowhere and everywhere, an illumination that seems to emanate from all points along a central, invisible horizontal line. Luminism, the school these two painters helped create, eventually transcended its Hudson River origins and led to the salt marsh and harbor views of artists such as Martin Johnson Heade and Fitzhugh Lane.

Hudson River painting climaxed in the work of Frederic Edwin Church and Albert Bierstadt. Church bathed his subjects in lighting that could range from the Turner-esque to the almost lurid; eventually, the valley could no longer contain him and he turned to grander subjects such as those depicted in *Heart of the Andes* and *Niagara*. Bierstadt, too, roved far from his Irvington-on-Hudson home. His great canvases, such as *A Storm in the Rocky Mountains* or *Domes of the Yosemite*, portray a landscape whose scale dwarfs the now cozy-looking Catskill and Hudson River scenes. But they are paintings which, nonetheless, owe nearly everything to the possibilities first perceived by Thomas Cole. ❑

RIGHT: Thomas Cole's painting illustrates a scene from J.F. Cooper's *Last of the Mohicans*.

THE ERIE CANAL: A MAGNIFICENT VISION

Once lambasted as "Clinton's Ditch," the Erie Canal was the engineering marvel of its day. Without it there would be no Empire State

Standing 6 ft 3 in tall, DeWitt Clinton was big in stature but bigger in imagination. As New York State Governor, his vision was monumental: to access the heartland's resources with a water route connecting the Great Lakes to the Atlantic Ocean. To do so required making a river where none existed, from Buffalo to Albany and the Hudson River, the waterway south. Clinton had already, as 10-time mayor of New York City, transformed it by leveling the topography and imposing the 1811 street grid. Now his vision was to transform the state.

Thomas Jefferson called his plan "little short of madness." The press derided it as "Clinton's Folly." But in 1817, Clinton persuaded the state to authorize $7 million for construction. Work was done by men, horses, mules, and pulleys, carving out of tough terrain a canal 363 miles (584 km) long, 40 feet (12 metres) wide, and 4 feet (1.2 metres) deep. Even the roads to haul in supplies had to be made. But the Erie Canal opened in 1825, three years ahead of schedule.

PHENOMENAL GROWTH

The canal was pivotal in shaping New York's economy and propelling its growth. The wealth generated by its port made New York City the commercial capital of the world. Wherever it went, the canal made change, creating jobs, sparking business, even speeding population shifts. From 1825 to 1860, waves of immigrants arrived as never before. Those heading west could sign on to work one way to Buffalo and just keep going. The canal had jump-started the young nation, and made New York the Empire State.

▽ **FLOUR CITY**
The second Erie Canal aqueduct, now Broad Street, was built across the Genesee River at Rochester in 1842. Flour mills made the city America's first boom town.

▽ **A GREAT LEGACY**
President Theodore Roosevelt saved the canal by enlarging the waterway in 1905–18. The entire New York State Canal System now measures 524 miles (843 km).

▷ **MANMADE CHANNELS**
The original Erie Canal featured 18 aqueducts and 83 locks, and rose 568 ft (173 meters) from the Hudson River to Lake Erie.

◁ **SHIPPING NEWS**
Barge traffic peaked in 1951, when 5.2 million tons were shipped on the canal. A mere 50,000 tons are shipped today.

LIVING ON THE CANAL

The Erie Canal may seem peaceful and romantic today, but life on the waterway was hard. Canal boats were up to 100 feet (30 meters) long but only 18 feet (5.5 meters) wide. They were pulled by mule teams who trudged the tow paths alongside the canal. Many boats were mom-and-pop operations, with the family living in the back. Sleeping accommodations were below and were very uncomfortable. Imagine ducking for a bridge. Canal bridges were built low to save construction costs, and boat passengers beneath had to lean forward so as not to get hit.

A boatman's life was hard and dirty. Boatmen swore and fought, for position going through a lock, and in the hundreds of brothels and saloons ashore. Thus another name for the canal arose: "The Ditch of Iniquity." But in the 1900s floating schools appeared. Students read texts in on-board libraries and at stopovers explored topics first-hand.

◁ **THE WORLD'S GRANARY**
Warehouses lined the banks of canal towns. Before, there was no fast, affordable way to transport grains to the port of New York. The canal cut freight costs by 90 percent.

△ **A RECREATION RESOURCE**
Today the canal's main use is recreational. Mule-drawn packet boats revisit canal journeys of the past, and the waterway is lined with bike paths and pleasure boats.

△ **CANAL VILLAGE**
Life on the canal is re-created in Rome's Erie Canal Village, where restored 19th-century buildings from around the area sit along the banks.

▷ **BOOM TOWNS**
The canal brought sudden prosperity and New York's major cities, such as Syracuse, shown here in 1906, lie along its route.

ALBANY TO SARATOGA

Maps:
Area 204
City 206

This region of New York's heartland developed early because it was close to the Hudson River. It includes the state capital, Albany, and the spa town of Saratoga Springs, with its famous racecourse

New York

The mallet strikes the solid wood base. Its sound resonates throughout the crowded chamber at the State Legislature in Albany, calling into session the State Assembly or Senate. About 150 miles (240 km) north of New York City, Albany is New York State's seat of government, its capital since 1797. One of a triad of capital-district cities, Albany began as the Dutch fur trading settlement Fort Orange in 1624 *(see page 26)*.

Schenectady and nearby Troy also developed as commercial centers because of their proximity to rivers. Around this triad lies a patchwork of places that began as mill towns and are now enjoying a revival – restoration, renovation, and reinterpretation of historic structures and sites are contagious. About 30 miles (48 km) north lies Saratoga Springs, whose preeminence as an international resort earned her the title "the Queen of the Spas" in the 19th century. Her mystique continues, as a small town community with a big city heart, a notorious past, and delightful attractions.

Throughout this region, clean air, open space, and nature are never far away. Non-invasive "industries," including 19 colleges and universities, dominate the workforce. The contemporary arts are flourishing, as are traditional crafts and historic festivals. Rich in local color, tradition, and the spirit of invention, the Capital-Saratoga region entered the new Millennium with vigor. As the Saratoga track announcer would say, this part of the state is "off and running."

LEFT: the upstate equestrian life.
BELOW: artwork at Empire State Plaza.

Albany, the state capital

Visitors arriving in **Albany ❶** on highways from the south or north enjoy an elevated view of the river known as the Mighty Hudson. Without the Hudson, Albany would not exist. Because the river offered a way to transport furs from the interior down to New Amsterdam, the Dutch West Indies Company founded their Albany outpost. The Hudson currents have borne Algonquin and Iroquois canoes, merchants and entrepreneurs galore, bargemen, and maritime traffic. Its surging water power ran early sawmills and paper mills and eventually heavy industry. Today, the Hudson's popularity includes recreational pastimes.

In the heart of Albany, the panoramic **Empire State Plaza ❹** (Madison Avenue and Swan, State, and Eagle streets; tel: 518/474-2418; open daily 6am–11pm) announces without a word the city's persona as the state capital. This iconographic creation, undertaken under the direction of Governor Nelson A. Rockefeller, was constructed between 1965 and 1979 for a hefty $1 billion. Futuristic and monumental, cast in white marble, its outdoor pedestrian concourse has topiary trees and reflecting pools. The Plaza has been praised as visionary and criticized as sterile, but since

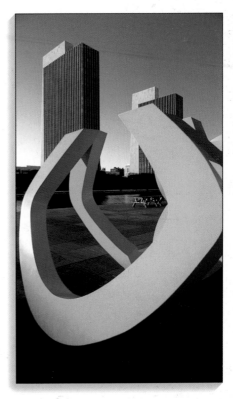

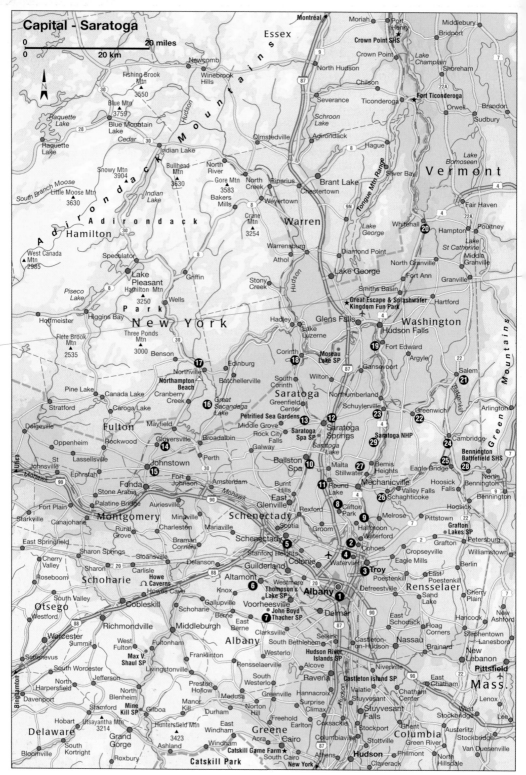

Capital - Saratoga

its opening it has been popular as a place to gather for free public events, especially the Fourth of July extravaganza fireworks. Best of all, it is user-friendly: those arriving by car can find parking directly underground, quickly reached from the exit ramp from I-787.

Maps:
Area 204
City 206

Across the Plaza along **State Street** rises the handsome **State Capitol** ❸ (Washington Avenue and State Street; tel: 518/474-2418; open daily; tours free), one of the last great monumental structures to be built entirely of masonry. From its sweeping exterior staircase on the river side, to its opulent dark interior hallways, the Capitol evokes a past grandeur. Constructed between 1867 and 1899 at a cost of $25 million, it embodies the visions of five architects. Thomas Fuller designed the first two stories in Italian Renaissance style; Henry Hobson Richardson chose Romanesque for the next two stories, including his *pièce de résistance*, the illustrious Million Dollar Staircase. As you tread upon its (some say haunted) winding steps, you'll see thousands of unnamed carvings, including over 300 stone portraits of famous New Yorkers and the carvers' friends and families. The Senate Staircase is known as "the Evolutionary Staircase" because of its depictions of a range of creatures.

The Capitol is most importantly the political heartbeat of the state. It belongs to every New Yorker, not just politicians. Special interest groups, arriving from all over the state, often demonstrate outside. The **Amtrak station Rensselaer** is just across the river (555 East Street, Rensselaer; tel: 800/872-7245 or 518/462-5763). When Jackie Kennedy came from Manhattan to lobby for the preservation of Grand Central Terminal (a victorious cause), she arrived via Amtrak.

The Cultural Education Center, a modern building at the Madison Avenue side of the plaza, houses the State Library and the **New York State Museum** ❻ (tel: 518/474 5843; open daily 9.30am–5pm; donation). The center's historical archives hold such unexpected treasures as original bird paintings by Louis Agassiz Fuertes, lifelong resident of New York and one of the world's greatest bird artists. The museum contains permanent exhibits on Native Peoples, the Wilderness, and the New York Metropolis; its Shaker collection is one of the worlds' most important. In partnership with major art institutions and the Smithsonian, it hosts guest art exhibits.

Along one side of the Plaza rise four monolithic office buildings; on the other is a tilted spherical building that almost seems to float in the air. Known as **The Egg** ❼, this unique structure hosts performing arts events in its two theaters (tel: 518/473-1061; tours Mon–Fri from 11am; entrance free). Next door, the **Observation Deck** ❽ atop the 42-story Corning Tower offers spectacular views of the Helderbergs, Catskills, and surrounding areas.

A visit to the 1857 **Executive Mansion** ❻ (138 Eagle Street between Madison and Park avenues; tel: 518/473-7521; tours by appointment), home of the state governor, should be scheduled at least two weeks in advance. Its historic interior is delightful.

This grand plaza – 98 acres (40 hectares) in all – continues below ground. The indoor concourse, filled with shops and occasional craft fairs, buzzes with state workers and visitors en route between buildings. Lin-

BELOW: the Senate Chambers at the State Capitol.

ing the walls is the excellent Plaza Art Collection, with 92 paintings, tapestries, and sculptures, mostly of the New York School. Pick up free guides at the **Visitor Center** (State Street; tel: 518/474-2418).

Among the restored 19th-century houses in neighborhoods beyond Swan Street is the former Dove Street home of bootleg-era gangster Legs Diamond. It is now owned by Pulitzer Prize-winning William Kennedy, who penned both *Legs* and *Ironweed*. The movie version of *Ironweed*, starring Jack Nicholson and Meryl Streep, was shot on location in Albany. **Lark Street**, one block west, offers eclectic shops and restaurants, similar in atmosphere to New York City's Greenwich Village. Spacious **Washington Park ⑥**, beyond Lark Street, offers places for solitude and play, as well as rare trees, a lake, and historic monuments.

The Albany Heritage Area, near the Hudson, is the site of the original Dutch settlement. The Visitors Center here (25 Quackenbush Square; tel: 800/258-3582 or 518/434-1217) provides information, trolley tours, and a free walking tour map. First Church Albany (110 North Pearl Street; tel: 518/463-4449; open by appointment), founded in 1642, is New York's second-oldest church. It contains the nation's oldest pulpit, bought in 1656 for the cost of 25 beaver skins. The 1931 Palace Theater (corner of Clinton and North Pearl streets) is home to the Albany Symphony Orchestra (tel: 518/465-4663). As a young writer, Herman Melville lived at 3 Clinton Square. On North Pearl and up along Columbia Street are great architecture plus venues for the arts: the Capital Repertory Theatre (111 N. Pearl Street; tel: 518/462-4531), the College of St Rose Art Gallery (125 State Street; tel: 518/485-3900), and the **Albany Center Galleries ⓗ** (23 Monroe Street; tel: 518/462-4775). At Eagle and Pine streets, step inside the Greek Revival New York State Court of Appeals and look at the State Seal on the lobby dome.

The **Albany Institute of History and Art ①** (125 Washington Avenue; tel: 518/463-4778; open daily; entrance fee), focuses on the history, art, and culture of the upper Hudson River Valley. A three-story atrium with tiered balconies was unveiled in 2001. To the north is the Federal-style **Ten Broeck Mansion ⓙ**, home of the Albany Historical Association (9 Ten Broeck Place; tel: 518/436-9826; entrance fee).

From here it is a bit of a hike down to attractions nearer the Hudson. Those arriving by bus will already be downtown. The **Albany Bus Terminal** (tel: 800/225-6815 or 231-2222) is near the palatial Dutch **Old D & H Building** (Broadway and State Street). Built as headquarters for the Delaware and Hudson Railroad, the Administrative Offices of the **State University of New York** (SUNY) ⓚ now occupy the premises. The weathervane at the top of the tower is a replica of Henry Hudson's ship, the *Half Moon (see page 26)*. It is the largest working weathervane in North America.

TIP

"Albany Remembered Tours" offers custom tours including a Capitol Hill Stroll and Legs Diamond theme tours (100 State Street; tel: 518/427-0401; open daily).

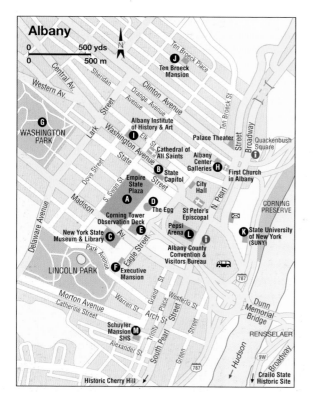

Albany

The **Pepsi Arena** (51 S. Pearl Street; tel: 518/487-2000) hosts concerts, trade shows, and events. World championship football featuring the Albany Firebirds and NCAA ice hockey with the Albany River Rats are hard-hitting crowd-pleasers. Concert audiences come for headliners such as Tina Turner.

The Pastures, at the river end of Madison Avenue, is an ongoing restoration of 19th-century homes built around gardens where cows once used to graze. Future city plans include a pedestrian bridge linking downtown with the historic waterway. **Dutch Apple Cruises** (137 Broadway Avenue, corner of Quay and Madison avenues; tel: 518/463-0220; open Apr–Oct daily; entrance fee) offers narrated scenic cruises. Nearby stands the USS *Slater*, the last surviving World War II destroyer escort (for tours tel: 518/431-1943; children under 6 free). To the north, the **Corning Preserve**, part of the Mohawk-Hudson Bikeway, offers great river views and a biking trail.

South of the Pastures is **Schuyler Mansion State Historic Site** (32 Catherine Street; tel: 518/434-0834; open mid-Apr–Oct Wed–Sun; Nov–mid-Apr by appointment; entrance fee). This small stately mansion, built in 1761, was home to Revolutionary War general and socialite Philip Schuyler. He welcomed as guests George Washington, Ben Franklin, and other dignitaries. Farther south, **Historic Cherry Hill** (523½ South Pearl Street; tel: 518/434-4791; open Feb–Dec Tues–Sat 10am–3pm, Sun 1–3pm; entrance fee) was home to five generations of one Albany family, from 1787 to 1963.

You can explore the Shaker legacy at the **Shaker Heritage Society**, America's first Shaker settlement (1848 Shaker Meeting House, Albany-Shaker Road; tel: 518/456-7890; open Tues–Sat; entrance fee). It includes a museum and self-guided walking tours of the grounds, Ann Lee Pond, and the Nature Preserve.

Maps:
Area 204
City 206

BELOW:
the New York State
Capitol at Albany.

Pumpkins and field corn are popular autumn decorations.

BELOW: a Rensselaerville Victorian inn decorated for Christmas.

Mill towns and blue-collar workers

Wherever the Hudson or Mohawk rivers or their tributaries afforded force to power a mill, a settlement grew. Forests and water power such as that of the cascading Cohoes Falls, helped establish the area as one of the timber capitals of the nation. North of Albany, I-787 ends in **Cohoes** ❷, a 19th-century cotton knitting center once known as "Spindle City." Start at the Cohoes Music Hall/Riverspark Visitor Center (58 Remsen Street; open Tues–Fri noon–5 pm, Sat 11am–4pm). The Music Hall for concerts and performing events is upstairs in this 1874 building (tel: 518/237-7999 for performance details).

A side trip to Cohoes Commons offers great buys in designer clothes and furniture (tel: 518/237-0524). Harmony Mills Historic District also offers many shopping outlets as well as a tie to the past in its historic buildings.

At nearby Waterford, the oldest continually incorporated village in the United States, the Champlain and Erie canals meet. Watching the "Waterford Flight" (which begins with Lock Two) in operation from the observation deck at Lock Six can amaze even the most jaded. The locks move boats from the Hudson to the Mohawk, raising them 169 ft (50 meters) in 1.5 miles (3 km) by controlling water elevations. It the highest rise of lift locks in this distance in the world.

Troy ❸ (exit 7 from I-87) grew up around small mills to become an important steel and iron center during the Civil War, and then a leading manufacturer of shirts and collars. Now its period architecture makes it a mecca for filmmakers, and its Victorian Stroll in December is one of the northeast's premier holiday events (tel: 518/270-2959). Captain JP Cruise Line offers cruises on the Hudson aboard its triple-deck, 600-passenger Mississippi paddlewheeler (278 River Street; tel: 518/270-1901; open May–mid-Oct; entrance fee).

Map
on page
204

The arts are also important to Troy's economy, evidenced by a multimillion-dollar renovation of its arts and entertainment districts. The Troy Savings Bank Music Hall is a celebrated concert hall (32 Second Street; tel: 518/273-0038). Professional theater is staged by the New York State Theater Institute (Schacht Fine Arts Center, Russell Sage College Campus; tel: 518/274-3256; box office open Mon–Fri 9am–5pm; performances Fri–Sat 8pm, Sun 2pm). The Rensselaer County Historical Society operates the 19th-century Hart-Cluett House Museum (59 Second Street; tel: 518/272-7232; open Feb–Dec Tues–Fri 1–4pm, Sat 10am–4pm; entrance fee). Another of Troy's most famous landmarks is Rensselaer Polytechnic Institute (RPI), a university world-renowned for its technological research.

The man who gave rise to Uncle Sam, the mythical recruiter of Americans to war service, was a Troy meatpacker named Sam Wilson. During the War of 1812, he stamped the barrels of beef he shipped to American soldiers "US Beef." Many assumed this stood for Uncle Sam's beef. Sam Wilson is buried in Oakwood Cemetery (101st Street; tel: 518/272-7520); a statue at River and Fulton Streets pays him tribute.

In nearby **Watervliet** ❹ is the Watervliet Arsenal Museum, housing a collection of rare cannons and items related to the arsenal's history (Broadway, Route 32; tel: 518/266-5805; open Mon–Thur 10am–3 pm; entrance free).

Historic Schenectady

A first association with **Schenectady** ❺ (reached via I-90 and Route 5) may be General Electric and the wizardry of Thomas Edison, but the town is of equal architectural importance. In colonial times, settlers erected a wall as a barrier

BELOW:
the Vischer Ferry
Nature Preserve.

against Indian attack. The Stockade District, the state's oldest registered Historic District, derives its name from that defensive wall, long since gone. This multi-block area around Washington Avenue and Front Street and bounded by the Mohawk River, includes homes built from the late 1600s through the 1900s, in styles from Dutch to Victorian. Start at the Dora Jackson House, where the Schenectady County Historical Society is located (32 Washington Avenue; tel: 518/374-0263; entrance fee). Pick up a free self-guided walking tour map and sample their exhibit of 18th- and 19th-century furniture, toys, and artifacts.

For information on local history and architecture, try the Schenectady Museum, which also has a Planetarium, and an archive of electrical history (Nott Terrace Heights; tel: 518/382-7890; open Tues–Fri 10am–4.30pm, Sat–Sun noon–5pm; entrance fee).

Union College (Union Street; tel: 518/388-6000), designed by the French architect Joseph Jacques Ramee and completed in 1814, was the first college chartered in the state. Offering many events open to the public, the college has attractive grounds, formal gardens, and noteworthy buildings. See the 16-sided, ivy-covered, Venetian Gothic Nott Memorial. Another garden worth visiting is the Central Park Rose Garden (Central Park and Wright avenues; tel: 518/382-5152; open June–Oct daily), where there are 3,000 fragrant rose bushes.

Finally, make a trip to Proctor's Theatre (432 State Street; box office tel: 518/346-1083 or 382-3884), a fully restored 1926 Vaudeville-era theater that presents top talent in Broadway musicals and other fine events.

From the Schenectady Amtrak station, you can go south to Albany or north to Saratoga Springs, Fort Edward, and Whitehall. There are limited stops daily, so pick up a schedule (tel: 800/USA-RAIL).

BELOW: Troy was the birthplace of Uncle Sam, America's favorite mascot.

Schenectady to Saratoga

The best way to visit places between Schenectady and Saratoga is by car. The first stop is **Altamont ❻** (Route 146, south of Schenectady), where the Altamont Fairgrounds host colorful traditional music festivals (tel: 518/765-2815 or 888/414-3378). Then take Route 157 to **Voorheesville**, where **John Boyd Thatcher State Park ❼** offers views of the Hudson-Mohawk Valley and the Adirondacks. An Indian ladder trail along Helderberg Escarpment goes among some of the richest fossil-bearing formations in the world (Route 157; tel: 518/872-1237; open summer 8am–10pm, fall–spring 8am–6pm).

The **Vischer Ferry Nature Preserve** is a gem in the center of **Clifton Park ❽** (exit from I-87), a sprawling residential community that is home to many of the thousands who work in Albany. The preserve offers breathing space, with trails to historic portions of the Erie Canal. There's also a canoe launch (tel: 518/371-6667). In nearby **Halfmoon ❾**, Crescent Cruise Lines offers narrated Erie Canal cruises (tel: 518/373-1070).

Approaching **Ballston Spa ❿** (exit 12 from I-87, or Route 50 north) puts you decidely en route to the springs. The National Bottle Museum (76 Milton Avenue; tel: 518/885-7589; open June–Sept daily, Oct–May Mon–Fri; entrance fee) is a testament to the élan with which the waters have been bottled. Part of Ballston's main street appeared in the film *The Way We Were*, which starred Barbra Streisand and Robert Redford, and has not changed much in the years since. Ballston's town-wide sidewalk sales and auctions are fun-filled treasure hunts. Brookside Museum (6 Charlton Street; tel: 518/885-4000; open Tues–Fri 10am–4pm, Sat noon–4pm; entrance fee), a former resort hotel, is now a fine local museum, on the hillside by the Old Iron Spring.

The quickest route into Saratoga from Albany is I-87, but in terms of vernacular appeal it can't touch **Route 9**, the pre-speedway connector north and south. It's not Route 66, but it has sections of pure regional character: caving-in barns and slouching frame houses; places to buy handmade wooden whirligigs; oldtime motel cabins; and other vanishing Americana. At **Round Lake ⑪**, pull off and drive slowly through this time warp of a Victorian village. The entire village of gingerbread houses, with its narrow tree-shaded streets, is on the National Historic Register. The Auditorium houses the 1847 Ferris tracker pipe organ, played during public recitals (tel: 518/899-7141).

The approach to Saratoga Springs along Route 9 goes past the Malta Drive-in Theater (tel: 518/587-6077), one of the few operative drive-ins around. Here you can watch first-run features on a slightly out-of-focus open-air screen with a sound speaker hung on your window, and chomp on hot dogs and popcorn purchased during intermission from the refreshment building in the middle of the field. Angled upward toward the screen, your car sits unevenly on a hump of grassy dirt. Everything is slightly precarious and uncomfortable, especially the mosquitoes. In today's world, this is nostalgic Nirvana.

Saratoga Springs

The first non-native of note who came to the Saratoga area was probably Sir William Johnson. In 1771 his Mohawk friends, who believed the curative waters of the High Rock Spring could help his wounded knee, carried him on a litter from his Johnstown home *(see page 217)* to the spring. Johnson told his friends about the spring, including George Washington, who wanted to buy it. In time, settlement followed, as resort-minded entrepreneurs were drawn by the promise of health and profit from the magical waters.

Saratoga Springs ⑫ has been born and reborn countless times, always reemerging in a mélange of class, culture, and warring elements that gives the city its distinctive character. It was the site of the country's first Temperance Society in 1808, yet in 1811 Gideon Putnam started the elegant Congress Hall to attract a clientele used to more hedonistic pleasures. By the 1820s, visitors coming for the therapeutic waters could also enjoy billiards, orchestras, ballroom dancing, and other diversions – all activities the Temperance Society stood against. By 1864 the existing race track had been built and the first Travers Stakes was held. Casino gambling was introduced in 1869; in the 1920s came Prohibition-era bootleggers and criminals large and small. Along with the wealthy who had money to gamble came those conniving to win at something, at anything.

Map on page 204

There are recitals on the famous pipe organ at the Round Lake auditorium.

BELOW:
an idyllic scene at Round Lake.

A fountain bubbles outside the artists' retreat at Yaddo.

But the waters drew other types as well. In the 20th century, a large summer Jewish population came not so much to socialize as to heal. The east side of the city sprouted boarding houses whose small porches with four or five rockers duplicated in miniature the vast porches of the big hotels. Farmlands attracted other New Englanders and European immigrants: Irish, Italians, Slovak, and more. Their willingness to work hard and their skills in masonry, iron and steel, and agriculture were needed in small industry and to serve the tourist trade.

And in the midst of the high rollers – like the Vanderbilts and Whitneys – and low rollers – like Damon Runyon's fictive but all-too-real trackside bookies – a creative community was being nourished. In a woody locale where Edgar Allan Poe had once worked, the Trask family would endow Yaddo, the world-renowned artists' retreat that opened in 1926 (Union Avenue past the Race Track; tel: 518/584-0746; rose gardens open dawn to dusk; entrance free). Skidmore College (enter from Woodlawn Avenue or North Broadway; tel: 518/580-5450), founded in 1903, would round out the holistic appeal of this area with its fine educational facilities and offerings.

Exploring Saratoga

Mid-19th-century visitors would have come by train into the heart of Saratoga Springs. Then the Saratoga trunk was not merely the rage but a necessity, for holding the voluminous gowns women wore as they strolled tree-lined Broadway or whirled demurely on the dance floor at one of the majestic hotels, the Grand Union or the United States. Those hotels are long gone and so is the grand train station. Still, the **Amtrak Saratoga** stop, west of town, is popular (West Avenue; tel: 800/USA-RAIL or 518/587-8354). In the summer Amtrak

BELOW: flag day parade at Saratoga.

adds a special Saratoga car exclusively for those coming to experience the high racing season between July and August *(for Amtrak, see page 308)*.

Approaching Saratoga by road from the south, the **Saratoga Spa State Park** (between Routes 9 and 50; tel: 518/584-2000; open daily) is an immediate reminder of the pulse of the city's identity, its carbonated springs. Created by the state in 1909 to preserve the springs and surrounding land, the site grew to its present 2,200 acres (890 hectares), encompassing health, recreational, and cultural facilities. Top attractions are the Gideon Putnam Hotel and Conference Center (tel: 518/584-3000), an elegant locale for a romantic getaway; and the Saratoga Performing Arts Center (tel: 518/587-3330; season June–Sept), which includes productions by the New York City Ballet, the Philadelphia Orchestra, a jazz festival, and special concerts and events. There are also assorted mineral springs and baths, picnic areas, and the Spa Little Theater (tel: 518/587-4427), where other theater productions are staged and, during the summer, the Lake George Opera Festival. For the sports-minded, there is a 1,200-ft (400-meter) skating rink, tennis courts, swimming pools, two golf courses, and miles of hiking, biking, and cross-country skiing trails through woods and forests.

Just past the entrance to the park stands a low-lying structure that was once the Washington Baths, and is now the country's only museum devoted to professional American dance. The National Museum of Dance (99 South Broadway; tel: 518/584-2225; open Tues–Sun; entrance fee) features galleries with fabulous costumes, a Hall of Fame, a café and gift shop, and peaceful grounds.

Arriving by bus, you will be let off on South Broadway at the **Bus Terminal** (tel: 518/584-0911). However you arrive, a convenient starting point for visitors is the **Saratoga Springs Urban Cultural Park Visitor Center** at the Drink Hall

Map on page 204

BELOW: the Roosevelt Spa at Saratoga Springs.

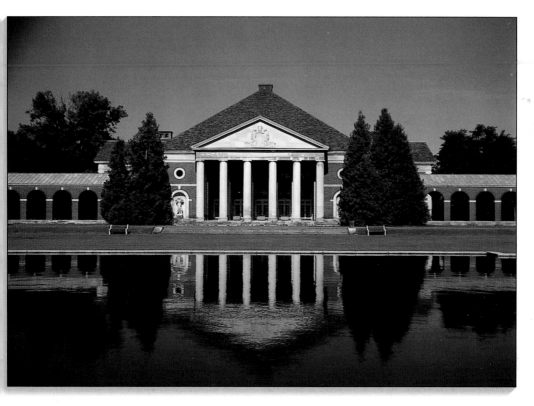

Spirit of Life *by*
Daniel Chester
French graces
Congress Park.

(297 Broadway; tel: 518/587-3241). An orientation center helps you get your bearings; there are displays and tasteful souvenirs on offer.

Diagonally across from the Visitor Center is the entrance to **Congress Park**. Inside, the Canfield Casino houses the Saratoga Historical Society Museum, the Walworth Memorial Museum (tel: 518/584-6920; entrance fee), the Ann Grey Gallery, and a good gift shop. The open areas on the ground floor are transformed each year according to the theme of Mary Lou Whitney's annual racing season party. Stroll the landscaped grounds. In the 19th century, tourists bought goods here at the summer Abenaki encampment. The Canfield Casino, opened in 1869 and enlarged in 1873, is the oldest gambling casino in the country, although casino gambling is now illegal in the area.

One can exit the park on the Broadway side and discover the eclectic mixture of specialty shops and eateries, with prices for every budget from the ridiculously low to sky-high. Explore the side streets off Broadway, too. On Phila Street are two well-known spots: the Lyrical Ballad Bookstore antiquarian booksellers (7–9 Phila Street; tel: 518/584-8779); and **Caffè Lena**, the country's oldest continuously operating coffee house (47 Phila Street; tel: 518/583-0022; open Thur–Sun; cover charge). Bob Dylan and Pete Seeger both performed here early in their careers.

One of the milder-tasting mineral springs is the **Old Hathorn** at Spring and Putnam streets. This carbonated spring has the highest mineral content of all the springs. The **High Rock Spring**, where the Mohawks brought the wounded Sir William Johnson, is on High Rock Avenue. Continuing along High Rock, there is a café in what was once the Van Raalte Knitting Company. A short way beyond is the **Old Red Spring** (intersection of Excelsior and High Rock

BELOW:
the Old Hathorn
mineral spring.

avenues). The Old Red Spring is sometimes called "the beauty spring" as it is popular for skin ailments and often used on the eyes.

Behind Congress Park, Union Avenue runs in an east-west direction. No more fitting pathway to the historic race track (or Saratoga Lake, beyond) could be conceived than this, lined with one remarkable building after another. You will see a range of styles: Italianate (Nos. 43, 67, 85); Queen Anne (Nos. 28, 55, 84, 115, 149, 203); High Gothic (Nos. 104, 143); Colonial Revival (Nos. 48, 72, 125, 134); Second Empire (No. 139); and Romanesque (No.148). This urban "architectural casebook" includes the modest No. 100, a Vernacular Cottage.

The **Saratoga Race Course** (Union Avenue; tel: 888/285-5961 or (during meetings) 518/584-6200; post time 1pm Wed–Mon, July 28–Sept 6; entrance fee) is the nation's oldest thoroughbred track and perhaps the most beautiful, with its Victorian grandstand and grounds. It has been the scene of thousands of races, but it has also appeared in countless novels and films; among the more recent is *Billy Bathgate*, starring Nicole Kidman. When the grounds and Saratoga-area extras were dressed in Prohibition-era attire, the clock turned back. Some would say this flavor of the past is always in the Saratoga air – it was at Saratoga in 1919 that Man O' War suffered his only defeat– while in 1930, Jim Dandy came down a muddied track at 100 to 1, beating Gallant Fox, the Triple Crown winner.

Early morning is the best time to experience behind the scenes at the track. You can take a free tram tour of the Backstretch, tour the grounds, or watch the Paddock show and Starting Gate demonstration (tel: 518/584-6200). Breakfast at the track has been a tradition since after the Civil War. From 7am to 9.30am, you can sit trackside and order a buffet breakfast; admission is free.

The Fasig-Tipton Horse Sales, held once a year in August, are a chance to see some of the country's most outstanding horses up close as they are led in to be sold.

BELOW: neck-and-neck at Saratoga Race Course.

Across from the racecourse, the National Museum of Racing and Thorough-bred Hall of Fame has noteworthy displays from "the sport of kings" (191 Union Avenue; tel: 518/584-2225; open daily; entrance fee).

A few streets away beyond Nelson Avenue, Saratoga Harness Racing is held at the Saratoga Equine Sports Center between July and August (tel: 518/587-2110 for times and dates). The Saratoga Harness Racing Museum and Hall of Fame located here features exhibits of sulkies (the wheeled vehicle jockeys ride harnessed to the horse) and an antique horseshoe display (tel: 518/587-4210; open Tues–Sat 10am– 4pm; entrance free). Saratoga Polo Matches are held during August on Seward Street (tel: 518/584-8108).

West of Saratoga

You need a car to explore the areas beyond Saratoga in any direction, and you will do best to choose one direction a day. Heading toward North Broadway, turn left at the traffic light at Broadway and Church Street (which becomes Route 9N). Like Route 9, this was once a main highway, and it is studded with small towns and hamlets, rustic attractions, and beautiful scenery, from the Greenfield Center area to Lake George.

A must-see in this area for the geology buff is the **Petrified Sea Gardens** ⓭, 3 miles (5 km) west of the city off Route 29 on Petrified Sea Gardens Road (named Lester Park Road from the other direction). This natural-history park includes a 500-million-year-old fossil ocean reef. Gardens and trails lead to deep crevices and formations made from cryptozoan rocks, known as cabbage rocks because of their swirling patterns (tel: 518/584-7102; open Thur–Sun 11am–5pm; entrance fee).

TIP

Broadway and its side streets have a number of antiques shops and thrift shops for vintage goods. But for real local color, take the old route north to Glens Falls (Rte 9, out Maple Avenue) for antiques sold in one-of-a-kind, memorable setups and locales.

BELOW: away from the races, rural bliss.

Route 29w passes through **Broadalbin** en route to the turnoff for **Gloversville ⑭** and **Johnstown ⑮**, about 30 miles (50 km) west of Saratoga. Known in their heyday as the center of tanning and the leather industry, both places have small-town charm and good museums and historical sites. In Gloversville, visit the Fulton County Museum for colonial and Indian artifacts and leather-making displays (tel: 518/725-2203).

The Johnstown Historical Society Museum (17 N. William Street; tel: 518/627-0769; open daily; entrance fee) is a restored 18th-century cottage, with 18th- and 19th-century artifacts from various wars and information on Elizabeth Cady Stanton, a native of the area. Stanton is known for her pioneering achievement in Women's Rights, working with Susan B. Anthony *(see page 268)*.

Fittingly, Johnstown bears a version of the name of Sir William Johnson. This man of many talents founded the town as a trading outpost. An Irish immigrant, he inherited his uncle's lands in the Mohawk Valley in 1738 and earned a reputation among the Iroquois as an amiable and fair trader. He learned the native languages and often wore Indian clothing. Later, working with Joseph Brant and the Mohawks, Johnson and the British defeated the invading French in the 1755 Battle of Lac du Saint Sacrement. Thereafter Johnson was awarded a baronetcy and appointed Superintendent of Indian Affairs. Johnson married Catherine, niece of Chief Hendricks of the Mohawks, and later lived with Molly Brant, the outspoken sister to Chief Joseph Brandt, respected as a military strategist. **Johnson Hall State Historic Site** is Johnson's restored 1763 Georgian mansion and grounds (Hall Avenue; tel: 518/762-8712; open Wed–Sun; entrance free). It contains furnishings, dioramas, and a camera obscura. In Johnson's time, the picnic area outside would have often been filled with visitors, for he

Map on page 204

BELOW:
snowed under at
Greenfield Center.

TIP

A popular annual
event in Corinth is the
Bluegrass Festival in
August (tel: 518/654-
9424)

conducted his affairs here: daily visits from Joseph Brant, scores of Mohawk and other native peoples, and British leaders and politicians were a matter of course.

From Broadalbin, Route 30N leads to **Great Sacandaga Lake** , where **Northville** and **Edinburg** nestle at one end. Here, where nights are colder and distances between places far, red hunting plaids, thick boots, and a determination to work with, in, or in spite of, the weather, are in the air. At the Lapland Lake Nordic Vacation Center in Northville, former US Olympian Olavi Hirvonen and family run their year-round resort. The cross-country ski center has lodging and offers instruction. In other seasons, overnight guests enjoy swimming, fishing, hiking, and canoeing on a 70-acre (28-hectare) wilderness lake (tel: 800/453-SNOW or 518/863-4974). For lakeside camping, try the Northampton Beach State Campground on the Great Sacanadaga Lake in Northville (tel: 800/456-CAMP or 518/863-6000).

On Route 9N heading south toward Saratoga, **Corinth** is home to Adirondack Wildwaters for rafting (tel: 518/696-2953); and River Road Campgrounds (tel: 518/654-6630), with acres of natural beauty on the upper Hudson. Locals and dealers turn out on Saturday nights at Corinth Auction Service (Saratoga Avenue, Route 9N; tel: 518/654-7209; open Sat 6pm; entrance free). Some come just to hear auctioneers Charlie and Richie Witherbee rib the regulars.

North and east of Saratoga

Fort Edward on Route 4 is another Amtrak stop. There are guided tours at the Old Fort House Museum, a six-building complex centered around a 1772 toll house and featuring other 18th-century buildings (29 Broadway; tel:518/747-9600; open June–Labor Day, Labor Day–Oct Sat–Sun only; entrance fee).

BELOW: a relic
of times past.

Going north, **Whitehall** ⑳ is the next stop after Fort Edward, at the northern edge of the Capital-Saratoga Region. The birthplace of the US Navy, Whitehall has a number of unusual attractions. The Bridge Theater puts on live productions on a bridge over Lock 12 of the Champlain Canal (Clinton Street Bridge; tel: 518/499-2435 or 800/644-2435; July–Sept daily; entrance fee).

Map on page 204

The Skene Manor "Castle on the Hill" is an 1874 Victorian manor open to the public (8 Potters Terrace; tel: 518/499-1906; open May–Dec Wed–Sun, Jan–Apr Fri–Sun; entrance free). For local history, visit the Skenesborough Museum along the Champlain Canal. Exhibits include wooden ship models (Skenesborough Drive; tel: 518/499-1155; open mid-June–Labor Day Mon–Sat 10am–4pm, Sun noon–4pm; Labor Day– mid-Oct Sat 10am–3pm, Sun noon–3pm; entrance fee). The Whitehall Antique Center features 50 dealers and their wares (Route 4; tel: 518/499-2501).

The 1870 Rexleigh Covered Bridge south of **Salem** ㉑ on Route 22 is worth a visit as a fine example of the style. This Salem along the Battenkill is not, however, the Salem of the Witch Trails, which took place in Massachusetts.

Raggedy Ann and Andy dolls bring back childhood memories.

The Hand Melon Farm on Route 29 between Schuylerville and **Greenwich** ㉒ (tel: 518/692-2376) has "pick your own" strawberries and sells famous Hand melons during the summer. Nearby, you can ski at Willard Mountain (tel: 800/457-SNOW or 518/692-7337); or golf at Windy Hills Golf Course, (tel: 518/695-4902). The Country Peddler Shop is in a restored livery in the downtown historic district. Then take the family to the **Washington County Fairgrounds** for animals, crafts, rides, and games on a Midway meant for excitement and fun by night or day.

BELOW: clowning around.

Schuylerville ㉓ was named for the same General Schuyler of the Albany area, as was the 1877 **Schuyler Monument** (tel: 518/664-9821; entrance free). The cornerstone of the 154-ft (47-meter) granite monument was laid exactly 100 years after Burgoyne's surrender to Gates at the Battle of Saratoga. Outside are bronze statues of military heroes Schuyler and Gates. One plaque in the Schuyler Monument shows Mrs Schuyler setting fire to grain fields to keep them from the enemy. The General Philip Schuyler House was built in 27 days to replace one burnt by the retreating British in 1777 (south of Fishkill on Route 4; tel: 518/664-9821). Today there are living history programs and craft and cooking demonstrations on the site where Schuyler, ever the host, entertained during the summer months.

Cambridge ㉔ is as American as apple pie, and indeed this traditional dish was first served at the venerable Cambridge Hotel, still on Main Street. Nearby, Hubbard Hall Projects sponsors music and art events in an 1878 opera house (tel: 518/677-2495). If it is outdoor adventure you want, head for Battenkill Sports Quarters on the Battenkill River, for camping, canoeing, kayaking, tubing, fly fishing, barbecues, and picnicking (tel: 800/676-8768 or 518/677-8868).

One of the most delightful nearby visits may be to the New Skete Monastery, whose gift shop is stocked with cheesecakes, fruitcakes, and other monastery-made items (tel: 518/ 677-3810).

Most art fans know the name of Grandma Moses

Map
on page
204

for her wonderful paintings of American life, but not so many know that at her home in **Eagle Bridge** , her grandson Will Moses is still turning out handsome work in the Moses tradition. At the Mount Nebo Gallery in town you can buy his limited edition prints and etchings while standing only a few yards away from the place Grandma Moses called home (tel: 800/328-6326 or 518/686-4334). Grandma Moses is buried in Maple Grove Cemetery, Wood Memorial Park, in the **Hoosick Falls Historic District**.

In **Schaghticoke** ㉖ are the **Schaghticoke Fairgrounds**, which hold a draft horse show, firemen's day with fireworks, demolition derby, the Royal Hanneford Circus, and a Family Fun Fair (tel: 518/753-4411; held around Labor Day; entrance fee). For another exhilarating outdoor experience, visit the Maze at Liberty Ridge Farm, a 10-acre (4-hectare) corn field maze, where getting lost is all the more fun (29 Bevis Road, Schaghticoke; tel: 518/664-1515; open Aug–Oct; entrance fee).

Revolutionary relics

Throughout the area around **Stillwater** ㉗, events are staged relating to the decisive 1777 Battle of Saratoga, especially during the summer months. A lot of local pride is wrapped up in laying claim to some part of this military turning point, when British General Burgoyne surrendered to General Gates. The truth is, the victory happened over a period of four-plus weeks, during which time there were clashes and rebuffs, battles and retreats, and various places saw action of one sort or another (*see page 35*). Look for Revolutionary War reenactments, demonstrations, musket drills, heritage days, costumed dramas, and more. The events at the official battlefield sites may be the more informative,

BELOW: whittling away the time.

but the ones put on by local individuals and spirited groups can often be more fun.

Stillwater holds an annual "18th Century Day" every August, with period demonstrations, puppet shows, farm animals, and more (tel: 518/664-9821, ext 224). But at the **Bennington Battlefield State Historic Site** ㉘ in Hoosick Falls, (tel: 518/279-1155) you can really immerse yourself in history while you picnic on the actual hilltop where, in 1777, American militia men defeated General Burgoyne's forces.

Then there is a self-guided driving tour at the **Saratoga National Historical Park** ㉙ in Stillwater (648 Route 32; tel: 518/664-9821, ext 224; battlefield open daily 9am–5pm; tour road open Apr–Nov 9am–dusk; entrance fee).

Once you have had your fill of Revolutionary War memorabilia, you can return to Saratoga Springs taking the road that goes along Saratoga Lake. As you are driving, you might ponder the lake's history and legends, such as what might have given Rattlesnake Hill its name, or where the great boxer Jack Dempsey trained, or what Moon's Lake House was once like when a resident Indian cook named George Crum really burnt some fried potatoes by mistake and came up with the original potato chip. If all that doesn't make you thirsty for some Saratoga spring water, nothing will. ❑

The Dutch-Indian Legacy

In 1664 Dutch governor Peter Stuyvesant surrendered New Netherlands to the British, who would rename it New York and Fort Orange as Albany. Apart from that, much of life went on as usual. The colony's population was then about two-thirds Dutch, with the British next in number. Germans, French, Finns, and Jews were present in small number, as were slaves brought by the Dutch from Angola and Brazil. The Dutch and English became the landed merchant class, while the ranks of artisans, farmers, and shopkeepers grew.

When the Dutch arrived, American Indians already had established trading routes along land and water, and they hunted beaver pelts on Indian lands. From the Indian peoples, the Dutch learned trapping, hunting, and how to clear forests and survive in the wilderness, as well as what crops would grow. Demand for beaver skins by the Dutch, French, and British heightened inter-tribal competition and struggles between the French and English. Eventually liberal charters granted Albany exclusive rights to the fur trade. The beaver's presence on the state seal reflects its importance to the state in its infancy.

As Indians lost ground, the settlers acquired it. Under the patroonship system *(see page 28)*, a person could claim miles of land along the Hudson if it was colonized within four years. In the Fort Orange area, an Amsterdam diamond merchant, Kiliaen Van Rensselaer, succeeded as a patroon and the Crailo State Historic Site, former home of the Van Rensselaers, is now a Museum of the Dutch (9½ Riverside Avenue, Rensselaer; tel: 518/463 8738; open Apr–Dec Wed–Sun; entrance fee). During Albany's Tulip Festival each May, women wearing Dutch costumes scrub State Street, and Kinderkermis (a children's fair) enlivens Washington Park.

The Indians' fate was to be caught between loyalties during the Revolution. Siding with the British, many were killed. Some relocated to Canada. However, pockets of Indian settlements remain in the Capital-Saratoga region, and Indian presence is felt through place names; at pow wows and festivals; and along their foot trails, which became today's highways. Resources they valued are still important, such as corn, beans, and squash, and Saratoga's mineral springs. The Saratoga Springs city seal depicts an Indian family at a spring.

The New York State Museum and Johnstown sites contain important collections on Native Peoples. Some residents trace their ancestry to the Algonquin or Iroquois; some to other northeastern peoples such as the Abenaki, who summered at an encampment in Saratoga Springs.

Local government also owes much to the original League of Five Nations, formed around 1500 as a way for warring Iroquois tribes to co-exist *(see page 25)*. The nation's founding fathers Benjamin Franklin and James Madison were inspired by its example when they developed their plan of government for the liberated colonies.   ❑

RIGHT: Peter B. Jones's sculpture *Yoin jot geh cot* is a tribute to the native Seneca people.

THE ADIRONDACKS

The mountain landscape of the Adirondacks has been the setting for many notable events, from fierce Revolutionary battles to the international stage of two Winter Olympics

Map on pages 226–7

New York

The Adirondack Mountains range across the largest park preserve in the northeastern United States, an area of nearly 6 million acres (2,400,000 hectares) occupying most of New York State north of the Mohawk River. Rugged and densely forested, the Adirondacks were the last part of the state to be explored and settled. Well into the 19th century, this was the domain of moose, bear, and wolves, and it was only after the 1849 publication of Joel T. Headley's *The Adirondacks, or Life in the Woods* that the outside world paid much attention to the vast region.

Created not by folding and thrusting but by erosion along fault lines separating harder, more resistant masses of rock, the Adirondacks are a part of Canada's Laurentian Plateau. Among the range's High Peaks, clustered roughly 25 miles (40 km) west of Lake Champlain, are 42 summits exceeding 4,000 ft (1,200 meters). Highest is Mount Marcy, at 5,344 ft (1,630 meters), where the waters that form the Hudson River first gather at Lake Tear of the Clouds. The best Adirondack views, however, are from free-standing Whiteface Mountain at 4,872 ft (1,485 meters), which offers 85-mile (135-km) vistas that take in much of Lake Champlain and Vermont's Green Mountains to the east, the St Lawrence River valley and the city of Montreal to the north, and many of the other High Peaks to the west and south.

PRECEDING PAGES: North Country snow. **LEFT:** hiking in the Adirondacks. **BELOW:** ski jumper at Lake Placid Olympic complex.

Settling the mountains

When outsiders did begin to penetrate the Adirondacks, they arrived largely in the persons of loggers, who harvested vast tracts of virgin timber; hunters and anglers, whose activities are handsomely portrayed in the paintings of Winslow Homer; and, most spectacularly, the super-rich of the post-Civil War era, who amassed private holdings of tens of thousands of acres and built the legendary Adirondack "Great Camps," several of which still survive. Financial barons such as J. P. Morgan, Collis P. Huntington, and Alfred G. Vanderbilt created a style of backwoods rustication unlike anything seen before or since in the United States, traveling to remote sidings via private railway car and "roughing it" in a fashion perhaps only equaled by the titled possessors of European hunting lodges.

The modern history of the Adirondacks began in 1894, when the New York state legislature created Adirondack Park. Like Catskill Park to the south, Adirondack Park is a complicated amalgam of public and private land. Of the total acreage, a bit less than half is in public ownership and is legally required to be kept "forever wild." The remainder consists of private holdings, subject to stringent constraints regarding development and resource extraction. It is a

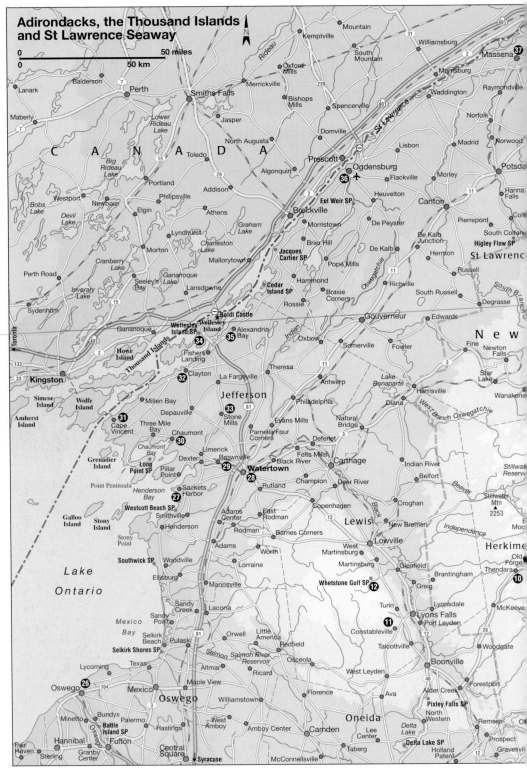

Adirondacks, the Thousand Islands and St Lawrence Seaway

N

0 ——————— 50 miles
0 ——————— 50 km

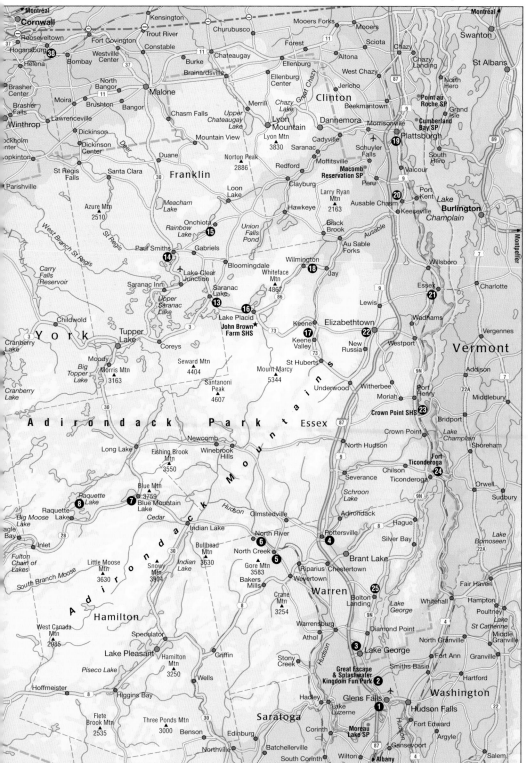

There are trails for hiking and biking in the Adirondacks.

rare year that does not see some sort of protest from property-rights activists among the fewer than 100,000 inhabitants of the park, who feel that their prerogatives as landowners are infringed by enforcement of its regulations.

As it did for those long-ago subjects of Winslow Homer's paintings, the Adirondacks continue to provide splendid opportunities for fishing, hunting, wildlife observation, hiking and boating. The region is threaded by around 6,000 miles (9,700 km) of rivers, many of which connect some 2,300 lakes to create canoe routes as diverse and rewarding as any in the eastern United States. In winter, reliably cold temperatures and abundant snowfall provide ideal conditions for skiing (downhill and cross-country) and snowshoeing. Lake Placid, in the shadow of Whiteface Mountain, hosted the Winter Olympic Games in both 1932 and 1980.

Although roads paved and unpaved snake through the Adirondacks, this is territory that demands to be seen at a hiker's pace, or from water level in the distinctive local craft – part canoe, part rowboat – called an Adirondack guide boat. Come to think of it, there's another piece of regional craftsmanship that makes an ideal vantage point from which to appreciate these mountains. It's called an Adirondack chair, and its broad sloping seat and big enveloping arms welcome anyone who wants to savor the solitude of a remote lake at dusk, listening for the eerie laugh of the loons.

The southern Adirondacks

BELOW: giants of the North Country.

A good place to start a tour of the area is the home of paper heiress Charlotte Pruyn and her husband, Louis Fiske Hyde, who began construction of their Italian Renaissance villa in **Glens Falls ❶** in 1912. When it was finished, they

SAVING THE ADIRONDACKS

The campaign leading to the 1894 establishment of Adirondack Park was a prototype for the wilderness preservation efforts of our own time. Among the most effective weapons in the preservationists' arsenal, then as now, were sympathetic comments from public figures. "The chief argument for the preservation of the Adirondack forests," wrote the silviculturist C.S. Sargent in 1885, "must rest upon the act that they are necessary to the existence of many important streams which head among them, and which will be seriously injured, and perhaps ruined by the denudation of their water-sheds." Landscape architect Frederick Law Olmsted, designer of Central Park, took a similar approach, arguing in that same year on behalf of "the profit to the state... from preserving and enlarging the value of the region as a resort for recreation and health." But it was Julian Hawthorne, son of Nathaniel, who pleaded for the region's protection in the most modern terms. He hoped "that the Adirondacks will never be interfered with by the worshipers of real estate and manufactories... The mere knowledge that such a place as the Adirondacks has ceased to exist would be a cause of genuine sorrow even to those who had never personally enjoyed the pleasure and enjoyment of being there."

Map on pages 226–7

filled it with a brilliant collection of American and European art spanning five centuries. Along with the paintings, they collected sculpture, tapestries, and period furnishings. Their home and gallery now form The Hyde Collection (161 Warren Street; tel: 518/792-1761; open Tues–Sun; entrance free).

Head northwest on Route 9/28, past the **Great Escape and Splashwater Kingdom Fun Park** ❷ in Queensbury (Route 9; tel: 518/792-3500; open Memorial Day–Labor Day; entrance fee), the state's largest theme park, to **Lake George Village** ❸, at the southern end of the 32-mile-long (52-km) lake by the same name. This popular tourist resort has swimming beaches, a raft of attractions, and numerous boat rides, including shoreline cruises on the paddlewheeler *Minne-ha-ha* (Steel Pier; tel: 518/668-5777 or 800/553-2628; open May–Oct; entrance fee). Fort William Henry Museum (Route 9; tel: 518/668-5471; open May–Oct; entrance fee), overlooking the village, is a replica of a stronghold built by the British in 1755 and attacked by the French and Indians under the command of General Montcalm. The slaughter that ensued was described by James Fenimore Cooper in his book *The Last of the Mohicans*. Activities such as musket firing are demonstrated at the living history museum. The ruins of the actual fort are in Lake George Battlefield Park (tel: 518/668-3352; open May–Columbus Day; parking fee), behind the museum. Nearby, Prospect Mountain Veterans Memorial Highway (Route 9s; tel: 518/668-5198; open Memorial Day–late Oct; entrance fee) climbs 5½ miles (9 km) to a parking area near the summit, where a van whisks visitors to an observation center at the top.

North on Route 9 in **Pottersville** ❹, at Natural Stone Bridge and Caves (555 Stone Bridge Road; tel: 518/494-2283; open Labor Day–Columbus Day; entrance fee), the Ausable River has carved out a 180-ft (55-meter) stone arch,

TIP

Adirondack Park Visitor Interpretive Centers in Newcomb (Route 28N; tel: 518/582-2000; open year round; entrance free) and Paul Smiths (Route. 30; tel: 518/327-3000) are excellent places to learn about the park.

BELOW: cloud-clad Lake George.

Kayaks are a peaceful mode of transport on the Adirondack lakes.

gigantic potholes, unusual rock formations, and a series of underground waterways. Two caves are lighted for exploration. Rental shoes are available for those who don't have sturdy footwear, and visitors can mine for gemstones.

To the southwest, in **North Creek** ❺, a chairlift at Gore Mountain Ski Area (Peaceful Valley Road; tel: 518/251-2411 or 800/342-1234; open summer and fall Sat–Sun; entrance fee) takes visitors to the summit. Some of the country's best whitewater rafting is up ahead at Hudson River Gorge. A number of outfitters in town arrange trips. The Upper Hudson River Railroad (Main Street at Railroad Place; tel: 518/251-5334; open May Sat–Sun, June Fri–Sun, July–Aug daily, Sept Fri–Mon, Oct Wed–Sun; entrance fee) travels along the Hudson River and through the wilderness to a refurbished station in Riparius.

From 1878 to 1983 Barton Mine (Barton Mine Road; tel: 518/251-2706; open June–Labor Day daily, Labor Day–Columbus Day Sat–Sun; entrance fee) in **North River** ❻ was an active, open-pit garnet mine. Visitors get a short lecture on the mine's history and geology, and then have a half-hour to collect garnets (there are plenty lying around). North Creek is one of the entrance points to Siamese Ponds Wilderness Region, a 112,000-acre (45,000-hectare) hiking and camping area. For information contact the Adirondack Mountain Club (RD 3, Box 3055, Luzerne Road, Lake George 12854; tel: 518/668-4447).

Central and western Adirondacks

BELOW: the steamer
Mohican at Lake
George Village.

Farther west on Route 28 the Hudson River flows into **Indian Lake** just east of the village center. Hudson River Gorge is just to the west of town. Continue into **Blue Mountain Lake** ❼ to the excellent Adirondack Museum (Route 30; tel: 518/352-7311; open mid-June–mid-Oct, entrance fee), where the story of how

Map on pages 226–7

people lived, traveled, worked, and played in the Adirondacks from the early 1800s to the present is told at 23 indoor and outdoor exhibit areas. Among the highlights are financier August Belmont's private railroad car and a fine collection of handmade canoes and guideboats. The visual and performing arts Adirondack Lakes Center for the Arts (Route 28; open Sept–June Mon–Fri, July–Aug daily; entrance fee) exhibits and sells regional arts and crafts, and hosts a theater, music, and dance series. The trailhead to the top of Blue Mountain, a fairly steep round-trip of 4 miles (6.5 km), is off Route 30 half a mile (1 km) north of the museum.

West on Route 28, on **Raquette Lake ❽**, is the consummate Adirondack Great Camp, Sagamore (Raquette Lake; tel: 315/354-5311; open May–Nov; entrance fee), built in 1897 by William West Durant, and the summer home of the Alfred Vanderbilt family for more than 50 years. After Vanderbilt drowned on the *Lusitania* in 1915, his widow continued to entertain family and friends at the 27-building complex for the next 39 years. Tours of the National Historic Landmark are available and, with advance reservations, guests can stay overnight. Members of the knowledgeable Bird family at Bird's Boat Livery (Route 28; tel: 315/354-4441; open July–Aug Mon–Sat; entrance fee) give an excellent tour of the lake aboard a covered pontoon boat as they go about their business of delivering mail.

Inlet is the "Gateway to the Moose River Recreation Area," the Adirondacks' largest block of public land. More than 435 species of plants and trees, including 18 varieties of orchids and 28 varieties of ferns, thrive on the 50,000 acres (20,200 hectares). In **Eagle Bay**, detour north past Big Moose Lake, the setting for the 1906 drowning murder that inspired Theodore Dreiser's novel *An American Tragedy*, to remote Stillwater Reservoir. The Norridgewock River Boat (Norridgewock Lake Road; tel: 315/376-6200; open July–Aug Thur–Tues; entrance fee) gives narrated wilderness cruises and provides transportation to a rustic overnight lodge and cabins on Beaver River.

Continue west on Route 28 to the tourist town of **Old Forge ❾**, the starting point for the Fulton Chain of Lakes, a popular 18-mile (29-km) canoe route that winds through a network of lakes and requires just 1.7 miles (3 km) of portage. Several businesses in town rent canoes and offer whitewater rafting and tubing trips. Old Forge Lake Cruises (Route 28; tel: 315/369-6473; open Memorial Day–Columbus Day; entrance fee) provides narrated scenic tours of the Fulton Chain. The Arts Center at Old Forge (Route 28; tel: 315/369-6411; open daily; entrance free) hosts a range of changing exhibits on local arts, photography, and crafts.

One mile (2 km) south in **Thendara ❿**, the Adirondack Scenic Railroad (Route 28; tel: 315/369-6290; open May–Columbus Day; entrance fee) provides scenic excursions along Moose River through some of the most remote areas of the Adirondacks.

A chairlift at McCauley Mountain Ski Area (off Route 28; tel: 315/369-3225; open late June–mid-Oct Thur–Mon; entrance fee) whisks visitors to the top of the mountain for great views of the surrounding area.

BELOW: summer vacation at Raquette Lake.

On September 13, 1901, Vice-President Theodore Roosevelt paused for lunch at Lake Tear-of-the-Clouds while hiking on Mount Marcy. Suddenly, a ranger appeared with the news that President McKinley, shot the week before, had died. Roosevelt descended the mountain as President of the United States.

Detour south to **Remsen** to visit Steuben Memorial State Historic Site (Starr Hill Road; tel: 315/831-3737; open late May–Labor Day Wed–Sun; entrance free), a replica of the home the Prussian officer Steuben built on the 16,000 acres (6,500 hectares) granted to him for his invaluable assistance in preparing the Continental Army for battle.

In **Constableville** ⓫ in 1819, William Constable, Jr inherited 4 million acres (1½ million hectares) of Adirondack wilderness and built a Georgian mansion patterned on a family-owned estate in Ireland. Five generations of Constables lived there until 1947, after which Constable Hall (tel: 315/397-2323; open late May–mid-Oct Tues–Sun; entrance fee) became a museum. The house contains original furnishings and family possessions.

Farther north, near Lowville, **Whetstone Gulf State Park** ⓬ (Route 26; tel: 315/376-6630; open late May–mid-Sept; entrance fee) straddles a 3-mile-long (5-km) gorge. A 5-mile (8-km) trail (quite steep in parts) leads to the top of a plateau and spectacular vistas. There's good largemouth bass and tiger muskie fishing in the 500-acre (200-hectare) reservoir. A road just before the park entrance (West Road to Corrigan Hill Road) goes to the top of the mountain.

Route 812 out of Lowville goes through **Croghan** and the American Maple Museum (Route 812; tel: 315/346-1107; open Memorial Day–June Fri–Mon, July–early Sept Mon–Sat; entrance fee), whose three floors of exhibits are dedicated to preserving the history and growth of maple syrup-making in North America. Locally famous Crogan Bologna is made in town.

The whimsical outdoor sculpture park along Route 812 in **Indian River** is the work of octogenarian folk artist Veronica Terrillion, who invites visitors to enjoy her work from the side of the road.

BELOW:
trout fishing on
the Ausable River.

Lakes and high peaks

Head east on Route 3 past **Cranberry Lake**, one of the state's loveliest and most undeveloped lakes, to **Tupper Lake**, a plain town which still bears traces of its days as a lumbering and sawmill hub. The National Historic Landmark Beth Joseph Synagogue (Lake Street; tel: 518/359-7229; open July–Aug Tues–Fri; entrance free), built in 1905 by Russian immigrants, is the oldest synagogue in the Adirondacks and retains its original fixtures and furnishings. Adirondack Park's 20,000-acre (8,000-hectare) St Regis Canoe Area is just to the north.

Map
on pages
226–7

In winter 1888 writer Robert Louis Stevenson, suffering from tuberculosis, settled at a cottage in the town of **Saranac Lake** ⑬ (which is actually on Flower Lake) to receive care at a world-famous sanitarium. Today the Robert Louis Stevenson Memorial Cottage (11 Stevenson Lane; tel: 518/891-1462; open July–Sept Tues–Sun; entrance fee) houses the country's largest collection of the author's personal effects. The historic Hotel Saranac (101 Main Street; tel: 518/891-2200) is a popular spot with visitors to the region. Excursion trains leave from the 1904 Union Depot (19 Depot Street; tel: 518/891-0971) for Lake Placid in summer and fall.

Wildflowers bloom in the mountains and fields in summertime.

Detour north to **Paul Smiths** ⑭ to visit the Adirondack Park Visitor Interpretive Center (Ts 30/86; tel: 518/327-3000; open daily; entrance free) and White Pine Camp (tel: 518/327-3030; open late June–mid-Oct; entrance fee), the "Great Camp" which served as the 1926 "Summer White House" for President Calvin Coolidge.

In **Onchiota** ⑮, artifacts and exhibits in the Six Nations Indian Museum (County Route 30; tel: 518/891-2299; open July–Labor Day Tues–Sun; entrance fee) tell the story of the region's native population.

BELOW:
motel strip at Lake George Village.

Much of the infrastructure built for the 1932 and 1980 Olympic Games at the chic alpine village of **Lake Placid** ⑯ is still used today to train athletes. Olympic Center (village tel: 518/523-1655 or 800/462-6236; seasons vary; entrance fee for museum, self-guided tour, ice shows, or skating) is the largest facility of its kind in the world and has four indoor rinks. Displays at the Lake Placid Winter Olympic Museum chronicle the Olympic years. The McKenzie-Intervale Ski Jumping Complex (Kodak Sports Park; tel: 518/523-2202; open late May–late Oct; entrance fee) has a chairlift and an elevator to the Sky Deck at the top of a 26-story, 393-ft (120-meter) jump tower. An Olympic Sites Passport provides one-time admission to the Ski Jump Complex, Mount Van Hoevenberg Sports Complex, the Winter Olympic Museum, and a gondola ride to the top of Little Whiteface (tel: 800/462-6236 for information).

Detour a short distance to the John Brown Farm State Historic Site (Route 73; tel: 518/523-3900; open early May–late Oct Wed–Sun; entrance free). The militant abolitionist who was hung by the US Government in 1859 lived and is buried here. Nearby, at the Mount Van Hoevenberg Sports Complex (Route 73; tel: 518/523-4436; seasons vary; entrance fee), visitors can ride down the country's only dedicated bobsled run, shoot targets and rent mountain bikes.

Keene and **Keene Valley** are at the heart of the High Peaks Region. On the left side of the road between Keene Valley and St Huberts, Roaring Brook Falls drops nearly 200 ft (60 meters).

North of Lake Placid on Route 86, in **Wilmington** , the Ausable River has carved a deep ravine at the base of Whiteface Mountain at High Falls Gorge (off Route 86; tel: 518/946-2278; open Memorial Day–Columbus Day; entrance fee), creating a dramatic 700-ft (213-meter) waterfall. The Cloudsplitter Scenic Gondola at Whiteface Mountain Ski Area (Route 86; tel: 518/946-2223; seasons vary; entrance fee) transports passengers to the top of Little Whiteface. Visitors can also drive up the mountain on the paved Whiteface Mount Veterans Memorial Highway, where an in-mountain elevator at the summit takes passengers to the very top of the state's fifth-highest mountain. At Santa's Workshop (Route 431, Whiteface Mountain Memorial Highway; tel: 518/946-2211 or 800/835-2251; open June–Columbus Day; entrance fee), Mr Claus and his elves oversee activities at the nation's first Christmas theme park.

Champlain Valley and Lake George

Plattsburgh , on Lake Champlain, has been struggling to regain its footing for the past few years since a nearby US Air Force Base closed. But it's no stranger to tough battles: colonists engaged the British here (and lost) in the 1776 Battle of Valcour Island, and in 1814 American Commodore Thomas MacDonough defeated the British at the Battle of Plattsburgh. Both battles are immortalized in dioramas at the Clinton County Historical Museum (48 Court Street; tel: 518/561-0340; open Feb–Dec Tues– Fri; entrance fee). The Federal-style 1797 Kent-Delord House Museum (17 Cumberland Avenue; tel: 518/561-

1035; open Feb–Dec Tues–Fri; entrance fee), home to three generations of the Delords family, retains its original furnishings as well as pieces brought by the British, who commandeered the home in 1814. Works by artists including Rockwell Kent, Ansel Adams, Rubens, and Picasso are on exhibit at the Plattsburgh State Art Museum, SUNY (101 Broad Street; tel: 518/564-2474; open daily except pubic holidays; donation).

In Ausable, the Ausable River has carved a dramatic, 1.5-mile-long (2-km) gorge, creating **Ausable Chasm ⓴** (Route 9; tel: 518/834-7454 or 800/537-1211; open mid-May–early Oct; entrance fee), a landscape of cliffs, caves, crevasses, waterfalls, and rapids. One of the country's oldest – and upstate New York's most popular– tourist attractions takes visitors on a ¾-mile (1.2-km) trail through the gorge to a dock, where they board a boat for the rest of the tour. Two-mile (3-km) raft, kayak, and inner tube rides are available.

It's hard to imagine that the sleepy little village of **Essex ㉑** in the foothills of the Adirondacks was a booming shipbuilding center and port in the mid-1800s. Today, most visitors come here to catch the Lake Champlain Ferry (tel: 802/864-9804; open when lake is ice-free; entrance fee) to Charlotte, Vermont. But the entire village is included on the National Register of Historic Places and the varied styles of the buildings provide a fascinating glimpse into the evolution of American architecture. The oldest building in town is the Essex Inn (16 Main Street; tel: 518/963-8821), which has operated as a hostelry almost continually since it was built in 1853. Also built in 1853, the 20-room Greek Revival house Greystone (Elm Street; tel: 518/963-8058; open Memorial Day– Labor Day Sat–Sun; entrance fee) reflects the taste of 19th-century aristocracy.

To the southwest, in **Elizabethtown ㉒**, exhibits at the Adirondack Center

Map on pages 226–7

LEFT: rowing home.
BELOW: navigating through scenic Ausable Chasm.

Historic cannon and other artifacts are on display at the fort.

Museum (Route 9 and Court Street; tel: 518/873-7477; open mid-May–mid-Oct; entrance fee) focus on the history of the Champlain Valley. Among the highlights are a sound-and-light show about the French and Indian War and a log cabin kitchen. John Brown's wife spent a night at the 1808 Deers Head Inn, one of the Adirondacks' oldest hostelries, while the body of her husband was in the Essex County Court House (Court Street) en route to his final resting place *(see page 233).*

Back on Lake Champlain, south on Route 9N, the Victorian village of **Westport** has a number of historic inns and the Depot Theater (Route 9; tel: 518/962-4449; open June–Sept; entrance fee) headquartered in a restored railway station.

The French built Fort St Frederic in 1734 on what is now **Crown Point State Historic Site** ㉓ (Route 903; tel: 518/597-3666; open mid-May–mid-Oct Wed–Sun; entrance fee). In 1759, the British seized the fortification and rebuilt and renamed it. The visitor center has exhibits on its history and archeology.

The bas-relief *La Belle France* by sculptor Auguste Rodin was presented to the State of New York in 1912 by the French to honor Samuel de Champlain, who discovered Lake Champlain in 1609. It was incorporated into the Champlain Memorial Lighthouse, dedicated in 1909 to replace an earlier beacon at this narrow waist of the lake (tel: 518/597-1309; open Memorial Day–Labor Day, Mon–Fri; entrance fee) on the New York side of the Lake Champlain Bridge.

During the 1800s, a vein of iron ore was discovered at Crown Point and the region became a bustling mining town centralized in an area of town appropriately named Ironville. The Penfield Homestead Historical Museum (Ironville Road; tel: 518/597-3804; open May–June, Sept–Oct Wed–Sun, July–Aug daily; entrance fee), a complex of buildings in the Ironville Historic District, includes the Crown Point Iron Company works and the home of industrialist-inventor

BELOW: flying the flags at Fort Ticonderoga.

Map on pages 226–7

Allen Penfield, who in 1831 became the first person to use electricity for powering industrial machinery.

In 1755 the French built a fort overlooking Lake Champlain to control the waters between the American colonies and Canada. Fort Carillon was seized by the British four years later, and then by Ethan Allen and his Green Mountain Boys in 1775 *(see page 35)*. Two years later the British took the fort back and burned it to the ground. **Fort Ticonderoga** ㉔ (Fort Road; tel. 518/585-2821; open early May–late Oct; entrance fee), rebuilt on its original foundations according to the French plan, is a living history museum housing a world-renowned collection of muskets, powder horns, and artifacts. During July and August there are fife and drum parades, cannon and mortar drills, and musket firings. Tours of the 1920s King's Garden are offered from June to September. There are panoramic views of the lake and surrounding mountains from the top of nearby Mount Defiance (tel: 518/585-2821; open early May–mid-Oct; entrance free). A paved road goes to the overlook, where British cannons are still in place. The Hancock House (Moses Circle; tel: 518/585-7868; open Wed–Sat; donation) is a replica of John Hancock's now demolished house in Boston. The Heritage Museum (Montcalm Street; tel: 518/585-2696; open July–Labor Day daily, June–Oct Sat–Sun; donation) has displays on the technology of mills and local history.

Route 9N continues along the western side of Lake George, through the resort town of **Hague** to **Bolton Landing** ㉕ and the Marcella Sembrich Opera Museum (Route 9N; tel: 518/644-9839; open June–Sept; donation), the "Woodland Retreat" of the celebrated Metropolitan Opera diva who lived here from 1921 to 1934. The collection includes an autographed photo of Enrico Caruso, a 1905 Steinway piano used by Paderewski, and Sembrich's costumes and personal effects. ❑

Militia leader Ethan Allen supposedly demanded surrender of Fort Ticonderoga "in the name of the Great Jehovah and the Continental Congress." But some reports have him bellowing at the British commander, "Come out of there, you damned rat!"

BELOW: a young patriot at the fort's summer parades.

THE THOUSAND ISLANDS AND ST LAWRENCE SEAWAY

Map on pages 226–7

The bordering waterways between Canada and the United States attract a range of water-lovers from canoeists to anglers, but the region also has its fair share of historic mansions and battlefields

New York's "North Coast" encompasses the easternmost of the Great Lakes, Lake Ontario, and the source of one of the world's great rivers, the St Lawrence. The Thousand Islands-St Lawrence Seaway region, which New York State shares with the Canadian province of Ontario, is a realm whose history and economy – as well as the opportunities it offers to visitors – have been defined by water.

The grand river highway between the Great Lakes and the sea loomed large in the struggles between France and Britain and their Indian allies for control of North America, and Lake Ontario itself was the locale for the opening hostilities of the War of 1812. Nearly a century and a half later, the St Lawrence Seaway became a model of cooperation between nations as Canada and the United States built locks, dredged shallows, and constructed channels to enable ocean-going freighters to pass between the continental heartland and the Atlantic.

Recreation in the region centers upon the uncluttered Lake Ontario shoreline, dotted with state parks, and upon the Thousand Islands, an archipelago that extends eastward for some 35 miles (56 km) of the St Lawrence, beginning at its source. Much of the islands' acreage is parkland, and the bewildering array of channels that run between their wooded shores offers some of the finest boating and fishing in New York State. These are prime waters for pike, bass, and the legendary muskellunge, a toothy fighter that can reach 5 ft (1.4 meters) and 60 lbs (27 kg) in size. The "Muskie" is a fitting denizen for a part of New York where just about everything – lake, river, islands, and seaway – is scaled to heroic proportions.

Much of the route outlined below follows the New York State Seaway Trail, a 454-mile (730-km) scenic driving route that parallels Lake Erie, the Niagara River, Lake Ontario, and the St Lawrence River.

Along Lake Ontario

Oswego ㉖, at the mouth of the Oswego River, got its name from the Native American "Osh-we-geh," meaning "pouring out place." Although the river is one of the few in the United States that flows north, the city is a popular starting point for 24-mile (40-km) barge canal trips "down" river to Three Rivers. The Oswego County department of Promotion and Tourism publishes a free guide called *Oswego River Canalling* (County Office Building, 46 East Bridge Street, Oswego 13126; tel: 315/349-8322), which tells about historical points en route. Exhibits at the H. Lee White Marine Museum (West First Street Pier;

LEFT: making a friend at Wellesley State Park.
BELOW: sightseeing on the St Lawrence River.

By some estimates, there are actually some 2,000 islands in the Thousand Islands region of the St Lawrence River. But many island-counters come up with fewer than 1,000, insisting that an "island" has to support at least one tree.

tel: 315/342-0480; open Memorial Day–Sept; entrance fee) focus on the history of the Oswego harbor and Lake Ontario. The museum's tugboat LT-5, active in the 1944 invasion of Normandy, is anchored in the harbor. In 1755 the British built Fort Ontario State Historic Site (Foot of E. 7th Street; tel: 315/343-4711; open May–Sept Wed–Sun and Mon holidays; entrance fee) to protect their interests in the region and remained here 20 years after the Revolution ended, attempting to make the fledgling government reimburse British loyalists for property it seized. The fort was attacked and rebuilt four times, most recently in 1844. During World War II it served as the only refugee camp in the US for Holocaust victims. Today it's a living history museum, with costumed guides giving tours of the buildings. The Italianate Richardson-Bates House Museum (135 E. 3rd Street; tel: 315/343-1342; open Tues–Sun; entrance fee), built around 1867, has five period rooms with Victorian furnishings.

Head north on Route 104B, past Selkirk Shores State Park. Detour east on Route 13, alongside the Salmon River through **Pulaski**, the self-proclaimed "Salmon Capital" where, with advance reservations, guests can stay overnight at the 1838 Selkirk Lighthouse (6 Lake Road Extension; tel: 315/298-6688). More than 4 million trout and salmon are raised each year at the Salmon River Hatchery (2133 County Route 22; tel: 315/298-5051; open Mar–Nov daily; entrance free) in **Altmar** for the stocking of lakes Erie, Ontario, and Champlain *(see page 361)* and their tributaries. Spawning seasons – salmon in October and steelhead in late March/early April – are the most interesting times.

Back on Route 104B, continue to the resort town of **Sackets Harbor** ㉗, on the shores of Black River Bay. The Seaway Trail Discovery Center (West Main and Ray streets; tel: 800/732-9298 or 315/646-1000; open May–Oct daily, call

BELOW: the catch of the day.

Map
on pages
226–7

Stained-glass
windows are part of
the decoration at
Boldt Castle.

for Nov–Apr hours; entrance fee) has nine rooms of information on the trail in a newly restored 1817 limestone Federal-style building. During the War of 1812 two battles were fought on what is now Sackets Harbor Battlefield State Historic Site (505 W. Washington Street; tel: 315/646-3634; open Memorial Day–Labor Day Wed–Sun; entrance free). Several of the original buildings have been restored. Many of the buildings at Madison Barracks (85 Worth Road; tel: 315/646-3374; open year-round; entrance free), a military post during and after the War of 1812, have also been restored. The property is now an apartment complex and guests can sleep in the quarters occupied by Ulysses Grant when he was a young officer here in the late 1840s. Kids learn about farming while having fun at Old McDonald's Children's Village (14471 County Route 145; tel: 583-5737; open May–Oct; entrance fee), where more than 200 tame animals live in their own "fantasy" village in the middle of a working dairy farm.

Watertown ㉘ is the headquarters of several whitewater rafting companies and the Jefferson County Historical Society Museum (228 Washington Street; tel: 315/782-3491; open year-round except major holidays; entrance fee), set in an 1878 mansion with High Victorian furnishings, American Indian artifacts, and Civil War memorabilia.

Head out toward Cape Vincent on Route 12E, through **Brownville** ㉙, home to the 150-year-old Brown Mansion (216 Brown Boulevard; tel: 315/782-7650; open year-round; call for hours). Chaumont Barrens (Van Alstyne Road; tel: 716/546-8030, ext 21; open daily) in **Chaumont** ㉚ is a 2-sq-mile (5-sq-km) "alvar" landscape characterized by windswept vegetation, and is the only place in the northeastern US to see the prairie smoke flower. Chaumont Bay is the largest freshwater bay in the world.

BELOW: Boldt
Castle dominates
Heart Island.

This St Lawrence skiff-putt is part of the Antique Boat Museum collection.

Northwest of Three Mile Bay turn off Route 12E onto Route 6 to the tip of **Cape Vincent** ③. Here, the 1854 Tibbetts Point Lighthouse (33469 Route 6; tel: 315/654-2481), now a visitor's center and youth hostel, stands where the St Lawrence River flows out of Lake Ontario. In town, the Cape Vincent Historical Museum (James Street; tel: 315/654-4400; open July–Aug daily; donation) has displays on local history. Horne's Ferry (Horne's Dock: tel: 315/783-0638; open May–late Oct; fee) transports vehicles across the St Lawrence to Wolfe Island, in Canada.

Along the river and Seaway

Follow Route 12E along the banks of the St Lawrence to **Clayton** ③, a one-time shipbuilding and lumbering port surrounded on three sides by water. One of the region's most impressive museums is the Antique Boat Museum (750 Mary Street; tel: 315/686-4104; open mid-May–mid-Oct daily; entrance fee), with the world's largest collection of inland recreational boats. Visitors can ride in a triple-cockpit mahogany Hacker Craft, lunch on a 40-ft (12-meter) pleasure cruiser, and row a replica of an early 20th-century St Lawrence River Skiff.

The works of some of the country's finest artists are on exhibit at the American Handweaving Museum/Thousand Islands Craft School (314 John Street; tel: 315/686-4123; open Jan–June Mon–Fri, July–Dec Mon–Sat; donation). The Thousand Island Museum (403 Riverside Drive; tel: 315/686-5794; open July–Labor Day daily; entrance fee), in a historic 1903 Town Hall and Opera House, replicates an early 20th-century village square and displays exhibits on local history as well as an excellent collection of muskies and decoys. The 1897 Thousand Islands Inn (335 Riverside Drive; tel: 315/686-3030

BELOW:
the Martello tower at Sackets Harbor on Lake Ontario.

TODAY'S NORTHWEST PASSAGE

From the time of Jacques Cartier's discovery of the St Lawrence River in 1535, explorers and entrepreneurs sought to exploit this great waterway as an avenue of trade. At first, the goal was the elusive "Northwest Passage" to the Orient. But as North America's true geography was puzzled out, the more immediate object was to use the St Lawrence to reach the Great Lakes.

The first obstacle was the shallow Lachine Rapids near the island of Montreal. Dollier de Casson, the Sulpician priest who more or less ran Montreal in the late 17th century, partially completed a canal around the rapids, but his work was abandoned as too costly. For the next 150 years, canoes and other shallow-draft vessels were all that the river would admit. By the 1830s, Canadians had built the Lachine Canal and Welland canals to bypass rapids between Montreal and Lake Ontario. In 1932, Canada completed the fourth Welland Canal, enabling vessels of up to 23½-ft (7-meter) draft to reach Lake Erie.

But that wasn't enough. Recognizing the need to modernize passage along the length of the St Lawrence so that merchant vessels could move between the Canadian-US heartland and the Atlantic, the two nations agreed in the 1950s to create the St Lawrence Seaway.

Map
on pages
226–7

or 800/544-4241) is the last of the more than two dozen grand hostelries built to lodge the masses of tourists that thronged to the region in the late 1800s.

To learn about agriculture in this part of the state, detour southeast on Route 180 for 12 miles (18 km) to the Northern New York Agricultural Historical Society Museum (Route 180; tel: 315/658-2353; open June–late Sept Wed–Mon and May by appointment; entrance fee) in **Stone Mills** ㉝, a 38-acre (15-hectare) complex including an 1873 meeting house, a one-room schoolhouse, and a carriage house with antique wagons. Farm crafts are demonstrated on weekends.

Thousand Island salad dressing was first served to the public in the dining room of the Thousand Islands Inn in the early 1900s.

The Thousand Islands International Bridge, opened in 1938 by Canadian Prime Minister William Lyon Mackenzie King and US President Franklin D. Roosevelt, is actually three bridges in one – a 4,500-ft (1,500-meter) suspension bridge, and two smaller rigid-frame arch spans. The (toll) bridge crosses to 2,630-acre (1,060-hectare) **Wellesley Island State Park** ㉞ (tel: 315/482-2722; open year-round; entrance fee in summer), a terrific place to swim and picnic. The 600-acre (240-hectare) Minna Anthony Common Nature Center (44927 Cross Island Road; tel: 315/482-2479; open daily; entrance free), inside the park, has a museum, hiking trails and wildlife sanctuary. At the end of the island is Thousand Islands Park, a community of brightly colored Victorian homes.

Hart House (tel: 315/482-5683 or 888/481-5683), now an elegant bed-and-breakfast, was part of the original 80-room mansion that George C. Boldt, owner of New York City's Waldorf-Astoria Hotel *(see page 141)*, moved here when he bought Hart (now Heart) Island. One of the Thousand Island's other major attractions is accessible via water taxi from the docks of the busy tourist village of **Alexandria Bay** ㉟. In 1900 Boldt began construction of a 120-room Rhineland-style castle, complete with a drawbridge and Italian gardens, for his

BELOW: barge traffic on the St Lawrence Seaway.

Map
on pages
226-7

wife. When she died unexpectedly in 1904, he immediately ceased work and Boldt Castle (Heart Island; tel: 315/482-2520; open mid-May–mid-Oct; entrance fee), 80 percent completed, fell into disrepair. Since 1977, millions of dollars have been spent restoring the structure and the Yacht House, with its collection of antique wooden boats (a free shuttle transports visitors from Heart Island).

Continue north on routes 12/37 to reach the Frederic Remington Art Museum (303 Washington Street; tel: 315/393-2425; open Wed–Sun; entrance fee) in **Ogdensburg** ㊱, at the junction of the Oswegatchie and St Lawrence rivers. The artist, born in nearby Canton, is renowned for his paintings and bronzes of soldiers, cowboys, and Native Americans. The museum houses the country's largest collection of his works as well as his tools, personal notes, and furnishings from his home. The Ogdensburg-Prescott International Bridge (1 Bridge Plaza; tel: 315/393-3620; toll) into Canada is the world's 18th-longest suspension bridge. Plaques in Greenbelt Riverfront Park (Riverside Drive; tel: 315/393-1980) chronicle the War of 1812 Battle of Ogdensburg. Soldiers from both sides sought protection in the 1809–10 Custom House (127 Water Street), the country's oldest federal government building.

Observing the Seaway

BELOW:
antiques shop on
Wellesley Island.
RIGHT: pit-stop on
the St Lawrence at
Alexandria Bay.

Since it opened to commercial trade in 1959, more than 1.5 billion tons of cargo have been transported through the St Lawrence Seaway. In **Massena** ㊲, the observation deck at the Dwight D. Eisenhower Visitors' Center (Barnhart Island Road; tel: 315/769-2049; open Memorial Day–Labor Day; entrance free) provides a perfect vantage point for watching vessels navigate the Eisenhower Locks, where 22 million gallons of water are used during each transit to raise and lower ships more than 100 ft (30 meters) in less than 10 minutes. The center has exhibits both on the Seaway and President Eisenhower. Drive underneath the Seaway's Wiley-Dondero Ship Canal to the St Lawrence-FDR Power Project Visitors Center (Barnhart Island Road; tel: 315/764-0226, ext 304 or 800 262-6972; open daily; entrance free), where hands-on displays teach you how electricity is made. There are panoramic views of the countryside and the Moses-Saunders Power Dam from the observation deck, 116 ft (35 meters) above the river. Civil War artifacts, period furnishings, and boxing gloves that belonged to John L. Sullivan are among exhibits at the Massena Museum (200 East Orvis Street; tel: 315/769-8571; open Mon–Fri; entrance free).

Hogansburg ㊳, where the St Lawrence and St Regis rivers meet, is the sovereign land of the St Regis Indian Reservation, also called Akwesasne ("Where the Ruffed Grouse Drums"). The Akwesasne Cultural Museum and Learning Center (Route 37; tel: 518/358-2240; open Mon–Sat; donation) preserves the culture of the Akwesasne Mohawk people, whose history dates back thousands of years. The museum has more than 3,000 artifacts, including photographs, medicine masks, and a collection of black-ash splint baskets. The Akwesasne Mohawk Casino (Route 37; tel: 518/358-2222; open year-round; entrance free) has more than 1,000 slot machines and a variety of gaming tables. ❑

CENTRAL-LEATHERSTOCKING

Map
on page
250

From sports meccas to Revolutionary war sites and riverside villages, the once industrial central region of New York State today offers plenty of attractions for tourists

New York

S
mack in the middle of New York State lies the Central-Leatherstocking region, a land of lush hills, glimmering lakes, one-stoplight hamlets, Revolutionary War sites, family farms, languishing industrial towns, and the mighty Mohawk River. The nickname "Leatherstocking," referring to the leather leggings worn by the area's early Yankee settlers, originates from the writer James Fenimore Cooper, America's first internationally recognized writer, who grew up in this once densely forested region and set many of his novels here, including *The Pioneers (see page 65)*.

Cooperstown

Many travelers begin their tour of Central-Leatherstocking in James Fenimore's hometown, **Cooperstown ❶**, first settled in 1790 by his father, William Cooper. Now home to the world-renowned National Baseball Hall of Fame, Cooperstown likes to think of itself as "the most famous small town in America." It centers on an old-fashioned Main Street lined with lots of small businesses, a towering flag pole, and one lone traffic light. To the town's immediate north lies deep, spring-fed Otsego Lake, often dotted with brightly colored sailboats, while all around are gentle, green rolling hills.

The **National Baseball Hall of Fame and Museum** (25 Main Street; tel: 607/547-7200; open daily; entrance fee) sits near the eastern end of town, a handsome, three-story brick edifice, always crowded with eager fans of all ages. Established in 1939, the museum is packed with exhibits covering every conceivable aspect of America's favorite pastime. Plenty of memorabilia is on display, such as Jackie Robinson's warm-up jacket, Hank Aaron's locker, and Willie Mays' glove, along with exhibits devoted to such subjects as famous ballparks, the World Series, women's baseball, all-star games and baseball stamps.

Just down Main Street from the Hall of Fame are a multitude of baseball souvenir shops selling everything from T-shirts to baseball cards, and Doubleday Field, the oldest baseball diamond in the world. The site of the first official game, played in 1839, the field is available for rent and is very popular among amateur teams. Adjoining the field is Doubleday Batting Range (tel: 607/547-5168), where aspiring ballplayers can test their skills against an adjustable Tru-Pitch machine – the same kind used by the major leagues.

But Cooperstown is home to much more than baseball. Less than 1 mile (2 km) from the village center are two more first-class museums, both run by the New York State Historical Association, and the 1902 Otesaga Hotel (60 Lake Road, Route 80; tel: 607/547-9931 or 800/348-6222). One of the state's grandest

PRECEDING PAGES: autumn harvest. **LEFT:** the rustic life. **BELOW:** sculpture of Babe Ruth at the National Baseball Hall of Fame.

The grand Otesaga Hotel serves a fantastic buffet lunch.

historic hotels, the Otesaga boasts stately columns out front and a wide inviting porch overlooking Otsego Lake out back – the perfect place for a cool drink on a summer's day.

The Fenimore Art Museum (Lake Road; tel: 607/547-1400; open May–Sept daily, Oct–Apr Tues–Sun; entrance fee) holds the state's premier collection of folk art, fine art, and Native American art. The main exhibits are housed in a historic mansion, with rooms devoted to such subjects as landscape painting and the Cooper family, while downstairs is the $10 million wing built in 1995 to house the Eugene and Clare Thaw Collection of American Indian Art. Perhaps the most important privately owned collection of its kind, the assemblage includes about 700 works spanning 2,500 years of Native American culture.

Across the street from the Fenimore stands the Farmers' Museum (Lake Road; tel: 607/547-1400; open May–Sept daily, Oct–Apr Tues–Sun; entrance fee), a living history village composed of over a dozen pre-Civil War buildings. Founded in 1943 and one of the first of its kind in the country, the museum is

spread out along one wide street, lined with a general store, printing office, early wallpaper "factory," church, farmstead, doctor's office, and pharmacy. In the Main Barn near the entrance hang intriguing exhibits on early American rural life, while everywhere guides in period dress demonstrate nearly forgotten arts such as broom-making and blacksmithing. One of the museum's more idiosyncratic exhibits is its 2,900-lb (1,300-kg) Cardiff Giant. Supposedly unearthed in nearby Cardiff in 1869 by a local farmer, the sleeping stone man drew thousands of visitors from all over the country and was declared to be authentic by at least one Harvard professor. Only after the farmer had raked in tens of thousands of dollars was the statue proven to be a hoax.

At the northern end of Otsego Lake stands another attraction for which Cooperstown is famous: the Glimmerglass Opera House (7300 Route 80; box office 18 Chestnut Street, tel: 607/547-2255). During July and August, an acclaimed opera festival takes place in this partially open-air theater beneath the stars; tickets must be reserved well in advance.

Also at the northern end of Otsego Lake is the serene **Glimmerglass State Park** (East Lake Road, off Country Road 31; tel: 607/547-8662; open daily; entrance fee in summer), featuring a wide swimming beach, hiking trails and a neo-classical mansion known as Hyde Hall. After decades of disrepair, Hyde Hall is now being meticulously restored (tel: 607/547-5098; tours May–Oct).

Head 2 miles (3 km) northwest of Cooperstown on Route 28/80 to reach the tiny hamlet of **Fly Creek**, home to the Cooperstown Bat Company (tel: 607/547-2415). In this factory-shop, visitors can watch baseball bats being cut and turned, or buy personalized bats engraved with their names. Also of interest is the 1856 Fly Creek Cider Mill (288 Goose Street, off Route 28/80; tel: 607/547-9692),

Map on page 250

TIP

During summer, when Cooperstown crawls with traffic, park in one of the park-and-ride lots on routes 80 and 28 and ride the free trolley into town.

BELOW:
Otsego Lake at Cooperstown.

where apples are pressed in a wooden, water-powered cider mill. All original equipment is used and lots of homemade apple products, including cider and apple butter, are for sale.

Caves and valleys

Old-time skills are demonstrated at the Farmers' Museum.

From Cooperstown, it's about a half-hour drive south on Route 28 and southwest on Interstate 88 to **Oneonta ❷**, a small city on whose outskirts is another sports mecca – the National Soccer Hall of Fame (18 Stadium Circle, off Brown Street, Exit 13 off Interstate 88; tel: 607/432-3351; open June–Sept daily; call for off-season hours; entrance fee). Housed in a state-of-the-art complex situated on a 61-acre (25-hectare) campus, the museum traces the history of soccer in the US from its 1860 beginnings to the present. Included are a Hall of Fame atrium, exhibits on famous games and famous players, film and video clips, and lots of interactive games aimed at both adults and kids. Out back stretch nine soccer fields on which tournaments are played throughout the summer; teams of all ages and abilities come here from all over the country to compete.

Interstate 88 heads northeast from Oneonta to **Howes Cave**, about an hour's drive away. Though not much of a town, Howes Cave boasts by far the oldest and most commercialized tourist attraction in central New York, **Howe Caverns ❸** (Caverns Road, off Route 7, Exit 22 off Interstate 88; tel: 518/296-8990; open daily; entrance fee). An underground labyrinth of cathedral-like caves filled with gleaming stalactites and stalagmites, Howe Caverns were discovered in 1842 by farmer Lester Howe, who soon began conducting torturous eight-hour cave tours involving much scrambling. A modern-day visit is a much easier affair: it begins with an elevator ride descending 156 ft (47 meters), proceeds

BELOW: the Main Barn at the Farmers' Museum

along paved walkways lit by blue and pink lights, and culminates with a boat ride on a small, mysterious underground lake. Guides with megaphones describe the caverns' history and highlights along the way.

Spelunking fans might also want to stop at the nearby Secret Caverns (Caverns Road; tel: 518/296-8558; open Memorial Day–Labor Day daily; Sept–Oct and Apr–May Sat–Sun; entrance fee). Considerably less commercialized than Howe Caverns, the Secret Caverns have been left in as natural a state as possible. Stone steps lead down to the caves, complete with a thundering, 100-ft-high (30-meter) underground waterfall, and there are no megaphones or boat rides here.

Also not far from Howe Caverns is the Iroquois Indian Museum (Caverns Road; tel: 518/296-8949; open Apr–Dec daily; entrance fee), a modern edifice designed in the shape of an Iroquois longhouse. Both historic artifacts, including arrowheads and pottery, and modern Native American art such as watercolors and baskets, are on display. Special programs featuring dance and crafts demonstrations are presented on the weekends. Downstairs is a Children's Museum, with many hands-on exhibits, and upstairs is an excellent bookshop.

Route 7 heads east out of Howes Cave toward the quaint, historic town of **Schoharie** ❹. The hamlet centers on the 1874 Schoharie Pharmacy & Soda Fountain (261 Main Street; tel: 518/295-7300), equipped with an antique soda fountain serving over 20 flavors of ice cream sodas, and the Old Stone Fort Museum (North Main Street; tel: 518/295-7192; open May–Oct Tues–Sun; entrance fee). Built in 1772, the gray stone complex was ferociously attacked by the British in 1780, but never gave way. On display are war artifacts from the Revolution through to World War II, and exhibits on early rural New York life.

Map on page 250

To date, over 350 weddings have taken place underground in Howe Caverns.

BELOW: exploring Howe Caverns.

Out back there are a restored carriage shed, schoolhouse, and period barns.

From Schoharie, head north on Routes 30 and 30A to reach Route 20. Now a quiet highway traveling through much idyllic countryside, Route 20 was once known as the Great Western Turnpike. Many early 19th-century settlers, impatient with the stony farmlands of New England, traveled along here to reach what would become the great grain fields of the Midwest.

Cherry Valley is named for the wild cherries that thrive in the surrounding countryside.

One of the major stops along Route 20 in those days was **Cherry Valley** ❺, which in 1815 boasted 15 taverns, its own marble works, iron foundries, tanneries, and distilleries. However, the building of the Erie Canal in 1825, followed soon thereafter by construction of the New York Central Railroad, diverted traffic away from Cherry Valley, turning it into the sleepy village that it is today. To get a taste of the area's past, stop into the Cherry Valley Museum (49 Main Street; tel: 607/264-3303; open daily Memorial Day–Oct; entrance fee), which houses everything from 19th-century ink wells and children's clothes to Civil War uniforms and an 1885 fire engine.

The Mohawk River Valley

Directly north of Cherry Valley and Route 20 runs the wide Mohawk River, named after the Mohawk Indians, an Iroquois tribe who first settled the area some 10,000 years ago. Much later, in the 1720s, the German and Dutch arrived, establishing farms along the river, and during the Revolutionary War the area's loyalties were badly divided between its many resident Tories and their Mohawk allies and the Colonials. The Erie Canal follows large sections of the Mohawk River, and from the mid-1800s until the mid-1900s, the Mohawk River Valley was known for its many industries, manufacturing everything from carpets to clothing, baby foods to bubble gum. Only a few of these factories are still in operation today.

BELOW: Little Falls in the fall.

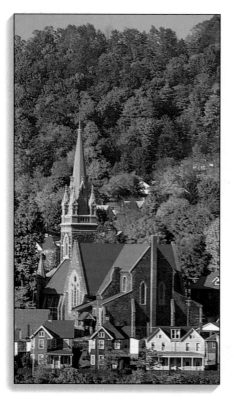

One stop well worth making in the Mohawk River Valley is the small town of **Canajoharie** ❻, Iroquois for "The Pot That Washes Itself." The name comes from a large geological pothole in a gorge just south of the village, while in the town proper is the Canajoharie Library and Art Gallery (2 Erie Boulevard; tel: 518/673-2314; open Mon–Sat; entrance free). Upstairs, the place appears to be nothing more than a simple local library, but downstairs is a vaulted hall which houses a small but stunning collection of paintings by such American masters as Winslow Homer, Thomas Eakins, and Albert Bierstadt.

About 15 miles (20 km) east of Canajoharie lies **Auriesville** ❼, home to one of the region's more unusual attractions, the National Shrine of the North American Martyrs (Route 5s at Noeltner Road; tel: 518/853-3033; open May–Oct daily; entrance free). Spread out over a shaded, park-like area that contains a large church, chapel, and the Stations of the Cross, the National Shrine is dedicated to Father Isaac Joques and seven other Jesuit priests who were killed by the Mohawks in the 1640s *(see page 28)*. In 1930, the Catholic Church canonized the eight martyrs as the first saints of North America, and the shrine attracts busloads of pilgrims throughout the summer.

Auriesville was also the birthplace of the Blessed

Map on page 250

Kateri Tekakwitha, born in 1656 to a Christian Algonquin mother and a Mohawk chief. Tekakwitha was the first laywoman in North America honored as "Blessed," and is said to have performed many miracles. A shrine dedicated to her memory, the Kateri Tekakwitha Memorial Shrine (Route 5; tel: 518/853-3646; open May–Oct daily; entrance free), is located in nearby **Fonda ❽**. On site are a snug wooden church, the Stations of the Cross and the Mohawk-Caughnawaga Museum, with a large collection of Iroquois artifacts and modern art, and the only completely excavated Native American village in the US.

From Fonda, Route 5 wanders leisurely westward past the picturesque hamlets of Palatine Bridge and St Johnsville. On Route 10 just north of Palatine Bridge is **Stone Arabia ❾**, home to two lovely churches, the 1788 Stone Arabia Reformed Church and the 1792 Stone Arabia Trinity Lutheran Church. In **St Johnsville ❿** is Fort Klock, a restored homestead and fur trading post originally built in 1750 (Route 5; tel: 518/568-7779; open Memorial Day–Oct Tues–Sun; entrance fee). An early 19th-century schoolhouse, blacksmith's shop, cheese house, and Dutch barn stand behind the house, moved here from nearby areas.

Next along Route 5 comes **Little Falls ⓫**, a former Erie Canal mill town that now features an appealing restored waterfront lined with a dozen or so restaurants and shops. Little Falls is also home to Lock 17, which at 40 ft (12 meters) tall is one of the highest lift locks in the world. Tankers and pleasure craft still pass through here daily. On Route 169, about 3 miles (5 km) southeast of downtown Little Falls, stands the **Herkimer Home State Historic Site ⓬** (tel: 315/823-0398; open May–Oct Wed–Sat, call for hours off-season; entrance fee). The restored home of Revolutionary War General Nicholas Herkimer, who led the Colonial militia in the bloody Battle of Oriskany *(see page 35)*, the

BELOW: rolling along through central New York.

Playful pumpkins make good autumn decorations.

house was once considered to be one of the grandest homes in the Mohawk River Valley. Costumed guides now conduct tours of the homestead.

Not far from Little Falls is **Ilion** ⓭, a small but congested town that has been the site of the Remington Arms Factory since 1816. The plant was founded by Eliphalet Remington, Jr, who made his first rifle at his father's forge, and the company is still one of the area's largest employers. The factory houses the small Remington Firearms Museum, showcasing both antique and modern firearms, and offers guided tours during the week (14 Hoefler Avenue; tel: 315/895-3200 or 800/243-9700; museum open Mon–Sat; call for tour information; entrance free).

Utica

Just beyond Ilion lies **Utica** ⓮, Central-Leatherstocking's largest city with a population of almost 70,000. Once an important industrial city, best known for its knitting mills, Utica has since fallen on hard times, but is still filled with handsome, early 20th-century buildings, many of them located downtown along Genesee Street, as well as several other attractions worth a stop.

Foremost among them is the Munson-Williams-Proctor Institute (310 Genesee Street; tel: 315/797-0000; open daily; entrance free), housed in a building designed by Philip Johnson. A first-class institution that's both an art museum and a performing arts center, it contains more than 5,000 works by the likes of Pablo Picasso, Salvador Dali, Henry Moore and Hudson River School painter Thomas Cole *(see page 199)*. The Fountain Elms, an Italianate villa once lived in by the Proctor and Munson families, is next door to the art museum.

Not far from the Munson-Williams-Proctor Institute is a completely different

BELOW:
land of the giants.

Map on page 250

type of visitor attraction, the Matt Brewery (Court and Varick streets; tel: 315/732-0022 or 800/765-6288; tours daily, call for hours and reservations; entrance fee). One of the oldest breweries in the nation, founded in 1888, the Matt Brewery is the maker of Saranac beer, among others, and when operating at full capacity can produce 2.4 million bottles of beer a day. Guides in period dress take visitors through the plant, past the brewhouse, refrigerated tanks, and bottling department. The tour ends with a stop in a restored 1888 tavern, where visitors are offered a complimentary mug of draft or root beer.

A good stop for families traveling through the city is the popular Utica Zoo (Steele Hill Road at Memorial Parkway; tel: 315/738-0472; open daily; entrance fee), located next door to the Roscoe Conkling Park, designed by Frederick Law Olmsted of Central Park fame *(see page 143)*. The zoo houses about 300 species of mammals, birds, and reptiles, as well as a Children's Zoo. Another good stop for families is the Children's Museum (311 Main Street; tel: 315/724-6129; open Tues–Sun; entrance fee), thought by many to be the finest children's museum between New York City and Toronto. The cheery establishment has a wide variety of hands-on exhibits for all ages, along with a re-created Native American longhouse and a laser light experimentation station.

From Utica, it's a short drive northwest on Route 69 to the **Oriskany Battlefield** ⓑ (Route 69; tel: 315/768-7224; open May–Labor Day Wed–Mon; entrance fee), marked by a 100-ft-tall (30-meter) obelisk. Now a National Park, Oriskany was the site of the bloodiest battle of the American Revolution. Hundreds of British and American soldiers were killed and the US General Nicholas Herkimer was fatally wounded *(see page 35)*. Today, a small museum commemorates the battle and National Park rangers offer tours of the site.

BELOW: the Fountain Elms villa is now a museum.

Rome to Canastota

Route 69 continues northwest to **Rome** ⑯, another large upstate city that has fallen on hard times in recent decades. Much of downtown Rome was razed during the urban renewal projects of the 1960s, giving the city an oddly flat and empty feel. For tourists, Rome's primary attraction is the Fort Stanwix National Monument (112 East Park Street; tel: 315/336-2090; open Apr–Dec daily; entrance fee), also run by the National Park Service. Built in 1976, the monument is said to be one of the most accurately reconstructed log-and-earth fortifications in the world. Included within its sturdy bulwarks are barracks, a guard house, sentry boxes, officers' quarters, and a small museum. Special events are often staged. The original Fort Stanwix was built by the British in 1758 at the headwaters of the Mohawk River. The Americans captured the fort in 1776, and in 1777 successfully withstood a three-week-long siege waged by the British. Thereafter, the settlement was renamed Rome, in tribute to the "heroic defense of the Republic made here."

Not far from Fort Stanwix is the Rome Historical Society Museum (200 Church Street; tel: 315/336-5870; open year round Mon-Fri, July–Aug Sat–Sun; entrance free). Exhibits showcase everything from the area's colonial past to its more recent industrial history. Also in Rome, a few miles west of Fort Stanwix, is the Erie Canal Village (Erie Boulevard, Route 46/49w; tel: 315/337-3999; open Memorial Day– Labor Day daily; entrance fee). Built along the banks of the original Erie Canal, the village re-creates the life of 19th-century canawlers, or canal workers. The attractive settlement, composed of buildings moved here from throughout the area, includes a 1858 Canal Store, the 1862 Verona Cheese Factory, and the 1862 Bennett's Tavern, which still serves cold draft and root beer, pretzels, and pickled eggs. Visitors can also climb aboard the packet boat *Independence*, pulled along the canal by mules; rides last about 45 minutes.

Southwest of Rome and just north of **Oneida** ⑰ is the big, glitzy Turning Stone Casino (5218 Patrick Road, Exit 33 off Interstate 90, Verona; tel: 315/361-7711 or 800/771-7711; open daily). The first legal casino in New York State, opened in 1993 (a second one has since opened in Akwesasne, near the Canadian border), the Turning Stone offers blackjack, craps, roulette, baccarat and other games, along with a large luxury hotel, a golf course, and upscale boutiques and restaurants. There are no slot machines, however, and no liquor is served in the casino.

Meanwhile in Oneida proper, a genteel town of wide, shady streets and plush lawns, is the Mansion House (170 Kenwood Avenue; tel: 315/363-0745; tours offered Wed–Sun, call for hours; entrance fee). Once home to the Oneida Community, a Utopian society that flourished in the mid-1800s, the handsome redbrick house contains many photographs, letters and historical documents from the community's heyday. Tours of the house are led by descendants of the original Oneida Society, and just down the street is the Oneida Silversmiths Factory Store (606 Sherrill Road, Sherrill Shopping Center; tel: 315/361-3661), which offers discounts on traditional Oneida flatware.

Travelers interested in Native American history and

BELOW: Fort Stanwix National Monument.

Map on page 250

culture will want to visit the Shako:Wi Cultural Center, housing the simple but interesting Oneida Nation Museum and a gift shop stocked with books and handicrafts (5 Territory Road, Route 46S; tel: 315/363-1424; open daily; entrance free). Exhibits showcase archeological artifacts, historical photographs, silverwork, and beadwork.

Route 5 heads west from Oneida to the cozy, old-fashioned town of **Canastota ⑱**, where many historic buildings still line the old Erie Canal. The Canal Town Museum downtown (122 North Canal Street; tel: 315/697-3451; open June–Aug Mon–Sat; Apr–May and Sept–Oct Tues–Fri; entrance free) is a casual place filled with exhibits depicting the history of the canal and local businesses. On the outskirts of town, the International Boxing Hall of Fame Museum (1 Hall of Fame Drive, Exit 34 off Interstate 90; tel: 315/697-7095; open daily; entrance fee) is housed in a modern building showcasing the robes, gloves, fist casts, and memorabilia of boxing greats. The museum was founded in Canastota in 1984 largely because two major boxing champs, Carmen Basilio and Billy Backus, were native sons.

Cazenovia and Binghamton

An exceptionally picturesque town to the south of Canastota is **Cazenovia ⑲**. Centered around three unique country inns – the Scottish-themed Brae Loch, the 1835 Lincklaen House, and the 1890 Brewster Inn – Cazenovia boasts a long main street lined with many attractive cafés and tourist-oriented shops.

Abutting the town to the south is Cazenovia Lake, a pristine, deep blue body of water rimmed with fine homes. On the outskirts of Cazenovia, find the Lorenzo State Historic Site (17 Rippleton Road, Route 13; tel: 315/655-3200;

BELOW: children's dance at the Oneida Community.

THE PERFECTIONISTS

Founded by John Humphrey Noyes in 1848, the Oneida Community was one of the longest lasting of the many Utopian societies that were established in the US in the 19th century. Also known as the Perfectionists, the Oneida Community believed that the second coming of Christ had already occurred, in AD 70. Therefore, the human race had already been freed from sin and personal perfection was possible. Men and women should give up all personal property and abandon marital vows in exchange for communal living that could include several sexual partners.

When the Perfectionists first settled in Oneida, they tried to make a living by farming. However, profits proved meager and after several lean years, they turned first to selling canned fruits and vegetables and then to producing the famed flatware that is still manufactured by Oneida Ltd. today. Both sexes shared equally in all the work, taking turns at various menial and managerial jobs. When not working, the Perfectionists improved their minds by reading the Bible and books about science and religion.

At its zenith, the Oneida Community numbered about 300, most living in the handsome Mansion House. In 1879, however, public criticism forced Noyes to move to Canada, and two years later the community disbanded.

Map on page 250

Six elaborate wood-carved carousels dot the Binghamton parks. Rides cost "one piece of litter."

BELOW:
antiques for sale.
RIGHT:
Victorian house.

open May–Oct Wed–Sat; entrance fee). This Federal-style mansion was built in 1793 by John Lincklaen, a land agent for the Holland Land Company, a sort of real estate developer that once controlled 3.3 million acres (1.3 million hectares) in western New York State. Out back is a fine carriage house filled with dozens of horse-drawn vehicles, and during the summer carriage races are staged.

South of Cazenovia much rich farmland flourishes, alternating with stretches of forest and more old-fashioned small towns. On Route 20 between **Madison** and **Bouckville** are an extraordinarily high number of antiques shops, one of the largest groupings in the state. A guide to the shops is available in local business and tourist offices. Colgate University in **Hamilton** (at Broad Street and Kendrick Avenue; tel: 315/228-1000) is built around a quadrangle flanked by early Georgian and neo-Gothic buildings. In **Earlville** ❷⓿, the Earlville Opera House (16 East Main Street; tel: 315/691-3550) is an unusual two-story theater that dates back to 1892. During the summer, much first-rate opera, theater, vaudeville, and music is presented here.

At the southwestern tip of the Central-Leatherstocking region sprawls **Binghamton** ❷❶, with a population of 58,000. Once a major industrial city, best known for its shoe factories, like Utica and Rome it has since fallen on hard times. Nonetheless, the city boasts several attractions. The downtown centers around Courthouse Square, along Court Street between State and Exchange streets. To one side is the neo-classical 1898 Broome County Courthouse, to another a Civil War Monument, and to a third the 1898 Old City Hall. The latter, a magnificent Beaux Arts building with an elegant interior staircase, now houses the upscale Grand Royale Hotel (800 State Street; tel: 607/722-0000 or 800/295-5599), complete with a classy bistro and polished front desk that was once used by the city's police sergeants.

For a dose of science and history, stop into the Roberson Museum and Science Center (30 Front Street; tel: 607/772-0660; open daily; entrance fee), housed in both a grand 1910 mansion and a modern building. You'll find everything from art and history galleries and period rooms to a planetarium and science exhibits. One room is devoted to Binghamton's native son Edwin Link, who developed the Link Flight simulator, and another to the region's folk art and ethnic history. The Roberson also operates the Kopernik Observatory on Underwood Road in nearby Vestal. Equipped with three powerful telescopes, it is open to the public most Friday nights.

Also in Binghamton is the Ross Park Zoo (60 Morgan Road; tel: 607/724-5461; open Apr–Nov daily, Jan–Mar Sat–Sun; entrance fee), the fifth-oldest zoo in the nation. Ross Park houses an unusually wide variety of rare creatures, including white tigers and snow leopards; one of its finest exhibits is "Wolf Woods," where timber wolves roam free.

About 14 miles (20 km) northeast of Binghamton, the **Chenango Valley State Park** (Route 369; tel: 607/648-5251; open daily; entrance fee in summer) beckons. Spread out over 1,000-plus serene acres (400 hectares), the park contains two glacial ponds, lacy waterfalls, an 18-hole golf course, hiking and nature trails, a bathing beach, and fishing sites. ❑

THE FINGER LAKES

Skinny glacial lakes, rolling vineyards, craggy gorges, progressive cities, and social history make this one of the most varied and interesting regions of upstate New York

Maps:
Area 264
City 265

New York

Stretching from Syracuse in the east to Rochester in the west, the Finger Lakes region encompasses six major lakes: Skaneateles, Owasco, Cayuga, Seneca, Keuka, and Canandaigua, as well as a handful of smaller ones. Exploring here means taking many winding back roads that loop in and out, up and down, past one lake after another, with lots of sleepy country hamlets and a few aging industrial towns in between.

When the French explorers first arrived in the Finger Lakes area in the 1600s, they found it already occupied by a confederacy of five Iroquois nations: the Mohawks, Seneca, Onondaga, Cayuga, and Oneida (a sixth, the Tuscarora, joined the confederacy in 1722). During the Revolution, all of the Iroquois except the Oneida sided with the British, and after the war thousands fled to Canada or were resettled on reservations that still dot the region *(see page 34)*. Many colonial soldiers, impressed by the fertile valleys they had seen during battle, returned to the area and were given land in lieu of payment for their military service. The region developed rapidly, and by the early 1800s, the once dense woodlands had become a busy agricultural region. Then, in 1825, the Erie Canal was completed *(see page 200)* and the Finger Lakes boomed. Inland ports grew up all along the canal and factories flourished. Social and religious movements proliferated as well, as Joseph Smith founded the Mormon religion in Palmyra, William Seward and Harriet Tubman championed the abolitionist movement in Auburn, and the first Women's Rights Convention convened in Seneca Falls. By the early 1900s, however, the Erie Canal had declined in importance, thanks largely to the new railroads, and the region settled down to become the somnolent agricultural land that it is today.

LEFT:
fruit of the vine.
BELOW:
country charms.

Syracuse

Syracuse ❶, the fourth-largest city in the state (population 164,000), marks the gateway to the Finger Lakes. Once known for its many flourishing industries, especially salt, furniture, agricultural tools and Franklin cars, Syracuse is still home to the Niagara Mohawk Power Corporation, Bristol Myers Squibb and Syracuse University, famed for its 50,000-seat Carrier Dome. Like many large cities, Syracuse suffers from its share of urban blight, but its downtown has experienced a small renaissance in recent years, with the restoration of many historic buildings.

The downtown area centers on **Clinton Square Ⓐ**, which once marked the intersection of the Erie Canal (now paved over and known as Erie Boulevard) and the Genesee Valley Turnpike (now Genesee Street). Much of the square is surrounded by mammoth 19th-century buildings, some as elaborate as small castles,

while to one side the **Jerry Rescue Monument** commemorates the rescue of an escaped slave, William "Jerry" McHenry, from a Syracuse jail by a vigilante abolitionist group. The rescue challenged the Fugitive Slave Act of 1850 and was one of the events leading to the Civil War.

Two blocks east of Clinton Square, the **Erie Canal Museum and Visitor Center** Ⓑ (318 Erie Boulevard; tel: 315/471-0593; open daily; entrance free) is housed in an 1850s building that was once a weigh station for Erie Canal boats. Inside is an interesting collection of historical exhibits on the canal and a 65-ft-long (20-meter) reconstructed canal boat. The center is also a good place to pick up tourist literature about Syracuse and the Finger Lakes. Two blocks south, the **Onondaga Historical Association Museum** Ⓒ (321 Montgomery Street; tel: 315/428-1864; open Tues–Fri; entrance free) is one of the finest county museums in the state. Large and well laid out, the museum covers virtually every aspect of the area's history, from early African-American settlers to the 50 breweries that once operated in Syracuse.

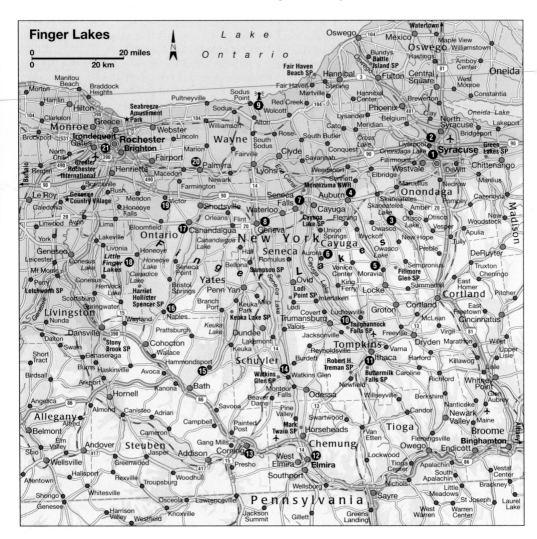

Take West Jefferson Street west of the museum to reach the 1928 **Landmark Theater** (362 South Salina Street; tel: 315/475-7979), an extravagant 2,922-seat auditorium that presents everything from Broadway shows to movies. The Landmark is especially known for its ornate gilded lobby, open weekdays and during performances. Just beyond the Landmark, the **Rubenstein Museum of Science and Technology** E, better known locally as MOST (500 South Franklin Street; tel: 315/425-9068; open daily; entrance fee), is a favorite destination for families. Situated in the old Syracuse Armory, an imposing fortress-like edifice, the museum has exhibits on such subjects as the human body, the earth, and the environment, and includes a planetarium and domed IMAX theater. The MOST sits on the edge of Armory Square, at the junction of Franklin and Walton Streets. Filled with historic brick buildings now housing popular music clubs and restaurants, the square is one of the busiest neighborhoods in Syracuse.

Farther south is the **Everson Museum of Art** F (401 Harrison Street; tel: 315/474-6064; open daily; donation). Housed in a 1968 building designed by I.M. Pei, it contains one of the world's largest collections of ceramics, along with early American portraits. Temporary exhibits usually focus on major American artists, such as Andrew Wyeth or Edward Hopper.

North of Syracuse in the suburb of **Liverpool** ❷ is the living history museum St Marie Among the Iroquois (Onondaga Lake Parkway, Route 370; tel: 315/453-6767; open Wed–Sun; entrance fee). It re-creates the 17th-century world of the French Jesuits and the Iroquois, who once lived side by side on the shores of nearby Onondaga Lake. Costumed guides forge horseshoes and bake bread in a reconstructed French fort, and the handsome museum is filled with artifacts and historical documents. Across the parkway is the Salt Museum

Maps:
Area 264
City 265

TIP

For blues and barbecue, stop into Dinosaur Bar-B-Cue (246 West Willow Street; tel. 315/476-4937). This Syracuse institution is frequented by bikers and bankers alike.

BELOW: winter wonderland.

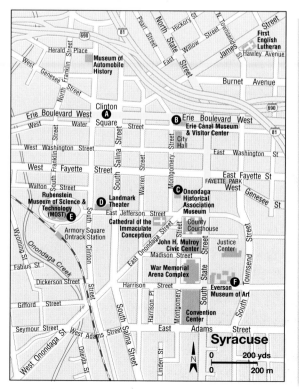

TIP

A 557-mile (890-km) hiking trail runs throughout the Fingers Lakes. For more information and maps, contact the Finger Lakes Trail Conference, P.O. Box 18048, Rochester, NY 14618-0048; tel: 716/288-7191.

(tel: 315/453-6715 or 6767; open May–Oct daily; entrance free). A simple affair with a handful of exhibits, the museum is situated on the edge of Onondaga Lake, whose rich salt deposits – once referred to as "white gold" – first drew settlers to the area. Now, alas, the lake is badly polluted.

Skaneateles and Owasco lakes

From Syracuse, it's a 40-minute drive west to **Skaneateles** ❸, the highest and arguably most beautiful of the six major Finger Lakes. Fifteen miles (20 km) long and 1½ miles (3 km) wide, Skaneateles is spring fed, crystal clear, and surrounded by woods. During the summer, colorful sailboats dot its waters. The only town on the lake is Skaneateles, located at the waters' northern edge. Mostly spread out along one long main street (Route 20), the village is filled with 19th-century wooden homes and brick storefronts, many now housing tourist boutiques, antiques shops, and restaurants. The village's anchor is the **Sherwood Inn** (tel: 315/685-3405 or 800/374-3796), a rambling colonial inn that was once a stagecoach stop and is still the area's premier hostelry.

On the edge of the lake, directly across from the Sherwood Inn, Clift Park is equipped with a small gazebo where bands perform during the summer. Docked at the end of the park's small pier are two classic wooden boats operated by the Mid-Lakes Navigation Co. (tel: 315/685-8500 or 800/545-4318). From May to September, the boats offer sightseeing, lunch and dinner cruises of the lake.

To obtain good land views of Skaneateles Lake, drive south along either Route 41 to the east or Route 41A to the west. Route 41A heads away from the shoreline at the lake's southern end to New Hope Mills (5983 Glen Haven Road; tel: 315/497-0783; open Mon–Sat; entrance free), a still-operating flour

BELOW: trout-fishing at Seneca Lake.

mill that dates from 1823 and is powered by a 26-ft (8-meter) waterwheel.

To the west of Skaneateles Lake is **Owasco Lake**, which at 12 miles (15 km) long is the smallest of the Finger Lakes. Good views of Owasco can be had by taking either Route 38 south, which hugs the lake's western shore, or Route 38A south, which travels on a ridge above the lake to the east.

History buffs will want to visit **Auburn ❹**, at Owasco's northern end. A small industrial city, dotted with many handsome 19th-century buildings, Auburn has been home to a number of remarkable men and women, among them Harriet Tubman, the African-American leader; William H. Seward, the visionary statesman; and Theodore W. Case, the inventor of sound film. Sites connected with each of the three are still standing and open to the public. Near the center of town, the **Seward House** (33 South Street; tel: 315/252-1283; open year-round Tues–Sat, Tues–Sun in summer; entrance fee) is a lovely Federal-style mansion and one of the most interesting house museums in New York State. Almost everything inside is original, including Seward's furniture, top hats, snuff box collection, 10,000 books, tea from the Boston Tea Party, and personal letters from the likes of Abraham Lincoln.

Down the street is the **Harriet Tubman Home** (180 South Street; tel: 315/252-2081; call for hours). Born into slavery in Maryland around 1820, Tubman escaped in her late twenties and thereafter made 19 trips south, rescuing more than 300 slaves. In her later years, Tubman settled in Auburn largely because her close friend and fellow abolitionist, William Seward, lived nearby. Today, her home is a simple affair, equipped with her original bed and Bible, while nearby stands a homespun museum filled with exhibits on famous African-American women. Plans are in the works to greatly expand the museum exhibits.

Map on page 264

The Frederick Douglass monument in Rochester honors the great abolitionist.

BELOW:
Seward House.

The MacKenzie-Childs pottery occupies a lovely old farmstead in Aurora.

Also in Auburn is the **Cayuga Museum and Case Research Lab** (203 Genesee Street; tel: 315/253-8051; open Tues–Sun; entrance free). The museum is devoted to Cayuga County History and is only moderately interesting, but the lab focuses on Theodore Case and his discovery of sound film. Displays include the first sound camera and projector, original lab equipment, and correspondence between Case and Thomas Edison.

At the southern end of Owasco Lake, about a 20-minute drive from Auburn, is **Moravia ⑤**, a small hamlet whose main claim to fame is that it was the birthplace of Millard Fillmore, the 13th president of the United States. He was born in a humble log cabin, a replica of which now stands in the Fillmore Glen State Park (Route 38; tel: 315/497-0130; open daily; entrance fee in summer). Spread out over 857 wooded acres (347 hectares), split by a deep ravine, the park also contains five waterfalls, numerous hiking trails, a small beach, and a campground.

Cayuga Lake

After Owasco Lake comes Cayuga, the longest of the Finger Lakes, stretching out for 38 miles (60 km). Iroquois for "boat landing," Cayuga is known for its good fishing. Carp and large-mouth bass swim in its shallow waters, and in its deeper ones, northern pike and lake trout.

One of the few settlements on Cayuga's eastern shore is **Aurora ⑥**, a picture-perfect 19th-century village that is on the National Register of Historic Places. At the center of town is the Aurora Inn (Main Street, Route 90; tel: 315/364-8888), a hospitable, antiques-filled establishment offering meals, accommodations and free walking tour maps of the village. On the outskirts of town is MacKenzie-Childs (3260 North Main Street, Route 90; tel: 315/364-7123; shop open Mon–Sat, tours Mon–Fri), a classy design studio best known for its terra-cotta pottery.

Seneca Falls ⑦, at the northwestern end of Cayuga Lake, is the small industrial town where the first Women's Rights Convention was held in 1848. The convention came about largely through the efforts of Elizabeth Cady Stanton, who had moved to the town from Boston with her abolitionist husband in 1847 *(see page 38)*. Often home alone, Stanton felt overwhelmed by childcare and housework. She also noticed the worse plight of her poorer neighbors and, on July 13, 1848, shared her discontent with four friends. That led to the planning of the Women's Rights Convention, held only six days later, during which Stanton delivered the Declaration of Sentiments: "We hold these truths to be self-evident; that all men and women are created equal..." About 300 people of both sexes attended.

The history of the convention, its leaders, and the times in which they lived is well documented at the Visitors Center of the **Women's Rights National Historic Park** (136 Fall Street; tel: 315/568-2991; open daily; entrance fee). Run by the National Park Service, the center also contains exhibits on many other women's issues, including employment, fashion, and sports. Next door is the Wesleyan Chapel, where the historic convention took place. Unfortunately, all that remains of the church today are two brick walls and part of the roof, but nearby is a

Map on page 264

140-ft-long (42-meter) wall inscribed with the Declaration of Sentiments.

Also part of the park is the **Elizabeth Cady Stanton House** (32 Washington Street; open daily; entrance free), located about a mile (2 km) from the Visitors Center. Although few original furnishings remain, the house has been meticulously restored and the Visitors Center's rangers give interesting tours of the residence. Nearby is the **National Women's Hall of Fame** (76 Fall Street; tel: 315/568-8060; open May–Oct daily; Nov–Apr Wed–Sun; entrance fee). Though a somewhat static place, it does contain photos, plaques and tape recordings honoring the achievements of dozens of American women working in a variety of fields. The Seneca Falls Historical Society Museum (55 Cayuga Street; tel: 315/568-8412; open year-round Mon–Sat, daily in summer; entrance fee), housed in a handsome Queen Anne-style mansion, contains 23 elaborate period rooms, all outfitted with antiques and mannequins in period dress.

Bird lovers will want to head 5 miles (8 km) east of Seneca Falls to the **Montezuma National Wildlife Refuge** (3395 routes 5 and 20 East; tel: 315/568-5987; open Apr–Nov daily; entrance free). Spread out over 6,300 acres (2,550 hectares) of swamplands, marshlands and fields, the refuge is a haven for migrating and nesting birds; about 315 species have been spotted here since the refuge was established in 1937. On site are a small visitors center, nature trail, driving trail and two observation towers.

To the west of Seneca Falls, past scrappy **Waterloo**, lies **Geneva ❽**, one of the larger towns in the region (population 15,000). South Main Street, which runs through its center, is lined with many fine homes and Hobart and William Smith Colleges. Hobart was once known as the Medical College of Geneva and, in 1847, admitted Elizabeth Blackwell to the incoming class. Blackwell,

BELOW: sunset on Seneca Lake.

who graduated two years later, was the first woman ever granted a medical diploma in the United States.

The only mansion on Geneva's South Main Street that is open to the public is the Federal-style Prouty-Chew House and Museum (543 South Main Street; tel: 315/789-5151; open year-round Mon–Sat, daily in summer; entrance free). Built in 1829 by a Geneva attorney, the house was enlarged several times over the decades and features many period rooms, along with changing exhibits on local history and art. Geneva's best-known visitor attraction, however, is the 1839 **Rose Hill Mansion** (Route 96A; tel. 315/789-3848; open May–Oct daily; entrance fee), which sits on the eastern outskirts of town. Built in a grand Greek Revival style, with six Ionic columns out front, the house was once home to Robert Swan, an innovative farmer who installed the country's first large-scale drainage system on his land. The house is filled with fine Empire-style furniture, while out back is a carriage house.

Lakewood Vineyards has tastings and wines for sale.

Take a 30-mile (50-km) detour north of Geneva on Route 14 to reach **Sodus Point** ❾, overlooking Lake Ontario. The village has lovely lake views, a well-kept public beach, and the 1870 Old Sodus Point Lighthouse and Maritime Museum (7606 North Ontario Street; tel: 315/483-4936; open May–Oct Tues–Sun; entrance free). Sodus Point is also home to the unusual Chimney Bluffs, located on the east side of town off Route 141. Rising up 150 ft (45 meters), the bluffs are all pinnacles, spires and peaks – part of a drumlin (elongated hill carved by a glacier) that has been eroded and shaped by the elements.

BELOW: Finger Lakes is the country's second-largest wine region.

Returning to Seneca Falls, Route 414 meanders south to Route 96, heading toward Trumansburg and Ithaca. Along the way are some of the many vineyards for which the Finger Lakes region is famous *(see page 356)*. Among them

Map on page 264

are the large Swedish Hill Vineyard (4565 Route 414; tel: 315/549-8326 or 800/549-WINE; open daily; entrance free) and the smaller Knapp Winery, Vineyards and Restaurant (2770 County Road 128; tel: 607/869-9271 or 800/869-9271; open daily; entrance free). Both produce excellent wines.

Off Route 96 just south of Trumansburg is the **Taughannock Falls State Park** ❿ (Route 89; tel: 607/387-6739; open daily; entrance fee in summer). Centering on a skinny, 215-ft-tall (65-meter) waterfall, the park offers lake swimming, fishing, boating, hiking, and an imaginative playground for kids. During the summer, a wide variety of concerts are presented here.

Ithaca and Elmira

South of Trumansburg, at the very southern tip of Cayuga Lake, the small, progressive city of **Ithaca** ⓫ is home to both Cornell University and Ithaca College. The city's downtown is compact and flat, but all around are steep hills, gorges, and waterfalls. Ithaca Commons, in the middle of Ithaca's downtown, is a pedestrian mall filled with fountains, trees and benches. At the Commons' western end is Clinton Hall (110 North Cayuga Street), packed with shops and restaurants, and Clinton House (116 North Cayuga Street), a historic hotel now housing arts organizations and an informal visitors center. Abutting the Commons to the north is the DeWitt Mall (Seneca and Cayuga streets), a former school building that now holds about 20 shops, galleries and restaurants. Among them are the Upstairs Gallery (tel: 607/272-8614), showcasing the work of local artists, and the cooperatively owned Moosewood Restaurant (215 North Cayuga Street; tel: 607/273-9610), a casual place famed nationwide for its best-selling cookbooks and natural foods.

One of Ithaca's strange claims to fame is as the birthplace of the ice cream sundae, supposedly first concocted here in 1891.

The **DeWitt Historical Society Museum of Tompkins County** (401 East State Street; tel: 607/273-8284; open Tues–Sun; entrance free) is on the edge of downtown, overlooking Sixmile Creek. Come here to learn about Ithaca's beginnings and its surprising film history; for several years, beginning in 1914, long before Hollywood, the city was the center for the nation's motion picture business. Recently renovated, the museum also presents many temporary exhibits on such subjects as alternative medicine and folk art.

On a hill overlooking downtown and Cayuga Lake is **Cornell University**, built around a peaceful green lined with ivy-covered buildings. Founded by Ezra Cornell and Andrew D. White in 1865, Cornell was one of the first educational institutions in the country to admit all qualified students, regardless of sex, race or class. Free walking tours of the campus leave from the Information and Referral Center (Day Hall, Tower Road and East Avenue; tel: 607/254-INFO). For most travelers, the most compelling reason to visit Cornell is the Herbert F. Johnson Museum of Art (Central Avenue; tel: 607/255-6464; open Tues–Sun; entrance free). Housed in a striking, largely glass building designed by I.M. Pei, the museum features a strong collection of Asian and contemporary art.

On the hills behind the university proper are the Cornell University Plantations (1 Plantations Road; tel: 607/255-3020; open daily; entrance free), 2,800 acres

BELOW: Lucifer Falls in Robert Treman State Park.

(1,130 hectares) filled with dozens of specialty gardens, an arboretum, and nature trails. Maps of the plantation are available in a small gift shop near the entrance, while brochures describing the various gardens are on site. Also connected with the university is the Sapsucker Woods Sanctuary, which contains the Cornell Lab of Ornithology (159 Sapsucker Woods Road; tel: 607/254-BIRD or 800/843-BIRD; open Mon–Sat; entrance free). Over 4 miles (6 km) of trails loop through the 220-acre (90-hectare) Sapsucker Woods, named after the yellow-bellied birds who breed here every year. Much of the Cornell Lab is closed to the public, but it does have an interesting Visitors Center with changing bird-related exhibits and an excellent gift shop selling an enormous selection of bird books, birdhouses, and bird paraphernalia of every conceivable kind.

A good stop for families visiting Ithaca is the cheery, bustling **Sciencenter** (601 1st Street; tel: 607/272-0600; open daily; entrance fee). The museum boasts over 100 exhibits, many of them hands-on, that teach kids about everything from gravity to heat. On the outskirts of Ithaca are two state parks. **Buttermilk Falls State Park** (off Route 13 south of downtown; tel: 607/273-5761; open daily; entrance fee in summer) centers around a series of waterfalls that plunge more than 500 ft (150 meters). A hiking trail follows the falls and at their base is a natural swimming hole. Five miles (8 km) south of Ithaca, **Robert H. Treman State Park** (off Route 13; tel: 607/273-3440; open Apr–Nov daily; entrance fee in summer) has 1,025 acres (415 hectares) of rugged terrain.

From Ithaca, Route 13 heads southwest toward **Elmira ⑫**. Elmira was once the summer home of Mark Twain, and visitors interested in literary history will want to make a stop at the **Mark Twain Study**, located on the Elmira College campus (Park Place, Route 14; tel: 607/735-1941; open June–Labor Day daily,

BELOW:
Taughannock Falls.

or by appointment; entrance free). The study was moved here from its original location on a hilltop on the outskirts of town. Built in the shape of a Mississippi steamboat pilot house, it contains many of his personal effects, including his trunk, desk, and old Remington typewriter. Twain, under his real name Samuel Clemens, is buried in Woodlawn Cemetery (1200 Walnut Street).

Also in Elmira is the Arnot Museum (235 Lake Street; tel: 607/734-3697; open Tues–Sun; entrance fee), a restored neo-classical mansion that boasts a fine collection of both European and American paintings, most from the 18th and 19th centuries. Behind the mansion is a modern wing that houses temporary exhibits and selections from the museum's Asian and pre-Columbian collections.

Harris Hill rises on the western outskirts of Elmira. The **Harris Hill Soaring Center and National Soaring Museum** are located here (Harris Hill Road, off Route 352; tel: 607/734-0641 soaring center, 607/734-3128 museum; rides June–Labor Day daily, Sat–Sun spring and fall; museum open daily; entrance fee). Harris Hill has been attracting gliding fans since the 1910s; in the museum are 12 antique gliders and exhibits on the history of the sport.

Glassworks and motor-racing

One of the most popular visitor attractions in New York State is the state-of-the-art **Corning Museum of Glass**, located in the small city of **Corning ⓭**, west of Elmira. Following a $62 million renovation, the museum (1 Museum Way; tel: 607/974-2000 or 800-732-6845; open daily; entrance fee) now includes the Glass Innovation Center, which tells of the latest scientific developments in glassmaking; the Hot Glass Show, where visitors can watch the art of glass-blowing; the Steuben Factory, filled with skilled craftspeople at work; and the Glass Sculpture Gallery. The heart of the institution, however, remains its historical wing, which showcases more than 10,000 glass objects dating from 1400 BC to the present. Among the many striking objects on display are an 11-ft-high (3-meter) Tiffany window and dozens of exquisite paperweights.

From the Glass Museum, a wide walkway heads over the Chemung River to downtown Corning, clustered around historic Market Street. Here, brick sidewalks lead past bustling restaurants and shops, including the Vitrix Hot Glass Studio (77 West Market Street; tel. 607/936-8707), where artisans demonstrate ancient glassblowing techniques.

Near the east end of Market Street is the Rockwell Museum (111 Cedar Street; tel: 607/937-5386; open daily; entrance fee), housed in the restored Old City Hall and said to be the most comprehensive collection of western art in the East, amassed by Corning denizen Robert F. Rockwell. Everything from works by sculptor Frederic Remington and painter Albert Bierstadt to Navajo rugs and Native American art is on display.

Also in Corning is the Benjamin Patterson Inn Museum Complex (59 W. Pulteney Street; tel: 607/937-5281; open Mar–Dec daily; entrance fee). This clutch of historic buildings includes the inn, with a women's parlor and ballroom, and an 1860s barn filled with antique farm implements. Guides are on hand to conduct tours and answer questions.

Map on page 264

The author's typewriter is on display at the Mark Twain Study.

BELOW: Susan B. Anthony's grave in Rochester's Mount Hope Cemetery.

Take Route 414 north from Corning to reach **Watkins Glen** 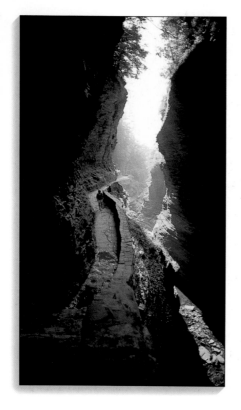, nestled in woods at the southern edge of Seneca Lake. One of the deeper bodies of water in the US (618 ft/188 meters), Seneca Lake rarely freezes over, and is known for its first-rate trout fishing. Named after a deep gorge that cuts through its center, tiny Watkins Glen and the steep roads surrounding it were the speedway of the American Grand Prix throughout the 1950s and 1960s. Back then, as many as 75,000 spectators crowded the usually sleepy streets to watch racecar wizards tear by. Today, world-class auto racing still takes place here, but at the Watkins Glen International Raceway (County Route 16, off Route 14/414s; tel: 607/535-2481; entrance fee), on the outskirts of town.

A good place for casual hiking is the **Watkins Glen State Park** (Route 14/414; open May–Nov daily; tel: 607/535-4511; entrance fee). Centering on the gorge that is the town's namesake, the park has a 1½-mile (2.5-km) Gorge Trail made up of stone steps and stone paths that take hikers past 19 waterfalls. Also in the park is an Olympic-size swimming pool and at night, a light-and-sound show known as Timespell is presented.

Route 14 leads south out of Watkins Glen to Montour Falls, a small industrial community that boasts a National Historic District made up of 24 brick buildings erected in the 1850s. The 165-ft-high (50-meter) Chequagua Falls, illuminated at night, plunges through the center of town – a startling sight. Along Route 14 just north of Watkins Glen are several more good wineries; among them are the Hermann J. Wiemer Vineyard (3962 Route 14; tel: 607/243-7971), best known for its Rieslings, and Glenora Wine Cellars (5435 Route 14; tel: 607/243-5511 or 800-243-5513), known for its sparkling wines. Glenora has panoramic views of Seneca Lake and presents first-rate jazz concerts during the summer.

Keuka Lake

To the west of Watkins Glen lies **Hammondsport** , a picturesque village tucked between steep hills at the southern edge of **Keuka Lake**. Shaped like a "Y," Keuka is the only one of the Fingers Lakes with an irregular outline; its name means "canoe landing" in Iroquois. Hammondsport was the site of the nation's first winery, the Pleasant Valley Wine Company, established here in 1860. The Visitor Center (8260 Pleasant Valley Road, County Road 88; tel: 607/569-6111; open May–Oct daily, Nov–Apr Mon–Sat; entrance free) displays historic exhibits and a film, screened inside a 35,000-gallon former wine tank.

Hammondsport was also once home to Glenn Hammond Curtiss, a pioneering aviator born here in 1878. Though not as well known as the Wright brothers, Curtiss made the world's first pre-announced flight on July 4, 1908, piloting his "June Bug" aircraft 5,090 ft (1,550 meters) up. Curtiss also developed the US Navy's first amphibian airplane. The Glenn H. Curtiss Museum (8419 Route 54; tel: 607/569-2160; open Apr–Dec daily; Jan–Mar Thur–Sun; entrance fee), housed in cavernous hangars, contains about a dozen antique airplanes, along with antique bicycles, motorcycles, propellers, and engines.

Throughout the Keuka Lake region, and especially northeast of Hammondsport between **Dundee** and

BELOW: Watkins Glen State Park.

Penn Yan, are scattered several small Mennonite communities. Horse and carts driven by men and women dressed in dark blue and black often appear clip-clopping down routes 14A, 11, 374, and 27, where there are occasional hand-written signs advertising Mennonite quilts, furniture, or produce for sale. Many Mennonite families operate booths at the Windmill Farm and Craft Market (Route 14A, midway between Penn Yan and Dundee; tel: 315/536-3032; open May–Dec Sat), one of several farmers' markets in the Finger Lakes region.

Canandaigua Lake to Palmyra

The farthest west of the six major Finger Lakes is Canandaigua Lake. Iroquois for "the Chosen Place," Canandaigua is a popular weekend retreat for Rochesterians and as such, is considerably more commercialized than the other lakes.

The tidy hamlet of **Naples** ⑯ sits at the southern end of Canandaigua. Built around a historic Old Town Square, Naples is one of the best places in the Finger Lakes to sample grape pies, a regional specialty. Made with dark grapes, the pies are only available in the autumn, during the harvest season. About 8 miles (11 km) northeast of Naples is the Cumming Nature Center (6472 Gulick Road; tel: 716/374-6160; open daily; entrance free). Owned and operated by the Rochester Museum and Science Center, the 900-acre (365-hectare) preserve has 6 miles (9 km) of themed trails, such as the Iroquois Trail, leading through forests and wetlands. Near the entrance is a small visitors center.

At the northern end of Canandaigua Lake is **Canandaigua** ⑰, a bustling resort town. Main Street, the central thoroughfare, is lined with trees, tourist shops, and historic buildings. One of these is the Granger Homestead and Carriage Museum (295 North Main Street; tel: 716/394-1472; open May–Oct

Map on page 264

 TIP

The Hill Cumorah Pageant, held every July in Palmyra, commemorates Joseph Smith's meeting with Angel Moroni. First held in 1937, it is the largest and oldest outdoor pageant in the US.

BELOW: café society on Rochester's Park Avenue.

Tues–Fri, June–Aug daily; entrance free). Once owned by Gideon Granger, US Postmaster General under presidents Jefferson and Madison, the 1816 Federal-style mansion is notable for its carved moldings and original furnishings. Out back is a carriage museum holding dozens of gleaming coaches.

East of Main Street is the Sonnenberg Gardens and Mansion (151 Charlotte Street; tel: 716/394-4922; open May–Oct daily; entrance free), a serene, 50-acre (20-hectare) estate that contains nine formal gardens, an arboretum, and an imposing 1887 mansion that visitors are free to wander through at will. The classic Rose Garden is filled with over 4,000 rose bushes.

West of Canandaigua Lake are the **Little Finger Lakes** ❶❽, made up of four small bodies of water: Honeoye, Canadice, Hemlock, and Conesus. Honeoye has a village of the same name and Conesus is a lake of choice among Rochester's second-home owners. Canadice and Hemlock serve as reservoirs, however, and remain largely undeveloped. At the southern end of Honeoye, the Harriet Hollister Spencer State Park (Canadice Hill Road, Route 37; open daily), largely undeveloped, has good views of the lake. Along the far southwestern edge of the Finger Lakes is the magnificent Letchworth State Park *(see page 294)*.

From Canandaigua, it's a short drive northwest to **Victor** ❶❾, home to the Ganondagan State Historic Site (1488 Victor-Bloomfield Road; tel: 716/924-5848; visitor center open May–Oct Wed–Sun; trails open daily; entrance free). During the 17th century, an important Seneca Indian village of 4,500 people stood on this site, but it was completely destroyed in 1687 by the French, who wished to eliminate their competitors in the fur trade. Ganondagan today has a small visitors center with exhibits on the Seneca Nation, an impressive reconstructed bark longhouse, and three walking trails that lead over gentle terrain past interesting interpretive plaques.

Northeast of Victor is **Palmyra** ❷⓿, a compact town lined with brick buildings. Palmyra was once home to Joseph Smith, the founder of the Mormon religion, and it was here, on Hill Cumorah outside town, that he allegedly received the gold tablets from the angel Moroni in 1827. Many sites in Palmyra are connected with the Mormon religion, and all welcome non-believers. Downtown is the handsome, recently restored Grandin Building (217 East Main Street; tel: 315/597-5982; open daily; entrance free), housing the printing press that published the first copies of the Book of Mormon in 1829–31. On the outskirts of town is the well laid-out Hill Cumorah Visitor Center (603 Route 21; tel: 315/597-5851; open daily; entrance free), which offers an introduction to Mormon history, beliefs and practices. Nearby is the Joseph Smith Historic Farm Site (29 Stafford Road; open daily; tel: 315/597-4383; entrance free), a simple, white farmhouse where he lived until age 22. He received his first vision in the Sacred Grove behind the house when he was only 14.

Rochester and Lake Ontario

Travel west of Palmyra about 40 minutes to reach **Rochester** ❷❶, the metropolis that marks the western edge of the Finger Lakes region. New York's third-largest city (population 230,000), Rochester is best

Rochester was America's first boom town; its population increased 13-fold between 1825 and 1845, largely thanks to the Erie Canal.

BELOW: the Seneca longhouse at Ganondagan State Historic Site.

Maps:
Area 264
City 277

known for its high-tech industries, including Eastman Kodak, Xerox and Bausch & Lomb. Many major educational and cultural institutions are also based here. Although downtown Rochester has its share of urban blight, what's most striking about the city are its many plush neighborhoods filled with large residential homes. The Genesee River Gorge, with attractive parks, runs through the center.

At the northern end of downtown stretches Brown's Race, four brick buildings that once housed water-powered mills; Brown's Race sits at the edge of the 96-ft-tall (29-meter) High Falls. One of the restored buildings contains **The Center at High Falls A** (60 Brown's Race; tel: 716/325-2030; open Wed–Sun; free), with exhibits on the area's history, while others hold shops and restaurants. Spectacular laser light shows are beamed over High Falls from May to October.

The renowned **Eastman School of Music** and the **Eastman Theatre B** (435 E. Main Street) opened in 1922. Chuck Mangione, Wynton Marsalis, and Mitch Miller are among the famous musicians who studied here. The Rochester Philharmonic Orchestra performs in the Eastman Theatre, which has a lavish interior and 35-ft (11-meter) chandelier made of over 20,000 handmade crystals. With 3,094 seats, it was the largest theater in the country at the time. Over 700 concerts a year are held here and in Kilbourn Hall; most are free and open to the public (tel: 716/274-1100 for concert hotline).

Also downtown is the **Strong Museum C** (1 Manhattan Square, corner of Chestnut Street and Woodbury Boulevard; tel: 716/263-2700; open daily; entrance fee). Long known for its outstanding collections of Americana and folk art, the Strong has recently reinvented itself as a busy hands-on museum for kids. The many special collections are still here, but they take a back seat.

East of the Strong is the **Rochester Museum and Science Center D** (657

'Wings of Progress' top the Times Square Building in downtown Rochester.

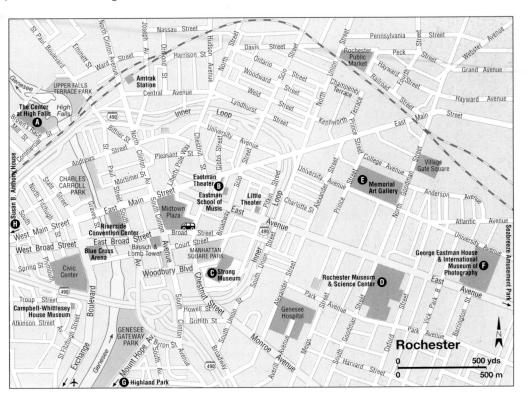

Maps:
Area 264
City 277

Apples are a prime product of upstate New York.

BELOW: minding the shop at Genesee Country Village.

East Avenue; tel: 716/271-1880; open daily; entrance fee), housing a first-rate selection of science and history exhibits. One of the most interesting is "At the Western Door," which documents the history and culture of the Seneca Nation. Connected with the University of Rochester is the **Memorial Art Gallery E** (500 University Avenue; tel: 716/473-7720; open Tues–Sun; entrance fee), a small gem containing a little bit of everything, from pre-Columbian sculpture to late 20th-century paintings. In its center is an enclosed sculpture garden featuring many works by Rochesterian artist Albert Paley.

Farther east is the **George Eastman House and International Museum of Photography F** (900 East Avenue; open Tues–Sun; tel: 716/271-3361; entrance fee). The founder of Eastman Kodak lived with his mother in this 50-room Georgian mansion for much of his life. It is furnished with period pieces from the late 1800s and early 1900s, and has lovely gardens. Adjoining the house is a fascinating museum on the history of photography, with early cameras and four picture galleries with changing exhibits.

On Rochester's south side, **Highland Park G** (bounded by Mount Hope, Highland and Elm avenues and Goodman Street; open daily; entrance free) has an arboretum designed by Frederick Law Olmsted in 1888. One of the city's biggest events, the Lilac Festival, takes place here every May, when the park's 1,200 lilac blushes are in bloom. The park is also home to the 1911 Lamberton Conservatory (180 Reservoir Avenue), housing a tropical forest, orchid collection, and cacti. Nearby is the 1898 Frederick Douglass statue, the first public statue to honor an African-American. The escaped slave, abolitionist, and writer settled in Rochester in 1847 and published his newspaper here for 17 years.

The simple wooden **Susan B. Anthony House H** (17 Madison Street; tel: 716/235-6124; open Memorial Day–Labor Day Tues–Sun; entrance fee) was home to the women's rights advocate from 1866 until her death in 1902, and fellow reformers Elizabeth Cady Stanton and Frederick Douglass were frequent guests. The house contains such memorabilia as typewriters, clothes, letters, and photographs. .

About 15 miles (20 km) north of Rochester is Lake Ontario and the **Seabreeze Amusement Park** (4600 Culver Road; tel: 716/323-1900 or 800-395-2500; open June–Labor Day daily; May Sat–Sun; entrance fee). First established in 1879, the park has about 75 rides, among them the 1920 Jack Rabbit, one of the few surviving wooden rollercoasters. Also on Lake Ontario is the **Ontario Beach Park** (Lake and Beach avenues; tel: 716/256-4950; open daily), with an Art-Deco bathhouse, fishing pier, and the 1905 Dentzel Menagerie Carousel, one of the oldest in the US.

Twenty miles (28 km) southwest of Rochester is the **Genesee Country Village and Museum** (1410 Flint Hill Road; tel: 716/538-6822; open May–Oct Tues–Sun; entrance fee), where 57 restored 19th-century buildings are spread out around a village square. Among them are a log cabin, fly tier's shop, Greek Revival mansion, pharmacy, and doctor's office. Costumed guides demonstrate the folk arts of the pre-industrial age, while nearby is a Nature Center with 3 miles (5 km) of hiking and nature trails. ❏

Exploring the Vineyards

One of the Finger Lakes' most famous attractions is its many wineries. When the glaciers that created the lakes retreated, tens of thousands of years ago, they left behind not only magnificent bodies of water but also ideal grape-growing conditions by depositing a layer of topsoil on the shale beds above the lakes. The deep lakes also provide protection from what otherwise would be a very cold climate by moderating the temperatures along their shorelines.

Viniculture in the Finger Lakes began in 1829 when a Reverend Bostwick planted a few grapevines near his home in Hammondsport on Keuka Lake, to make sacramental wine. His efforts were surprisingly successful and his neighbors took note. Before long, vineyards ringed the village and in 1860, 13 Hammondsport businesspeople banded together to form the country's first commercial winery, the Pleasant Valley Wine Company *(see page 356)*. Other would-be viticulturists followed suit, and within a few years, grapes were growing around Keuka, Canandaigua, and Seneca lakes.

For decades, the vineyards of the Finger Lakes produced only native American Concord, Niagara, and Delaware grapes, which are seldom used in the making of fine wines. About 30 years ago, however, a few people began experimenting with the more complex European Vinifera grape. Again, efforts were surprisingly successful and today excellent Chardonnays, Rieslings, and sparkling wines are produced throughout the region.

One of the stranger tales in the chronicles of Finger Lakes wine history is that of the battle waged over the name "Taylor." In 1970, Walter S. Taylor, a grandson of the founder of Taylor Wine, was kicked out of the company after publicly attacking its "incompetence, greed, and jealousy." He and his father Greyton then began their own winery in Hammondsport, now known as the Bully Hill Vineyards (8843 Taylor Memorial Drive; tel: 607/868-4814; open May–Oct daily; entrance free). Then in 1977, Coca-Cola bought Taylor Wine and sued Walter for using his family name on his own labels. Walter took the case to court and lost, only to become a local hero. This and other aspects of Taylor history are documented in the Taylor Museum, adjacent to the Bully Hill Vineyards.

Today, the Finger Lakes region boasts over 60 wineries, each one distinctly different from the next. Some are large, some small, some house their own restaurants and gift shops. Most hug the shores of Cayuga, Seneca, or Keuka lakes, and each lake has its own wine-growing association that publishes free maps and brochures, available throughout the region.

Most wineries welcome visitors, and are open May to October daily, with more limited hours off-season. Tastings are usually free.

For a complete list of wineries in the Finger Lakes region and elsewhere in New York State, contact the New York Wine and Grape Foundation, 350 Elm Street, Penn Yan, New York 14527; tel: 315/536-7442. ❑

RIGHT: the soil and climate of the Finger Lakes produce first-class grapes for making wine.

GREATER NIAGARA

Maps:
Area 284
City 286

The most famous waterfalls in the world, Niagara Falls form a natural boundary between the United States and Canada. Nearby are New York's second city, Buffalo, and some stunning state parks

New York

F ormed about 12,000 years ago, Niagara Falls has long been regarded as one of the world's great natural wonders. Spilling over a ledge that is 180 ft (55 meters) high and two-thirds of a mile (2 km) wide, they gush 40 million gallons (150 million liters) of water a minute into a spectacular water hole churning with waves, whirlpools, eddies, and mists. As early as 1678, one of the Falls' first white visitors, missionary Father Louis Hennepin, wrote: "Betwixt the Lake Ontario and Erie, these is a vast and prodigious Cadence of Water… The universe does not afford its Parallel…"

Nestled into the far northwestern region of New York State, Niagara Falls is bordered by Lake Ontario to the north and Canada to the west. A little farther south lies Lake Erie and Buffalo, the second-largest city in the state (population 328,000), while to the east flourishes much fertile farmland. Most of the area wasn't settled until the early 1800s, and so it is more Midwestern than Eastern in feel, with few colonial or even Revolutionary War historical sites.

PRECEDING PAGES:
Niagara Falls.
LEFT: on the Hurricane Deck at Cave of the Winds.
BELOW: *Maid of the Mist* skirts the falls.

Buffalo

Many travelers enter the region through **Buffalo ❶**, whose Greater Buffalo International Airport is serviced by numerous national airlines; the Amtrak railroad also stops here. Once the domain of the Iroquois, Buffalo was first incorporated by white settlers in 1816, but didn't flourish until the Erie Canal was completed in 1825. Marking the transportation break between the Great Lakes and the Erie Canal, the town soon became known for its many warehouses and employment opportunities, which attracted thousands of immigrants, mostly from Ireland and Germany. Throughout the 1800s, the city boomed.

Then, in 1901, Buffalo hosted the Pan-American Exposition, a 350-acre (140-hectare) science, design and architecture fair that attracted 8 million visitors. In the late summer of that year, however, President William McKinley, in Buffalo to visit the exposition, was assassinated by anarchist Leon Czolgosz. The city continued to prosper until the mid-20th century, thanks to its thriving steel industry, but that tragic event seemed to mark the beginning of the end of Buffalo's early promise. In the early 1970s, the steel mills closed down, plunging the city into a serious depression, and although it has largely recovered, it is now much quieter than it was in yesteryear.

A good place to begin a tour of Buffalo is Niagara Square, which centers on the McKinley Monument, honoring the late president. Dominating one side of the square is the Art-Deco **Buffalo City Hall ⓐ**, with a 28th-floor observation deck with great views of the city (65 Niagara Square; tel: 716/851-4200, ext 5027;

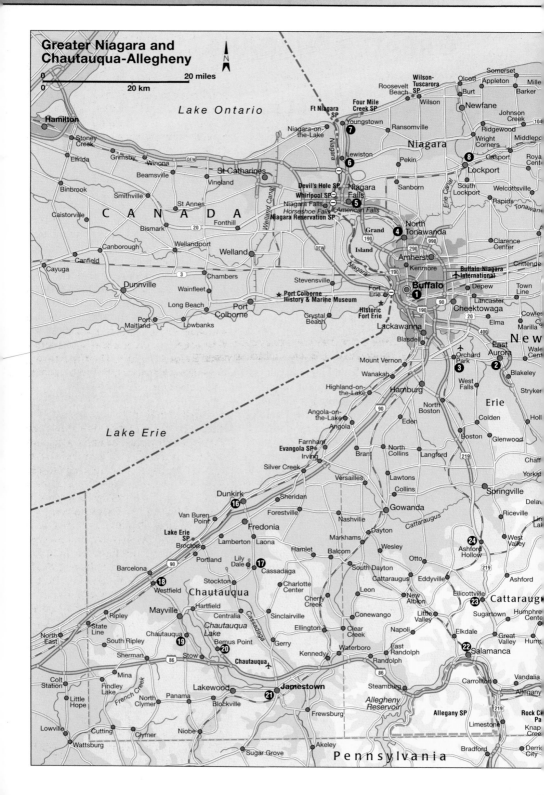

Greater Niagara and Chautauqua-Allegheny

N

0 ———————— 20 miles
0 ———————— 20 km

Lake Ontario

CANADA

Hamilton
Stoney Creek
Elfrida
Grimsby
Winona
Beamsville
Binbrook
Smithville
St Annes
Caistorville
Bismark
Fonthill
Canborough
Wellandport
Cayuga
Canfield
Welland
Dunnville
Chambers
Wainfleet
Long Beach
Port Colborne
Port Maitland
Lowbanks
Crystal Beach

St Catharines
Vineland

Welland Canal

Port Colborne History & Marine Museum
Stevensville
Fort Erie
Historic Fort Erie

Lake Erie

Niagara-on-the-Lake
Ft Niagara SP **7**
Lewiston **6**
Devil's Hole SP
Whirlpool SP
Niagara Falls
Niagara Reservation SP
Horseshoe Falls
5 American Falls
Niagara Falls **Niagara**

Roosevelt Beach
Wilson-Tuscarora SP
Wilson
Youngstown
Ransomville
Pekin
Sanborn

Somerset
Olcott
Appleton
Mille
Burt
Barker
Newfane
Johnson Creek
Ridgewood
Wright Corners
Middlepo
Gasport
Roya
Cent
8 Lockport
South Lockport
Welcottville
Rapids
Tonawa

Grand Island
4 North Tonawanda
Amherst
Kenmore

Buffalo-Niagara International
1 Buffalo
Lackawanna
Blasdell

Clarence Center
Crittende
Town Line
Depew
Lancaster
Cheektowaga
Cowles
Elma
Marilla

Mount Vernon
Wanakah
Highland-on-the-Lake
Hamburg
Angola-on-the-Lake
Angola
Farnham
Evangola SP
Irving
Silver Creek

Orchard Park
3
West Falls
2 East Aurora
Wale
Cent
Blakeley
Stryker

Erie

New

North Boston
Eden
Boston
Colden
Glenwood
Holl

North Collins
Brant
Langford
Chaff
Yorks

Dunkirk **16**
Van Buren Point
Fredonia
Lake Erie SP
Brocton
Barcelona
Portland
Lamberton
Laona
Hamlet
Balcom
Sheridan
Forestville
Nashville
Dayton
Markhams
Wesley
Otto
Versailles
Lawtons
Collins
Gowanda
Cattaraugus

Springville
Riceville
West Valley
Ashford Hollow **24**
Ashford
Lin
Lal
Delav

18 Westfield
Stockton
Charlotte Center
Cherry Creek
Lily Dale **17** Cassadaga
South Dayton
Cattaraugus
Eddyville
Leon
New Albion
Little Valley
Ellicottville
Sugartown
Humphre
Cente
23 Cattaraug

Ripley
State Line
Mayville
Hartfield
Centralia
Sinclairville
Chautauqua
South Ripley
19 Chautauqua Lake
Bemus Point
20
Gerry
Ellington
Clear Creek
Conewango
Napoli
Elkdale
Great Valley
Hump
22 Salamanca

North East
Sherman
Stow
Chautauqua
Kennedy
Waterboro
East Randolph
Randolph
Steamburg

Colt Station
Mina
Findley Lake
Lakewood
21 Jamestown
Blockville
Frewsburg

Little Hope
North Clymer
Panama
Allegheny Reservoir
Allegany SP
Carrollton
Vandalia
Allegany
Rock Ci
Pa

Lowville
Cutting
Clymer
Niobe
Akeley
Sugar Grove
Limestone
Bradford
Derri
City
Knap
Cree

Wattsburg

Pennsylvania

Cattaraug

Nashville

20

QEW

Niagara

190

290

990

90

400

219

86

3

20

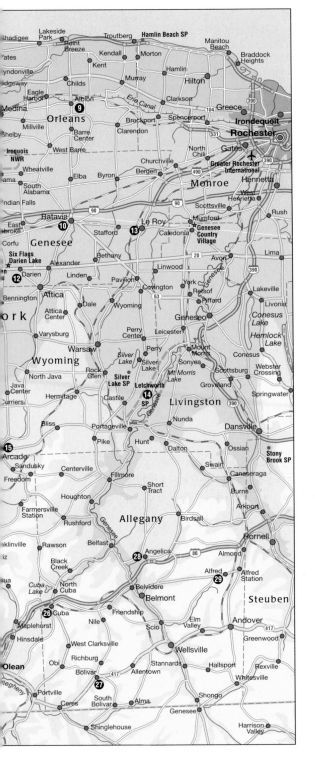

open Mon–Fri; entrance free). Along Main Street downtown is Buffalo Place, a pedestrian-only thoroughfare serviced by the sleek Metro Rail. Most of the southern end of Buffalo Place is lined with large office buildings, including the Ellicott Square Building (295 Main Street) which, when it was completed in 1896, was the largest commercial office building in the world.

At the northern end of Buffalo Place, the 20-block area known as the Theater District extends as far west as Delaware Avenue and as far north as Tupper Street. A half dozen or so theaters and cabarets thrive here, along with galleries, restaurants, and shops. A highlight among them is **Shea's Performing Arts Center Ⓑ** (646 Main Street; tel: 716/847-1410), an opulent 1926 movie palace filled with mirrors, marble and gilt. Almost destroyed in the 1970s by a wrecker's ball, Shea's is now being fully restored, and offers a busy schedule of cultural events ranging from theater and rock shows to movies and dance (see page 346).

Guided missiles

At the southern end of downtown the **Buffalo and Erie County Naval and Military Park Ⓒ** (1 Naval Park Cove, foot of Pearl and Main streets; tel: 716/847-1773; open Apr–Oct daily, Nov Sat–Sun; entrance fee) sprawls across 6 acres (2.5 hectares). This maritime park is dedicated to all branches of the armed forces, but most of its exhibits concern the US Navy. Highlights include the USS Little Rock, a 610-ft-long (186-meter) guided missile cruiser, and the USS Croaker, a submarine that sank 11 Japanese vessels during World War II. Also on site are guided missiles, a PT boat, an Army M41 tank, and the Servicemen's Museum, offering a good model ship collection.

Just north of downtown is **Allentown**, the nation's second-largest historic district. Roughly bounded by Main Street to the east, Edward Street to the south, North Street to the north, and Cottage and Pennsylvania streets to the west, Allentown is primarily made up of

Victorian buildings, many now housing restaurants, shops, and boutiques. In the heart of Allentown is the **Theodore Roosevelt Inaugural National Historic Site D** (641 Delaware Avenue; tel: 716/884-0095; open daily; entrance fee), housed in the 1881 Wilcox Mansion. Roosevelt was formally inaugurated here following the assassination of President McKinley. On display is everything from historic documents to the handkerchief that assassin Leon Czolgosz used to cover his handgun. Self-guided audio walking tours of historic Buffalo can also be picked up at the Roosevelt site. Allentown is also home to the Anchor Bar (1047 Main Street), a Buffalo institution. This is the lively Italian restaurant where Buffalo chicken wings, dipped in blue cheese, were invented.

Delaware Park E, about 4 miles (6 km) north of downtown, is ringed with some of Buffalo's finest cultural institutions. Foremost among them is the **Albright-Knox Art Gallery F** (1285 Elmwood Avenue; tel: 716/882-8700; open Tues–Sun; entrance fee). World famous for its collection of contemporary American and European art, including works by the likes of Picasso, Matisse, Miró, and Pollock, the Albright-Knox also houses a good general collection that spans the history of art. The gallery regularly stages temporary exhibitions.

Across from the Albright-Knox is the **Buffalo and Erie County Historical Society Museum G** (25 Nottingham Court; tel. 716/873-9644; open Tues–Sun; entrance fee), which holds an interesting array of exhibits on everything from Buffalo manufacturing (Pierce Arrow cars, pacemakers, kazoos) to the area's vibrant ethnic history. The museum is housed in the only remaining permanent building from the 1901 Pan-American Exposition; it is modeled after the Parthenon in Athens. Also nearby is Buffalo State College, home to the **Burchfield-Penney Art Center H** (1300 Elmwood Avenue; tel. 716/878-6011;

According to architectural historian John D. Randall, Buffalo boasts a wider range of American and European architectural forms than any other city in the world.

BELOW:
Shea's Performing Arts Center, a gilded palace.

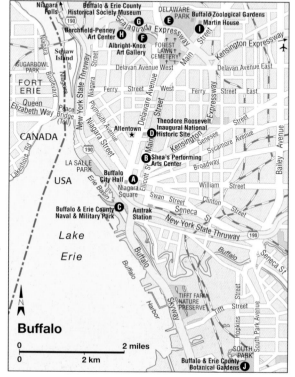

open Tues–Sun; entrance free). Renowned watercolorist Charles Burchfield taught at the college, and the center is a low-key affair focusing primarily on his work and that of other contemporary western New York artists.

Meanwhile, Delaware Park is a peaceful, 350-acre (140-hectare) oasis of green, designed by Frederick Law Olmsted of Central Park fame in the 1870s. Within the park, you will find the Buffalo Zoological Gardens (300 Parkside Avenue; tel. 716/837-3900; open daily; entrance fee). Highlights of the gardens include "Habicat," where lions and tigers roam free, a tropical rainforest, and a large herd of the city's namesake.

Abutting Delaware Park to the south is the historic Forest Lawn Cemetery (1411 Delaware Avenue; tel: 716/885-1600; open daily), spread out over low hills. Near the entrance are a cluster of small Iroquois graves and a tall monument honoring the famed Seneca orator Red Jacket, whose Indian name "Sa-Co-Ye-Wat-Ha" means "he who keeps them awake".

If you're interested in modern architecture, be sure to stop at the **Martin House** ❶ (175 Jewett Parkway; tel. 716/856-3858; open Sat–Sun tours only; entrance fee). One of Frank Lloyd Wright's most important works, this long, horizontal building incorporating many open spaces is characteristic of his famous Prairie style *(see page 94)*.

On the opposite end of town is the **Buffalo and Erie County Botanical Gardens** ❶ (2655 South Park Avenue; tel. 716/696-3555; open daily; entrance free). This park was also designed by Olmsted, but in it reigns a pristine, white conservatory built by the famed greenhouse architectural firm of Lord and Burnham in the 1890s. A fairytale-like creation made up of domes, fan-windows and glass, the conservatory also contains 12 small interconnected greenhouses.

Map on page 286

There are great views from the observation deck at Buffalo City Hall.

BELOW: inside City Hall.

The Roy;croft Inn provides historic accommodations.

BELOW: the Roycroft campus, a national landmark.

Around Buffalo

Several unique attractions can be found in two small towns just south of Buffalo. **East Aurora ②** was once home to the Roycrofters artists group. Now a National Historic Landmark District, the former Roycroft Campus still stands at the corner of Main and Grove streets. Included within the 14-building complex are several artisans' workshops (still-operating), the Elbert Hubbard-Roycroft Museum (363 Oakwood Avenue; tel: 716/652-4735; open June–Oct Wed, Sun), and the magnificently restored Roycroft Inn (40 South Grove Street; tel. 716/652-5552 or 800/267-0525). Only recently reopened for guests, the inn has many pieces of Roycroft furniture.

Also in East Aurora is Vidler's 5 & 10 (690–4 Main Street; tel: 716/652-0481), a delightfully creaky store filled with display cases from the 1920s. For sale are such things as penny candy, marbles, magic cards, mousetraps, and sewing notions, and almost everything is priced under $1.

Not far from East Aurora lies the suburb of **Orchard Park ③**, home to two sporting institutions. The Pedaling History Bicycle Museum (3943 North Buffalo Road, Route 240/277; tel: 716/662-3853; open Apr–Dec daily, Jan–Mar Fri–Mon; entrance fee) is America's only all-bicycle museum. This modern, well laid-out establishment displays over 200 bicycles, including unicycles and courting tandems. Other exhibits trace the history of the bicycle. And no reference to Buffalo would be complete without mention of the Buffalo Bills, the National Football League team that plays in Orchard Park's Ralph Wilson Stadium (1 Bills Drive; tel: 716/649-0015; season Sept–Jan). Tickets are available to most games, but should be ordered well in advance if you want to avoid disappointment.

FROM SOAP TO ART

In the early years of the 20th century, Elbert Green Hubbard (1856–1915), former soap salesman and advertising executive, founded "The Roycroft," an idealistic Arts and Crafts colony in East Aurora, New York. "The love you liberate in your work is the love you keep," Hubbard said, and before long his community was an enormous success, attracting artists and artisans from all over the country. At its peak, more than 500 Roycrofters were working with their mentor as bookbinders, printers, coppersmiths, potters, silversmiths, innkeepers and, in particular, furniture makers. The Roycrofters became famed nationwide for their simple, heavy, beautifully designed oak furniture, which is still in great demand today.

Inspired by the Arts and Crafts Movement founded by William Morris in England, Hubbard was as much a philosopher, writer and publisher as he was an organizer. "Fences are for those who cannot fly!" was but one of his many inspirational sayings, and he published a popular magazine known as *The Philistine*, which was subtitled "A Periodical of Protest."

On May 7, 1915, Hubbard and his wife Alice died tragically in the sinking of the SS *Lusitania*, which was torpedoed by a German U-boat.

River Road heads north out of Buffalo, toward Niagara Falls, to pass through **North Tonawanda** ❹, once home to the Herschell Carrousel Factory. In its heyday during the 1920s and 1930s, the factory produced over 50 carousels a year. Those days are now long gone, but the old factory still houses an informal workshop and the Herschell Carrousel Factory Museum (180 Thompson Street, off River Road; tel: 716/693-1885; open July–Aug daily; Apr–June and Labor Day–Dec Wed–Sun; entrance fee). On display are many hand-carved animals dating back to the early 1900s, new carvings, and various historical exhibits. Out back is a working 1916 carousel that kids of all ages are welcome to ride.

Map on page 284

Niagara Falls

From North Tonawanda, River Road continues onto **Niagara Falls** ❺, a name that refers to both the city and the waterfalls. The city itself is rather flat and gray, surrounded by industrial plants, but it does have several interesting visitor attractions. The spectacular Falls, meanwhile, can be viewed from a variety of vantage points, each one with something slightly different – and equally fascinating – to offer.

Located along the Niagara River between the United States and Canada, Niagara Falls are actually three falls in one: the American and Bridal Veil Falls on the New York side, and the Horseshoe Falls on the Ontario side. The Niagara River flows between Lake Ontario and Lake Erie, over the Niagara Escarpment, while just beyond the falls it descends into a 7-mile-long (11-km) canyon known as Niagara Gorge. On the US side, much of Niagara Falls lies within the **Niagara Reservation State Park** (off Robert Moses Parkway; tel: 716/278-1796; open daily; entrance fee). The main entrance to the park is at Prospect

BELOW: hand-carved horses.

Point. Here, a visitor center is filled with good introductory exhibits to the area, and screens an informative film. Viewmobiles, or small trolleys, leave from behind the center to travel throughout the park, April to October.

The best place to view the falls on the New York side is at Prospect Point itself, which sits at the edge of the American Falls' 1,000-ft (300-meter) brink. Here, foamy turbulent waters gush straight downward, while rainbows often form in the mid-morning mist. Looming over one side of Prospect Point is the Observation Tower, an aging structure with glass-enclosed elevators that rise 200 ft (60 meters) above the falls, offering dramatic views. The *Maid of the Mist* boats, a tourist attraction since 1846, dock at the bottom of the tower. The boats head straight into the bases of the falls, passing close enough to touch.

Goat Island sits above the waterfalls, a small, wooded spit of land offering great views. The Bridal Veil and American Falls tumble down on one side, the Horseshoe Falls on the other, while from all around comes thunderous sound. The "Cave of the Winds" trip descends from Goat Island's western end; guides lead visitors along wooden walkways down to the base of Bridal Veil Falls.

At the northern end of the park, overlooking the Niagara Gorge beyond Prospect Park, is the Schoellkopf Geological Museum (tel: 716/278-1780; open Apr–Oct daily). Inside are many multimedia exhibits on the falls' geological history. A footpath leads from the museum down into the gorge, and guided walking tours are led by the park's naturalists.

As stunning as the American and Bridal Veil Falls are, Niagara's most spectacular waterfall is the Horseshoe Falls, best viewed from Queen Victoria Park (tel: 905/468-4257) on the Canadian side. Queen Victoria Park can be reached via the Rainbow Bridge, which passes near Prospect Point. Proof of

BELOW: braving the elements at Cave of the Winds.

citizenship (such as a passport or voter's registration card) is required to cross over. Both more built up and more sophisticated than the US side, it is beautifully landscaped with lots of flowers, and dotted with one tourist museum after another. Among them are Tussaud's Wax Museum and Ripley's Believe It or Not Museum. A highpoint of a visit to the Canadian side is the "Journey Behind the Falls," which allows visitors to walk behind Horseshoe Falls.

Back on the US side, a major attraction is the Aquarium of Niagara Falls (701 Whirlpool Street; tel: 716/285-3575; open daily; entrance fee). Inside, there are over 2,000 marine animals, including Atlantic bottlenose dolphins, electric eels, and many varieties of shark.

Map on page 284

Around Niagara

Throughout western New York, and especially in the Niagara Falls region, are numerous sites connected with the Underground Railroad. Among them are St John's A.M.E. Church (917 Garden Avenue, Niagara Falls), an early African-American church, and the Thomas Root Home (3016 Upper Mountain Road, Pekin), where escaped slaves once hid in a 5-by-10-ft (1.5 by 3-meter) cellar. One of the best ways to learn about these sites is with Motherland Connextions tours (tel: 716/282-1028) in Niagara Falls.

Travel north of Niagara Falls on Robert Moses Parkway to visit **Whirlpool State Park**, which offers excellent views of a giant swirling whirlpool, and Devil's Hole State Park, perched above the Niagara River's lower rapids. Both parks feature hiking trails (tel: 716/278-1770). The **New York Power Authority Niagara Project** (5777 Lewiston Road; tel: 716/285-3211; open daily; entrance free), one of the world's largest hydroelectric plants, sits across from the two

In 1901, 63-year-old Annie Taylor, a schoolteacher, went over the Horseshoe Falls in a wooden barrel and survived. She was the first daredevil to do so.

BELOW: Bridal Veil Falls overlook on Luna Island.

Scarecrows guard the fields and orchards of upstate New York.

BELOW:

pick your own at Brown's Berry Patch, near Albion.

parks. The project's visitor center does a good job of explaining the principles of hydroelectric power, and contains many hands-on exhibits. Also on display are exhibits about the area's history.

Off Lewiston Road directly across from Devil's Hole State Park is University Drive, which leads to Niagara University and the Castellani Art Museum (Senior Drive, off University Drive; tel: 716/286-8200; open Wed–Sun; entrance free). The museum contains a permanent exhibit of contemporary art, as well as a small collection of Hudson River School paintings *(see page 199)* and changing exhibits on the region's folk art.

Historic **Lewiston ❻** is a 19th-century village filled with many National Historic Landmarks. Among them is a McDonald's restaurant, housed in the 1824 Frontier House (460 Center Street). At the southern edge of town, the 200-acre (80-hectare) Artpark (150 South 4th Street; tel: 716/754-9001, box office: 800/659-7275; open daily; parking fee in summer) is the only state park in the country devoted to the visual and performing arts. Many cultural events are staged here throughout the summer, including theater, storytelling, acrobatics, and dance. Also on site is a Hopewell Indian burial mound, dating back over 2,000 years.

Continue north to **Youngstown ❼** to visit Old Fort Niagara (off Robert Moses Parkway in Fort Niagara State Park; tel: 716/745-7611; open daily; entrance fee in summer), a striking gray stone complex with breathtaking views of Lake Ontario. Strategically located at the mouth of the Niagara River, Fort Niagara was originally established by the French in 1726, and was occupied by US soldiers until the early 1900s. Today, costumed guides in military dress roam the complex, staging frequent military musters and fire-and-drum drills.

Route 18 hugs the shore of Lake Ontario between Youngstown and Monroe County, offering scenic views of the lake, orchards, and farmland.

The historic town of **Lockport ❽** lies about 20 minutes directly east of Niagara Falls on Route 31 and is best visited for its cluster of Erie Canal attractions. Lockport Locks & Canal Tours (tel: 716/433-6155 or 800-378-0352) give 2-hour cruises on the canal. Next door to the embarkation point, the Erie Canal Heritage Center (210 Market Street; tel: 716/433-6155; open May–Oct daily; off season by appointment) has a small museum that documents the canal's history from its beginnings in 1812 to the present *(see page 200)*.

Exploring the west

Continue east along Route 31, through fertile farm country, until you reach the quiet village of **Albion ❾**, centered on the 34-building Courthouse Square Historic District (along Route 98). At its heart is the 1858 Orleans County Courthouse, complete with a shiny silver dome and old-fashioned courtroom crowded with wooden pews.

Three miles (5 km) north of town, in the hamlet of Childs, is the Cobblestone Museum (14393 Ridge Road West, Route 104; tel: 716/589-9013; open June–Labor Day Tues–Sun; entrance fee), housed in a cobblestone church. Approximately 1,000 of these unique buildings constructed of cobblestones – small rounded stones small enough to hold in one hand – stand all across western New York. The museum documents the masonry's history and technique.

To learn more about the settlement of western New York, stop into the Holland Land Office Museum (131 West Main Street; tel: 716/ 343-4727; open Mon–Sat; entrance fee) in **Batavia ❿**. The museum explains how, in the early

Map on page 284

BELOW:
Old Fort Niagara.

1800s, New York State was divided into several enormous land tracts by investors, who then sold off plots at about $2 an acre to pioneers. One of the largest of these investors was the Holland Land Company, made up of bankers from Amsterdam. Established in 1940, Batavia Downs (8315 Park Road, Batavia; tel: 716/343-3750) is the oldest parimutuel harness track in the US. Races run July to October, Wednesday to Saturday at 7.30pm.

Nature lovers will want to head northwest of Batavia on Route 63 to reach the **Iroquois National Wildlife Refuge ⓫** (1101 Casey Road, in Basom, off Route 63; tel: 716/948-5445; open year-round Mon–Fri, mid-Mar–May Sat–Sun; entrance free). Once covered by a glacial lake, the refuge is now a 10,818-acre (4,378-hectare) preserve for migrating birds and other animals. On site is a small visitors' center with exhibits on local flora and fauna.

In **Darien ⓬**, not far from the wildlife refuge, is the Darien Lakes State Park (10289 Harlow Road, off Sumner Road; tel: 716/547-9242; open daily; entrance fee in summer), a good stop for families. The park centers on a large lake with fishing and swimming and features 19 miles (30 km) of nature trails.

Across from the park, Six Flags Darien Lake (9993 Allegheny Road, off Sumner Road; tel: 716/599-4641; open June–Labor Day daily, May–Sept Sat–Sun; entrance fee) is an enormous entertainment complex with more than 100 rides, shows, and attractions. Among them are one of the nation's top-10 wooden rollercoasters, a water park, and the excellent Darien Lake Performing Arts Center.

Continue east of Batavia on Route 5 to reach **Le Roy ⓭**, a somewhat depressed town that's nonetheless still filled with many fine old Victorian homes and leafy trees. Le Roy is best known as the birthplace of Jell-O, invented in 1897 by Pearl Bixby Wait, a local carpenter. A small exhibit on the wobbly dessert is displayed in the Le Roy House and Jello Gallery (23 East Main Street; tel: 716/768-7433; open Tues–Fri, Sun; entrance free), a handsome stone building that also serves as the local history museum.

BELOW: railroad bridge near Letchworth Gorge.

Grand Canyon of the East

In the southeastern corner of the Greater Niagara region, straddling a boundary that crosses over into the Finger Lakes, is magnificent **Letchworth State Park ⓮** (off Route 19A in Castile; tel: 716/493-3600; open daily; entrance fee in summer). One of the most dramatic sights in the state, the 17-mile-long (22-km) Letchworth Gorge, also known as the "Grand Canyon of the East," plunges through the park's center, while all around is dense forest.

Most of Letchworth Gorge was purchased in 1859 by industrialist William Letchworth, who wished to preserve the natural wonder for future generations. At the time, the area was being targeted for development, with other local businessmen hoping to turn it into a hydroelectric plant, but Letchworth succeeded in conserving its beauty.

One main road runs through the park along the gorge, and there are lots of scenic vistas and hiking trails along the way; the trails range in length from around half a mile to 7 miles (1–12 km). At the

Map on page 284

southern end of the park, the grand, yellow-and-white Glen Iris Inn (tel: 716/493-2622) overlooks the most spectacular of the gorge's waterfalls, the Mid Falls. Once the home of William Letchworth, this Victorian-era hostelry is now equipped with 15 pleasant guestrooms, a library stocked with regional books, a gift shop, and an attractive restaurant *(see page 338)*.

Across from the Glen Iris Inn, the **William Pryor Letchworth Museum** (tel: 716/493-3600; open mid-May–Oct daily) is a hodgepodge affair filled with many exhibits on natural and local history. Among them are several displays relating to Mary Jemison, the "white woman of the Genessee." Of Irish extraction, Jemison was taken prisoner by the Seneca at age 15 and lived among them for the rest of her life. She married, bore seven children, and eventually became a Seneca leader. Mary Jemison's grave, moved here by William Letchworth in 1910, stands on a hill behind the museum. Beside it is the Council House in which the last Iroquois council on the Genesee River was held in 1872.

To the west of Letchworth State Park, heading back toward Buffalo, is the small town of **Arcade ⑮**. Surrounded by fertile dairy country, Arcade was a major shipping center for cheese around the turn of the 20th century, and many fine Victorian homes still stand sentinel along its West Main Street. Arcade's main visitor attraction, however, is the Arcade and Attica Steam Railroad, equipped with vintage orange-and-black carriages that date back to 1915.

The train leaves from the Arcade and Attica Railroad Station (278 Main Street; tel: 716/492-3100; rides given Memorial Day–Oct Sat–Sun, July–Aug Wed and Fri; entrance fee). The station is notable for its double-pitched hipped roof. The entire rail excursion lasts 90 minutes, and actors in period dress entertain travelers along the way. ❑

BELOW: Letchworth State Park.

CHAUTAUQUA-ALLEGHENY

With lakes, beaches, forests, woodland, and mountains,
this relatively undiscovered part of the state is
a great place for getting away from it all

Map
on page
284

New York

Tucked into the far southwestern corner of New York State is its least discovered region, Chautauqua-Allegheny. Bounded by Lake Erie to the west and Pennsylvania to the south, the area is mostly made up of small towns and farmland. To the south are the dark rolling foothills of the Allegheny Mountains, which grow considerably higher as they continue on into Pennsylvania, while to the southwest lies Chautauqua Lake, a popular resort area that is also home to the famed Chautauqua Institution.

Harbor towns

Interstate 90 and Route 20 lead southwest from Buffalo *(see page 283)* into **Dunkirk** , as good a place as any to begin a tour of the region. A sprawling, low-key industrial city named after the town in France, Dunkirk centers on a small but busy harbor. The town's main visitor attraction is the Historic Dunkirk Lighthouse and Veteran's Park Museum (1 Lighthouse Point Drive, off Route 15; tel. 716/366-5050; open June–Aug Thur–Tues, Apr–May and Sept–Dec Mon–Sat; entrance fee). Here, volunteers guide visitors through the old keeper's quarters, which still look much as they did back in the 1940s, and up into the 95-ft-high (29-meter) lighthouse tower. Also on site is a museum dedicated to the armed forces and various dry-docked small boats.

Just south of Dunkirk, **Fredonia** is a pretty town of solid brick buildings and tree-lined streets. The nation's first gas tank was installed here in 1821, making it possible to light the entire village with gas lamps – an all-but-unheard-of feat at the time. Today, Fredonia boasts the 1891 Fredonia Opera House (9–11 Church Street; tel. 716/679-0891), an ornate historic theater, open during performances only.

Route 60 continues south from Fredonia to the town of **Cassadaga** ⑰, best known as the home of the Lily Dale Assembly (5 Melrose Park, off Route 60; tel. 716/595-8721; open late June–Aug daily; entrance fee). Founded in 1879 by the Fox sisters of Rochester, Lily Dale sits on the shores of a peaceful lake. Today this spiritualist community attracts mediums from all over the country, and Lily Dale offers daily services, lectures, the laying-on of hands, and sessions with clairvoyants throughout the summer. Most lectures are delivered in an 1883 open-air auditorium. Also on site are a Healing Temple, Forest Temple and inspirational Stump, where mediums demonstrate their skills. The general public is welcome to attend most events, but the private sessions with clairvoyants must be booked well in advance. Overlooking the lake is the creaky Victorian-era Maplewood Hotel, offering inexpensive accommodations to both clairvoyants and more ordinary folk alike.

LEFT: a rural backwater.
BELOW: Dunkirk Lighthouse.

Park outhouses are one way of getting back to nature.

Hugging the shore of Lake Erie from Dunkirk west to the Pennsylvania border is Route 5, also known as the Seaway Trail. Marked by green-and-white route markers, the Seaway Trail is the largest national recreational trail in the US. East of Dunkirk, it continues all along New York's northern coastline, following the Niagara River, Lake Ontario, and the St Lawrence River.

Numerous fine recreational parks are located on or just off the Seaway Trail; among them is the Lake Erie State Park (Route 5; open daily; entrance fee in summer; tel: 716/792-9214), to the southwest of Dunkirk. Situated on a small bluff overlooking Lake Erie, the 335-acre (135-hectare) park has a pleasant beach, hiking and nature trails, and a campsite with scenic vistas.

Barcelona Harbor is a hamlet so tiny it might pass by in a blink. Nonetheless, it is home to the handsome, well-preserved Barcelona Lighthouse, built in 1829 and originally powered by natural gas. Alas, the lighthouse is now privately owned and so closed to the general public, but next door is a small park and boat launching dock with superb views of Lake Erie.

Route 394 heads south from Barcelona Harbor to the town of **Westfield** ⓲. Many of the solid brick storefronts along Main Street house antiques shops, while on the outskirts of downtown is the imposing 1818 McClurg Mansion, now home to the Chautauqua County Historical Society Museum (Main Street, at Route 394; tel: 716/326-2977; open Tues–Sun; entrance fee). Inside are restored period rooms, Native American artifacts, and an exhibit on Grace Bedell. At age 11, Grace sent a letter to Abraham Lincoln, then campaigning for the 1860 election, and suggested that he would look better if he grew whiskers. Surprisingly, Lincoln followed her advice and asked to meet her the following year when his train stopped in Westfield. A bronze Lincoln-Bedell Statue across

BELOW: Griffis Sculpture Park at Ashford Hollow.

Map on page 284

from the museum commemorates the event, and a bouquet of flowers lies at Lincoln's feet. Grace was so nervous that she dropped them.

Chautauqua and Chautauqua Lake

The historic town of **Mayville** sits at the northern end of Chautauqua Lake, centered around the handsome, 19th-century Chautauqua County Courthouse on Main Street. The *Chautauqua Belle*, a replica of a 19th-century paddlewheel steamship, leaves from the town dock during the summer on 1-hour cruises of the lake (15 Water Street; tel: 716/753-2403; call for schedule). At 22 miles (35 km) long and 1,400 ft (425 meters) high, Chautauqua is a lovely and busy lake, often dotted with many brightly colored sailboats and other small craft. "Chautauqua" is said to be Iroquois for "two moccasins fastened together," an apt description for this long, thin body of water, indented in the middle.

Chautauqua ⑲, just south of Mayville, is the home of the Chautauqua Institution (Route 394; tel: 716/357-6200 or 800/836-ARTS; open June–Aug daily; entrance fee), a large, self-contained Victorian village that is a sort of educational camp for adults. Vacationers come here for a week or two at a time to rent a room or cottage, and take courses in subjects from Greek drama and philosophy to foreign languages and computers. Day visitors are welcome to browse in the institution's small museum, tour the grounds, use the beaches, and attend many of the lectures, concerts, and other events.

Midway down Chautauqua Lake is its narrowest crossing point. The tiny, flat Bemus Point-Stow Ferry (tel: 716/753-2403), which operates whenever there is a passenger, runs between its two shores. The ride takes a mere five minutes. **Bemus Point** ⑳ is a small, old-fashioned resort village sprinkled with

Chautauqua Lake is renowned for its giant muskies, as well as bass and wall-eye. The record muskie caught in the lake weighed 51 lb 3oz (23 kg).

BELOW: home, sweet home.

THE CHAUTAUQUA INSTITUTION

A village unto itself, complete with winding streets and gingerbread-style Victorian homes, the Chautauqua Institution was founded in 1872 as a vacation school for Sunday School teachers. Its mission, according to co-founder Dr John Heyl Vincent, was "self-improvement in all our faculties, for all of us through all time, for the greatest good of all people." Although rooted in Christianity, Chautauqua was open to all who wished to come, and the idea of learning and self-improvement in a pastoral setting immediately caught on. Soon other "mini-chautauquas" and "traveling chautauquas," all advertising "pure, wholesome entertainment," sprouted up all over the country. The Chautauqua Movement, as it became known, pioneered several important developments in adult education, including correspondence courses and the "great books" curricula. Today, the Chautauqua is filled with palatial buildings, auditoriums, meeting halls, restaurants, a bookshop, an 18-hole golf course, and four beaches fronting Chautauqua Lake. One of the highlights is its 1881 Athenaeum Hotel. Once the largest wooden frame building in the country, the Athenaeum presides over an emerald green lawn overlooking the lake. The hotel was wired for electricity by Thomas Edison himself.

gift shops and restaurants. At one end stands the creaky old Hotel Lenhart (20–22 Lakeside Drive, tel: 716/386-2715). Though worn around the edges, the rambling, mustard-colored hostelry is a classic, lined with long front porch filled with rocking chairs *(see page 329)*.

Jamestown to Salamanca

Follow Route 17 and 60 south of Chautauqua Lake to **Jamestown ㉑**, a hilly city that was once a leading furniture manufacturing center. Founded in 1811, Jamestown's earliest settlers included a number of skilled woodworkers who made furniture. In the 1850s, Swedish cabinetmakers, attracted by that industry, began to arrive, and by the late 1800s Jamestown was predominantly Swedish. Today, much of the city is still of Swedish descent.

The comedienne Lucille Ball also grew up in Jamestown and her memory is honored in the **Lucy-Desi Museum** (212 Pine Street; tel: 716/484-7070; open May–Oct daily; Nov–Apr Sat–Sun; entrance fee). The daughter of a telephone linesman and a concert pianist, Ball was born in 1911 into a family that encouraged her theatrical interests. At age 15 she landed her first showbusiness job as a chorus girl in a Broadway musical, but it wasn't until 1940, when she was cast in the movie *Too Many Girls* with future husband Desi Arnaz, that she got her first big break. On display in the museum are plenty of pictures and memorabilia, along with taped interviews with some of Lucy's childhood friends and videos of the *I Love Lucy* TV show.

Off a cobblestone street on the outskirts of Jamestown is the **Roger Tory Peterson Institute of Natural History** (311 Curtis Street; tel: 716/665-2473; open Tues–Sun; entrance fee). Peterson also hailed from Jamestown, and the

Throughout her life, Lucille Ball purchased her favorite Swedish rye bread from Jones Bakery (209 Pine Street, Jamestown; tel: 716/484-1988). After she became famous, she had it shipped to her home in Hollywood.

BELOW: teepee near Salamanca.

Map on page 284

institute is a striking modern building that houses nature exhibits (mostly for kids), an art gallery, library, and gift shop. Paintings by Peterson and other naturalists are always on display.

Head east of Jamestown on Route 17 to reach **Salamanca ㉒**, the only city in the nation situated on a Native American reservation. The Seneca lease the land to the US government on a long-term basis; the current lease, signed in 1990, is due to expire in 2031, with an option to renew.

A must-stop in Salamanca is the **Seneca-Iroquois National Museum** (794 Broad Street Extension; tel: 716/945-1738; open June–Labor Day daily; Labor Day–May Mon–Fri; closed Jan; entrance fee). Compact and well laid out, this museum covers the history of the Seneca Nation from prehistory to the present day. Exhibits explain everything from the complex Iroquois clan system to their use of medicinal plants. To one side is a small theater where a slide show is presented; to the other are cases filled with magnificent *wampum* belts.

Handmade earrings are on display at the Seneca-Iroquois National Museum.

Also in Salamanca is the Salamanca Rail Museum (170 Main Street; tel: 716/945-3133; open Apr–Oct daily, Oct–Mar Tues–Sun; entrance fee). Housed in a restored 1912 passenger depot, the museum is packed with exhibits on the Buffalo, Rochester and Pittsburgh Railway. One exhibit focuses on the early Seneca railroad workers, another on George Pullman of Pullman car fame.

South of Salamanca is the largest state park in New York, the 65,000-acre (26,300-hectare) **Allegany State Park** (Exit 17 or 18 off Route 17; tel: 716/354-9121; open daily; entrance fee in summer). Laced with over 90 miles (150 km) of hiking and biking trails, some of them over rugged terrain, the park also contains two lakes with fishing, boating, and swimming in season. Row boats can be rented and children's programs are presented year-round.

BELOW: boathouse blues.

Ellicottville to Olean

Route 219 heads north of Salamanca to the bustling resort village of **Ellicottville ㉓**. Especially popular during the ski season, Ellicottville is home to the Holiday Valley Resort (28 Parkside Drive; tel: 716/699-2377), which operates 52 slopes and 12 ski lifts during the winter, and an 18-hole golf course and three-pool swimming complex in summer. Also in town is the Nannen Arboretum (28 Parkside Drive; tel: 716/699-2377; open daily; free), planted with more than 250 varieties of rare trees and shrubs. The plants are landscaped into small gardens, and to one side is a shallow reflective pool.

The best reason to visit **Ashford Hollow ㉔** is to see the Griffis Sculpture Park (Route 219; tel: 716/257-9344; open daily; donation), perched on a hilltop with great views of the valley below. Created by Buffalo artist Larry Griffis, the park is filled with magical, 20-ft-high (6-meter) humanoid sculptures that seem to frolic and dance against their backdrop of meadows and trees.

Farther east, **Olean ㉕** is a busy, scrappy city that was once an important junction of the Erie and Pennsylvania Railroads. Back then, the town was a receiving depot for local oil refineries (no longer in operation); the name "Olean" comes from the Latin *oleum*, meaning oil. **Rock City Park** (Rock City

Map
on page
284

Road, 505 Route 16s; tel: 716/372-7790; open daily; entrance fee), built around an enormous outcropping of quartz conglomerate, rises about 7 miles (11 km) outside Olean. Formed some 320 years ago, the outcropping has since been eroded in parts into all sorts of odd shapes. It affords wide-ranging views of the striking Allegheny Mountains.

Allegany County

Allegany County, one of the least known and most beautiful counties in New York State, begins beyond Olean. Largely located in the foothills of the Allegheny Mountains, it is blanketed with a dark rolling landscape and some 23 state forests, covering about 46,000 acres (18,600 hectares). Allegany County has no large cities and few "tourist attractions"; instead there are lots of scenic back roads and villages to explore.

Cuba ㉖ is a low-key local resort clustered around Cuba Lake, a popular haunt of fisherfolk. Once part of the Genesee Valley Canal system, Cuba Lake was the world's largest man-made body of water during the mid- to late 1800s. Downtown, the Cuba Cheese Shoppe (53 Genesee Street; tel: 716/968-3949), proffers a large selection of New York-made cheeses and other gourmet foods. Along South Street between Grove Street and Steven Avenue, there is a handsome Victorian-era historic district.

In the southwestern corner of the county is the village of **Bolivar** ㉗, home to the Pioneer Oil Museum (Main Street; tel: 716/268-1433; call for hours; donation). The first oil drill in the nation was set up in Allegany County in 1867, and a few wildcat oil drills still dot the landscape. However, most of the region's small, remaining oil reserve is too difficult to access. The museum, run entirely by volunteers, documents this local oil history; on display are many historical photographs, documents, tools, and other artifacts relating to the local oil industry.

One of the prettiest villages in Allegany County is **Angelica** ㉘. Founded in 1800, it is laid out around a large, circular park. Handsome churches and public buildings line the park's circumference, while down the side streets are many grand Victorian homes. Along Main Street, there are a number of interesting antiques shops.

Also worth exploring is the village of **Alfred** ㉙, nestled into rolling hills near the eastern edge of the county. Alfred is home to Alfred University, world-renowned since the early 1900s for its College of Ceramics. Many of the roofs here are made of orange terra cotta, an incongruous sight against the surrounding dark woods.

Near the university campus is the **International Museum of Ceramic Art** (200 North Main Street; tel: 607/871-2421; open Tues–Sun; entrance free). Currently housed in an informal arts center, this small museum showcases ceramics and glass from the university's collection of over 8,000 pieces. Objects on display range from antique pottery shards to contemporary sculpture, by both American and foreign artists. A new, larger museum facility, which will be located on campus, is presently under construction. ❑

BELOW:
a rockin' place.
RIGHT:
golden boughs.
OVERLEAF:
autumn wedding.

INSIGHT GUIDES
Travel Tips

New Insight Maps

Maps in Insight Guides are tailored to complement the text. But when you're on the road you sometimes need the big picture that only a large-scale map can provide. This new range of durable Insight Fleximaps has been designed to meet just that need.

Detailed, clear cartography
makes the comprehensive route and city maps easy to follow, highlights all the major tourist sites and provides valuable motoring information plus a full index.

Informative and easy to use
with additional text and photographs covering a destination's top 10 essential sites, plus useful addresses, facts about the destination and handy tips on getting around.

Laminated finish
allows you to mark your route on the map using a non-permanent marker pen, and wipe it off. It makes the maps more durable and easier to fold than traditional maps.

The first titles
cover many popular destinations. They include Algarve, Amsterdam, Bangkok, California, Cyprus, Dominican Republic, Florence, Hong Kong, Ireland, London, Mallorca, Paris, Prague, Rome, San Francisco, Sydney, Thailand, Tuscany, USA Southwest, Venice, and Vienna.

INSIGHT GUIDES
The world's largest collection of visual travel guides

CONTENTS

Getting Acquainted

The Place

Area: New York State is located in the northeastern United States and occupies 47,224 sq. land miles (122,310 sq. km) and a total mass of 54,475 sq. miles (141,090 sq. km), bordered to the east by Connecticut, Massachusetts and Vermont; to the south by Pennsylvania, New Jersey and the Atlantic Ocean; to the west by Lake Erie and the Canadian province of Ontario; and to the north by the Canadian provinces of Ontario and Quebec.

Capital city: Albany

Population: 18.14 million

Nickname: The Empire State

Religion: 80 percent Christian (both Protestant and Catholic), with Judaism (7 percent), Islam (0.8 percent), Buddhism (0.2 percent), Hinduism (0.6 percent) plus Sufism and various others (1.5 percent) also represented

Time Zone: Eastern Standard Time, three hours ahead of California and five hours behind London (GMT)

Currency: US dollar ($)

Weights and measures: Imperial

International dialing code: (1)

Local dialing codes: In New York City, Manhattan 212 and 646; 718 for Brooklyn, the Bronx and Staten Island; 516 for Long Island; 914, 518 and 607 for the Hudson and Catskills areas; 518 for Albany and the Adirondacks; 315 and 607 for the Thousand Islands and Finger Lakes; 716 for Chautauqua-Allegheny and Niagara

Toll Free Numbers: 1-800 and 1-888 numbers are only free when dialed within the United States

Electricity: 110 volts AC. Adaptors can be bought at most airports as well as local hardware stores

Climate

New York State's gorgeous scenery provides a perfect setting for the drama of the seasons. Autumn, as in New England, is perhaps the most breathtaking: the colors of the foliage make a brilliant spectacle. Upstate, winters can be harsh, with temperatures below freezing and heavy snowfall. But the beauty of this wilderness blanketed in snow is hard to match.

In New York City and its environs, particularly Long Island, winter is not usually as harsh, although snowfalls and temperatures are unpredictable, with snow falling as late as April.

Throughout the state, summers can be hot but pleasant, especially in the mountains and along Long Island's beach-lined seashore. In New York City, however, summers as a rule are humid and oppressive, and can be unbearable without an air-conditioned hotel room.

Average Temperatures

New York City:

	°F	°C
January	37/24	(3/-4)
April	57/42	(14/6)
July	82/66	(28/19)
October	69/66	(21/19)

Buffalo, New York State:

	°F	°C
January	34/20	(1/-7)
April	56/42	(13/6)
July	81/61	(27/16)
October	63/45	(17/7)

Economy

Major industries include agriculture and manufacturing, with dairy products (cheese, butter and milk) generating the heftiest percentage of farm income. Cash-earning crops around the state include apples and other fruit, along with various other produce. Machinery, high-tech electronics, cameras and imaging supplies, and aircraft parts make up a large part of the state's manufacturing base, while construction is another important source of local employment.

In New York City, international finance, publishing and advertising, as well as shipping and transportation, account for billions of dollars in annual assets. The tourism industry and the large numbers of conventions held here also help create jobs as well as attract millions of dollars; this is increasingly true throughout the state as well.

Government

The current New York State constitution has been in effect since 1894, and sets the guidelines for how the state government, based in Albany, works. Led by a governor who serves a four-year term, it includes the State Legislature divided into a 61-member Senate and a 150-member assembly. (Members of each serve two-year terms.) Major political parties, as in the rest of the country, are the Republicans and the Democrats, with a smattering of Libertarians, Conservatives and Social Democrats.

New York City is governed by a mayor and a strong city council, made stronger by a US Supreme Court ruling that the former Board of Estimate, which was made up of the mayor, the city comptroller and presidents of each of the five boroughs, was unconstitutional.

Culture and Customs

In fast-paced New York City, few people seem to have time for anything not on their schedule. Even asking for directions on the street is best done with an awareness of this, ideally while moving at the same pace and in the same direction of the informant. Despite their reputation for rudeness, most New Yorkers are helpful to visitors, depending of course on how often they've been asked the same question that day.

Upstate, life proceeds at a more leisurely pace, particularly in the small towns that often personify

Facts about New York

- Broadway, one of the world's most famous streets, was originally an Indian warpath
- In 1883, circus impressario PT Barnum led 21 elephants across the Brooklyn Bridge to convince New Yorkers it was safe to cross
- Established in 1803, the New York Post is the oldest newspaper in the country
- At 110 stories, 1,377 feet (420 meters) the World Trade Center's Rooftop Promenade is the world's highest open-air observation platform
- Grand Central is the largest train station in the world
- Charles Feltman, a Coney Island vendor, introduced the hot dog to the world in 1889
- During the winter of 1902, the East River was completely frozen over and it was possible to walk from Brooklyn to Manhattan on the ice
- Before being landscaped in 1858, Central Park was full of quarries, pig farms and swamps

America at its best. Remember, however, that tourism in some places (excluding major attractions like Lake Placid and Niagara Falls) is more the exception than the rule, so be prepared to chat about where you're from and where you're going. Even if your would-be informant hasn't a clue about giving you directions to where you're actually headed for, you may pick up helpful tips about a nearby restaurant or worthwhile local attraction.

Planning the Trip

What To Bring

Like Paris, New York City is a fashion capital and New Yorkers generally dress to be seen. Fashion can change according to the part of town you're in, however, with Upper East Side attire on the elegant side, Soho and the Villages more casual (black is always good), and Midtown and Lower Manhattan's Financial District (during the weekdays) conservative and business-like.

In rural areas, dress is more practical and traditional, and especially in the state's northern areas, where clothing is generally geared toward the outdoors. (Even up there, some of the nicer restaurants and clubs may require men to wear a jacket and tie.)

Because New York's climate is so variable, it's a good rule of thumb to bring a raincoat no matter what time of year you arrive. If you're in the mountains or near the Great Lakes, a sweater or jacket will come in handy even in summer, as evening temperatures can drop drastically. Thermal underwear, scarves, gloves, proper foot gear and a heavy coat are as necessary for a north country winter as they can be in Manhattan, so plan accordingly. Summer on Long Island and elsewhere dictates bathing suits, sunglasses and an extra towel for the beach.

Passports and Visas

To enter the United States you will need a passport, a passport-size photograph, evidence of intent to leave the United States after your visit and, depending on your country of origin, a visitor's visa.

Customs Regulations

For a full breakdown of customs allowances write to the **US Customs Service**. Meat or meat products, illegal drugs, seeds, plants, fruits and firearms are among the prohibited goods. Do not bring in any of these or any duty-free goods worth more than $400 (returning Americans) or $100 (foreign travelers). Visitors over 21 are allowed to bring in 200 cigarettes, 3lbs of tobacco or 50 cigars and one liter of alcohol.

A non-resident may claim, as free of duty and internal revenue tax, articles up to $100 in value for use as gifts for other persons, if you remain in the US for at least 72 hours and the gifts accompany you. This $100 gift exemption or any part of it can be claimed only once every six months. You may include 100 cigars within this gift exemption, but alcoholic beverages may not be included. Do not giftwrap your articles, as they must be available for inspection.

Articles bought duty-free in foreign countries are subject to US Customs duty and restrictions, but may be included in your exemption.
US Customs Service
PO Box 7407
Washington, DC 20044
Tel: (202) 927-6724

Health

Depending where your flight originated, proof of vaccination against cholera and other diseases may be required. Canadian citizens, as well as British residents of Canada and Bermuda, are normally exempt from these requirements, but check for specific regulations in your home country.

If you need prescription medication, ask your doctor to write a prescription that gives the generic name before you leave; it's also helpful to take an extra prescription for glasses, if you wear them. During summer in upstate New York, insect repellant is a must.

It's also wise to invest in a traveler's health plan before

Public Holidays

The United States has gradually shifted most of its public holidays to the Monday closest to the actual dates, thus creating a number of three-day weekends throughout the year. If a holiday falls on a Sunday, the Monday after is also a holiday and post offices, government offices, etc are closed. Holidays that are celebrated no matter what day they fall on are:

- **January** New Year's Day (1); Martin Luther King Jr's Birthday (15)
- **February** President's Day (3rd Monday)
- **May** Memorial Day (last Monday)
- **July** Independence Day (4)
- **September** Labor Day (1st Monday)
- **October** Columbus Day (2nd Monday)
- **November** Election Day (1st Tuesday, every four years); Veterans' Day (11) Thanksgiving (last Thursday)
- **December** Christmas Day (25).

departure, as medical care in New York City is excellent but expensive: emergency room treatment is generally a minimum of $50, while the average hospital room costs at least $300 a night.

Currency

The unit of currency in the US is the dollar ($), made up of 100 cents (¢). The following coins are in circulation at present: cent (1¢); nickel (5¢); dime (10¢); quarter (25¢); half-dollar (50¢); and $1. Banknotes come in the following denominations: $1, $2, $5, $10, $20, $50, $100 and up. Note that there are two types of $50 and $100 bills.

There is no limit to the amount of foreign or domestic currency that can be taken in or out of the country; travelers' checks or cash worth more than $100,000 must be declared, however.

It's best to bring a credit card (e.g. Visa, MasterCard), US dollar travelers checks for small sums ($20, $50), and also a small amount of cash in low-denomination notes. Credit cards are accepted almost everywhere, although not all cards at all places. They can also be used to withdraw money at ATMs (automatic teller machines) marked with the corresponding stickers (i.e. Visa, MasterCard, American Express, etc.). Bank cards from foreign countries (and other states)

can be used at ATMs using corresponding systems (such as Cirrus).

A few banks still charge a fee to change traveler's checks unless you have an account there, although traveler's checks (as long as they are in dollar amounts) are accepted in most hotels and good restaurants if accompanied by identification. Keep your passport handy.

In New York City, money can be exchanged on weekdays at branches of Thomas Cook, American Express and the Chase Manhattan Bank. Other banks that deal with international money transactions include Citibank and Westminster Bank USA, with branches throughout the state.

Among the foreign exchange centers in Manhattan that offer full services are Ruesch International and Harold Reuter & Co.

Thomas Cook
630 Fifth Ave
Tel: (1-800) 287-7362
American Express
374 Park Ave
Tel: (212) 421-8240
Chase Manhattan Bank
277 Park Ave
Tel: (212) 935-9935
Ruesch International
608 Fifth Ave
Tel: (212) 977-2700
Harold Reuter & Co
Grand Central Terminal
Tel: (212) 661-7600

Getting There

BY AIR

If all roads lead to Rome, most airlines lead to New York City. Thousands of planes land and take off from the city's airports every day. Kennedy International Airport and Newark International Airport, in nearby Newark, New Jersey, serves international flights and all major international carriers; LaGuardia Airport serves domestic flights.

Other airports in the state include Stewart International Airport in Newburgh; Greater Buffalo International Airport; Greater Rochester International Airport; Hancock International Airport in Syracuse; and Albany County Airport. These are served by most major US airlines, including American, Continental, Delta, Northwest, United and USAir.

BY SEA

The days of the great ocean liners have long passed, but there are still passenger ship sailings to New York City from the other side of the Atlantic, most notably the *Queen Elizabeth II*. For information call **Cunard Steam-Ship Co plc** in London. Tel: (++44-20) 7491-3930.

BY RAIL

Amtrak trains provide service to all the major cities in the state from Pennsylvania Station on Seventh Avenue and 32nd Street in New York City, including Poughkeepsie, Albany, Utica, Syracuse, Rochester and Buffalo. There are three major routes: "The Empire Corridor", which takes passengers north through the Hudson Valley and the Finger Lakes region to Buffalo and Niagara Falls, and stops at many of the smaller towns along the way; the "Adirondack", which travels north along the Hudson, through part of Adirondack Park and along the shore of Lake Champlain, stopping en route at Poughkeepsie,

Albany, Saratoga Springs and Plattsburgh, among other places, before ending in Montreal; and the "Lake Shore Limited", which basically follows the "Empire Corridor" route to Syracuse, Rochester and Buffalo, making fewer stops along the way (and ending at Chicago).

Amtrak trains to other parts of the US, as well as trains run by the **Long Island Railroad** also depart from Pennsylvania Station. Trains for Westchester County and nearby Connecticut are operated by the **Metro-North Commuter Railroad**, and depart from Grand Central Station on 42nd Street.

For schedules and information call the following numbers:
Amtrak
Tel: (212) 582-6875 or toll-free from within the US (1-800) 872-7245.
Long Island Railroad
Tel: (718) 217-5477
Metro North Railroad
Tel: (212) 532-4900 or (1-800) METRO-INFO

BY ROAD

The New York State Thruway (Interstate 87) stretches north to Albany from New York City, then veers west through Utica, Syracuse and Rochester to Buffalo. Other highways include Interstate 88, which connects Schenectady and Binghamton; Interstate 81, which joins Binghamton to the Thousand Islands and St Lawrence Seaway; and State Route 17, which travels northwest from Newburgh to Lake Erie, linking Jamestown, Elmira and Binghamton along the way.

A scenic driving alternative is provided by US Route 9, which meanders north-south from New York City all the way to the Canadian border. Routes 5 and 20 are also scenic alternatives.

The major artery to many destinations on Long Island is the Long Island Expressway (Interstate 495), sometimes called the world's biggest parking lot (especially during rush hour), which can be accessed from New York City via the Triborough Bridge or the Midtown Tunnel and runs from Manhattan to Riverhead. Route 25A runs parallel to the Expressway at many points, and is slower (with traffic lights) but less congested.

It's worth noting that car rentals in New York City can be almost three times as expensive as elsewhere in the state, although prices depend on the size and type of car (*see page 315*). Check with an airline or travel agent before you go to find out about special package deals that provide rental cars for reduced rates.

By Bus
Greyhound Bus Lines operates buses throughout the state, with all departures from the Port Authority Bus Terminal in New York City (Eighth Ave and 41st St). Regional services are provided by Adirondack Trailways, Shortline/Hudson Transit Lines and Blue Bird Coach Lines.
Greyhound Bus Lines
Tel: (1-800) 231-2222
Adirondack Trailways
Tel: (1-800) 225-6815;
in Albany (518) 436-9651;
in Kingston (845) 339-4230
Shortline/Hudson Transit Lines
Tel: (1-800) 631-8405;
in New York City (212) 736-4700
Coach USA
Tel: in Syracuse (315) 471-4777;
in Rochester (716) 334-2222

Practical Tips

Business Hours

Normal business hours are 9am to 5 or 6pm, but shops, particularly in New York City, tend to stay open much later and sometimes open earlier. Needless to say, there is no lunchtime closing, which for many stores is the busiest time of day. Some stores stay open on Sun.

Generally, banks are open 9am–3pm, Mon–Fri, although more and more open earlier than 9am (as early as 7am), and stay open later (as late as 7pm) at least one day a week. They are often open on Sat too.

Media

NEWSPAPERS & MAGAZINES

New York is the media capital of the country, with New York City offering three major dailies (the *New York Times*, *Daily News*, and *New York Post*), as well as informative weekly magazines such as *Time Out New York*, *New York* and the *New Yorker*, all of which offer extensive listings of things to do and see that week, as does the weekly *Village Voice*. The *Wall Street Journal*, as well as *Forbes*, *Fortune*, *Time* and *Newsweek*, are also published in New York City.

Every city in the state has its own newspapers and usually magazines, which are the best sources of information for finding out what's going on while you're there. Useful regional publications include *Adirondack Life*, *Hudson Valley and Kaatskill Life*, and are available on newsstands, in airports and bookstores as well as other retail outlets (like food markets).

RADIO & TV

Radio in New York is varied. On the FM waveband, a few of the most popular stations are: WQXR-FM 96.3 (classical), WFUV-FM 90.7 (folk, blues, Irish) and WBGO-FM 88.3 (jazz); on the AM band, check out WOR-AM 710 (talk radio) and WINS-AM 1010 (24-hour news). For news about Metro New York City area traffic and other bulletins, stay tuned to WINS (1010 on the AM dial) radio station, which broadcasts 24 hours a day, as do most other commercial stations.

In New York City there are seven major broadcast TV stations on the VHF band (2, 4, 5, 7, 9, 11 and 13), plus local stations (21, 25 and 31) that specialize in educational, foreign-language or public television programs, and a couple (41, 47) that broadcast in Spanish on UHF. Dozens more are available on cable, including CNN, TNT, HBO (Home Box Office) and the local Public Access stations.

Upstate, the viewing is less varied, although cable is now available in all but the most remote (or mountainous) regions.

Postal Services

Post office hours vary in central big-city branches and in smaller cities and towns. Hotel personnel will answer questions about the business hours of the nearest post office. Stamps may be purchased from vending machines, found everywhere from airports to stores.

In New York City, the Post Office on Eighth Avenue between 31st and 33rd streets is open 24 hours a day for stamps, express mail and certified mail.

Telecommunications

Public telephones can be found in hotel lobbies, restaurants, drugstores, street corners and other general locations. If you're using a phone card or credit card, make sure that the particular phone is under the local carrier (Bell Atlantic), not a private company, or

Emergency Numbers

Police, Ambulance, Fire: tel 911
Deaf Emergency Line (NYC): tel: (1-800) 342 4357.

the rates will be as much as three times more than they should be; by law, these are identified by a sticker or posted notice on the phonebox.

The cost of a local phone call is 25¢. Long distance calls are cheaper after 5pm and lowest on weekends and after 11pm. Check the yellow pages of the phone book for a list of local and international area codes, or dial "0" and inquire.

Western Union will take telegram and telex messages by phone; check the local phone directory or call local information (411 or 555 1212). Most hotels offer fax services, but faxes can also be sent from copy shops and private mailing facilities such as Mail Box Etc.

Internet and E-mail

Internet service via telephone lines is available throughout New York State; in cities, rooms in better hotels are often equipped with high-speed access portals. To send and receive e-mail on the road, consider establishing an account with a provider such as Hotmail, through which you can send and receive messages at locations such as Internet cafés, which are increasingly easy to find in cities.

There's free computer access at the New York Public Library's Science, Industry and Business branch at Madison Avenue and 34th Street (tel: 212/592-7000).

Mobile Telephones

Cellular telephone service is available throughout the more settled areas of New York State, although it becomes spotty in the countryside and non-existent in deep rural areas such as the Adirondacks. Wireless mobile phone service, an alternative to cellular advertised as having a clearer sound, is available in large metropolitan areas only.

Consulates in New York City

Australia: 636 Fifth Ave, tel: 408-8400
Canada: 1251 Ave of the Americas, tel: 596-1700
France: 934 Fifth Ave, tel: 606-3600
Germany: 460 Park Ave, tel: 572-5600
Ireland: 345 Park Ave, tel: 319-2555
Italy: 690 Park Ave, tel: 737-9100
Mexico: 8 East 41st, tel: 689-0456
The Netherlands: 1 Rockefeller Plaza, tel: 246-1429
New Zealand: 780 Third Ave, tel: 832-4038
South Africa: 333 East 38th St, tel: 213-4880
United Kingdom: Third Ave, tel: 745-0202

Medical Services

Insurance is a must, as medical treatment is expensive.

For immediate medical attention, head for the nearest hospital emergency room: generally, whether you have medical insurance or not, they are required to treat you, and credit cards are usually accepted for on-the-spot payment. Most hospitals throughout the state have 24-hour emergency rooms. You usually have a long wait before you see the doctor, but the care is thorough and professional.

While in New York City, you can call a 24-hour doctors-on-call service, tel: (718) 238-2100; for dental emergencies, tel: (212) 679-3966. Kaufman's Pharmacy, 50th St and Lexington Ave, tel: (212) 755-2266, is open 24 hours a day, seven days a week.

Security & Crime

New York City has long had a reputation for high levels of – often violent – crime, but in recent years it has, according to the statistics, become safer than most large US cities. So long as you use common sense, following these guidelines,

New York State Tourist Offices

New York State
New York State Division of Tourism
PO Box 2603, Albany, NY 12220
Tel: (518) 474-4116; (1-800)
ENJOY-NY for accommodations.
Info; www.iloveny.state.ny.us.

New York City
NYC & Co.
810 Seventh Ave, New York,
NY 10019
Tel: (212) 484-1222
www.nycvisit.com

Long Island
Long Island Visitors Bureau
350 Vanderbilt Pkwy, Hauppage,
NY 11788
Tel: (516) 951-3440, (1-800)
441-4601; www.licvb.com

Hudson Valley
Columbia County Tourism
401 State St, Hudson, NY 12534
Tel: (518) 828-3375, (1-800)
724-1846
Duchess County Tourism
3 Neptune Rd, Poughkeepsie,
NY 12601
Tel: (914) 463-4000, (1-800)
445-3131
Westchester Visitors Bureau
235 Mamaroneck Ave,
White Plains, NY 10605
Tel: (914) 948-0047, (1-800)
933-9282

Catskills
Delaware County Chamber of Commerce
97 Main St, Delhi, NY 13753
Tel: (607) 746-2281, (1-800)
642-4443
Greene County Promotion Dept
PO Box 527, Catskill, NY 12414
Tel: (518) 943-3223, (1-800)
542-2414
Sullivan County Visitors Association
100 North St, Monticello,
NY 12701
Tel: (914) 794-3000
Ulster County Tourism
County Office Bldg, Kingston,
NY 12401
Tel: (914) 340-3566, (1-800)
342-5826

Capital-Saratoga
Albany County Convention & Visitor Bureau
25 Quackenbush Sq,
Albany, NY 12207
Tel: (518) 434-1217, (1-800)
258-3582
Washington County Tourism
County Office Bldg, Fort Edward,
NY 12828
Tel: (518) 746-2290

Adirondacks
Adirondack Regional Tourism Council
PO Box 2149, Plattsburgh,
NY 12901
Tel: (518) 846-8016, (1-800)
487-6867
Plattsburgh/North Country/Lake Champlain Regional Visitors Center
Box 310, Plattsburgh, NY 12901
Tel: (518) 563-1000
Franklin County Tourism
63 West Main St, Malone, NY
12953
Tel: (518) 481-1704, (1-800)
709-4895
Hamilton County Tourism
Box 771, White Birch Lane,
Indian Lake, NY 12842
Tel: (518) 648-5239

Thousand Islands & St Lawrence Seaway
Oswego County Promotion & Tourism
46 East Bridge St, Oswego,
NY 13126
Tel: (315) 349-8322, (1-800)
248-4386.
Thousand Islands International Tourism Council
Box 400, Collins Landing,
Alexandria Bay, NY 13607
Tel: (315) 482-2520, (1-800)
8-ISLAND (from US and Canada)

Central-Leatherstocking
Leatherstocking Country
327 North Main St, PO Box 447,
Herkimer, NY 13350
Tel: (315) 866-1500
Oneida County Convention & Visitors Bureau
PO Box 551, Utica, NY 13503

Tel: (315) 724-7221, (1-800)
426-3132 (US and Canada)

Finger Lakes
Finger Lakes Association
309 Lake St, Penn Yan, NY 14527
Tel: (315) 536-7488, (1-800)
KIT-4FUN
Greater Rochester Visitors Association
126 Andrews St, NY 14604
Tel: (716) 546-3070, (1-800) 677-7282
Ithaca/Tompkins County Convention & Visitors Bureau
904 East Shore Dr, Ithaca,
NY 14850
Tel: (607) 272-1313, (1-800)
284-8422 (US and Canada)
Syracuse Convention & Visitors Bureau
572 Salina St, Syracuse, NY 13202
Tel: (315) 470-1800
Tioga County Chamber of Commerce
188 Front St, Oswego, NY 13827
Tel: (607) 687-7440, (1-800)
671-7772

Greater Niagara
Buffalo Visitors Center
617 Main St, Buffalo, NY 14203
Tel: (716) 852-2356, (1-800) BUFFALO
Niagara Falls Convention & Visitors Bureau
310 Fourth St, Niagara Falls,
NY 14303
Tel: (716) 285-2400
Orleans County Tourism Office
Route 31 West, Albion, NY 14411
Tel: (716) 589-7004, (1-800)
724-0314

Chautauqua-Allegheny
Allegheny County Tourism
City Office Bldg, Belmont, NY 14813
Tel: (716) 268-9229, (1-800)
836-1869
Cattaraugus County Tourism
303 Court St, Little Valley,
NY 14755
Tel: (716) 938-9111
Salamanca Chamber of Commerce
784 Broad St, Salamanca,
NY 14779
Tel: (716) 945-2034

you shouldn't encounter any threatening situations:

• Don't carry large sums of money or wear flashy or expensive jewelry;

• Hang on to your purse or shoulder bag and keep your wallet in your front pocket;

• Women especially should avoid traveling alone late at night;

• Don't enter strange or deserted areas alone;

• Walk purposefully, with confidence, even if you're lost – if you look like you don't know your way around, you may appear vulnerable;

• If you need to take the subway at night be sure to stand near either the token booth, a transit police officer or in the designated "off-hour waiting areas". Never ride in a car with just a few people in it. In general, buses and taxis are safer than the subway;

• If you are unfortunate enough to be mugged, walk or take a taxi to the nearest police station and report the crime. The police probably won't be of much help in finding your assailant, but they can do the paperwork for any insurance claims. There's no good response to a mugger. Your best bet is to give him whatever he asks for and hope that's the end of it.

Elsewhere in the state, especially in cities, the same precautions could apply; if you've rented a car, don't leave your belongings in the vehicle unlocked or unattended.

In an emergency if 911 doesn't respond, dial "0" or, time permitting, turn to the inside front cover of a local telephone directory, which lists emergency numbers for the area. Other vital telephone numbers are generally contained on a detachable page near the front.

Lost Property

Your chances of retrieving lost property are not high, but the occasional public-spirited individual may turn items into the nearest police precinct or station. In New York City, to inquire about items left on public transportation, tel: (718) 625-6200. For items left in taxis, tel: (212) 840-4734.

Lost or stolen credit cards

American Express
Tel: (1-800) 528-4800
Visa
Tel: (1-800) 227-6800
Carte Blanche/Diners Club
Tel: (1-800) 525-9135
MasterCard
Tel: (1-800) 826-2181

Disabled Travelers

Information about rights and facilities in New York City is available from the **Mayor's Office for People with Disabilities**, 52 Chambers St, Room 206, New York, NY 10007, tel: (212) 788-2830.

Student Travelers

For $20 ($21 by mail) and proof of status, the **Council on International Educational Exchange** (CIEE, 205 East 42nd St, New York, NY 10017, tel: 212/822-2600) issues student identity cards for discounts on some services, including admission to museums.

Gay Travelers

New York City's prominence as a gay center dates back to the Stonewall Riots of the late 1960s (*see page 129*) and continues with the annual Gay Pride Parade up Sixth Avenue in June.

The **Gay and Lesbian Switchboard** (tel: 212/777-1800) exists specifically to provide information to gay men and women about all aspects of gay life in New York City, including bars, restaurants, accommodations, legal counseling, etc. Many bookshops (such as the **Gay & Lesbian Bookstore**, 548 Hudson St, tel: 212/989-4850) stock the *Gay Yellow Pages*, along with various other useful publications.

Religious Services

In metropolitan areas such as New York City, Albany, Syracuse, Rochester and Buffalo, churches representing virtually all Christian as well as Jewish (Orthodox,

Taxes

Value added tax is never included in the prices displayed at tills in New York, therefore, you pay the basic price plus 8.25 percent sales tax. There is also a 13.25 percent tax on all hotel rooms. This so-called room tax is supplemented still further by a transient occupancy tax of $2 per room per night.

Conservative, and Reform), Muslim, Buddhist, Hindu, and other places of worship offer regular services. In New York City, it is often possible to find services in a variety of languages.

Outside major cities or resort areas, Jewish services – particularly Orthodox – may be more difficult to locate, although services sponsored by Hillel organizations on larger college campuses are often available. Likewise, mosques and temples are unlikely to be found outside cities.

In small towns and rural areas, religious services are often held only once on the specified weekly observance day. This is particularly true of rural Catholic churches, which frequently have one priest who serves parishes in several communities. Inquire about worship times several days in advance.

Tipping

The majority of New Yorkers in the service industries (hotels, restaurants, transportation) regard tips as a God-given right, not just a pleasant gratuity. The fact is, many of them rely on tips to make up for what are often miserly salaries. Unless service is bad, tip bellmen and hotel porters a minimum of 50¢ per bag (or a dollar if just one bag); hotel maids $1 per day, doormen expect $1 for merely opening car doors or calling cabs; waiters 15 percent of the bill, taxi drivers 10–15 percent of the total fare, cloakroom attendants $1; and at the bar, it's usually $1 per drink.

Getting Around

On Arrival

There are a number of ways to get to Manhattan, 15 miles (24 km) from John F Kennedy International Airport in Queens. The cheapest method is to take the shuttle bus marked "Subway" to the Howard Beach/JFK Airport subway station, where the "A" train connects directly with Manhattan for $1.50. However, if you're unfamiliar with the subway system, take the more expensive New York Airport Service to midtown Manhattan (every 15–30 minutes until midnight). The fare is under $15; for more information, tel: (718) 706-9678.

Gray Line Air Shuttle minibuses (daily, 7am–11pm) stop at most hotels in Manhattan between 23rd and 63rd streets and cost about $14. For information, tel: (212) 315-3006 or (1-800) 451-0455.

The most comfortable way to get to Manhattan is by taxi. This costs a flat rate of $30, plus bridge and tunnel tolls and a 15 percent tip. Be aware that visitors straight off an airplane are often besieged by private taxi drivers offering rides into the city at vastly inflated prices. While most are reputable enough, unless you have great savvy and a keen sense of direction it's best to stick to the official taxi stands of yellow (licensed) cabs for rides.

From Newark International Airport 16 miles (26 km) east of Manhattan, there are bus connections, including **Olympia Trails Airport Express Bus**, tel: (212) 964-6233 or (718) 622-7700 to Pennsylvania Station, Grand Central Terminal and the World Trade Center (fares are $11 and above). The Gray Line Air Shuttle minibuses

(between $14–19) again pick up and drop off at hotels. A taxi from Newark is around $40; in the other direction, it is the amount on the meter plus $10, bridge and tunnel tolls and a 15 percent tip.

From LaGuardia Airport, only 8 miles (13 km) east of Manhattan in Queens, **New York Airport Service** buses (every 30 minutes, $10) connect with midtown Manhattan; **Gray Line Air Shuttle** minibuses (under $14) connect with several hotels; taxis are metered and cost between $18–26, with bridge, tunnel tolls and 15 percent tip extra.

Carey Transportation operates buses from both JFK and LaGuardia air terminals to a drop-off point opposite Grand Central Terminal.

New York City Streets

Getting your bearings in Manhattan is remarkably easy. Apart from Lower Manhattan, where the thoroughfares twist and turn and may even be named, all the straight thoroughfares running from west to east are called 'streets' and are numbered from south to north (1st, 2nd, 3rd, etc). In addresses, the addition of a "West" (W) or an "East" (E) after the address number show whether it lies to the west or east of Fifth Avenue.

The avenues run north-south, intersecting with the streets at right angles. They too are numbered, from (starting in the east) First to Twelfth Avenue. Some have their own names, eg York Avenue, Lexington Avenue, Park Avenue and Madison Avenue; and Sixth Avenue is officially called Avenue of the Americas. One street doesn't conform to this pattern: Broadway cuts across the island diagonally.

Transportation in New York City

THE SUBWAY

The New York City subway system, despite its reputation overseas, is one of the most efficient ways to get around. Four million people use

it each day without problem and the city couldn't function without it.

As far as your personal safety on the subway is concerned, a few basic rules should be followed:
• Always stick with the crowd whenever you get on or off a train. Avoid remote entrances or exits.
• Have the exact amount of money for the trip ready; keep your wallet or purse hidden.
• Don't get into carriages that are empty or unilluminated.
• Remember to keep a firm grip on your bags.
• Don't ride the subway between 10pm and 7am.
A subway token costs $1.50 and is bought at the official booth in the station. A single fare allows you to travel as far as you like. The MetroCard – a stored-value plastic card available in denominations from $3 to $120 – allows unlimited transfers throughout the system, including buses. Note that express trains leave out certain stations, local trains make all stops on a particular line.

Traveling at peak times (7.30–9am and 4.30–7pm) is not recommended, unless you like crowds. Free subway maps are sometimes available from the token booths or tel: (718) 694-4903. They are also available at Grand Central Terminal, Pennsylvania Station, the Port Authority Bus Terminal and the New York Convention and Visitors Bureau, now called NYC & Co. (*see page 311*).

Finally, make sure you know the direction you're traveling in – downtown (southwards) or uptown (northwards), and look out for your stop early – signs are hard to see.

BUSES

Buses are safer and more pleasant than the subway, and connect most of the east-west streets (the subway is north-south oriented).

A bus trip costs either $1.50 or one token. Have the exact amount ready – drivers provide no change. If you want to switch buses or move onto the subway, ask the driver for a free transfer ticket. You can also use the MetroCard. In rush hour it can often be faster to walk or take the subway.

Manhattan bus maps are (sometimes) available from token booths at subways, or at the Times Square Visitor Information Center and the official city visitor information center (*see page 311*).

TAXIS

Taxis normally have to be hailed, although there are taxi ranks at Grand Central Terminal as well as elsewhere. You can't call a cab: only private car services can be ordered over the telephone.

All licensed taxis (i.e. yellow with a medallion on the hood)

have electronic meters that print out receipts if required. A nightly surcharge of 50 cents is in effect from 8pm–6am, and a tip of 10–15 percent is expected. Cabbies are usually reluctant to break anything larger than a $20 bill, so be sure to ask before you set off whether the driver has change.

Specialist Tours in New York City

New York offers a wide variety of package tours and tour programs, ranging from hotel-and-theater packages in New York City to canoe expeditions in the Adirondacks. A **New York City Tour Package Directory** is available from the NYC Convention and Visitors Bureau (also called NYC & Co, *see page 311*). For information about tours elsewhere in the state, contact the **Division of Tourism**, 1 Commerce Plaza, Albany, NY 12245, Tel: (518) 474-4116 or (1-800) 225-5697.

Bus tours
Gray Line New York Tours
900 Eighth Ave at 42nd St
Tel: (212) 397-2620
A wide range of hop-on, hop-off double-decker bus and other itineraries. Tours last between two and eight hours.
New York Apple Tours
777 Eighth Ave
Tel: (212) 944-2400
More double-decker hop-on, hop-off bus tours.

Boat tours
Circle Line Sightseeing
Pier 83 at the western end of 42nd St
Tel: (212) 563-3200
Tours ranging from 30-minute speedboat rides to a three-hour trip around the entire island, showing all aspects of Manhattan from the water.
Circle Line Seaport
Pier 16, South St Seaport
Tel: (212) 630-8888
One-hour cruises of New York Harbor, plus special music cruises and more speedboat rides.

NY Waterway
Pier 78, West 38th St and Twelfth Ave
Tel: (1-800) 533-3779
Converted ferries; rides up the Hudson and around Manhattan.

Helicopter Tours
Liberty Helicopter Tours
Heliport at West 30th St and Twelfth Ave
Tel: (212) 967-6464
Manhattan from the sky – not exactly cheap, but exhilarating.

Walking Tours
Adventure on a Shoestring
300 West 53rd St
Tel: (212) 265-2663
Tours through particular neighborhoods and special themes, eg sites with literary associations.
Municipal Art Society
457 Madison Ave
Tel: (212) 935-3960
Tours focusing on history and architecture.
Museum of the City of New York
1220 Fifth Ave and 103rd St
Tel: (212) 534-1672
Sunday walking tours.

Guided Themed Tours
Art Horizons International
330 West 58th St
Tel: (212) 969-9410
Art-related tours covering everything from artists' lofts to neighborhoods of particular architectural interest.
Backstage on Broadway
228 West 47th St
Tel: (212) 575-8065
Behind the scenes at Broadway's top theaters.

Bite of the Apple Central Park Bicycle Tours
2 Columbus Circle
Tel: (212) 541-8759
Tours across Central Park.
Harlem Spirituals/New York Visions
690 Eighth Ave
Tel: (212) 391-0900
Harlem jazz and gospel tours, plus sightseeing in Brooklyn and the Bronx.
Harlem Your Way
128 West 130th St
Tel: (212) 690-1687
Walking tours of Harlem, including gospel churches and jazz clubs.
Heritage Trails New York
61 Broadway
Tel: (212) 269-1500
or (1-888) 4-TRAILS
Historical points of interest in the Financial District.
Urban Park Rangers
1234 Fifth Ave
Tel: (212) 360-2774
Tours with nature themes in various parks throughout the city. For Central Park tours, call the Ranger Station at (212) 628-2345.

You can also take organised tours of some important buildings and cultural institutions of note, such as the following:
Carnegie Hall
Tel: (212) 247-7800
Gracie Mansion
Tel: (212) 570-4751
Metropolitan Opera House
Lincoln Center
Tel: (212) 875-5350
NBC Studios
Rockefeller Center
Tel: (212) 664-3700

Getting around by taxi can be expensive if you have a long way to go, or if traffic is heavy. However, if you're going a fairly short distance, or there are several of you, a cab may be the cheapest form of transport. They're generally safe (although some cab-drivers don't speak very good English and can give passengers hair-raising rides) and convenient, especially at night. By law, taxis must take you anywhere in the five boroughs, and to any of the airports.

One New York axiom worth noting: you can never get a cab when it rains. Be prepared for a long wait for a cab in bad weather. It is also difficult to get a cab at rush hour.

If you lose any of your belongings in a taxi, call their lost property office: tel: (212) 302-8294.

PRIVATE TRANSPORTATION

If you can afford the extravagance, contact one of the numerous limousine companies listed in the yellow pages of the phone book and have a car and driver at your beck and call. These include **Carey Limousine**, tel: (212) 599-1122; **Smith Limousine**, tel: (212) 247-0711; and **Gotham Limousines**, tel: (1-888) 227-7997 (toll-free). A car and chauffeur can also be arranged through the concierge desk if you're staying at one of the better hotels.

Driving
Driving in New York isn't recommended, mainly because parking is expensive in garages or lots, and either risky or unavailable on the streets.

Transportation in New York State

PUBLIC TRANSPORTATION

Amtrak operates trains throughout the region and **Greyhound** is the main bus company. For addresses and information on train and bus travel throughout the state, *see page 308*.

Car Rental Companies

Alamo
Tel: (1-800) 327-9633
(305) 522-0000
Dollar
Tel: (1-800) 800-4000
(813) 877-5507
Enterprise
Tel: (1-800) 325-8007
(314) 781-8232
Hertz
Tel: (1-800) 654-3131
(405) 749-4424
National
Tel: (1-800) 227-7368
(612) 830-2345
Thrifty
Tel: (1-800) 331-4200
(918) 669-2499

DRIVING

Roads outside New York City are in good condition. The road system consists of Interstate Freeways (eg I-84), United States Highways (eg US95), State Highways or Routes (country roads) and Secondary State or County Roads (side roads).

The maximum speed limit in New York State is 65 mph (105 kph) on interstate highways; slower on rural and residential routes.

Except for in New York City, a right hand turn at a red light is permitted unless otherwise indicated. Drivers going in either direction sighting a school bus that has stopped to load or unload children must stop their vehicles completely before reaching the bus, and may not proceed until the warning signal lights on the bus have been switched off. Finally, hitchhiking (or picking up hitch-hikers) is strongly discouraged, especially near urban areas.

For suggested driving routes around the state, you can write to the **New York State Thruway Authority**, PO Box 189, Albany NY 12201. Also, the **Adirondack North Country Association (ANCA)** has created a combination historic/scenic "driving trail" system that covers 14 counties. For a map, send $2 to ANCA, 183

Broadway, Saranac Lake, NY 12983; for more information tel: (518) 891-6200.

Car Rental
Driving around Manhattan is not much fun, although car rental companies don't lack for business, mostly from people heading out of town. Because Manhattan is linked to the rest of New York City (and to New Jersey) by 16 bridges and four tunnels, finding your way out can be a challenge. Study a map before you start, and get verbal directions.

In Manhattan itself, try **Budget Car Rental**, at various locations (tel: 1-800/331-1212). Other car rental companies represented throughout the state include **Avis Rent A Car** (240 West 54th St, tel: 212/980-9469), **Dollar**, **Hertz**, **National** and **Thrifty**. If you are considering renting a car, check out the conditions. In general, national chains have the best selection of cars and the most expensive services. Smaller, local agencies tend to cost less, but their selection and services are limited. Collision insurance is often covered in the base rental fees, which vary according to car model, but you should check; it's also a good idea to take out liability insurance if you're not covered by your insurance or credit-card company.

To rent a car you must be over 21 years of age and have a national or, better, international driving license. Some car rental firms add a surcharge for drivers aged under 25. Credit cards are necessary for all car rentals in the US.

Where to Stay

Choosing a Hotel

New York City may have some of the finest hotels in the world, but they're also some of the most expensive. Although dormitory-style hostels and budget hotels offer rates as low as $25–$90 a night, the average room costs between $200 and $250 with no upper limits for luxury hotels.

However, even the priciest establishments often have special weekend rates, which are worth inquiring about. In addition, several US reservation services, including **Quikbook**, offer discounts of 50 percent or more on upscale rooms.

Accommodations throughout the rest of the state are much less expensive (with a few exceptions, such as The Point resort in the Adirondacks), and the variety goes well beyond simple hotel rooms to country inns, roadside motels, holiday cabins, forest lodges, lakeside cabins, even dude ranches available by the night or the week.

Prices at upstate resorts are generally highest during the summer "high" season, although Christmas and major winter holiday weekends attract the skiing crowd to places like Lake Placid. In New York City as well as other cities, most large hotels offer weekend rates that are generally less than weekday prices. Check with your travel agent or airline for infor-mation about special packages.

Remember that telephone calls from rooms can be astronomically expensive, so check with the front desk before dialing (in recent years, however, several hotels have begun offering free local calls).

Also remember that state and city levies are high, with a 13.25

percent room tax added to hotel bills, plus an additional "transient occupancy tax" of $2 per room, per night. It all adds up.

Quikbook
Tel: (1-800) 789-9887
Fax: (212) 779-6120
e-mail: info@quikbook.com
www.hoteldiscount.com

Hotels are listed by region in the same order as the Places section of this guide, and then alphabetically by town. New York City hotels are listed by price category. Where indicated, some rates may be MAP (Modified American Plan), which means breakfast and dinner are included in the price.

New York City

Hotel rooms in Manhattan are expensive by any standards. The average room costs $265 a night, and in many cases it's considerably more. But it is possible to find bargains – and even some top hotels offer special weekend rates. Most hotels have deluxe rooms that cost more, and many offer special promotional or corporate rates that bring prices down a notch. Of the assorted reservation services that specialize in up to 70 per cent discounts on regular room rates, you could try **Big Apple Manhattan Hotels**, tel: (1-800) 823 9568; www.big-apple-manhattan-hotels.com.

Inexpensive

Best Western Manhattan
17 West 32nd St
Tel: (212) 736-1600
Fax: (212) 790-2760
Situated near the Empire State Building, the Best Western Manhattan has 176 comfortable rooms, decorated with Manhattan themes and equipped with data ports, voicemail and other conveniences. A lobby café, rooftop bar and moderately priced suites add to the appeal. Rates are slightly higher on weekends.

Chelsea Hotel
222 West 23rd St
Tel: (212) 243-3700
Fax: (212) 675-5531

A few cheap "student rooms" are available in this bohemian landmark (*see page 133*), which otherwise falls into the moderate or expensive category.

Comfort Inn Midtown
129 West 46th St
Tel: (212) 221-2600
Fax: (212) 764-7481
Close to Broadway, this Beaux Arts Revival-style hotel has 79 standard rooms with nice touches. Prices rise in fall-to-Christmas season.

The Ellington Hotel
610 West 111th St
Tel: (212) 864-7500
Fax: (212) 749-5852
A 1920s apartment building on the Upper West Side that has been converted into a pleasant, very reasonably priced hotel. Rooms are contemporary and feature new marble baths. Popular with visitors to nearby Columbia University, especially families of its students.

Habitat Hotel
130 East 57th St
Tel: (212) 753-8841
Fax: (212) 829-9605
A well-appointed budget hotel with a convenient Midtown location between Park and Lexington avenues. Rooms with shared baths are priced under $100; rooms with private baths are slightly more.

Malibu Hotel
2688 Broadway at 103rd St
Tel: (212) 663-0275
Fax: (212) 678-6842
Popular with students and younger travelers, the Malibu features neat, compact rooms with cable TV, CD player, etc. The cheapest rooms share bathrooms, but perks include passes to local attractions. Con-tinental breakfast included in rates.

The Milburn
242 West 76th St
Tel: (212) 362-1010
Fax: (212) 721-5476
The Milburn is on a quiet street off Central Park West, close to the Museum of Natural History. Some rooms have kitchenettes; there's also a laundry facility.

Pickwick Arms
230 East 51st St
Tel: (212) 355-0300
Fax: (212) 755-5029

Convenient Midtown location not far from the UN, set on a relatively quiet, tree-lined block between Second and Third avenues, with a pocket park across the street. The rooms are postage-stamp sized at this popular budget hotel.

Quality Hotel East Side
161 Lexington Ave
Tel: (212) 545-1800
Fax: (212) 790-2760
Refurbished early 20th-century hotel with 100 reasonably priced rooms, some with views of the Empire State Building.

Washington Square Hotel
103 Waverly Place
Tel: (212) 777-9515
Fax: (212) 979-8373
In the heart of Greenwich Village, with small but cheerful rooms, plus a fitness center and restaurant/bar that also serves high tea. A favorite with savvy young Europeans.

Wyndham Hotel
42 West 58th St
Tel: (212) 753-3500
Fax: (212) 754-5638
Off Fifth Avenue and close to Central Park as well as Midtown shopping, this delightful 1920s-era hotel has 134 spacious rooms. A bargain considering the location.

Moderate

The Bentley Hotel
500 East 62nd St
Tel: (212) 644-6000
Fax: (212) 207-4800
Sleek, contemporary high-rise hotel located on the Upper East Side and featuring some spectacular views. Rooms are more spacious than usual, and breakfast is included in the rates. There's free *cappuccino* on offer at the library off the lobby.

Best Western Seaport Inn
33 Peck Slip
Tel: (212) 766-6600
Fax: (212) 766-6615
A converted 19th-century warehouse in Lower Manhattan adjacent to South Street Seaport Museum. The 72 rooms are furnished in Federal-era style and generally priced on the low side of moderate; more expensive ones come with Jacuzzis.

Casablanca Hotel
147 West 43rd St
Tel: (212) 869-1212
Fax: (212) 391-7875
Romantic boutique hotel with a Moroccan theme just off Times Square. Rick's Café serves a complimentary breakfast, free tea in the afternoon and wine and cheese in the evening. Special summer and corporate rates notwithstanding, the Casablanca verges on the expensive category.

The Empire Hotel
44 West 63rd St
Tel: (212) 265-7400
Fax: (212) 245-3382
Almost within hearing distance of Lincoln Center, this midsize hotel is popular with visiting culture lovers and has a steakhouse on site. Also convenient for Central Park, theaters, and museums.

The Franklin
164 East 87th St
Tel: (212) 369-1000
Fax: (212) 369-8000
Chic hotel with a classic video library and complimentary continental breakfast. Great Upper East Side locale; free parking, too.

Gramercy Park Hotel
2 Lexington Ave at 21st St
Tel: (212) 475-4320
Fax: (212) 505-0535
Located off one of the city's only private squares, this genteel hotel is comfortable in a faded, frumpy way. Classic old-fashioned lobby cocktail lounge.

Holiday Inn Downtown
138 Lafayette St
Tel: (212) 966-8898
Fax: (212) 966-3933
The Holiday Inn Downtown, located on the borders of Chinatown, Little Italy and Soho, features pleasant, recently renovated rooms and has more atmosphere than you might expect from a chain.

Holiday Inn Wall Street
15 Gold St
Tel: (212) 232-7700
Fax: (212) 425-0330
Bargain weekend rates are available at this 138-room lower Manhattan refuge for aspiring dotcom moguls, which otherwise falls firmly into the moderate price

Price Guide

The following price categories indicate the cost of a double room in high season:
$$$ Expensive: $200 and more (NYC), $125 and more (NYS)
$$ Moderate: $125–200 (NYC), $85–125 (NYS)
$ Inexpensive: $85–125 (NYC), under $85 (NYS)

category. Rooms are wired for Internet access, and amenities include the Platinum Café.

The Marcel
201 East 24th St
Tel: (212) 696-3800
Fax: (212) 696-0077
Small boutique hotel near the increasingly fashionable Flatiron District. The Marcel features compact but comfortable rooms that attract a fashion-crowd clientele.

On The Ave Hotel
2178 Broadway at 77th St
Tel: (212) 362-1100
Fax: (212) 787-9521
A recent addition to the Upper West Side, On The Ave Hotel features stylish, comfortable rooms with queen- or king-size beds. Some rooms have views of the Hudson River or Central Park. A short walk from the Museum of Natural History and Lincoln Center. Rates hover around the low side of moderate and sometimes below even that.

The Paramount Hotel
235 West 46th St
Tel: (212) 764-5500
Fax: (212) 354-5237
Stylish and hip, the Paramount is a Times Square pioneer. Its interior was designed by Philippe Starck, and its rooms, though small, are futuristically equipped. There's a lobby restaurant and a popular cocktail lounge.

The Roger Williams Hotel
131 Madison Ave
Tel: (212) 448-7000
Fax: (212) 448-7007
Located in Midtown's pleasant Murray Hill neighborhood, the Roger Williams has stylish rooms that, although small, are stocked with a VCR and CD player. Complimentary

Price Guide

The following price categories indicate the cost of a double room in high season:

$$$ Expensive: $200 and more (NYC), $125 and more (NYS)

$$ Moderate: $125–200 (NYC), $85–125 (NYS)

$ Inexpensive: $85–125 (NYC), under $85 (NYS)

services include buffet breakfast, evening *cappuccino* on tap and desserts, too.

Hotel Wales
1295 Madison Ave at 92nd St
Tel: (212) 876-6000
Fax: (212) 860-7000
A small jewel located close to Central Park and Metropolitan Museum of Art. The rooms are old-fashioned, and some rates are more expensive than moderate, but the price includes breakfast and afternoon tea.

Expensive
The Algonquin Hotel
59 West 44th St
Tel: (212) 840-6800
Fax: (212) 944-1419
Gracious, stuffy and just quirky enough to be interesting, the Algonquin was famous as the meeting place of the literary Round Table in the 1920s. Clubby and close to the theater district.

The Carlyle
35 East 76th St
Tel: (212) 744-1600
Fax: (212) 717-4682
Posh and formal. The Carlyle includes an elegant restaurant as well as the Café Carlyle's sophisticated bar/cabaret.

The Drake
440 Park Ave at 56th St
Tel: (212) 421-0900
Fax: (212) 371-4190
Classical, old world-style hotel, with spacious rooms. The bar is a popular after-work rendezvous.

The Lowell
28 East 63rd St
Tel: (212) 838-1400
Fax: (212) 319-4230
Elegant and subdued, just off high-powered Madison Avenue. Famous

for its elegant tea salon, which is open to non-guests.

The Mark
25 East 77th St
Tel: (212) 744-4300
Fax: (212) 472-5714
Spacious rooms with Neo-Classical decor combine with top-quality service and a discreet Upper East Side location to make this a favorite with visiting celebrities.

The Mercer
99 Prince St
Tel: (212) 966-6060
Fax: (212) 965-3838
Located in the heart of Soho, The Mercer features 75 loft-like rooms, access to nearby health club facilities and a very fashionable restaurant, Mercer Kitchen, which attracts the young and gorgeous.

The Millenium Hilton
55 Church St
Tel: (212) 693-2001
Fax: (212) 571-2316
A sleek lower Manhattan business hotel with all the usual high-tech conveniences, plus an outstanding health club, pool and restaurant. Moderately priced weekend packages often available.

Morgans
237 Madison Ave
Tel: (212) 686-0300
Fax: (212) 779-8352
A discreet, stylish hideout for the glitterati. The service is among the best in town, and there's a trendy restaurant and bar with separate entrances for guests' privacy.

The Pierre
2 East 61st St at Fifth Ave
Tel: (212) 838-8000
Fax: (212) 758-1615
Landmark hotel on Central Park. The Pierre's rooms are large and elegant, and service is the best.

The Plaza
768 Fifth Ave at 59th St
Tel: (212) 759-3000
Fax: (212) 759-3167
A New York classic, and the last word in old-world style. (Ask for a room with a view of Central Park.) Moderate rates in summer.

The Regency Hotel
540 Park Ave at 61st St
Tel: (212) 759-4100
Fax: (212) 826-5674

A bastion of stylish tranquility with a cozy bar, evening entertainment and a reputable restaurant. The rooms are sumptuously decorated, and equipped with all modern communication necessities. It's famous for its movie and showbiz clientele and its long-term residents include the likes of Yankees team owner George Steinbrenner.

The Royalton
44 West 44th St
Tel: (212) 869-4400
Fax: (212) 575-0012
Across the street from the Algonquin, but light years away in atmosphere. The Royalton is ultra-chic, or coldly futuristic depending on your point of view. The service is superb and the lobby restaurant is frequented by literary types.

Soho Grand Hotel
310 West Broadway
Tel: (212) 965-3000
Fax: (212) 965-3244
This 15-story landmark on Soho's West Broadway blends nicely into the neighborhood, with industrial-chic decor on the ground floors and stark neutrals in the rooms upstairs. There's also a wonderful lobby bar. One of the few hotels in the city that welcomes pets.

TriBeCa Grand Hotel
2 Ave of the Americas
Tel: (212) 519-6600
Fax: (212) 519-6700
Sister hotel of the Soho Grand and located a few blocks away, below Canal Street, the 203-room, triangular-shaped TriBeCa Grand is one of downtown's newest and coolest places to stay. Features include a dramatic atrium lounge with continuous food-and-drink options, 24-hour concierge service, and ergonomically designed rooms with high-speed Internet access and extra-large windows.

W New York
541 Lexington Ave
Tel: (212) 755-1200
Most of the rooms are on the small side at this somewhat sybaritic spa hotel, but the facilities include a full-service health club that offers aromatherapy and massage. The lobby bar and nouvelle health-style restaurant are both extremely

popular, and the hotel is convenient to major Midtown landmarks like Grand Central Terminal.

Waldorf-Astoria
301 Park Ave
Tel: (212) 355-3000
Fax: (212) 872-7272
The most famous hotel in New York during its gilded heyday in the 1930s and 1940s has been restored to something approaching its former glory. The grand look of the lobby and public areas combine H.G. Wells's heroic view of the future with Cecil B. DeMille's image of Cleopatra's Egypt. Ultra-luxurious and centrally located in Midtown.

Long Island

Bridgehampton
The Enclave Inn
2668 Montauk Hwy, NY 11932
Tel: (631) 537-0197
or (1-877) 998-0800
Fax: (631) 537-5436
Recently remodeled inn on private, wooded grounds has 10 units with private bath, air conditioning, refrigerators and TV with VCR. There's a heated outdoor pool and beach passes for guests. A 4-night minimum stay is required during peak holiday times. **$$–$$$**

Cutchogue
Top o' the Mornin'
26350 Main Rd, NY 11935
Tel: (516) 734-5143
Three charming second-floor bedrooms with private baths in an historic farmhouse on the town's busy main road. **$$**

Freeport
Freeport Motor Inn & Boatel
445 South main St, NY 11520
Tel: (516) 623-9100
Fax: (516) 546-5739
Sixty waterfront rooms with cable TV, in-room movies and refrigerators at a marina. **$**

Greenport
The Bartlett House Inn
503 Front St, NY 11944
Tel: (516) 477-0371.
Year-round B&B with 10 elegantly

furnished, air-conditioned rooms with private baths, fireplaces, and phones. **$$–$$$**

Hampton Bays
Colonial Shores Resort
8 West Tiana Rd, NY 11946
Tel: (631) 728-0011
Fax: (631) 728-0897
Waterfront resort complex with motel rooms, waterfront cottages, and one- and two-bedroom suites with kitchens, baths and private decks. There's a private beach, pool, barbecue area, paddleboat and motor boat, and lawn games. Open year round. **$$–$$$$**

Melville
Melville Marriott
1350 Old Walt Whitman Rd, NY 11747
Tel: (631) 423-1600
Fax: (631) 423-1790
Suffolk County's largest full-service hotel has a glass-enclosed lobby, 371 luxury rooms, and 24 suites. Amenities include an indoor pool, fitness center, restaurant, and business center. **$$$**

Montauk
Montauk Manor
236 Edgemere St, NY 11954
Tel: (631) 668-4400
Fax: (631) 668-3535
The "Castle on the Hill", on 12 acres overlooking Gardiners Bay and Block Island Sound, has 140 studio, one- and two-bedroom fully equipped suites, indoor and outdoor heated pools, a sauna, fitness center, and courtesy van to nearby beaches. Open year round. **$$$–$$$$**

Montauk Yacht Club Resort & Marina
32 Star Island Rd, NY 11954
Tel: (631) 668-3100
or (1-888) MYC-8668
Fax: (631) 668-3303
Many of the 107 deluxe rooms overlook the marina; most have balconies and some have water-front views. There's a heated indoor pool and two outdoor pools, a fully-equipped fitness center, nine tennis courts, and a waterfront restaurant. Open mid-Apr–mid-Nov. **$$$–$$$$**

Port Jefferson
Danfords Inn on the Sound
25 East Broadway, NY 11777
Tel: (631) 928-5200
or (1-800) 332-6367
Fax: (631) 928-3598
Many of the 85 rooms and suites overlooking the village harbor are equipped with fireplaces and balconies. There's a full-service marina, health club, and a waterfront restaurant with entertainment Fri evenings. Open year round. **$$–$$$$**

Holly Berry Bed & Breakfast
415 West Broadway (Rte 25A), NY 11777
Tel: (631) 331-3123
Fax: (631) 473-2945
This bed and breakfast is in a restored 1800s farm house perched on a hill above the village, with beautifully-appointed, air conditioned suites. Continental breakfast is served by candlelight in the French country dining room. Open year round. **$$**

Sag Harbor
The Inn at Baron's Cove
31 West Water St, NY 11963
Tel: (631) 725-2100
Fax: (731) 725-2144
Each of the 66 rooms at this new, two-story inn overlooking the harbor have kitchenettes, air conditioning, phones and cable TV. There is a tennis court and a swimming pool. Standard units sleep up to three people, deluxe lofts sleep up to five, and there are one-bedroom suites. Choose from meadow, pool or harbor views. Open year round. **$$–$$$$**

Sag Harbor Inn
West Water St, NY 11938
Tel: (516) 725-2949
or (1-800) 828-0838
Fax: (631) 725-5009
All of the deluxe 42 rooms at this waterfront resort have a private balcony or terrace, a private bath with a separate vanity area, a direct dial phone, cable color TV and a climate control; some are directly on the water. The outdoor pool is open May–Oct, and Continental breakfast is included in the rate. **$$$–$$$$**

Shelter Island
Ram's Head Inn
Ram Island Dr, NY 11952
Tel: (516) 749-0811
Fax: (516) 749-0059
1929 Colonial-style resort on a
bluff has 17 guest units, a private
beach, sauna, tennis courts,
sailboats and kayaks, an excellent
restaurant and live music. Open
year round. **$$–$$$$**

Stony Brook
Three Village Inn
Tel: (516) 751-0555
Fax: (516) 751-0593
The Colonial inn overlooking Stony
Brook Harbor was built in 1751,
and became the home of Long
Island's first millionaire in 1835.
Today the restored inn has 26
individually decorated rooms with
private bath and cable TV in the
main building and a modern wing.
Rooms with fireplaces available on
request. The restaurant serves
Long Island and New England fare,
including seafood pie, prime rib,
and boiled lobster. **$$–$$$**

Westhampton
1880 House
Two Seafield Lane, NY 11978
Tel: (516) 288-1559
or (1-800) 346-3290
Just a few blocks from the beach; 2
large suites with sitting rooms and
private baths in the farmhouse, and
a third in a 100-year-old barn. The
year-round inn has a swimming pool
and tennis court. **$$–$$$**

The Hudson Valley

Amenia
**Troutbeck Inn & Conference
Center**
Leedsville Rd, NY 12501
Tel: (845) 373-9681
Slate-roofed, English-style country
estate on 422 acres overlooking
the Webatuck River, this is a
corporate conference center during
the week and a country inn on
weekends. Many of the elegant
rooms have fireplaces and canopy
beds. The dining room has an
excellent reputation. Rates are MAP
and include an open bar. **$$$$**

Cold Spring
Hudson House
2 Main St, NY 10516
Tel: (845) 265-9355
The state's second-oldest continu-
ously operating inn has been nicely
restored and has 13 air-conditioned
rooms and two suites, including
several with a river view and private
balcony. The restaurant serves an
uninspired Continental breakfast
(included in rate) but a fine lunch
and dinner. **$–$$**

Pig Hill Bed & Breakfast
73 Main St, NY 10516
Tel: (845) 265-9247
Handsome Georgian town house
right in town has eight beautifully
decorated rooms with fireplaces
and private baths. In season,
guests can request that breakfast
be served in the garden. **$–$$**

Cornwall
Cromwell Manor Inn B&B
Angola Rd, NY 12518
Tel: (845) 534-7136
Formal antebellum mansion, *circa*
1820, on seven secluded mountain
acres. Nine air-conditioned rooms
with private baths (and several with
woodburning fireplaces and
jacuzzis) in the inn, and four with air
conditioning and private bath in the
1764 Chimneys Cottage. A gourmet
breakfast is served in the dining
room or on the verandah. **$$–$$$$**

Croton-on-Hudson
Alexander Hamilton House
49 Van Wyck St, NY 10520
Tel: (914) 271-6737
Fax: (914) 271-3927
Historic 1889 Victorian inn on a cliff
overlooking the Hudson River; has
eight rooms and four suites with

Price Guide

The following price categories
indicate the cost of a double
room in high season:
$$$ Expensive: $200 and more
(NYC), $125 and more (NYS)
$$ Moderate: $125–200 (NYC),
$85–125 (NYS)
$ Inexpensive: $85–125 (NYC),
under $85 (NYS)

private baths, cable TV and phones;
five have fireplaces and two have
jacuzzis. The inn has an on-site pool
and is air-conditioned. **$–$$$$**

Dover Plains
Old Drovers Inn
Old Rte 22, NY 12522
Tel: (845) 832-9311
Fax: (845) 832-6356
Beautifully restored 1750 colonial
inn originally a stop for cattle
drovers; has four elegant, antiques-
filled guest rooms with private
baths. American breakfast and full
dinner (*see page 334*) are included
on weekends. **$$$–$$$$**

Goshen
**Anthony Dobbin's Stagecoach
Inn**
268 Main St at Maplewood Tce,
NY 10924
Tel: (845) 294-5526
Former stagecoach stop has seven
rooms (five with private bath) in a
25-room, antiques-furnished estate.
There's an elevator, and fireplaces
throughout. Breakfast, catered
dinners and afternoon tea
(weekends) are served in the
elegant dining room. **$–$$**

Highland
Rocking Horse Ranch
Rte 44/55
Tel: (845) 691-2927
or (1-800) 647-2624
Fax: (845) 691-6434
The state's largest dude ranch is a
popular year-round family vacation
destination. Amenities include three
heated pools, waterskiing, boating,
tennis, skiing in winter and, of
course, horseback riding. Rates are
MAP. **$$$–$$$**

Kingston
Holiday Inn
503 Washington Ave, NY 12401
Tel: (845) 338-0400
Fax: (845) 338-0400
One of the nicer of the chain's
properties has 212 recently
redecorated rooms and five suites,
an indoor recreation complex with
indoor and outdoor pools, a fitness
center, and a sauna. There's a
restaurant on the premises. **$$**

Alternative accommodations in New York City

Suite Hotels
Manhattan East Suite Hotels
Tel: (212) 465-3600
or (1-800) ME-SUITE
Fax: (212) 465-3697
Staying here is like renting an apartment, complete with hotel amenities – such as housemaid service – and fully equipped kitchens. There are several options when it comes to this type of accommodation, but these 10 all-suite properties located around Midtown and the Upper East Side are the original and the best. From $190 for a studio to $400 or more for a two-bedroom suite.

Bed and Breakfasts
Advance booking (at least two weeks) and a minimum two-night stay required.

B&B Network of New York
134 West 32nd St, Suite 602,
New York, NY 10001
Tel: (212) 645-8134
City Lights Bed & Breakfast
Box 20355, Cherokee Station,
New York, NY 10021
Tel: (212) 737-7049
Fax: (212) 535-2755
Urban Ventures
38 West 32nd St, Suite 1412,
New York, NY 10001
Tel: (212) 594-5650
Fax: (212) 947-9320

Student and Budget Accommodations
New York International Youth Hostel
891 Amsterdam Ave at 103rd St
Tel: (212) 932-2300
Fax: (212) 932-2574
www.hostelling.com

Set in a landmark Upper West Side building, this hostel charges from $25 nightly for dormitory-style accommodations ($3 off for members) with a/c. Amenities include a coffee bar, self-service laundry and kitchen facilities. Maximum stay of seven nights. (see also hostels, page 331)
YMCA-Vanderbilt
224 East 47th St
Tel: (212) 756-9600
Fax: (212) 752-0210
The best of the city's YMCAs. Some rooms have private baths, and there's a swimming pool, fitness facilities and an International Café on the premises. Singles start at $72, doubles at $86. One-bedroom suites are available, too.

New Paltz
Mohonk Mountain House
Lake Mohonk, NY 12561
Tel: (845) 255-1000
or (1-800) 772-6646
Fax: (845) 256-2100
The National Historic Landmark inn complex is tucked away on 2,200 acres overlooking the Shawangunk Mountains and Lake Mohonk. Many of the 261 rooms at the hostelry built in 1869 have balconies and fireplaces, but there is TV only in the public rooms. There are six guest cottages. The grounds, with formal gardens, greenhouses, a 9-hole golf course and a Victorian maze, are absolutely magnificent. Activities include tennis and trail rides. Kids' Club has programs for children ages 2–12. Rates are MAP, and the restaurant (see page 334) has a deservedly fine reputation. $$$–$$$$

Rhinebeck
Beekman Arms
4 Mill St (Rte 9), NY 12572
Tel: (845) 876-7077
Fax: (845) 876-7077
America's oldest continuously-operated hotel opened in 1766.

Rooms tend to be small but pleasant, and have private baths. Guests can opt to stay at one of the other buildings, which include the 1844 Delamater House next door, one of the few remaining examples of American Gothic residences. The tavern serves regional cuisine. $$–$$$

Staatsburg
Belvedere Mansion
Rte 9, NY 12580
Tel: (845) 889-8000
This Greek Revival hilltop estate overlooks the Hudson River. It offers 16 "cottage" rooms in a building facing the mansion – each with its own entrance and bath – or one of the smaller "cozies". Amenities include an outdoor pool, gazebos, a pond, and restaurant (see page 335). Rate includes a gourmet breakfast (served al fresco overlooking the pond in season). $–$$$

Tarrytown
Castle at Tarrytown
400 Benedict Ave, NY 10591
Tel: (845) 631-1980
The Relais & Chateaux property,

one of the region's most luxurious lodgings, is a 45-room castle in the style of a Norman fortification. It was built at the turn of the 20th century on 10 acres overlooking the Hudson River. The European-style hotel has 31 opulent rooms and suites, and an elegant restaurant with three distinct dining rooms, including the Oak Room imported from France. $$$$

West Point
Hotel Thayer
US Military Academy, Thayer Rd, NY 10996
Tel: (845) 446-4731
or (1-800) 247-5047
Fax: (845) 446-0338.
On the grounds of the famous military academy, the hotel overlooking the Hudson was built in 1926 and completely renovated a few years ago. Many of the 148 guestrooms have river views. The Sunday champagne brunch is a local favorite. Breakfast (not included in rate) is served on a terrace overlooking the valley. The hotel is popular, so advance reservations are highly recommended. $

Price Guide

The following price categories indicate the cost of a double room in high season:

$$$ Expensive: $200 and more (NYC), $125 and more (NYS)

$$ Moderate: $125–200 (NYC), $85–125 (NYS)

$ Inexpensive: $85–125 (NYC), under $85 (NYS)

The Catskills

Boiceville
Onteora, The Mountain House
96 Piney Point Rd, PO Box 357, NY 12412
Tel: (914) 657-6233
The magnificent estate on the side of Mount Ticetonyk overlooking the Esopus River was built by mayonnaise king Richard Hellman. One of the five bedrooms has a private bath; all have magnificent views. Public areas include the multi-windowed Great Room and a southwest deck. Rate includes gourmet breakfast. **$$–$$$$**

Callicoon
Villa Roma
Villa Roma Rd, NY 12723
Tel: (845) 887-4880
Full-service resort with 215 air-conditioned rooms and a host of activities including fishing, swimming, horse-drawn sleigh rides, rafting trips, golf and children's programs. Rates are MAP. **$$–$$$**

DeBruce
DeBruce Country Inn
DeBruce Rd, NY 12758
Tel: (914) 439-3900
In the Catskill Forest Preserve, 15 guest rooms, pool, fitness center, woodland hiking trails. **$$**

Delhi
Buena Vista Motel
Rte 28, Andes Rd, NY 13753
Tel: (607) 746-2135
Fax: (607) 746-2135
Clean, comfortable rooms and efficiency units with cable TV, air conditioning and private bath. Rate includes Continental breakfast. **$**

Fleischmanns
River Run B&B
Main St, NY 12430
Tel: (914) 254-4884
This 20-room Queen Anne style house, *circa* 1887, has nine comfortable guest rooms with some shared baths, a parlor with fireplace and piano, and wraparound porch. Rates include a full breakfast, and children and pets are welcome. **$**

Forestburgh
Inn at Lake Joseph
400 St Joseph Rd, NY 12777
Tel: (914) 791-9506
Victorian country estate on a 250-acre mountain lake and surrounded by forest and wildlife preserve was the retreat of Cardinal Spellman. It has 10 rooms in the main house (some with fireplaces and whirlpool baths), and rooms in an Adirondack-style carriage house. The lake has excellent bass fishing. **$$$**

Jeffersonville
The Sunrise House B&B
PO Box 132, NY 12748
Tel: (845) 482-3778
Fax: (845) 482-5570
Restored 100-year-old farmhouse on 45 acres has three elegantly decorated guest rooms with cable TV and private bath. Wraparound porch, heated pool and sun room. Rate includes a full breakfast. **$**

Kiamesha Lake
The Concord
Concord Rd, NY 12751
Tel: (914) 794-4000
or (1-800) 431-3850
Renowned family-style resort has 1,225 rooms with all modern amenities, an 18-hole golf course, 40 tennis courts, a fitness center, and nightly entertainment. Winter activities include snowmobiling, ice skating and skiing. Full children's program. Rates are MAP. **$$–$$$**

Lewbeach
Beaverkill Valley Inn
Beaverkill Rd, NY 12753
Tel: (845) 439-4844
Fax: (845) 439-3884
This National Historic Site developed by Laurance Rockefeller

in 1893 is secluded in the Catskills Forest Preserve; has 20 rooms with private bath and 8 with shared bath. The inn is popular with flyfishers. There's a pool and restaurant. **$$$–$$$$**

Livingston Manor
The Guest House
223 DeBruce Rd, NY 12758
Tel: (845) 439-4000
"Retreat to the world of the Rich and Famous on 40-acre estate" on the Willowemoc River; European decor. There are four rooms with private baths in the inn and three rooms in cottages on the grounds. Amenities include indoor and outdoor jacuzzi/ swimming pools, fly fishing, and a huge breakfast buffet. Winter spa packages are available. **$$$–$$$$**

Monticello
Kutscher's County Club
Anawana Lake Rd, NY 12701
Tel: (914) 749-6000
or (1-800) 431-1273
450-room, informal family resort with a full roster of activities, including an 18-hole golf course, tennis, swimming, a year-round ice skating rink and nightly entertainment. There's nursery/toddler care, and day camp and teen programs. Rates are MAP. **$$$**

Narrowsburg
The Commodore Murray, 1830
58 Fifth St, NY 12764
Tel: (845) 252-7220
Swimming, fishing and whitewater canoeing and rafting are the primary focus of guests at this three-story mansion on the Delaware River, but there are plenty of places to curl up and read a book. There are four guest rooms with shared bath. Pets and children over 15 permitted. **$**

Tannersville
Eggery Inn
County Rd 16, NY 12485
Tel: (518) 589-5363
Fax: (518) 589-5774
Rustic, three-story (no elevator) mountaintop inn overlooking Hunter Mountain; 11 rooms with private

bath and 2 with shared bath; cozy common room with a wood-burning Franklin stove and an antique player piano. Rates include a hearty breakfast; dinner is served seasonally on Sat night. **$–$$**

Walton
Walton Motel
37 Stockton Ave, NY 13856
Tel: (607) 865-4724
At the foot of Bear Spring Mountain across from the Delaware River, the motel has 12 rooms of varying sizes, but all nicely decorated and with air-conditioning and views of the Catskill foothills. **$**

Windham
Albergo Allegria
Rte 296, Box 267, NY 12496
Tel: (518) 734-5560
Fax: (518) 734-5570
This 1892 riverfront gingerbread mansion has 21 cozy rooms with private bath, TV/VCR and phone; suites with jacuzzi and fireplaces. Rate includes a gourmet breakfast. **$–$$**

Capital & Saratoga Region

Albany
The Desmond Hotel
660 Albany Shaker Rd, NY 12211
Tel: (518) 869-8100
or (1-800) 448-3500
A large, comfortable, old-fashioned hotel with 322 rooms (some with balconies or private patios) decorated in colonial style and facing indoor courtyards. Most have California King canopy beds; all have coffee makers, hairdryers, irons and ironing boards. There are two restaurants, including the Scrimshaw Dining Room (*see page 336*), two heated pools, and a health club. **$$–$$$**
Mansion Hill Inn
115 Philip St
Tel: (518) 465-2038
Hostelry in several historic downtown buildings; modern, comfortable rooms with queen-sized beds, private baths, and cable TV; a lovely courtyard, and a fine restaurant. **$–$$**

Omni Albany Hotel
10 Eyck Plaza, NY 12207
Tel: (518) 462-6611
Fax: (518) 462-2901
Fifteen-story luxury chain hotel close to town and with 386 fully equipped rooms and suites, an indoor swimming pool and shopping area. **$$–$$$**
Wingate Inn
254 Old Wolf Rd, Latham, NY 12110
Tel: (518) 869-9100
or (1-800) 228-1000
New moderately priced hotel situated just outside the center of the city. Large, comfortable rooms with many business amenities, fitness room and whirlpool, business center. Good Continental breakfast. **$$**

Dundee
The Inn at Glenora Wine Cellars
5435 Rte 14, NY 14837
Tel: (607) 243-9500
or (1-800) 243-5513
Each of the 30 spacious rooms at this modern and comfortable inn next door to Glenora Wine Cellars has a balcony overlooking Seneca Lake, a private bath and a refrigerator. There's also an upscale restaurant on the premises. **$$**

Johnstown
Holiday Inn
308 North Comrie Ave, NY 12095
Tel: (518) 762-4686
Three-story, 100-room chain motor inn (no elevator) with an outdoor pool and restaurant. Pets are welcome. **$–$$**

Rock City Falls
The Mansion Inn
Rte 29, NY 12863
Tel: (518) 885-1607
Fax: (518) 885-6753
Both the guest and common rooms at this 1866 mansion of Venetian design are handsomely furnished with Victorian antiques. All rooms have baths and air-conditioning. Guests have use of the parlors, library, porches, outdoor swimming pool and grounds. A full gourmet breakfast is included in the rate. **$–$$**

Saratoga Springs
Adelphi Hotel
365 Broadway, NY 12866
Tel: (518) 587-4688
Fax: (518) 587-0851
Each of the 38 rooms at this opulent downtown historic hostelry is furnished differently. It's fun to see even if you're not staying here. Closed Nov–Apr. **$$–$$$$**
Gideon Putnam Hotel
Saratoga Spa State Park, NY 12866
Tel: (518) 584-3000
or (1-800) 732-1560
Fax: (518) 584-1354
Historic landmark hotel in 2,000-acre Saratoga Spa State Park has 132 nicely furnished rooms, including several parlor and porch suites. There's a golf course, tennis courts, and mineral baths on the premises. The restaurant has a fine reputation. MAP optional. **$$$–$$$$**
Harren-Brook Inn
738 Rte 9P, NY 12866
Tel and Fax: (518) 583-4009
On the shores of Saratoga Lake, this cozy inn has nine guest rooms with private baths and queen-sized beds, a breezy porch, and an inviting sitting room. **$–$$$**
The Inn at Saratoga
231 Broadway, NY 12866
Tel: (518) 583-1890
Fax: (518) 583-2543
Restored 1890 inn has spacious, nicely decorated rooms and two-room suites. Entertainment Fri–Sat in the dining room. Breakfast is included in the rates. **$$–$$$$**
Saratoga Downtowner Motel
413 Broadway, NY 12866
Tel: (518) 584-6160
Fax: (518) 584-2907
All rooms at this comfortable motel have a private bath and cable TV; indoor pool. A minimum stay of two nights is required during racing season (mid-Jul–mid-Aug). **$$–$$$**
Union Gables B&B
55 Union Ave, NY 12866
Tel: (518) 584-1558
Fax: (518) 583-0649
Elegant Queen Anne-style house with 10 beautifully decorated rooms with bath, TV, phone and refrigerator. Near the race track and popular during racing season. **$$–$$$$**

Schenectady
Holiday Inn-Downtown
100 Nott Terrace, NY 12308
Tel: (518) 393-41411
Fax: (518) 393-4174
Pleasant in-town motor inn has 184
rooms on four floors, a restaurant,
and an outdoor pool. **$–$$**

The Adirondacks

Bolton Landing
Bonnie View Resort
Rte 9, PO Box 330, NY 12814
Tel: (518) 644-5591
Landscaped and shaded 9-acre
lakefront resort with a motel and
cottages (some with fireplaces) with
private baths, air-conditioning, and
color cable TV. There's a private
sand beach, tennis court, boat
dock, rowboats, BBQ grills, and lawn
games and a playground for the
kids. Open May–Sept. **$–$$**

The Sagamore
Bolton Landing, NY 12814
Tel: (518) 644-9400
or (1-800) 358-3585
Fax: (518) 644-2626
Historic grand hotel on private Lake
George island has 350 pleasant
rooms and suites with all the
amenities in the main building and
in lakefront town houses. Facilities
include a spa and fitness center,
18-hole golf course, indoor and
outdoor tennis courts, water and
racquet sports, sightseeing cruises,
and excellent dining in six
restaurants. Spacious common
rooms overlook the lake. MAP
available. **$$$–$$$$**

Chestertown
Friends Lake Inn
Friends Lake Rd, NY 12817
Tel: (518) 494-4751
Fax: (518) 494-4616
Sixteen guest rooms and several
suites with turn-of-the-20th-century
furnishings, queen-size four-poster
beds, and private baths on three
floors (no elevator). Many have
panoramic views of the lake. The
excellent dining room serves New
American cuisine (see page 336).
There's a private beach for guests
and cross-country ski trails.
$$$–$$$$

Diamond Point
Chelka Lodge
Rte 9N, Lake Shore Dr,
NY 12824
Tel: (518) 668-4677
Lakefront resort away from the
hustle and bustle of downtown Lake
George has 25 rooms with air
conditioning, color cable TV, and
bath. There's a tennis court, private
sandy beach, fishing dock and
rowboats. Open May–mid-Oct. **$$**

Keene
Bark Eater Inn
Alstead Hill Rd, NY 12942
Tel: (518) 576-2221
Fax: (518) 576-2071
This former stagecoach stop in the
High Peaks has 19 lovely guest
rooms, a private beach, a library,
and a first-rate restaurant. There's
horseback riding and miles of cross-
country ski trails in the vicinity.
$$–$$$

Lake George
Still Bay Resort
Rte 9N, NY 12824
Tel: (518) 668-2584
or (1-800) 521-7511
All cottages and apartments at this
lakefront resort have air-
conditioning, showers and cable TV,
and are decorated in early American
decor. There's a private boathouse
and dock, and breakfast is served
on the lakefront patio. **$$**

Lake Placid
Adirondak Loj
Adirondak Loj Rd, NY 12946
Tel: (518) 523-3441
Fax: (518) 523-3518
Wilderness bed & breakfast lodge
and backcountry education center
10 minutes from downtown Lake
Placid and adjoining the High Peaks
wilderness; has been taking in
guests since 1890. There are four
private rooms and five rooms with
bunk beds. **$**

Mirror Lake Inn
5 Mirror Lake Dr, NY 12946
Tel: (518) 523-2544
Fax: (518) 523-2871
New England charm combines with
Adirondack style to create one of
the region's loveliest resorts. Most

of the 128 rooms have balconies
overlooking the lake. A new multi-
million dollar spa features all the
latest European specialties. There's
a private beach, tennis court,
indoor and outdoor pool, sauna and
jacuzzi and a superb restaurant.
(see page 336). **$$$–$$$$**

North Creek
The Copperfield Inn
224 Main St, NY 12853
Tel: (518) 251-2500
Fax: (518) 251-4143
Twenty-five spacious, individually
decorated rooms with marble baths
in a contemporary country inn.
Whirlpool bath, tennis court,
excellent restaurant, and
entertainment are housed in a
recreation of a 200-year-old
wilderness cabin. **$$$–$$$$**

Goose Pond Inn
Main St, NY 12853
Tel: (518) 251-3434
A charming, antique-filled, 1900s
four-room B&B, a mile (2 km) from
Gore Mountain. The breakfast
specialty (included in the rate) is
brandied French toast with sautéed
apples. **$–$$**

North River
Garnet Hill Lodge
13th Lake Rd, NY 12856
Tel: (518) 251-2444
or (1-800) 497-4207
Fax: (518) 251-3089
This remote resort on 600 acres
appears to be a rustic Adirondack
estate, but the rooms, with whirlpool
baths and hot tubs, are anything but.
Activities include tubing and fly
fishing. Breakfast is a highlight. **$–$$**

Saranac Lake
**The Hotel Saranac of Paul
Smith's College**
101 Main St, NY 12983
Tel: (518) 891-2200
or (1-800) 937-0211
Fax: (518) 891-5664
Historic 1927 restored hotel in
village center a block from the lake
has 92 rooms with TV. Both the inn
and restaurant (Lydia's) are a
training facility for the nearby hotel
management college. Ask for one of
the more spacious rooms. **$**

The Point
Star Route, HCR I, Box 65
Tel: (518) 891-5674
or (1-800) 255-3530
Fax: (518) 891-1152
One of the country's most highly
rated resorts and a member of the
exclusive Relais & Chateaux; has
11 elegant units at its "elegantly
rustic" lakefront sanctuary. Rates
are MAP. **$$$$**

The Wawbeek on Upper
Saranac Lake
553 Panther Mountain Rd,
NY 12986
Tel: 518-359-2656
or (1-800) 953-2656
Fax: (518) 359-2475
Authentic Adirondack Great Camp
on 40 acres with 1,700 ft (500
meters) of shoreline has a lodge
with six bedrooms with private bath,
and log cabins and cottages. Meals
are served in the handsome
waterfront restaurant. Boats and
breakfast are included in rate.
$$$–$$$$

Thousand Islands & St Lawrence Seaway

Alexandria Bay
Bonnie Castle Resort
Holland St, Box 219, NY 13607
Tel: (315) 482-4511
or (1-800) 955-4511
Waterfront resort complex with 128
guest rooms and 70 suites with
phones, air-conditioning, color TV,
refrigerators and balconies.
Amenities include indoor and
outdoor pools, tennis courts, sauna
and jacuzzi, a waterfront restaurant
with entertainment, and a lounge.
The inn is the homeport of Bonnie
Belle Mississippi Riverboat. Open
year round. **$–$$**

Edgewood Resort
Edgewood Park, NY 13607
Tel: (315) 482-9922
or (1-800) 334-3966
Fax: (315) 482-5210
Family resort on 40 acres with 150
rooms and suites with massive, log
beds, air-conditioning and cable TV:
most have water views and private
balconies. There's a private beach,
paddleboats, a canoe and boat
rental, outdoor pool, entertainment

in the 1,500-seat center, waterfront
dining, children's programs, a
playground, and an arcade. Open
Apr–Oct. **$–$$**

Fisherman's Wharf Motel
15 Sisson St, NY 13607
Tel: (315) 482-2230
Twenty-four air-conditioned rooms
with cable TV in a modern, two-story
motel overlooking the St Lawrence
River and Alexandria Bay harbor.
Guests can fish off the dock. Open
Apr–Oct. **$**

Riveredge Resort Hotel
17 Holland St, NY 13607
Tel: (315) 482-9917
or (1-800) ENJOY-US
Fax: (315) 482-5010
Most of the 129 air-conditioned
rooms, including loft and jacuzzi
suites, overlook the St Lawrence
River. There are indoor and outdoor
pools, a boat dock, and several
waterfront restaurants, including an
outdoor deck open daily from
Father's Day through Labor Day,
and the elegant Jacques Cartier
Dining Room (see page 337).
$$–$$$

Cape Vincent
Angel Rock Lodge
34311 NYS Rte 12 East, NY 13618
Tel: (315) 654-2495
This riverfront colony has eight
three-bedroom, fully equipped
housekeeping cottages which rent
by the week in summer and by the
night the rest of year. There's also
a seasonal riverfront RV, swimming
beach and fishing. Kayaks and
boats are available for rent and, in
winter, activities include ice fishing,
skating and tobogganing. **$**

Clayton
Thousand Islands Inn
335 Riverside Dr, NY 13624
Tel: (315) 686-3030
or (1-800) 544-4241
Most of the rooms at this downtown
1897 hostelry have views of the St
Lawrence River. They've been
restored to recreate the flavor of
the late 1800s, but have all the
modern conveniences. The
restaurant overlooking the river has
an excellent reputation. Open late
May–late Sept. **$**

Fisher's Landing
Island Boat House B&B
Occident Island, NY 13641
Tel: (315) 686-2272
or (1-800) 686-6056
The boathouse on this private
island has been converted into two
bedrooms, with private baths and
decks, overlooking the St Lawrence
and Rock Island lighthouse. The
larger has two double beds and a
sitting room, the smaller has a
double bed. Guests can swim, sail,
water ski, boat, or fish off the
boathouse deck. Breakfast is
served on the verandah. Open
Apr–Oct. **$$$**

Ogdensburg
The Stonefence Hotel, Motel
Riverside Dr, NY 13669
Tel: (315) 393-1545
or (1-800) 253-1549
Ten-acre resort complex on the St
Lawrence with a motel and shore-
side hotel with rooms and town
houses, some with river views.
Amenities include a beach, sauna,
whirlpool, tennis court, and marina
with boat rental. Patio dining is
available at the restaurant. **$–$$**

Pulaski
Historic Selkirk Lighthouse
6 Lake Rd, NY 13142
Tel: (315) 298-6688
National Register of Historic Places
property with four heated bedrooms
that sleep up to 10; common rooms
include a kitchen, living room with
cable TV, and a bathroom. The
lighthouse is part of a compound
with a charter fishing fleet and
cabin and boat rentals. (For
information: Lighthouse Marina, PO
Box 228, Pulaski 13142.) **$$**

Price Guide

The following price categories
indicate the cost of a double
room in high season:
$$$ Expensive: $200 and more
(NYC), $125 and more (NYS)
$$ Moderate: $125–200 (NYC),
$85–125 (NYS)
$ Inexpensive: $85–125 (NYC),
under $85 (NYS)

Sackets Harbor
The Jacob Brewster House B&B
107 South Broad St, NY 13675
Tel: (315) 646-4663 or 646-3107
Circa 1815 Georgian-style country
house with four meticulously
restored guest rooms furnished in
period decor; all have private baths.
Three have queen-size beds; one,
with twin beds, can be part of a
suite. The inn is open year round
and is non-smoking. **$**
Ontario Place Hotel
103 General Smith Dr,
NY 13685
Tel: (315) 646-8000
or (1-800) 564-1812
Thirty-eight air-conditioned and
wheelchair accessible rooms
overlooking the harbor in the center
of town. Accommodations range
from budget to luxury suites with
refrigerators, microwaves, and
whirlpool or jacuzzi. **$–$$$$**

Wellesley Island
Hart House Inn
21979 Club Rd, NY 13640
Tel: (315) 482-5683
or (1-888) 481-5683
The original cottage on the site of
Boldt Castle, built *circa* 1872, is
now an elegant B&B with canopy
beds, fireplaces and whirlpools.
Breakfast (included in rate) is
served by candlelight. There is a
wedding chapel on the grounds, and
the inn's owner is a justice of the
peace. Open year round. **$$–$$$**
Torchlite Motel & Efficiencies
Peel Dock Rd, Box 451, NY 13640
Tel: (315) 482-3550
(in winter, 315/682-6330)
There are great views of the St
Lawrence from all of the house-
keeping and motel units. Motel
rooms are air-conditioned and have
color TV. There is a pool and private
dock. Open May–Oct. **$**

Central-Leatherstocking

Binghamton
Hotel de Ville
800 State St
Tel: (607) 722-0000
or (1-800) 295-5599
Fax: (607) 722-7912

The Beaux Arts Renaissance 1897
building that once served as the
city hall and jail has been hand-
somely restored to house 59 guest
rooms of varying sizes and shapes
with all modern amenities. **$$–$$$**

Cazenovia
Brae Loch
5 Albany St, NY 13035
Tel: (315) 655-3431
Fax: (315) 655-4844
Twelve antiques-filled guest rooms
with Stickley furnishings, private
baths and TV; and an elegant
lakeside dining room which serves
American cuisine with a Scottish
flair (the Scottish buffet brunch
served Sun morning from Sept–mid-
Jun is popular). Rate includes
Continental breakfast. **$$**
The Brewster Inn
6 Ledyard Ave, NY 13035
Tel: (315) 655-9232
Fax: (315) 655-2130
The three-story mansion overlooking
Cazenovia Lake was once the
summer home of Benjamin
Brewster, co-founder of Standard Oil
Historic. Today, it's an elegant inn
with 17 guest rooms (including a
three-room deluxe suite) in the main
house and carriage house. All have
private bath, TV, air conditioning,
and phone; four have jacuzzi baths
and/or fireplaces. Dinner is served
by candlelight in the dining room;
cocktails are at the Terrace Bar
overlooking the lake. **$$–$$$**
Lincklaen House
79 Albany St, NY 13035
Tel: (315) 655-3461
Fax: (315) 655-5443
Built in 1835 as a stagecoach stop,
the brick inn has been thoroughly
renovated with a careful blending of

Price Guide

The following price categories
indicate the cost of a double
room in high season:
$$$ Expensive: $200 and more
(NYC), $125 and more (NYS)
$$ Moderate: $125–200 (NYC),
$85–125 (NYS)
$ Inexpensive: $85–125 (NYC),
under $85 (NYS)

historical accuracy and modern
conveniences. Each of the 18 guest
rooms and suites has cable TV,
stenciling, antiques, and colonial
furnishings; the rooms in the rear
are quieter. American cuisine is
served in the elegant dining room;
lighter fare is available in the Seven
Stone Steps Pub and the Hearth
Room. **$–$$**

Cooperstown
The Cooper Inn
Corner Main and Chestnut streets
Tel: (1-800) 348-6222
Circa 1812 historic inn in its own
park in the middle of town with 20
handsomely decorated rooms and
suites with phones, cable TV, air
conditioning, and private bath.
Guests have use of Otesaga Resort
Hotel facilities. **$$–$$$**
The Inn at Cooperstown
16 Chestnut St
Tel: (607) 547-5756
Fax: (607) 547-8779
Built in 1874 and fully restored in
1985, the Second Empire inn in
the Historic District is easily
recognized by the sweeping
verandah lined with rocking chairs.
Each of the 17 rooms has a queen
or twin beds, is individually
decorated, and has a private bath;
there is a TV and phone in the
lounge. Continental breakfast is
included. **$$–$$$**
Landmark Inn
64 Chestnut St, NY 13326
Tel: (607) 547-7225 or 547-4005
Fax: (607) 547-7240
Centrally located, classic 1856
mansion has nine rooms with
private bath, cable TV, refrigerator,
and air conditioning. An excellent
breakfast, included in the rate, is
served in the elegant dining room.
Children are welcome. **$$**
Otesaga Hotel and Restaurant
Lake St
Tel: (1-800) 348-6222
1909 Historic Hotels of America
hotel overlooking Lake Otesago has
135 nicely appointed rooms and
suites, pool and lake swimming,
boating, tennis courts and a
renowned golf course. Rates are
MAP and there are several
restaurants. **$$$–$$$$**

Little Falls
Gansevoort House
42 West Gansevoort St, NY 13365
Tel: (315) 823-3969
Turn-of-the-20th-century fireplaced home with guest rooms in the main house and a family suite with a private ground level entrance in the carriage house. There is a music room, a porch, and a garden. Continental breakfast is served Mon–Fri, and a full breakfast on weekends. **$**

Rome
Beeches-Paul Revere Motor Lodge
7900 Turin Rd, NY 13440
Tel: (315) 336-1776
Fax: (315) 339-2936
Traditional motel with an outdoor swimming pool; 73 rooms with mini-fridges and seven apartments. A special whirlpool suite sleeps 1–2 persons. The Beeches restaurant is right next door to the lodge (*see page 337*). **$**
Wright Settlement B&B
7966 Wright Settlement Lane, NY 13440
Tel: (315) 337-2417
Two rooms with shared bath at a 130-year-old house nestled on 55 acres, with a swimming pool and nature trails. **$**

Sharon Springs
Clausen Farms
Rte 20, PO Box 395, NY 13459
Tel: (518) 284-2839
Fax: (518) 284-2929
This Victorian estate/llama farm, perched on 60 acres high above the Mohawk Valley, has 11 guest rooms and suites: seven in the Casino, an 1892 Victorian Gentleman's Guesthouse (open Apr–Oct), and four in the main house (open year round). There's a swimming pool and an old-fashioned bowling alley. The rate includes a "more than you care to eat" breakfast. **$$**
Brimstonia Cottage
Main St
Tel: (518) 284-2839
Central 1840 Greek Revival bed-and-breakfast has several cozy guest rooms and magnificent gardens to stroll through. **$**

Utica
Iris Stonehouse B&B
Jct. Holland Ave & Derbyshire Place, NY 13502
Tel: (315) 732-6720
Two-story Tudor-style home with four guest rooms (two with private baths). The inn is non-smoking. **$**
Radisson Hotel-Utica Centre
200 Genesee St, NY 13502
Tel: (315) 797-8010
Fax: (315) 797-1490
Downtown, six-story hotel with 158 rooms, a heated indoor pool and fitness center, whirlpool and sauna, and two restaurants. **$$–$$$**

Finger Lakes

Albion
Tillman's Historic Village Inn & Restaurant
Rte 104W/98
Tel: (716) 589-9151
For more than 45 years the Tillman family has been operating an inn/restaurant in an 1824 stagecoach stop. There are four spacious rooms with private bath in the inn. The fine restaurant next door serves prime rib, hickory smoked ribs, seafood and more. **$$**

Auburn
Springside inn
6141 West Lake Rd, NY 13021
Tel: (315) 252-7247
Fax: (315) 252-8096
A creaky, rambling old-fashioned inn, parts of which date back to 1851, on the shores of Owasco Lake. The eight rooms are simple but clean, and share baths. **$**

Canadaigua
Inn on the Lake
770 South Main St, NY 14424
Tel: (716) 394-7800
or (1-800) 228-2801
Fax: (716) 394-5003
Many of the 134 rooms and suites at this lovely, two-story motor inn overlooking Lake Canandaigua have private balconies and lake views. Luxury rooms are available. There's a boat dock and ramp, and a restaurant. **$$–$$$$**
Morgan Samuels Inn
2920 Smith Rd, NY 14424

Tel: (716) 394-9232
Fax: (716) 394-8044
Handsome 1810 stone mansion nestled on 46 acres with six guest rooms with private baths, ten fireplaces, numerous balconies, and a tennis court. Breakfast is served by candlelight. **$$–$$$$**

Geneva
Belhurst Castle
Lochland Rd (Rte 14S), PO Box 607, NY 14456
Tel: (315) 781-0201
Fax: (315) 781-0201
Richardsonian Romanesque stone castle has 13 period rooms, including one in the turret. There are also rooms in several buildings behind the castle. The restaurant (with five dining rooms) has a superb reputation, with offerings such as Russian wild boar tender-loin and chateaubriand. **$$–$$$$**
Geneva-on-the-Lake
1001 Lochland Rd (Rte 14S), NY 14456
Tel: (315) 789-7190
or (1-800) 3-GENEVA
Fax: (315) 789-0322
The small, romantic, 30-room inn overlooking Seneca Lake was inspired by summer residences around northern Italy's lakes Garda and Maggiore. Many of the rooms have fireplaces; most have views of the lake. The formal gardens are magnificent, and rates include wine, fruit and flowers, a Friday evening wine and cheese party, and Continental breakfast on the terrace (weather permitting). **$$$–$$$$**
White Springs Manor
PO Box 607, NY 14456
Tel: (315) 781-0201
Fax: (315) 781-0201
The sister property of Belhurst Castle is an 1806 Georgian Revival mansion perched on a hill overlooking Seneca Lake. Each of the 12 guest rooms has a private bath and glass fireplace. Guests breakfast at the castle. **$$–$$$$**

Ithaca
Rose Inn
814 Auburn Rd (Rte 34N), NY 14851

Tel: (607) 533-7905
Fax: (607) 533-7908
Elegant 1850s hilltop Italianate mansion with 15 rooms with private bath, including four suites with jacuzzis and three with fireplaces. The hand-carved, mahogany circular staircase is a gem. The restaurant serves a *prix-fixe* dinner ($$$$) most evenings. **$$$**

La Tourelle Country Inn
1150 Danby Rd, Rte 96B,
NY 14850
Tel: (607) 273-2734
or (1-800) 765-1492
European-style inn with 35 spacious rooms and marvelous views. Set in 70 acres of countryside with hiking trails and tennis court. No restaurant, but the inn is adjacent to a steakhouse. Continental breakfast available. **$$**

Mumford

Genesee Country Inn
948 George St, NY 14511
Tel: (716) 538-2500
Fax: (716) 538-4565
Nine elegant rooms with private baths, TV and air-conditioning in a renovated 1833 mill overlooking ponds, waterfalls and gardens. The garden rooms have fireplaces and queen canopy beds. Guests can fish for trout in the pond. **$–$$$**

Naples

The Vagabond Inn
3300 Sliter Rd, NY 14512
Tel: (716) 554-6271
This secluded mountain top inn has a 60-ft-long (20-meter) Great Room with two massive fireplaces, a Japanese garden, and an in-ground pool. Each of the five guest rooms is unique; the Bristol has its own fireplace and jacuzzi. **$$–$$$$**

Penn Yan

Finton's Landing B&B
661 East Lake Rd, NY 14527
Tel: (315) 536-3146
Secluded Victorian B&B built in the 1860s on Keuka Lake as a steamboat landing has four rooms with private baths. Breakfast is served on the porch (weather permitting), and there's a private beach. The inn is non-smoking. **$–$$**

Pittsford

Oliver Loud's Inn
1474 Marsh Rd, NY 14534
Tel: (716) 248-5200
Fax: (716) 248-9970
Named after the original innkeeper, this handsome B&B is set in a restored 1810 stagecoach inn, overlooking the Erie Canal. Elegantly appointed rooms with private baths, antiques and period artwork; some canopy beds. A breakfast hamper is delivered to your room in the morning. Richardson's Canal House restaurant is on the premises. **$$$**

Rochester

Dartmouth House B&B
215 Dartmouth St, NY 14607
Tel: (716) 271-7872
or (1-800) 724-6298
A 1905, two-story mansion in the Cultural Historic District withfour elegantly decorated rooms with phones and private baths. A six-course breakfast (included in the rate) is served by candlelight. **$–$$**

Rochester Crowne Plaza
70 State St, NY 14614
Tel: (716) 546-3450
or (1-800) 243-7760
Large modern hotel in the heart of downtown, along the Genesee River, near to city center attractions. Luxurious rooms with all amenities, fitness center, pool, restaurant and sports bar. Caters for meetings and conventions. **$$**

The Lodge at Woodcliff
Woodcliff Dr
Routes 96 & I-490 in Perinton
Tel: (716) 381-4000
or (1-800) 365-3065
Beautiful, luxury hilltop hotel located 20 minutes from downtown, in Perinton. 250 rooms and suites, with indoor/outdoor pool, sports and golf club facilities. Superb gourmet restaurant with live music most nights. **$$$**

Skaneateles

The Gray House
47 Jordan St, NY 13152
Tel: (315) 685-0131
Fax: (315) 685-3259
An 1899 Victorian home turned

hospitable B&B. All four rooms are nicely outfitted and have private baths. The parlors are spacious, and the inn is within easy walking distance of downtown. **$–$$**

Sherwood Inn
26 West Genesee St, NY 13152
Tel: (315) 685-3405
or (1-800) 3SHERWOOD
Fax: (315) 685-8983
Built in 1807 as a stagecoach stop. All rooms and suites all have Stickley furniture, Oriental carpets, private baths, phones, TV, and air-conditioning; some have lake views. There's an excellent restaurant with a lovely patio that serves American cuisine with a Continental touch (breakfast, lunch and dinner in summer; dinner year round), and a tavern. Non-smoking. **$–$$$**

Sodus Point

Carriage House Inn
Corner Ontario and Wickham Blvd,
NY 14555
Tel: (315) 483-2100
or (1-800) 292-2990
Highly acclaimed 1870 Victorian inn on four acres overlooking Sodus Point Lighthouse. Rooms in the inn, in the stone Carriage House overlooking the lake, and in efficiencies that sleep up to four and have outside decks and gas grills. All units have private baths and TV; some are air-conditioned. Rates include full breakfast, and there's a private beach. **$$–$$$**

Syracuse

Bed & Breakfast Wellington
707 Danforth St, NY 13203
Tel: (315) 471-2433
or (1-800) 724-5006
Among the unique features of this 1914 Arts and Crafts brick and stucco Tudor-style home designed by architect Ward Wellington Ward are its canvas flooring, leaded glass windows,and many porches. Four of the five guest rooms have private baths, and the rate includes a gourmet breakfast. **$–$$**

Dickenson House
1504 James St, NY 13203
Tel: (1-888) 423-4777
Fax: (315) 425-1965

A stately English Tudor B&B with five exceedingly attractive antiques-filled guest rooms with private baths, phones and cable TV. A small garden is out back. **$$**

Greater Niagara

Batavia
Best Western Batavia Inn
8204 Park Rd, NY 14020
Tel: (716) 343-1000
Fax: (716) 343-8608
Seventy-five sunny and pleasant rooms in a two-story hotel with an outdoor pool and restaurant. **$$**

Buffalo
Adam's Mark Buffalo
120 Church St, NY 14202
Tel: (716) 845-5100
or (1-800) 444-ADAM
Fax: (716) 845-5377
Downtown hotel with 468 deluxe rooms overlooking the waterfront. Amenities include a glass-enclosed indoor pool, dry sauna and a sun deck. **$$–$$$**
The Beau Fleuve B&B Inn
242 Linwood Ave at Bryant,
NY 14209.
Tel: (716) 882-6116
or (1-800) 278-0245
Handsome, 1881 stick-style home in Linwood Historic Preservation District has five individually decorated guest rooms with down comforters, fans and coffee makers; central air-conditioning. Non-smoking. **$–$$**

Clarence
Asa Ransom House
10529 Main St, NY 14031
Tel: (716) 759-2315
Fax: (716) 759-2791
Several of the nine elegantly appointed guest rooms at this 1853 farmhouse built on the site of one of the country's earliest gristmills have fireplaces and/or private front porches and balconies. Dinner is served in the full-service restaurant Sun–Thurs. **$$–$$$**

East Aurora
Roycroft Inn
40 South Grove St, NY 14052
Tel: (716) 652-5552

Price Guide

The following price categories indicate the cost of a double room in high season:
$$$ Expensive: $200 and more (NYC), $125 and more (NYS)
$$ Moderate: $125–200 (NYC), $85–125 (NYS)
$ Inexpensive: $85–125 (NYC), under $85 (NYS)

Reservations: (1-800) 267-0525 Arts & Crafts champion Elbert Hubbard opened the inn in 1903, and the National Landmark has been meticulously restored to look much as it did then. All bedroom suites have modern amenities. There's a restaurant on the premises. **$$–$$$$**

Niagara Falls
Holiday Inn by the Falls
5339 Murray St, Ontario, Canada
Tel: (905) 356-1333
or (1-800) 263-9393
Next to the Skylon Tower and within walking distance of the falls, the hotel has 122 rooms with private balconies and luxury suites with whirlpool baths. There's a Nordic spa with an indoor pool, sauna and whirlpool and outdoor pool. **$$–$$$**
The Red Coach Inn
2 Buffalo Ave, NY 14303
Tel: (716) 282-1459
Fax: (716) 282-2650
Many of the 10 uniquely decorated rooms and suites at this 1920s English-style inn overlooking the Upper Rapids have water views. Some have kitchens and whirlpools. The restaurant's patio is a wonderful spot to dine. **$$$**

Tonawanda
Cavalier Motor Lodge
1120 Niagara Falls Blvd,
NY 14150
Tel: (716) 835-5916
or (1-800) 445-1390
Fax: (716) 835-6030
Two-story motel adjacent to a shopping mall has 51 air-conditioned rooms with remote control TV and phones. Rate includes breakfast. **$**

Chautauqua-Allegheny

Alfred
Saxon Inn
1 Park St, NY 14802
Tel: (607) 871-2600
Pleasant 26-room motel on the campus of Alfred University. **$–$$**

Bemus Point
Hotel Lenhart
20-22 Lakeside Dr, NY 14712
Tel: (716) 386-2715
Historic inn overlooking Bemus Bay has been owned and operated by the same family since 1881. There are 54 rooms ranging from large parlor types (first floor) to small singles (top floor). Some share baths. Rocking chairs line the wrap-around verandah overlooking the bay. MAP rates in summer. **$–$$**

Chautauqua
Athenaeum Hotel
Tel: (716) 357-4444
Fax: (716) 357-4175
The 1881 hotel on the grounds of the Institution (*see page 299*), wired for electricity by Thomas Edison, was once the country's largest wooden frame building. Open only during the Chautauqua season (late Jun–Aug), the hotel has 156 rooms with private bath, phone, TV and air-conditioning in the hotel and a newer annex. Some rooms have lake views, and the restaurant has a porch overlooking the lake. Guests must purchase gate and parking passes. **$$$$**

Dunkirk
Four Points Sheraton Dunkirk
30 Lake Shore Dr East,
NY 14048
Tel: (716) 366-8350
Fax: (716) 366-8899
Four-story motor inn with 132 pleasantly decorated rooms with cable TV and phones. There are indoor and outdoor pools, and a restaurant. **$–$$**

Ellicottville
Ellicottville Inn
4-10 Washington St
Tel: (716) 699-2373

Brick inn with 22 antiques-filled guest rooms, and a lively bar/lounge/restaurant. **$–$$**

Ilex Inn
6416 East Washington St, NY 14731
Tel: (716) 699-2002
Six pleasantly furnished and comfortable rooms in a Victorian farmhouse; some have air-conditioning. There's an outdoor, heated pool. **$**

The Inn at Holiday Valley Resort
Rte 219 & Holiday Valley Rd, NY 14731
Tel: (716) 699-2336
Fax: (716) 699-2336
Two-story, 102-room inn has rooms with cable TV and indoor and outdoor pools. The resort's 18-hole golf course and tennis courts are nearby. **$$–$$$**

Fredonia
The White Inn
52 East Main St, NY 14063
Tel: (716) 672-2103
or (1-888) FREDONIA
Fax: (716) 672-2107
Duncan Hines himself included the restaurant at this stately inn in his "Family of Fine Restaurants" back in the 1930s, and it's maintained its excellent reputation ever since. There are 23 beautifully decorated guest rooms with TV on three floors. **$$–$$$**

Jamestown
Comfort Inn
2800 North Main St, NY 14701
Tel: (716) 664-5920
Fax: (716) 664-3068
Breakfast is complimentary at this 101-room, two-story hotel on the outskirts of town. Some rooms have whirlpool baths, and microwaves and refrigerators are available for a fee. **$–$$**

Mayville
Webb's Lake Resort
Rte 394, NY 14757
Tel: (716) 753-2161
Fax: (716) 753-1383
Resort just 3 miles (5 km) from Chautauqua Institution has water-front motel-style guest rooms, hot tubs, a fitness room, tanning booths, a pool and a fine restaurant

Price Guide

The following price categories indicate the cost of a double room in high season:

$$$ Expensive: $200 and more (NYC), $125 and more (NYS)
$$ Moderate: $125–200 (NYC), $85–125 (NYS)
$ Inexpensive: $85–125 (NYC), under $85 (NYS)

(see page 340). Golf packages are available, and there's a candy factory on the grounds. **$–$$**

Westfield
William Seward Inn
6645 South Portage Rd, NY 14787
Tel: (716) 326-4151
or (1-800) 338-4151
Restored, 1837 country inn near Chautauqua Institution has rooms with private baths and decorated with antiques or reproductions. Some overlook Lake Erie and have double jacuzzis and/or gas log fireplaces. Rate includes a full gourmet breakfast. A gourmet dinner is served Wed–Sun. **$–$$$**

Camping

There are over a hundred state parks, and hundreds of private and public campgrounds throughout the state, from Long Island to the Adirondacks and the Finger Lakes, offering everything from tent and recreational vehicle sites to cabins.

For a copy of the **New York State Office of Parks, Recreation and Historic Preservation**'s Guide to New York State Operated Parks, call (518) 474-0456 or write to: State Parks, Empire State Plaza, Albany NY 12238. For a brochure on cabins, write to: Cabins, State Parks, Albany NY 12238, or call (1-800) 456-CAMP. For an online directory of private campgrounds, visit the website of the **Campground Owners of New York** at: www.rvdestinations.com/cony, or get their annually updated guide by sending the cost of postage to CONY/WWC PO Box 497 Dansville, NY 14437-0497

Hostels

Hostelling International – American Youth Hostels have hostels in New York City, Niagara Falls, Cape Vincent, Buffalo and Syracuse. Check out their website, at www.hiayh.org, or contact the American head office in Washington DC (733 15th St, NW, Suite 840, Washington DC 20005; tel: 202/783-6161; fax: 202/783-6171). Private hostels, which are listed in www.hostelhandbook.com, include:

New York City
Big Apple Hostel
119 West 45th St, NY 10036
Tel: (212) 302-2603
Great location in the heart of the Broadway theater district, Manhattan.

The Blue Rabbit
730 St. Nicholas Ave, NY 10031
Tel: (212) 491-3892
Small travelers hostel in a renovated five-story mansion in the historic Sugar Hill, north Manhattan. Some double rooms are available.

Central Park Hostel
19 West 103rd St, NY 10025
Tel: (212) 678-0491
New hostel on the Upper West side of Manhattan in a renovated brownstone building.

Jazz on the Park
36 West 106th St, Central Park West, NY 10025
Tel: (212) 932-1600
Large friendly hostel, with over 200 beds in dorms and private rooms; coffee bar with live music.

The Park View Hotel
55 West 110th St, Central Park North, NY 10026
Tel: (212) 369-5539
Located just north of Central Park; has good views of the park and a snack shop.

New York State
Belleayre Hostel
Box J, Main St, Pine Hill, NY 12465
Tel: (845) 254-4200
Hostel in the Catskills with cabins and private rooms. Hiking; lake.

Hi Buffalo
667 Main St, Buffalo, NY 14203
Tel: (716) 852-5222
Centrally located hostel.

Where to Eat

What To Eat

Fresh game, fish and produce from around the state is increasingly used by New York's finest restaurants, such as the Hudson River Club in Manhattan's World Financial Center. You can see and taste a representative sampling at any of the Greenmarkets that take place throughout the week and on weekends in most of New York City's five boroughs. The largest is located at Union Square, where farmers arrive at dawn to set up their stands. In summer, there are dozens of varieties of tomatoes, potatoes, lettuce and other vegetables, herbs and fruit, while in fall and winter, apples, beets, squash, hot cider and other staples take center stage. For a free copy of the New York State Guide to Farm Fresh Food, which comes in four regional versions (Metro, Eastern, Central and Western) and lists pick-your-own farms as well as roadside produce stands, farmer's markets and wineries, write to the **New York State Department of Agriculture and Markets** (1 Winners Circle, Albany, NY 12235, tel: 518/457-3880 or 1-800/554-4501). The same department can also provide a list of New York State's 58 county agricultural fairs.

Where To Eat

There are literally thousands of restaurants in New York City alone, of all sizes, types, specialities and qualities, and the following does not begin to hint at an "exhaustive" list. Cited here are those recommended with few or even no qualms at all. However, it's worth keeping in mind that (to the eternal dismay of travel

guides) even the best established eateries can disappear abruptly, not to mention changes in management or menu that cause listings to become out of date just as quickly.

It's also worth noting that reservations are often necessary and always recommended: At some top-of-the-line establishments, such as the Four Seasons and the River Café, they may be required a week or two in advance. Of course, not everyone who makes a reservation shows up at their appointed time, so you can always take the chance of waiting in line – although this can often be a tedious experience and won't add to your dining enjoyment.

To calculate the tip, it's easiest to simply double the sales tax shown on the bill, which equals about 17 percent at the current rate (15 percent is the norm). In restaurants with captains, it's customary to leave an additional five percent. It's a good idea to call ahead and find out which, if any, credit cards are accepted.

Finally, be aware that since April 1995, under Local Law 5, smoking has been prohibited in New York City restaurants with 35 seats or more – even at the bar, unless it's well ventilated and a proscribed number of feet away from the dining area. Needless to say, New Yorkers are rebels: some restaurants ignore the law, particularly in obscure downtown establishments frequented by the young and oblivious.

Restaurants are listed by region in the same order as the Places section of this guide, and then alphabetically by town. New York City restaurants are listed by price category.

New York City

Expensive
Le Bernardin
155 West 51st St (Midtown)
Tel: (212) 489-1515
Formal and a bit aloof, but famous for the delicacy of its seafood. One of the city's most elite establishments. Reservations necessary. All major credit cards.

Café des Artistes
1 West 67th St, off Central Park West (Upper West Side)
Tel: (212) 877-3500
Romance is in the air at this elegant French restaurant decorated by murals of naked nymphs. Good for that special occasion. Most major credit cards. Reservations recommended.

Chanterelle
2 Harrison St at Hudson St (TriBeCa)
Tel: (212) 966-6960
Another elegant and very regarded downtown spot, noted for its exquisite nouvelle French cuisine and *prix fixe* "tasting menu". Most credit cards. Reservations.

Le Cirque 2000
455 Madison Ave (Midtown)
Tel: (212) 794-9292
Very elegant French restaurant, where the socially elite hobnob amidst huge floral arrangements. Excellent food. Make reservations far in advance. Major credit cards.

The Four Seasons
99 East 52nd St (Midtown)
Tel: (212) 754-9494
A Manhattan favorite and remarkable for its modern decor. The menu changes with the seasons of the year (hence the name) and is wildly eclectic. Make reservations well in advance. Major credit cards.

Hudson River Club
Four World Financial Center at Vesey St (Lower Manhattan)
Tel: (212) 786-1500
Views of the Hudson, overlooking the adjacent boat basin's collection of visiting yachts. This is a very proper but very friendly restaurant featuring innovative regional cuisine, including venison and rabbit. Desserts are splendid, too. Most major credit cards. Reservations necessary for lunch.

Lutece
249 East 50th St (between Second
and Third avenues, Midtown)
Tel: (212) 752-2225
Located in a pretty townhouse and
acclaimed for decades as the best
French restaurant in New York, it
recently acquired a new owner and a
new chef; whether it will remain the
city's favorite remains to be seen.
Major credit cards. Reservations.

Montrachet
239 West Broadway
(below Canal St, in TriBeCa)
Tel: (212) 219-2777
Another elegant French restaurant,
serving light and inventive nouvelle
cuisine. Reservations necessary.
American Express only.

The River Café
1 Water St (Cadman Plaza West,
Brooklyn Heights)
Tel: (718) 522-5200
Make your reservations a week or
two ahead, if possible, as this
romantic barge restaurant,
beautifully situated on the East
River at the Brooklyn end of the
Brooklyn Bridge. It is justly famous
for its spectacular view of lower
Manhattan's skyscrapers. The
superior American cuisine lives up
to its setting. All major credit cards.

San Domenico
240 Central Park South at
Columbus Circle (Midtown)
Tel: (212) 265-5959
One of the most highly-rated Italian
restaurants in the city, it offers
unusual Bolognese fare, with an
exceptional variety of northern
Italian pastas and an extremely
wide wine list.

"21" Club
21 West 52nd St (Midtown)
Tel: (212) 753-1870
A clubby, one-time speakeasy which
attracts a socially prominent, well-
heeled, often famous clientele to
the banquettes of its downstairs
bar area. Famous for its
hamburgers, which, if you order
one, cuts the price down to
moderate. All major credit cards.
Reservations recommended.

Windows on the World
107th floor, One World Trade Center
(Lower Manhattan)
Tel: (212) 524-7000

Famed for its breathtaking views
and pricey menu. A tourist
attraction, but worth the experience
at least once. All major credit cards.
Reservations recommended.

Moderate
Jezebel
630 Ninth Ave at 45th St (Midtown
theater district)
Tel: (212) 582-1045
One of the city's most atmospheric
restaurants, serving soul food
beneath fringed lamps. Most major
credit cards. Reservations are a
good idea.

Knickerbocker Bar & Grill
33 University Place (Greenwich
Village)
Tel: (212) 228-8490
A bar/restaurant that epitomizes
New York: dark paneling and, in the
evening, live jazz. A great place for
steak or a burger. Open lunch and
dinner. Major credit cards.

Oyster Bar
Lower level, Grand Central Terminal
(Midtown)
Tel: (212) 490-6650
A New York institution, and a must
for seafood lovers, it serves the
best clam chowder in town. Most
major credit cards. Closed Sunday.

Patrissy's
98 Kenmare St at Lafayette St
(Little Italy)
Tel: (212) 226-2888
On Little Italy's northern outskirts,
this mildly formal hideaway has
good service and a solid menu of
Italian dishes. All major credit
cards. Reservations suggested.

Peter Luger
178 Broadway (Brooklyn)
Tel: (718) 387-7400
Brooklyn landmark, specializing in
steak. Exposed wood beams in the
bar. Reservations suggested.

Provence
38 MacDougal St (Greenwich Village)
Tel: (212) 475-7500
Romantic restaurant with French
cuisine; very popular. Open lunch
and dinner. Major credit cards.

Raoul's
180 Prince St (Soho)
Tel: (212) 966-3518
A dark French bistro, elegant and
trendy, with a satisfying menu and a

small garden. Most major credit
cards. Reservations recommended.

Rosa Mexicano
1063 First Ave at 58th St
(Upper East Side)
Tel: (212) 757-7407
Perhaps the most authentic Mexican fare in New York, with
delicious Margaritas and
guacamole prepared fresh at your
table. All major credit cards.
Reservations recommended.

Sparks Steakhouse
210 East 46th St (Midtown)
Tel: (212) 687-4855
The granddaddy of New York
steakhouses, and a great place for
consuming huge steaks cooked to
precision. All major credit cards.
Reservations necessary.

Price Guide

The following price categories
indicate the cost of a meal for
two, with wine:
$$$ Expensive: $100 and more
$$ Moderate: $65–100
$ Inexpensive: under $65

TriBeCa Grill
375 Greenwich St at Franklin St
(TriBeCa)
Tel: (212) 941-3900
Actor Robert De Niro's place in
which to see and be seen, serving
upscale bistro food at expensive
prices. Reservations required.

Union Square Café
21 East 16th St (Union Sq)
Tel: (212) 243-4020
Some of the friendliest service in
New York, and some of the most
interesting regional cuisine
anywhere, attracts a hip, youngish
crowd. Most major credit cards.
Reservations recommended.

Inexpensive
Broome Street Bar
363 West Broadway at Broome St
(Soho)
Tel: (212) 925-2086
A relaxed, cheap and casual pub/
restaurant with a menu of
hamburgers, quiche and thick
Reuben sandwiches of corned beef
and sauerkraut. No reservations.

Carnegie Deli
854 Seventh Ave at 55th St
(Midtown)
Tel: (212) 757-2245
New York's most famous delicatessen restaurant, where the cognoscenti regard the corned beef sandwich as a work of art. Very crowded, especially at lunchtime.

Dominick's
2335 Arthur Ave (The Bronx)
Tel: (718) 733-2807
An old-fashioned family-style eatery where you share tables with other diners. No menu, no credit cards. A true New York experience.

Excellent Dumpling House
111 Lafayette, just below Canal
Tel: (212) 219-0212
An unpretentious, unadorned spot on the outskirts of Chinatown, usually packed with locals and visitors who love its no-nonsense atmosphere and stellar dumplings (especially the vegetable dumplings, served steamed or fried). No reservations or credit cards accepted.

Fanelli's
94 Prince St (Soho)
Tel: (212) 226-9412
A friendly, unpretentious neighborhood bar and restaurant that's been around since the 19th century, and a favorite with local artists who've managed to hang on to their Soho rent-controlled lofts. Most major credit cards.

Florent
69 Gansevoort St, near Greenwich St (Greenwich Village)
Tel: (212) 989-5779
Deep in the heart of the meatpacking district, this 24-hour stainless-steel café serves everything from *escargot* to onion soup to a clientele that gets stranger as the night goes on.

Il Mulino
86 West 3rd St between Thompson and Sullivan (Greenwich Village)
Tel: (212) 673-3783
Large portions and a wide variety of pastas make this a perennial Village favorite. Not the fanciest Italian restaurant around, but perhaps the best-loved. Reservations suggested.

Landmark Tavern
626 Eleventh Ave at 46th St
(Midtown)
Tel: (212) 757-8595
A 19th-century establishment that's convenient if you're visiting the Intrepid Sea-Air-Space museum, but otherwise off the beaten track. Worth the trip, however, if you're longing for Irish stew and shepherd's pie. Major credit cards.

O Lavrador
138-40 101st Ave, Richmond Hill
(Queens)
Tel: (718) 526-1526
In an out of the way neighborhood, this Portuguese restaurant (the name means "The Farmer") specializes in seafood dishes typical of southern Portugal. Extremely reasonable. All major credit cards.

Sylvia's
328 Lenox Ave (Harlem)
Tel: (212) 996-0660
Hearty, Southern-style home-cooked meals and a favorite destination for Sunday brunch with a soulfood flavour. Credit cards accepted.

Long Island

Amagansett
The Lobster Roll Restaurant
Montauk Hwy
Tel: (516) 267-3740
Between Amagansett and Montauk, watch for the big sign that says "Lunch". It marks one of the area's most popular spots for fresh seafood. Lobster roll, grilled tuna, and steamers are among the specialties. Open for dinner, too. **$–$$**

Cutchogue
Cutchogue Diner
Main Rd
Tel: (516) 734-9056
Authentic diner serves up three classic meals daily, including breakfast specials such as Belgian waffles with fresh fruit. **$**

East Marion
Hellenic Snack Bar & Restaurant
Main Rd
Tel: (516) 477-0138
Award-winning Greek cuisine for more than 25 years. Fresh barbecued lamb, chicken and piglet are prepared on the

outdoor rotisserie; desserts are homemade; and there are always traditional favorites such as *Spanakopita, gyros* and fried calamari. Breakfasts are a standout. **$**

Glen Cove
La Pace
51 Cedar Swamp Rd
Tel: (516) 671-2970
Highly regarded, European-style restaurant serving entrées such as veal chop with wild mushrooms. Semi-formal attire requested at dinner; valet parking. **$$$**

Greenport
Claudio's
111 Main St
Tel: (516) 477-0627
Seafood is king at "the oldest same-family owned restaurant in the United States", overlooking the harbor. Their clam bar on the docks has entertainment on summer weekends. **$–$$**

Rhumb Line Restaurant
36 Front St
Tel: (516) 477-9883
Fresh seafood including fried oysters, steamed mussels and fried soft shell crab shares the limelight with burgers and steaks. **$–$$**

Jamesport
Jamesport Country Kitchen
Main Rd (Rte 25)
Tel: (516) 722-3537
Where the locals (and everyone else) go for the freshest seafood, burgers, steaks, and other homemade fare – all prepared with North Fork produce and wines. Reservations highly recommended. **$$**

Kings Park
Old Dock Inn
798 Old Dock Rd
Tel: (631) 269-4118
Seafood and steak share the limelight at this restaurant overlooking the Nissequogue River and the Sound. House specialties include Old Dock Seafood Special (baked clams, stuffed mushrooms, scallops, shrimp and crab leg) and veal Parmigiana. **$$–$$$**

New Suffolk
Legends
835 First St
Tel: (516) 734-5123
Some of the region's best fish and shellfish dishes (the steamers are succulent) served up in ample portions at this off-the-beaten-path spot. The homemade desserts are indeed legendary. **$–$$**

Riverhead
Peconic River Cruises
Riverhead Village Pier
Tel: (516) 369-3700
Lunch, dinner, cocktails and Sunday brunch (along with banjo entertainment) served aboard the *Peconic River Queen* as it cruises along. **$$**

Sag Harbor
Lucida Roadhouse
Rte 114
Tel: (516) 749-1900
Fresh local fish, margaritas, tapas, coconut shrimp, and Black Angus steak are just a few items served at this popular spot which has an outdoor pool table and stays open to midnight, Fri and Sat. **$–$$**

Hudson Valley

Chappaqua
Crabtree's Kittle House Restaurant and Country Inn
11 Kittle Rd
Tel: (845) 666-8044
The menu changes daily, but the food, ambiance and service at this 200-year-old inn are always excellent. Continental cuisine includes offerings such as wild salmon gravlax, and loin of free-range lamb. The wine cellar has more than 30,000 bottles. The inn has 12 guest rooms. **$$$**

Cold Spring
Northgate at Dockside Harbor
1 North St
Tel: (845) 265-5555
American regional cuisine and a wide variety of fresh seafood dishes are the specialties at this riverfront restaurant with a deck for seasonal dining. **$–$$**

Dover Plains
Old Drovers Inn
Old Rte 22
Tel: (845) 832-9311
Rough hewn timber and stucco combine with leather furnishings and gleaming silver in this 250 year-old inn (*see page 320*) to create a romantic atmosphere. Emphasis is on Mediterranean and American regional dishes: cheddar cheese soup and browned turkey hash are among the signature dishes. Reservations are required well in advance. **$$–$$$**

High Falls
DePuy Canal House
Rte 213
Tel: (845) 687-7700
American gourmet cooking by John Novi, the "father of New American cooking", in a 1797 stone tavern built to serve workers and travelers on the Delaware and Hudson Canal. From the balcony overlooking the kitchen patrons can watch the preparation of dishes such as veal shoulder braised and stuffed with smoked pork loin, and lamb loin with black truffle risotto. Open for dinner Thurs–Sun and Sun brunch. There are three guest rooms at the Locktender Cottage. **$$$–$$$$**

Highland
The Would Bar and Grill
120 North Rd.
Tel: (845) 691-9883.
The international menu, which changes seasonally, may include fried *escargot* wontons and pan-seared duck. The home baked breads and pastries are a specialty. **$$–$$$**

Hyde Park
Culinary Institute of America
433 Albany Post Rd
Tel: (845) 452-9600
Choose from four restaurants on the campus of the country's oldest culinary college: a casual café, fixed-priced Italian regional cuisine, classic French cuisine, or one specializing in regional American cuisine. Reservations are recommended (call 845/471-6608 Mon–Fri). **$–$$$$**

Kingston
Hoffman House Tavern
94 North Front St
Tel: (845) 338-2626
American and Continental cuisine served in a National Historic Landmark American Dutch rubble house. There's a cozy fire in winter, and a terrace for warm weather dining. Closed Sun. **$–$$**

Millbrook
Millbrook Diner
Rte 44
Tel: (845) 677-5319
An institution for more than 65 years, this classic diner has served celebrities including James Cagney and Ray Charles. American and Mediterranean dishes. **$–$$**

New Paltz
Mohonk Mountain House
Mohonk Lake
Tel. (845) 255-1000
A great location and an air of old-world formality (jackets at dinner), combined with excellent fare and superb service. Buffets and five-course dinners are served daily; the main dining room, without air conditioning, can get warm. **$$–$$$**

Pine Island
Ye Jolly Onion Inn
Rte 517, Pulaski Hwy and Orange County Rte 1, 10969
Tel: (845) 258-4277
The region's famous "black dirt" onions are the house specialty. They're served on steak, as onion rings, on the salad bar, and as deep-fried blossoms. **$–$$**

South Salem
Le Chateau
Rts 35/123
Tel: (845) 533-6631
Classic French food served in a Tudor-style mansion built by financier JP Morgan overlooking the Hudson River Valley. The setting is elegant, the service impeccable, and the food excellent. **$$$$**

Staatsburg
Belvedere Mansion
Rte 9, 12580
Tel: (845) 889-8000

Linen tablecloths and polished silver set the mood for elegant dining in a Greek Revival mansion/ B&B (*see page 321*) overlooking the Hudson River. Dishes include gâteau of wild mushrooms and braised lamb shank with saffron risotto, artichokes, and mint. Dinner only. **$$$$**

Stormville
Harralds
Rte 52
Tel: (845) 878-6595
Harralds' traditional French and International cuisine have consistently won accolades since the restaurant opened more than 25 years ago. The multi-course dinners are *prix fixe*, with a less expensive, fewer course dinner offered mid-week. Dinner only. No credit cards. **$$$–$$$$**

Tivoli
Café Pongo
69 Broadway
Tel: (845) 757-4403
Everything is made from scratch with mostly local ingredients at this charming restaurant which specializes in "neighborhood cuisine" and excellent baked goods. The decor is elegant, but kids are most welcome. There's outdoor seating, and weekend brunch is popular. **$–$$**

Wappinger Falls
Orchid Restaurant
41 Middlebush Rd
Tel: (845) 297-7969
Wondering what to order at this Russian-Armenian restaurant? Try the Zakruska – a sampler plate of appetizers, or the mixed platter which includes lamb, pork, and eggplant. **$$–$$$$**

The Catskills

Downsville
The Old Schoolhouse Inn & Restaurant
Main St
Tel: (607) 363-7814
Renovated, 1903 schoolhouse with Victorian atmosphere serves up American fare including prime rib, fresh fish and lobster. There are daily specials, a shrimp and salad bar, and excellent homemade desserts. Closed Mon. **$–$$**

Eldred
Eldred Preserve
Rte 55
Tel: (845) 557-8316
Brown, brook, golden and rainbow trout fresh from the preserve's ponds is the specialty at this restaurant nestled amid 2,000 acres of forest. The dining rooms look out on the ponds. There's a motel here, and lakes for boating and fishing. **$$**

Mount Tremper
Catskill Rose
Rte 212
Tel: (845) 688-7100
Creative dishes include appetizers such as potato wedges with Gruyere cheese and entrées such as chervil-stuffed broiled trout and smoked duckling with strawberry rhubarb sauce. Reservations highly recommended. Dinner only, Wed–Sun. **$$**

Rock Hill
Bernie's Holiday Restaurant
Rte 17
Tel: (845) 796-3333
Oriental and American dishes, lots of fresh seafood, and daily specials are featured at this very large and very popular restaurant. Dinner only, Tues–Sun. **$**

Stamford
Nicole's
Main St
Tel: (607) 652-2975
Popular local spot for good, solid American fare, including bountiful breakfasts. **$**

Windham
La Griglia
Rte 296
Tel: (518) 734-4499
Northern Italian cuisine served in an elegant country atmosphere. Early bird specials and a good Sunday brunch. Dinner only Mon–Fri. **$–$$**

Woodstock
New World Home Cooking
1411 Rte 212
Tel: (845) 246-0900
"New Wave" cooking featuring ethnic dishes from around the world: many of them wonderfully spicy (although there are plenty for those that don't like it hot). There's an outdoor patio. **$**

Wurtsboro
The Repast
Sullivan St
Tel: (845) 888-4448
Handsomely appointed Victorian restaurant specializes in country fare with dishes such as croissant sandwiches, prime rib and chicken with almonds. **$–$$**

Wyoming
Gaslight Village Café
Gaslight Commons, 1 Main St
Tel: (716) 495-6695
Housed in an 1846 building in the historic gaslight district, the restaurant serves a wide range of American favorites, including steak, burgers, seafood and pizza. **$**

Capital & Saratoga

Albany
El Loco
465 Madison Ave
Tel: (518) 436-1855
Popular Mexican restaurant serving up Tex-Mex and vegetarian fare. **$**
Jack's Oyster House
42 State St
Tel: (518) 465-8854
Fresh seafood is the specialty at the city's oldest restaurant, run by the same family for more than 80 years. **$$**
Miss Albany Diner
893 Broadway
Tel: (518) 465-9148

Price Guide

The following price categories indicate the cost of a meal for two, with wine:
$$$ Expensive: $100 and more
$$ Moderate: $65–100
$ Inexpensive: under $65

Landmark 1941 diner serves up all traditional diner fare. **$**

Nicole's Bistro at Quackenbush House
351 Broadway
Tel: (518) 465-1111
Casual, fresh American bistro has an excellent buffet, an outdoor garden and *prix fixe* dinners. **$–$$**

Scrimshaw Dining Room
The Desmond Hotel, 660 Albany Shaker Rd
Tel: (518) 869-8100
or (1-800) 448-3500
One of the region's more elegant dining rooms specializes in Continental cuisine, with appetizers such as oysters Rockefeller, and entrées including veal Oscar. Closed Sun. **$$$$**

Saratoga Springs
Hattie's
45 Phila St
Tel: (518) 584-4790
Serving up some of the area's best New Orleans-style food since 1938. Specialties include fried chicken and biscuits, and slow-cooked barbecued spare ribs; Creole dishes including blackened catfish are delicious, too. **$$**

43 Phila Bistro
43 Phila St
Tel: (518) 584-2720
Upscale bistro serving nouvelle American cuisine such as Thai-spiced lobster, and sesame crusted salmon filet. The wine list is outstanding. Reservations recommended. Closed Sun. **$$–$$$$**

The Old Bryan Inn
123 Maple Ave
Tel: (518) 587-2990
1773 restored inn offers casual dining with dishes such as prime rib and fettuccini Lily, a seasonal outside patio, entertainment, and a popular Sun brunch. **$$**

Schenectady
Glen Sanders Mansion
1 Glen Ave
Tel: (518) 374-7262
Continental fare such as lobster bisque with cognac cream and chives, and coconut sugar cane glazed tuna, are served elegantly in an historic stone home. A lighter

pub menu is served in the lounge. Lunch Mon–Fri, dinner nightly and Sun brunch. **$$$–$$$$**

Ruby's Silver Diner
167 Erie Blvd
Tel: (518) 382-9741
Old fashioned diner with excellent cooking and reasonable prices. **$**

Troy
Holmes and Watson
450 Broadway
Tel: (518) 273-8526
English-style pub offers traditional fare including steaks, burgers, and salads; there's a courtyard for seasonal dining. **$–$$**

Adirondacks

Chestertown
Friends Lake Inn
Friends Lake Rd
Tel: (518) 494-4751
Creatively prepared New American cuisine, homemade pâtés and breads and fabulous desserts complement the largest wine cellar in northern New York. **$$$–$$$$**

Eagle Bay
Big Moose Inn
Big Moose Rd
Tel: (315) 357-2042
Award-winning, casually elegant restaurant housed in a 1903 Adirondack Inn, with rooms above the restaurant. Among the specialties: roast duck, veal Oscar, and homemade desserts. **$$–$$$**

Keene Valley
Noon Mark Diner
Rte 73
Tel: (518) 576-4499
Classic diner serves up good, solid American fare and better than average homemade pie. **$**

Lake Placid
Averil Conwell Dining Room
Mirror Lake Inn, Mirror Lake Dr
Tel: (518) 523-2544
One of the region's most highly acclaimed restaurants serves regional American fare by candle-light overlooking the lake. Reservations suggested. **$$$–$$$$**

The Great Adirondack Steak & Seafood Company
34 Main St
Tel: (518) 523-1629
Steak and seafood are the obvious specialties at this casual, upscale eatery, and the Surf and Turf nightly special is the way to sample them both. **$$**

Tail o' the Pup
Rte 86, Ray Brook
Tel: (518) 891-5092
Old-fashioned roadside restaurant offers inside, outside and in-car dining.BBQ is the house specialty, but there are lots of other American favorites to choose from. **$**

Martinsburg
Greystone Manor
Rte 26
Tel: (315) 376-7714
One of the area's finer restaurants, housed in an 1803 mansion, serves specialties such as shrimp scampi and steak teriyaki. Open May–Oct, Tues–Sun. **$$–$$$**

North Creek
Smith's Restaurant
296 Main St
Tel: (518) 251-2363
The Adirondacks' oldest family restaurant has been serving German and American food since 1924. Homemade desserts, a full bar and box lunches to go. **$$**

Old Forge
The Old Mill Restaurant
Rte 28
Tel: (315) 369-3662
Housed in an historic mill, the cuisine is decidedly American, with specialties such as roast duck, shepherd's pie, and prime rib. Cocktails are served on the deck. Dinner only; Sun from 1pm; closed mid-Mar–Apr. **$–$$**

Saranac Lake
Casa del Sol
154 Lake Flower Ave
Tel: (518) 891-0977
Traditional Mexican specialties including *molé poblano* and *chillquiles* are served in this cheerful restaurant with an outdoor patio. No credit cards. **$**

Thousand Islands & St Lawrence Seaway

Alexandria Bay
Jacques Cartier Dining Room
Riveredge Resort & Hotel,
17 Holland St
Tel: (315) 482-9917
Continental cuisine, including
French rotisserie cooking, is
elegantly prepared and served
overlooking the St Lawrence River
and Boldt Castle. Dinner jackets
requested. **$$$–$$$$**

Fishers Landing
Foxy's Restaurant
On the Dock
Tel: (315) 686-3781
Homemade veal, fresh shrimp
scampi and pasta are few
specialties at this family-owned
Italian restaurant on a private dock
between Alexandria Bay and
Clayton. **$–$$$**

Oswego
Canale's Restaurant
156 West Utica St
Tel: (315) 343-3540
Good Italian home cooking served
up in large portions. Dinner only
Sat–Sun. **$–$$**
Rudy's
Washington Blvd
Tel: (315) 343-2671
Close to the SUNY Oswego campus,
the casual restaurant is popular for
fried fish platters, including fish and
chips, and clams. **$**

Sackets Harbor
Old Stone Row Restaurant
336 Brady Rd
Tel: (315) 646-2923
Creative American cuisine in an
upscale restaurant located at the
historic Madison Barracks. **$$–$$$**

Watertown
Sboro's Restaurant
836 Coffeen St
Tel: (315) 788-1728
Since 1933, the family-owned and
operated restaurant has been
serving simple but sophisticated
Italian-American specialties
including veal, pasta, antipasto,
and fresh fish. **$$–$$$**

Central-Leatherstocking

Cazenovia
Wheatberry Restaurant
63 Albany St
Tel: (315) 655-2102
Sunday brunch is a popular event at
this casual restaurant which specializes in International cuisine and
homemade desserts. **$–$$**

Cooperstown
Blue Mingo Grill
Sam Smith's Boatyard, Rte 80
Tel: (607) 547-7496
A variety of international cuisines
are served at this lovely lakeside
restaurant. Lunch offerings tend to
the traditional, with salads, fresh
grilled fish and pizzas. The dinner
blackboard menu changes daily,
and includes Thai, Indonesian and
French dishes. Open Mother's Day
to Labor Day. **$$–$$$**
Gabiella's on the Square
161 Main St
Tel: (607) 547-8000
Continental cuisine with a European
flair is served in casually elegant
surroundings. Two of the
restaurant's four dining rooms have
fireplaces. Popular spot for late
evening nightcaps. **$$–$$$**

Little Falls
Canal Side Inn
395 S. Ann St
Tel: (315) 823-1170
Highly regarded waterfront
restaurant in a renovated historic
building specializing in classic
French cuisine. There is an
extensive wine list. Dinner only. **$$$**

Old Chatham
**Old Chatham Sheepherding
Company Inn**
99 Shaker Museum Rd
Tel: (518) 794-9774
Contemporary American fare is
featured in this Georgian style,
1790s inn overlooking the Shaker
Museum. A roaring fireplace,
comfortable wing chairs, and
excellent food have made this one
of the region's most popular
restaurants. Reservations are a
must. There are eight guest rooms

in the main house and two
outbuildings. **$$$–$$$$**

Rome
The Beeches
7900 Turin Rd. (Rte 26N)
Tel: (315) 336-1700
or (1-800) 765-7251
Traditional American fare is the
specialty at this historic restaurant
surrounded by woods and
meadows. Closed Mon. **$$–$$$**
Savoy Restaurant
East Dominick St
Tel: (315) 339-3166
Family-owned and operated since
1908, Italian specialties including
homemade pasta share the menu
with traditional American dishes. **$$**

Schoharie
Historic Throop Drugstore
Main St
Tel: (518) 295-7300
Pharmacy/museum/restaurant has
an old-fashioned soda fountain,
homemade soups, sandwiches, and
freshly baked Danish. **$**

Sharon Springs
The Roseboro Hotel
Main St
Tel: (518) 284-2020
"Bohemian" family bistro in a
historic hotel in the process of
being restored serves up a wide
variety of creative dishes including:
homemade soups (including black
bean with corn chowder topping);
hot brie topped with apricot com-
pote; BBQ pork and chicken; and
Middle Eastern specialties. Breakfast dishes include burritos with
egg, cheese and potato. **$–$$**

Utica
Devereaux
37 Devereaux St
Tel: (315) 735-8628

Price Guide

The following price categories
indicate the cost of a meal for
two, with wine:
$$$ Expensive: $100 and more
$$ Moderate: $65–100
$ Inexpensive: under $65

Local landmark has great sandwiches, homemade soups, and – on weekends – live music. **$**

Finger Lakes

Benton Center (Penn Yan)
Millers' Essenhaus
1300 Rte 14A
Tel: (315) 531-8260
Homemade Mennonite specialties include split pea soup, shoe fly pie, and barbecues. **$–$$**

Canandaigua
Thendara Inn
4356 East Lake Rd
Tel: (716) 394-4868
Elegant American cuisine in an historic inn overlooking the lake. There's an outdoor patio for summer dining. Lunch is served in summer. The inn has five lovely guest rooms. **$$$**

Castile
Glen Iris Inn
Letchworth State Park
Tel: (716) 493-2622
The yellow-and-white Victorian inn (15 guest rooms) overlooking Mid Falls has a popular restaurant with great views and good seafood, burgers, salads and steak. **$$**

Clifton Springs
Warfield's Restaurant & Bakery
7 West Main St, Clifton Springs
Tel: (315) 462-7184
Relaxed dining in a landmark 1871 building with brick and oak walls and gorgeous tin ceilings. The menu includes country favorites with an international twist, such as roast pork loin with corn bread and Andouille sausage stuffing with Cajun cabbage. Many vegetarian choices. Extensive wine list and delicious bakery. **$$**

Ithaca
Joe's Restaurant
602 West Buffalo St
Tel: (607) 273-2693
The menu is Italian and the atmosphere 1950s casual at this popular restaurant where reservations are highly recommended. Dinner only. **$–$$**

Moosewood
215 North Cayuga St
Tel: (607) 273-9610
The authors of the well-known natural foods cookbook serve up their own recipes in a casual restaurant with an outdoor patio. **$–$$**

Turback's of Ithaca
919 Elmira Rd
Tel: (607) 272-6484
Venerable eatery housed in an 1852 Victorian mansion specializes in New York State dishes and wines. Dinner only. **$$–$$$**

Naples
Bob's and Ruth's
204 Main St, Old Town Sq
Tel: (716) 374-5122
Popular local spot; casual area and the upscale Vineyard Room. **$–$$**

Pittsford
Richardson's Canal House Inn
1474 March Rd
Tel: (716) 248-5200
The Erie Canal's oldest original building, a haven for canal builders in the early 1800s, houses one of the region's finest restaurants. *Prix fixe* dinners might include sautéed crab cakes and espresso and black pepper crusted rack of lamb, followed by apple raisin cake. Lighter fare is served in the pub. Oliver Loud's 19th-century Inn B&B is next door (see page 328).

Rochester
Dinosaur Bar-B-Q
99 Court St
Tel: (716) 325-7090
A genuine honky tonk rib joint, featuring a pit barbecue and Cajun and Cuban specialties. Live Blues music. Open late, and slinging BBQ til midnight. **$**

Savory Thyme Café
105 East Ave
tel: (716) 423-0750
This pleasant café, in the East End and cultural district near the Eastman Theatre, serves healthy international cuisine with an emphasis on vegetarian dishes. Dishes range from Guatemalan or Lebanese salad wraps to grilled

chicken pesto sandwiches, to organic Tex-Mex specialties. Open Mon–Wed 11am–5pm, Thurs–Sat 11am–9pm. **$**

Tapas 177
177 St Paul St
Tel: (716) 262-2090
Candlelit restaurant in the heart of downtown. Features 'fusion food,' with exotic touches and many wild game and seafood dishes. There is also a Martini menu, homemade sangria and many wines by the glass. Live music at weekends. **$$**

Sodus Bay
Papa Joe's Restaurant
Tel: (315) 483-6372
The town's only year-round restaurant is right on the bay, offers entertainment on the deck on summer weekends, and has a diverse American menu. A two-room apartment overlooking the bay is available nightly. **$–$$**

Seneca Lake
Veraisons Restaurant
Glenora Wine Cellars
5435 Route 14, Dundee
Tel: (607) 243-9500
or (1-800) 243-5513
Superb restaurant overlooking Seneca Lake, located at the Inn at Glenora Wine Cellars. Large windows give magnificent lake views from any table, or dine al fresco on the balcony. Entrées range from Frenched filet mignon to chicken and seafood dishes, accompanied by extensive Finger Lakes wine list. Light salads and sandwiches at lunchtime. **$$-$$$**

Skaneateles
Rosalie's Cucina
841 West Genesee St
Tel: (315) 685-2200
Many of the Northern Italian specialties here are prepared according to old family recipes. Among the standouts are *polla marsala* and *pesce diavolo*. **$$–$$$**

The Krebs
53 West Genesee St
Tel: (315) 685-5714
The motto at this local institution which opened its doors in 1899 is "Never Leave Hungry", and the *prix*

fixe "traveling buffets", including everything from shrimp cocktails to prime rib to pan fried chicken to homemade desserts, assure that nobody ever does. Lighter fare is served in the Tavern. **$$$–$$$$**

Syracuse
China Pavilion
2101 West Genesee St,
(Westvale Plaza)
Tel: (315) 488-2828
Hunan, Peking, Cantonese and Szechuan fare at one of the area's most popular Chinese restaurants. **$–$$**
Pascale Wine Bar & Restaurant
204 West Fayette St
Tel: (315) 471-3040
Creative French-American cuisine in an historic townhouse. Finger Lake wines are featured. **$$$**

Watkins Glen
Bully Hill Café
8843 Taylor Memorial Dr
Tel: (607) 868-3490
At the Bully Hill Vineyards, the café overlooking Keuka Lake serves a lovely lunch with dishes such as salads and pasta. Open May–Oct. **$**

Greater Niagara

Batavia
Miss Batavia
566 East Main St
Tel: (716) 343-9786
Classic diner serves big portions of traditional specialties including burgers, steaks, sandwiches and homemade desserts. **$**

Buffalo
Anchor Bar and Restaurant
1047 Main St
Tel: (716) 886-8920
Reputedly the place where buffalo wings were invented: they're still served up here with the traditional celery and blue cheese dip. Other items on the menu include steaks, burgers and fish. **$–$$**
Breckenridge Brewery
623 Main St
Tel: (716) 856-2739
Spacious restaurant with a Southwestern flair located in the Market Arcade complex prepares

many of its dishes with beer and lots of tasty spices. **$$–$$$**
The Coda
350 Pennsylvania Ave
Tel: (716) 886-6647
Across from Kleinhans Music Hall in a converted grocery store, the focus here is on classic as well as hearty country French dishes. The menu changes weekly. Dinner only. Closed Jul–Aug. **$$$**
The Hourglass
981 Kenmore Ave
Tel: (716) 877-8788
For more than 30 years this fine restaurant has been serving Continental cuisine, with specialties such as rack of lamb, duck breast, sweetbreads and seafood dishes; the desserts are all homemade. Closed Sun–Mon, lunch. **$$$–$$$$**
Justine's
Buffalo Hilton, 120 Church St
Tel: (716) 845-5100
Elegant dining in an intimate atmosphere, with creatively sauced meat, seafood and poultry dishes. Dinner only. **$$$$**

Le Roy
D & R Depot Restaurant
63 Lake St
Tel: (716) 768-6270
Traditional American fare including seafood, steak and chicken served in a beautifully restored 1901 train depot. Breads, pastries and desserts are homemade. **$$–$$$**

Lewistown
Riverside Inn
115 South Water St
Tel: (716) 754-8206
This classic American steak house overlooks the scenic Lower Niagara River and Niagara Gorge. House specialties include aged Angus beef and prime rib. Award-winning wine list. **$$–$$$**

Niagara Falls
The Embers-Open Hearth
Michael's Inn by the Falls,
5599 River Rd, Ontario, Canada
Tel: (905) 354-2727
Prime rib, steaks, chicken and other specialties prepared on a spit over the open hearth. Daily specials and a dessert cart. **$$–$$$**

Price Guide

The following price categories indicate the cost of a meal for two, with wine:
$$$ Expensive: $100 and more
$$ Moderate: $65–100
$ Inexpensive; under $65

Skyline Tower Dining Room
520 Robins St, Ontario, Canada
Tel: (905) 356-2651
or (1-888) 673-7344
Dine with a view: 775 ft (235 meters) above Niagara Falls in the Revolving Dining Room which specializes in Continental cuisine (reservations required), or in the family-oriented Summit Suite Dining Room, which serves a breakfast, lunch and dinner buffets May–Oct. The $2 elevator ride includes admission to the Observation Deck. **$–$$$$**

North Tonawanda
Steamers
1 Detroit St
Tel: (716) 693-0302
Riverfront patio dining, with specialties including steamers, chicken and prime rib steak. The non-air-conditioned dining room is pleasant when the weather is not horribly hot. **$$**

Sanborn
Schimschack's Restaurant
2943 Upper Mountain Rd
Tel: (716) 731-4111
A handsome, four-tiered restaurant on the edge of the Niagara Escarpment overlooking orchards and vineyards offers a romantic atmosphere for dishes including prime rib, baby back ribs and homemade pies. **$$–$$$**

Chautauqua-Allegheny

Bemus Point
Italian Fisherman
61 Lakeside Dr
Tel: (716) 386-7000
Seafood, Italian food, and steaks are served on a deck overlooking Lake Chautauqua. **$–$$**

Ye Hare n' Hounds Inn
64 Lakeside Dr
Tel: (716) 386-2181
Continental dining in a replica of an English inn overlooking Lake Chautauqua. There's an excellent selection of meat, poultry and seafood dishes as well as homemade desserts, including "Death by Chocolate". Dinner only. **$$**

Cassadaga
Lazzaroni's Lakeside
282 Dale Ave
Tel: (716) 595-2557
A large menu of American dishes – many with a Moroccan slant – are served on a patio overlooking the lake or by the hearth in the dining room. Desserts are homemade. **$$**

Cherry Creek
The Grainery
1494 Thornton Rd
Tel: (716) 287-3500
Homemade treats such as onion pie and lamb stew are served in a restored 100-year-old barn with a gift shop upstairs. **$$**

Elliotcottville
Dina's
15 Washington St
Tel: (716) 699-5330
Bistro-style atmosphere in a restored 1840 building. American, Italian and Mexican dishes and homemade pastries. **$$**

Jamestown
MacDuff's
317 Pine St
Tel: (716) 664-9414
Beef tournedos with stilton sauce and green peppercorns, veal with blackberry sauce, homemade ice cream, and 40 malt scotches are just a few treats awaiting diners. Lunch weekends only. **$$–$$$**

Mayville
Webb's Captains Table
115 West Lake Rd
Tel: (716) 753-3960
Popular spot overlooking Lake Chautauqua serves regional specialties and vegetarian dishes. The patio is open in nice weather. Reservations weekends. **$$–$$$**

Culture

New York City

The number and variety of entertainment options available are practically endless: open-air concerts in Central Park, jazz in Greenwich Village, cinemas, musicals, Broadway theaters, off-Broadway, off-off-Broadway, the Met, music and dance clubs. To keep pace with what's happening, consult the Friday edition of the *New York Times*, which contains a preview of the forthcoming weekend's events. Weekly publications containing culture sections include *New York Magazine; The New Yorker; Time Out New York, Village Voice*, and *New York Press*, which have excellent guides to events.

Art Galleries

There are well over 400 art galleries in the city in various neighborhoods – in Midtown, along 57th Street between Sixth and Park avenues, on the Upper East Side along upper Madison Avenue, in Chelsea (particularly around West 22nd and West 24th streets near Tenth Avenue) and, of course, Soho.

Some of Soho's best-known galleries have moved to Chelsea (including **Paula Cooper**), but despite its transformation into a shopping and dining mecca, Soho is still home to some 200 galleries, with a few major ones still on West Broadway (**OK Harris, Sonnaben, the Dia Center for the Arts**) and others on adjoining streets such as Greene (**Phyllis Kind, Sperone Westwater, PaceWildenstein**); Prince (**Louis K Meisel**); Wooster (**Brooke Alexander, Gagosian, Tony Shafrazi**); Mercer (**Sean Kelley, Holly Solomon**), and along lower

Broadway (**Thread Waxing Space, Center for Book Arts, Exit Art**).

As with restaurants and clubs, galleries spring up overnight and disappear just as quickly. Art fans should consult the weekly listings in magazines such as *New York* or *Time Out* as well as the art section of the *New York Times* on Friday and Sunday. Alternatively, head down to Soho where most galleries have free guides listing shows around town.

Cinema

As a general rule, and with some exceptions, many first-run movies get their first showing in Midtown Manhattan cinemas, the largest of which are in the Times Square area, with a group of others in the West 50s and on the Upper East Side. Newspapers and the *New Yorker, New York* and *Time Out New York* magazines carry complete listings for these as well as for dance, theater and musical performances around the city.

A score of local cinemas are devoted to revival, cult, experimental and genre films, including the **Film Forum**, (209 West Houston St, tel: 212/727-8110) and the **Walter Reade Theater** (tel: 212/875-5600) at Lincoln Center, where the annual New York Film Festival takes place every fall.

Theater

The main Broadway theaters are near Times Square (*see page 136*). These stage all the large-scale musicals. The alternative is off-Broadway, where performances scarcely differ in quality, but are performed in smaller theaters.

The vast majority of off-Broadway theaters, and indeed, the more experimental off-off-Broadway theaters, are downtown in the East Village area. Here you'll find the **Public Theater** complex (*see page 130*) where shows including *Hair* and *A Chorus Line* originated before being transferred to uptown venues. **Theater for the New City** at 155 First Ave, tel: (212) 254-1109; and **La Mama** at 74A East 4th St, tel: (212) 475-7710; are two of the showplaces for work by experimental theater artists, while along West 42nd Street between Ninth and Tenth avenues, the group of off-Broadway theaters known as Theater Row includes **Playwrights Horizons**, tel: (212) 279-4200. Other performance art and multi-media venues include: **The Kitchen**, 512 West 19th St, tel: (212) 255-5793; **P.S.1**, 22–25 Jackson Ave at 46th Ave, Long Island City, tel: (718) 784-2084; and the **Brooklyn Academy of Music**.

Dance

There are numerous internationally acclaimed modern dance troupes in New York City, like the Martha Graham Dance Company, the Alvin Ailey American Dance Theater, and the Dance Theater of Harlem, as well as the acclaimed New York City Ballet which performs at the Lincoln Center (*see page 147*). Venues around town where you might see them perform include:

Brooklyn Academy of Music
30 Lafayette Ave, Brooklyn
Tel: (718) 636-4100

City Center
131 West 55th St
Tel: (212) 581-7907
Dance Theater Workshop
219 West 19th St
Tel: (212) 924-0077
The Joyce Theater
175 Eighth Ave
Tel: (212) 242-0800

Music

New York offers every kind of music imaginable, from opera and classical music to jazz, pop, blues, country and reggae. Admission to many of the concerts is free: the summer concerts in Central Park, for instance, or the lunch-time concerts held in the Financial District and Midtown, which liven up the day for office workers.

The two largest concert halls in the city are **Carnegie Hall** (*see page 143*) and **Avery Fisher Hall**; the latter forms part of the Lincoln Center for the Performing Arts (*see page 147*), where the **Metropolitan Opera** is also located. Another fine opera company is the **New York**

City Opera, at the New York State Theater in Lincoln Center. Also located at the Lincoln Center are the New York Philharmonic and the Chamber Music Society. Another arena for classical music performances is the concert hall at the **Aaron Copeland School of Music**, at Queens College, tel: (718) 793-8080.

Popular venues for contemporary music include **Madison Square Garden** and **Radio City Music Hall** (*see page 140*), which presents a range of entertainment, from movies, Christmas and Easter pageants (starring the high-kicking Rockettes) to superstar rock concerts. **Town Hall**, **Beacon Theater** and the **Apollo Theater** in Harlem also host musical events (*see page 147*).

Annual events include the Brooklyn Academy of Music (BAM)'s Next Wave Festival (Sep–Dec, tel: 718/636-4100), and the New York Philharmonic's season at Avery Fisher Hall, (begins in Sept, tel: 212/875-5030). The New York City Opera performs at the New York State Theater (Sept–Nov, and starts again in Mar, tel: 212/870-5570).

New York State

ART GALLERIES

Long Island

Long Island is studded with private, museum and college galleries. Summer is a popular time for open-air shows at street fairs.
Adobe Artes
192 East Main St, Huntington
Tel: (631) 385-8410
Sells traditional and contemporary Native American art.
Ashawagh Hall
Fireplace Rd/Old Stone Hwy, Cold Springs
Tel: (516) 324-9802
Exhibits works of local artists.
Cold Spring Harbor Gallery
Main St/Shore Rd, Cold Spring
Tel: (516) 367-6295
Has changing exhibits highlighting the island's history.

Buying Broadway tickets

Useful numbers for tickets and information include **NYC/On Stage**, tel: (212) 768-1818; and **The Broadway Line**, tel: (212) 302-4111. Popular shows are often sold out months in advance, so anyone keen to see a specific show should order the tickets via their travel agent before arriving in New York – or call **Telecharge**, tel: (212) 239-6200, which takes a small fee but handles ticket sales for over 30 Broadway and off-Broadway theaters. There are several ways of getting hold of tickets in New York itself: if you are staying in a good hotel and don't mind tipping generously, the hotel concierge should be able to obtain tickets on your behalf. Otherwise go to the box offices, or to the Convention & Visitors Bureau (also NYC & Co., *see page 311*), where discounts may be available.

Half-price tickets on the day of performance can be obtained from **TKTS**, which has branches at Times Square and Tower 2 of the World Trade Center – the lines at the World Trade Center tend to be much shorter than those at Times Square. The general rule is first come, first served: you can't reserve. Only cash or travelers' checks are accepted.

TKTS Times Square
47th St/Broadway
Tickets for matinée performances from 10am; for evening performances from 3pm.

TKTS Tower 2 World Trade Center
Mezzanine level: Mon–Fri 11am–5pm, Sat 11am–3.30pm.
Limited tickets for matinée and Sunday performances are available on the day prior to and on the day of performance; evening perfomance tickets are available on the same day only.

Hudson Valley

Art Barn
Rte 207, Campbell Hall
Tel: (845) 427-9003
Exhibits works by local artists,
American folk art, and unusual
"world" art.

Graystone Gallery
21 North St, Middletown
Tel: (845) 341-1317
Displays international and Hudson
Valley works.

Kokopeli
50 Main St, Warwick
Tel: (845) 987-9933
Displays Native American jewelry,
sculpture, pottery, and other works
with emphasis on Southwestern
artists.

The Catskills

Fine Art Gallery
Sullivan County Government Center,
100 North St, Monticello
Tel: (845) 794-3000
Provides a showcase for works by
local artists.

Woodstock Guild
34 Tinker St, Woodstock
Tel: (845) 679-2079
Presents performances and contemporary art exhibitions, theater,
and films.

Capital-Saratoga Region

Albany Center Galleries
23 Monroe St, Albany
Tel: (518) 462-4775)
Exhibits works by regional artists.

**Faust Art Park and Sculpture
Garden**
136 McKinley Ave, Northville
Tel: (518) 863-2530
Works by local artists.

Mount Nebo Gallery/Will Moses
60 Grandma Moses Rd, Eagle Bridge
Tel: (518) 686-4334
or (1-800) 328-326
Exhibits works by local artists.

Valley Artisans Market
25 East Main St, Cambridge
Tel: (518) 677-2765
Co-operative exhibiting local works.

The Adirondacks

Adirondack Craft Center
93 Saranac Ave, Lake Placid
Tel: (518) 523-2062
Hosts exhibits by regional artists.

**Arts North/Arts Council for the
Northern Adirondacks**
23 North Main St, Westport 12293
Tel: (518) 962-8778
or (1-800) 667-4704
Provides information on art and
cultural events in the Adirondacks.

Gallery of Fine Arts at Locust Inn
Rte 9N/8, Hague
Tel: (518) 543-6035
Works of Adirondack and New
England artists.

Old Forge Arts Center
Main St, Old Forge
Tel: (315) 369-6411
Hosts exhibits by regional artists.

**World Awareness Children's
Museum**
227 Glen St, Glens Falls
Tel: (518) 793-2773
Exhibits children's art.

Central-Leatherstocking

Cooperstown Art Association
22 Main St, Coopertown
Tel: (607) 547-9777
Displays solo and group shows.

Gallery 53 Artworks
118 Main St, Cooperstown
Tel: (607) 547-5655
Hosts exhibits, readings, and
drama.

**Murdock and Murdock Fine Arts
Galleries**
East Main St, Milford
Tel: (607) 286-9941
Exhibits works by accomplished
artists.

Smithy-Pioneer Gallery
55 Pioneer St, Cooperstown
Tel: (607) 547-8671
Exhibits works by regional artists.

Thousand Islands & St
Lawrence Seaway

The Breakwater Gallery
379 Club St, Cape Vincent
Tel: (315) 654-4750
Work by local artists.

Made in Chenango
41 South Broad St, Norwich
Tel: (607) 334-3355
Co-operative showcasing local
artists.

St Lawrence Gallery
47382 Dingham Point Rd,
Alexandria Bay
Tel: (315) 482-2833
Work by local artists.

Salmon River Fine Arts Center
4882A North Jefferson St, Pulaski
Tel: (315) 298-7007
Fine gallery exhibiting works by local
artists.

Finger Lakes

Memorial Art Gallery
500 University Ave, Rochester
Tel: (716) 473-7720
Home to 10,000 works spanning
50 centuries.

Sola Art Gallery
DeWitt Mall, corner of Seneca and
Cayuga streets, Ithaca
Tel: (607) 272-6552

State of the Art Gallery
120 West State St, Ithaca.
Tel: (607) 277-1626

Upstairs Gallery
in the DeWitt Mall, corner of Seneca
and Cayuga sts, Ithaca
Tel: (607) 272-8614

Greater Niagara

Artisans Alley
10 Rainbow Blvd, Niagara Falls
Tel: (716) 282-0196
or (1-800) 635-1457
Exhibits of American crafts.

**Carnegie Art Center, Tonawanda
Council on the Arts**
240 Goundry St, North Tonawanda
Tel: (716) 694-4400
Built in the early 1900s. Has three
galleries.

University at Buffalo Art Gallery
Center for the Arts, SUNY-Buffalo
Tel: (716) 645-ARTS
Exhibits local works.

Chautauqua-Allegheny

Adams Art Gallery
600 Central Ave, Dunkirk
Tel: (716) 366-7450

Griffis Sculpture Park
6902 Mill Valley Rd, East Otto
Tel: (716) 257-9344
Exhibits works of regional and
national artists.

Portage Hill Gallery
South Portage Rd, Westfield
Tel: (716) 326-4478; 6439
Exhibits regional art.

Surroundings
73 East Main St, Westfield
Tel: (716) 326-7373
Exhibits works of regional and
national artists.

CINEMA

Long Island
Cinema Arts Centre
423 Park Ave, Huntington
Tel: (516) 423-7610
Independent and international films.

Hudson Valley
Palisades Center
1000 Palisades Center Dr,
West Nyack
Tel: (845) 348-1005
IMAX Theater projects films on six-story screens.
Upstate Films
26 Montgomery St, Rte 9, Rhinebeck
Tel: (845) 876-2515
Presents foreign, independent, documentary and animation films.

Central-Leatherstocking
Unadilla Drive-In
Rte 7, Unadilla
Tel: (607) 369-2000
A classic drive-in movie theater.

Finger Lakes
Little Theatres
240 East Ave, Rochester
Tel: (716) 232-3906
Shows art, foreign and independent films.

Chautauqua-Allegheny
There are historic, single-screen theaters in the Chautauqua Institution, Jamestown, and Fredonia.

DANCE

Hudson Valley
Kaatsbaan International Dance Center, Inc.
Tivoli
Tel: (845) 757-5106
Professional residence/ performance center which presents dance performances, workshops and events throughout the year.

Capital-Saratoga Region
Palace Theater
North Pearl St, Albany
Tel: (518) 465-4663
Home to the Albany Berkshire Ballet.

Greater Niagara
Buffalo Inner City Ballet
2495 Main St, Buffalo
Tel: (716) 833-1244

ENTERTAINMENT CENTERS

Long Island
Jillian's
Airport Plaza, Rte 110, Farmingdale
Tel: (631) 249-0708
A large adult-oriented complex with a dance club, an Internet Theater, multimedia bowling, video games, and billiards tables.

MUSIC

Long Island
Jones Beach Theater
Jones Beach
Tel: (516) 2210-1000
Hosts headliner performers.
Nassau Veterans Memorial Coliseum
1255 Hempstead Tpke, Uniondale
Tel: (516) 794-9300
Presents rock concerts, ice shows and other events.
Staller Center for the Arts
Stony Brook University, Stony Brook
Tel: (631) 632-7240
Has a main concert hall, three small theaters and an art gallery.
Tilles Center for the Performing Arts
CW Post College, Northern Blvd, Brookville
Tel: (516) 299-2752
Offers year-round entertainment at its 2,200-seat Main Hall and 500-seat concert hall.
Westbury Music Fair
Brushhollow Rd, Westbury
Tel: (516) 334-0800
Nationally known; attracts top-rated performers to its 3,000-seat theater-in-the round.

Hudson Valley
Bardovan 1869 Opera House
35 Market St, Poughkeepsie
Tel: (845) 473-5288
Home to the Hudson Valley symphony opera, the Bardovan hosts a full roster of events from opera to drama to young people's theatre, and a summer amphitheater.
The Big Band Sound
3 Rose Lane, Wappingers Falls
Tel: (845) 226-6072
The 19 members perform classic and big band jazz.
Caramoor Center for Music and the Arts
Girdle Ridge Rd, Katonah
Tel: (845) 232-5035
Hosts one of the summer's major musical events – classical, opera and jazz.
Eisenhower Hall Theatre
Tel: (845) 938-4159
West Point's Military Band performs at the academy's theater throughout the academic year.

The Catskills
Maverick Concert Hall
Woodstock
Tel: (845) 679-8217
Hosts chamber ensemble concerts at a historic, rustic concert hall in a woodland setting.

Capital-Saratoga Region
L'Ensemble Center for Chamber Music
54 State St, Albany
Tel: (518) 436-5321
Chamber music concerts.
Hubbard Hall Projects
25 East Main St, Cambridge
Tel: (518) 677-2495
Sponsors classical and folk music and a film series.
Palace Theatre
North Pearl St, Albany
Tel: (518) 465-4663
The Ibany Symphony Orchestra performs here.
Rensselaerville Institute
Rte 85, Rensselaerville
Tel: (518) 797-3783
Sponsors jazz and classical concerts.
Troy Savings Bank Music Hall
32 Second St, Troy
Tel: (518) 273-0038
Hosts jazz, classical and acoustic music.
Union College Memorial Chapel
15 Nott Terrace Heights, Schenectady
Tel: (518) 382-7890
Presents chamber music concerts.

Comedy

If you're looking for a laugh, the **Lake Ontario Playhouse** (103 West Main St, Sackets Harbor, Thousand Islands, tel: 315/646-2305) presents stand-up comics from the national circuit.

In Rochester, check out the **Downstairs Cabaret Theatre** (151 St Paul St, Rochester, tel: 716/325-4370).

The Adirondacks
de Blasiis Chamber Music Series
Hyde Collections' Helen Froehlich Auditorium,
169 Warren St, Glens Falls
Tel: (518) 793-0531
Performs chamber concerts.
Glens Falls Symphony Orchestra
Glens Falls Senior High School,
Sherman Ave, Glens Falls
Tel: (518) 793-1348)
Performs classical music concerts.
Glens Falls Civic Center
1 Civic Center Plaza, Glens Falls,
Tel: (518) 798-0366
Hosts a variety of concert programs throughout the year.
Lake George Opera Festival
PO Box 2172, Glens Falls 12801
Tel: (518) 793-3859
Stages operas from late Jun–early Jul.
Luzerne Chamber Music Festival
Lake Tour Rd, Lake Luzerne
Tel: (518) 696-2661
Presents renowned performing artists, and has free concerts Sat nights and Sun afternoons in the summer.

Central-Leatherstocking
Catskill Choral Society
PO Box 135, Oneonta
Tel: (607) 432-0147
Performs concerts from fall through spring.
Catskill Symphony Orchestry
PO Box 14, Oneonta
Tel: (607) 432-6670
Performs a series of concerts fall through spring.
Cooperstown Concert Series
PO Box 624, Coopertown 13326
Tel: (607) 293-6124

Sponsors a variety of cultural events ranging from early music to folk dance from fall through spring.

Thousand Islands & St Lawrence Seaway
Arts in the Park
Lamoureaux Park on Water St,
Cornwall, Ontario, Canada
Tel: (613) 933-3586
Free live theatrical and musical entertainment.
Music Hall
41 Lake St, Oswego
Tel: (315) 342-1733
Family concerts every second weekend.

Finger Lakes
Cayuga Chamber Orchestra
116 North Cayuga St, Ithaca
Tel: (607) 273-8981.
Clemens Center
116 East Gray St, Elmira
Tel: (607) 733-5639
or (1-800) 724-0159
Hosts concerts by contemporary artists, classical and country performers, and comedians.
Cortland Country Music Park
1804 Truxton Rd, Rte 13, Cortland
Tel: (607) 753-0377
Has live shows by some of the biggest names in country music.
Eastman School of Music/Theatre
60 Gibbs St, Rochester
Tel: (716) 274-1110
Hosts the Rochester Philharmonic Orchestra.
Finger Lakes Performing Arts Center
Finger Lakes Community College, Canandaigua
Tel: (716) 222-5000
Hosts the Rochester Philharmonic.
Rochester Philharmonic Orchestra
100 East Ave, Rochester
Tel: (716) 222-5000
Performs at venues throughout the region.
SUNY Genesee Performing Arts Center
1 College Circle, Genesee
Tel: (1-800) 525-2070
Presents renowned entertainers.

Greater Niagara
Buffalo Chamber Music Society
71 Symphony Circle, Buffalo
Tel: (716) 838-2383

Kleinhans Music Hall
Porter and Richmond sts, Buffalo
Tel: (716) 885-4632
Home to the Buffalo Philharmonic Orchestra.
University at Buffalo Department of Music Concert Series
105 Slee Hall, University at Buffalo, Amherst
Tel: (716) 645-2921

THEATER & EVENTS

Long Island
The Airport Playhouse
218 Knickerbocker Ave, Bohemia
Tel: (516) 589-7588
Presents full-scale Broadway musicals, comedies, and drama.
Cultural Arts Playhouse
714 Old Bethpage Rd, Old Bethpage
Tel: (516) 694-3330
Community theater with fully staged performances.
New York Dinner Theatre
390 Plandome Rd, Manhasset
Tel: (516) 869-9191
or (1-800) 383-6080
Performs comedies and interactive murder mysteries.

Hudson Valley
Broadway Theatre
UPAC, 601 Broadway, Kingston
Tel: (845) 339-6088
On the National Register of Historic Places; hosts theater and concerts.
Center for Performing Arts
Rte 308, Rhinebeck
Tel: (845) 876-3080
Features plays, musicals, dance concerts and stage readings.
Helen Hayes Performing Arts Center
117 Main St, Nyack
Tel: (845) 358-6333
A 700-seat facility hosting concerts, dance, and live theater.

The Catskills
Bearsville Theater
Rte 212, Bearsville
Tel: (845) 679-4406
Performs original drama.
Fern Cliff House
Rte 67A, East Durham
Tel: (518) 634-7424
Hosts live entertainment.

Forestburgh Playhouse & Tavern
Forestburgh
Tel: (845) 794-1194
Summer theater of Broadway
musicals and comedies.

Irish Cultural & Sports Centre
Rte 145, East Durham
Tel: (518) 634-2286
Presents theater, dance, music and
sporting events.

Shadowland Theater
157 Canal St, Ellenville
Tel: (845) 647-5511
The professional ensemble
performs May–Sept.

Capital-Saratoga Region

Capital Repertory Company
111 North Pearl St, Albany
Tel: (518) 462-4534
Professional company, presenting
music, contemporary, and world
premiere productions.

Colonial Little Theater
Johnstown
Tel: (518) 762-4325
Presents community theater.

The Egg
Empire State Plaza, Albany
Tel: (518) 473-1061
Presents a variety of
entertainment.

New York State Theater Institute
Schacht Fine Arts Center,
Russell Sage College Campus,
Troy
Tel: (518) 274-3256
A professional regional theater.

Palace Theater
North Pearl St, Albany
Tel: (518) 465-4663
Hosts rock acts and Broadway
shows.

Park Playhouse
Washington Park Lakehouse,
Albany
Tel: (518) 434-2035
Outdoor theater mounting
Broadway-style performances.

Pepsi Arena
51 South Pearl St, Albany
Tel: (518) 487-2000
The venue for sports and
entertainment.

Proctor's Theater
432 State St, Schenectady
Tel: (518) 346-1083
Hosts Broadway musicals, dance,
opera and movies.

Saratoga Performing Arts Center
Saratoga Spa State Park, Saratoga
Springs
Tel: (518) 587-3330
Hosts Broadway musicals, dance,
opera and movies

The Adirondacks

**Adirondack Lakes Center for the
Arts**
Rte 28, Blue Mountain Lake
Tel: (518) 352-7715
Hosts concerts, theater, dance, and
films, and has an art gallery.

Depot Theatre
Westport Train Station, Rte 9N,
Westport
Tel: (518) 962-4449
Performs summer theater in a 19th-
century train station.

Lake George Dinner Theatre
Holiday Inn-Turf, Canada St, Lake
George
Tel: (518) 668-5781

Terrace Room Dinner Theater
Georgian Resort, 384 Canada St,
Lake George
Tel: (518) 668-5401
or (1-800) 525-3436

Central-Leatherstocking

Anderson Center for Performing Arts
Vestal Parkway East, Binghamton
Tel: (607) 777-6802
Has indoor-outdoor stages with major
performers and experimental theater.

**Chenango County Council of the
Arts**
27 West Main St, Norwich
Tel: (607) 336-2787
Presents concerts, dance reviews
and theatrical productions.

**Cooperstown Theater and Music
Festival**
Rte 80, Cooperstown
Tel: (607) 547-2335
Hosts classical chamber music,
music and theater productions.

Earlville Opera House
22 East Main St Earlville
Tel: (315) 691-3550
Presents jazz, folk, drama,
classical, and a children's series.

Glimmerglass Opera
Rte 80, Cooperstown
Tel: (607) 547-2255
Internationally recognized; performs
both familiar and rarely performed
works.

Jericho Arts Council
15 North Main St, Bainbridge
Tel: (607) 967-7228
Presents Blue Grass bands, drama
groups and art.

Leatherstocking Theater
Rte 80, Cooperstown
Tel: (607) 547-1363
Has professional summer
theater.

Orpheus Theatre
PO Box 1014, Oneonta
Tel: (607) 432-1800
Fully-staged live musicals.

Stanley Performing Arts Center
259 Genesee St, Utica
Tel: (315) 724-4000
Presents classical music, opera and
theater.

*Thousand Islands & St
Lawrence Seaway*

Clayton Opera House
Clayton
Tel: (315) 686-3771
Summer stock is performed here.

Dinner Theatre at Lakeside
507 Culkin Hall, SUNY Oswego,
Oswego
Tel: (315) 341-2106
Hosts summer productions.

Finger Lakes

Bristol Valley Theatre
151 South Main St, Naples
Tel: (716) 374-9032
Presents summer theater.

**Cornell University Center for
Theatre Arts**
430 College Ave, Ithaca
Tel: (607) 254-2700
Hosts student and professional
theater and dance events.

Downstairs Cabaret Theatre
20 Windsor St, Rochester
Tel: (716) 325-4370
Performs musicals, comedies,
drama, and cabaret.

Geva Theatre
75 Woodbury Blvd, Rochester
Tel: (716) 232-GEVA
Presents comedy, drama, new
plays, classics and musicals.

Hangar Theatre
Cass Park, Rte 89, Ithaca
Tel: (607) 273-8588)
or (1-800) 724-0999
Sponsors professional regional
theater.

Ithaca Performing Arts Center
109 West State St, Ithaca
Tel: (607) 273-1037
Features ballet, musicals, dance,
film and concerts.
Landmark Theatre
362 South Salina St, Syracuse
Tel: (315) 475-7979
Hosts touring Broadway shows,
classic films and concerts.
Merry Go Round Playhouse
Emerson Park, Rte 38A, Auburn
Tel: (315) 255-1305
or (1-800) 457-8897
Professional summer theater
including singing and dancing.
Smith Opera House
82 Seneca St, Geneva
Tel: (315) 781-5483
Live performances and films.
Syracuse Stage
820 Genesee St, Syracuse
Tel: (315) 443-3275
Stages both classic and
contemporary plays.

Greater Niagara
Alleyway Theatre
1 Curtain Up Alley, Buffalo
Tel: (716) 852-2600
Variety of performances
Buffalo Ensemble Theatre
New Phoenix, 95 North Johnson
Park, Buffalo
Tel: (716) 855-2225
Variety of performances.
**Buffalo State College Performing
Arts Center**
1300 Elmwood Ave, Rockwell Hall
210, Buffalo
Tel: (716) 878-3005
Variety of entertainment.
Genesee Center for the Arts
1 College Rd, Bataviatel
Tel: (716) 345-0055, ext. 6438
Hosts performance and visual arts.
Historic Riviera Theatre
67 Webster St, North Tonawanda
Tel: (716) 692-2413
Kavinoky Theatre
320 Porter Ave, Buffalo
Tel: (716) 881-7668
Variety of entertainment.
Melody Fair Theatre
80 Melody Lane, North Tonawanda
Tel: (716) 692-6601
Presents theatre-in-the-round.
Morgan Opera House
Main St, Aurora

Tel: (315) 364-5437
Music and community and
professional theater.
Shea's Performing Arts Center
646 Main St, Buffalo
Tel: (716) 847-1410
Hosts musicals, dance and
concerts.
**Paul Robeson Theatre/African
American Cultural Center**
350 Masten Ave, Buffalo
Tel: (716) 884-2013
Exposes the talents of African-
Americans.

Chautauqua-Allegheny
Civic Center Theater
116 East 3rd St, Jamestown
Tel: (716) 664-2465
Fredonia Opera House
9–11 Church St, Fredonia
Tel: (716) 679-0891
Founded in 1891; presents drama,
music, family events and films.
Lucille Ball Little Theater
18–24 East 2nd St, Jamestown
Tel: (716) 483-1095
Rockefeller Arts Center
SUNY, Fredonia
Tel: (716) 673-3217
Presents nationally recognized
programs in music, theater and art.

Nightlife

New York City

When you think of nightlife in New
York, you're thinking New York City.
Not that upstate cities like Buffalo,
Rochester and Syracuse don't have
nightlife of their own; they do. But
New York City – and in particular,
Manhattan – is known throughout
the world as a place that stays up
all night: jazz clubs, swanky nightspots, down and dirty basement
rock clubs – they're all here, and
thriving (although many say not as
frenetic as they were in the 1980s,
something that may have more to
do with the aging population of baby
boomers than it does with the avail-
ability of nocturnal entertainment).

Nightlife in New York tends to get
under way at around 11pm, not
before. Most of the city's nightclubs
are very short-lived. Bars and clubs
that are "in" one month can be
"out" the next. The only way to find
out is to do your own research on
the spot, look in the local papers
(*see page 309*) and then hope to be
admitted by the all-powerful door-
man. The "right" clothes may help.
Most charge an entrance fee of
around $15 or $20 and around $4
for a drink.

DANCE AND MUSIC CLUBS

Bowery Ballroom
6 Delancey St
Well-known bands and great
acoustics make this venue well
worth a pilgrimage to the Lower
East Side.
CBGB & OMFUG
315 Bowery at Bleecker St
The club where punk rock started in
the US.

Hush
7 West 19th St
A stylish, intimate Flatiron District club with drinking, dining, and dancing all under one roof.

The Knitting Factory
74 Leonard St
An eclectic mecca for avant-garde sounds in the heart of TriBeCa, offering everything from jazz to rock and poetry.

The Pyramid Club
101st Ave
A Typical East Village hangout.

S.O.B.'S
204 Varick St
A Soho bastion of Latin-American and world music.

The Supper Club
240 West 47th St
A classy Midtown establishment offering everything from dancing to big-bands to big-name rock acts.

Twilo
503 West 27th St
A sprawling Chelsea dance club with well-known DJs and a largely gay crowd. Usually open all night.

Vinyl
157 Hudson St
A dance club without alcohol but with quirky hours, for instance, Sun 4pm–midnight. Extremely popular with youthful devotees of house and similar music.

Webster Hall
125 East 11th St
A large club in East Village with all-night dancing to everything from rock and reggae to house.

Wetlands
161 Hudson St, below Canal
Casual club in TriBeCa where regulars groove to the sounds of reggae, folk, jazz, and funk.

JAZZ CLUBS

The following classic clubs are all in the West Village:

Blue Note
131 West 3rd St
The very best of mainstream jazz and blues, from time-honored greats to more contemporary acts.

Sweet Basil
88 Seventh Ave South
Another venue for mainstream jazz.

Village Vanguard
178 Seventh Ave South
The club that helped to launch legendary talents including Miles Davis and John Coltrane.

BARS

Barmacy
538 East 14th St
Bar located in a former pharmacy.

Chumley's
86 Bedford St at Barrow
A "speakeasy" from Prohibition days.

The Greatest Bar on Earth
1 World Trade Center
The view from here is awesome, and the bar offers live music on some nights.

McSorley's Old Ale House
15 East 7th St
Old-fashioned tavern with sawdust floors.

Oak Bar in the Plaza Hotel
Fifth Ave/59th St
Cozy, elegant club atmosphere.

COMEDY & CABARET

Caroline's Comedy Club
1626 Broadway
Tel: (212) 757-4100
A plush setting for a continuous roster of unknown comic hopefuls along with some of the biggest names in the "biz".

Don't Tell Mama
343 West 46th St
Tel: (212) 757-0788
Very jolly, spot, long favored by the theatrical club. There's often a sing-along at the piano bar.

The Duplex
61 Christopher St
Tel: (212) 255-5438
A landmark of the gay West Village, attracting a friendly, mixed audience.

Rainbow & Stars
65th floor, 30 Rockefeller Plaza
Tel: (212) 635-5000
Traditional nightclub and cabaret acts in as lavish a setting as the famous Rainbow Room next door, and with just as dazzling a view of the city's lights.

New York State

NIGHTCLUBS/DISCOS

Long Island
More than 100 nightspots offer a large variety of entertainment. Many are on the South Fork and stay open until the wee hours.

Amazon Long Wharf, Sag Harbor
Tel: (516) 725-9000
Bands here play everything from jazz to Latin to reggae.

M80
1976 North Sea Rd, Southampton
Tel: (516) 283-5550
Dance club.

Stephen Talkhouse
161 Main St, Amagansett
Tel: (516) 267-3117
One of the island's oldest, most popular spots.

Take Five Supper Club
256 Elm St, Southampton
Tel: (516) 283-9772
Known for fine jazz.

Capital-Saratoga Region
Golden Grill
37 Phila St, Saratoga Springs
Tel: (518) 584-8834
QE2
12 Central Ave, Albany
Tel: (518) 434-2023

Finger Lakes
Common Ground
1230 Danby Rd, Ithaca
Tel: (607) 273-1505
Country Club
Bridge St and Erie Blvd, East Syracuse
Tel: (315) 445-2527

LIVE MUSIC VENUES

Hudson Valley
Bodles Opera House
39 Main St, Chester
Tel: (845) 469-4595
Singing waiters, comedy and music.

O'Neills Irish Castle
313 Manchester Rd, Poughkeepsie
Tel: (845) 454-5848
Irish music on weekends.

Rip Van Winkle Café
3 Hill St, Saugerties
Tel: (845) 247-0122
Presents a variety of music.

Turning Point
468 Piermont Ave, Piermont
Tel: (845) 359-1089
Hosts folk, folk-rock, jazz and blues.

The Catskills
Shannanigans
Depot St, Delhi
Tel: (607) 746-6158
Hosts local bands.
Tinker Street Café
59 Tinker St, Woodstock
Tel: (845) 679-2487
Hosts local bands.

Capital-Saratoga Region
In the Albany/Troy area, *Metroland*
(tel: 518/463-2500), a free weekly
publication, lists weekly
performances. The hot spots are:
Bogie's
297 Ontario St, Albany
Tel: (518) 482-4368
Caffe Lena
455-47 Phila St, Saratoga Springs
Tel: (518) 583-0022
The country's oldest continuously
run coffeehouse.
Eighth Step Coffee House
362 State St, Albany
Tel: (518) 434-1703
Lionheart Blues Café
258 Lark St, Albany
Tel: (518) 436-9530
Metro
17 Maple Ave, Saratoga Springs
Tel: (518) 584-9581
Valenti's Pub
729 Pawling Ave, Troy
Tel: (518) 283-6766

Finger Lakes
Daniel Webster's
110 Montgomery St, Syracuse
Tel: (315) 479-0377
Jazz.
Dinosaur Bar-B-Cue
246 West Willow St, Syracuse
Tel: (315) 476-4937
Blues.
Huckleberry's Inn
12 Columbus St, Auburn
Tel: (315) 253-5704
Rock, classic rock, and metal
bands.
Rongovian Embassy to the USA
Rte 96, Interlaken
Tel: (607) 387-3334
Jazz, reggae and blues.

Shep's Paradise
293 Clarissa St, Rochester
Tel: (716) 232-9886
Top names in jazz.
Under the Stone
3 Fennell St, Skaneateles
Tel: (315) 685-5975
Live rock and blues.

Dinner/Casino Cruises

Long Island
Boats on Long Island offer tours,
lunch, dinner and overnight cruises,
and some turn into floating casinos
when they reach international waters:
Eastern Star, the Cruising Country Inn
Tel: (1-800) 445-5942
Freeport Casino Cruises
Freeport
Tel: (516) 377-7400
Peconic River Cruises
Riverhead Village Pier, Riverhead
Tel: (631) 369-3700
Southbay Paddlewheel Cruises
Brightwaters
Tel: (631) 321-0199
Thomas Jefferson Paddle Steamer
Steamboat Landing, Glen Cove
Tel: (631) 473-0286
Viking Casino Cruises
Montauk
Tel: (631) 668-5700

The Adirondacks
Akwesasne Mohawk Casino
Rte 37, Hogansburg
Tel: (518) 358-241
90 table games; over 1,000
machines.
Lake George Steamboat Company
Steel Pier, Beach Rd, Lake George
Tel: (518) 668-5777
or (1-800) 553-BOAT)
Meals and narrated cruises; vessels,
include the Steamboat *MV Mohican*.
**Raquette Lake Navigation
Company**
Mick Rd, Raquette Lake
Tel: (315) 3540-5532
Lunch, dinner, sunset, and Sunday
brunch cruises.

Central-Leatherstocking
Turning Stone Casino
5218 Patrick Rd, Verona
Tel: (315) 361-7711
or (1-800) 771-7711
Table games and slot machines.

Festivals

In New York City and throughout
New York State, there are various
festivals and special events that
take place on an annual basis. Here
is a list of the main ones you might
want to catch:

January

Winter Antiques Show
Seventh Regiment Armory,
New York City
Chinese New Year Celebrations
Chinatown, New York City
Sometimes in early Feb.
Snowtown USA Celebration
Watertown
10 days of snow-sculpting contest,
sled-dog racing, etc.

February

**Sleigh Rally and Currier & Ives
Competition**
Chautauqua Institution,
Chautauqua
Horses and drivers in turn-of-the-
20th-century regalia.
Empire State Building Run-Up
New York City
Foot race to the top.
Winter Carnival
Saranac Lake
**Westminster Kennel Club Dog
Show**
Madison Square Garden,
New York City

March

New York Flower Show
Piers 90 and 92, New York City
International Cat Show
Madison Square Garden,
New York City
St Patrick's Day Parade,
New York City and Syracuse

April

Central New York Maple Festival
Marathon
Arts, crafts and an all-day pancake breakfast.

Festival of Gold
Niagara Falls
A million daffodils.

Cherry Blossom Festival,
Brooklyn Botanic Garden,
New York City

May

Hudson River Wildlife Festival
Kingston

Tulip Festival
Albany

Lake Ontario Spring Fishing Derby
Lockport

International Food Festival
Ninth Ave, New York City

OzFest
Chittenango
In honor of local author Frank Baum.

Dressage at Saratoga
Saratoga
Carriage rides and competitions at the Race Course.

Canoe Regatta
Clinton

June

Ithaca Festival
Ithaca
Food, mimes, musicians.

Hot-Air Balloon Festival
Jamesville Beach Park, Jamesville

Belmont Stakes
Belmont Park Race Track, Elmont

Clearwater's Great Hudson River Revival
Valhalla
Folk music; environmental displays.

New York Shakespeare Festival
Central Park, New York City
Outdoor performances throughout Labor Day.

Grand Encampment of the French and Indian War
Fort Ticonderoga, Ticonderoga
Recreation of battle.

Caramoor International Music Festival
Katonah
Outdoor concerts on estate, through Aug.

Season at Chautauqua
Chautauqua Institution, Chautauqua
Opera, lectures, dance and workshops, through Aug.

July

Adirondack Festival of American Music
Saranac Lake

Fourth of July Fireworks
East River, New York City

International Seaway Festival
The Tonawandas
Concerts, canoe race.

NY Renaissance Festival
Tuxedo
Jousting to medieval crafts, through to mid-Sept.

Mayors Cup Sailing Race
Lake Champlain, Plattsburgh

Music on the Mountain
Hunter Mountain, Hunter
Country and bluegrass.

August

Woodsmen's Field Days
Oneida County Fairgrounds, Boonville
Lumberjack competitions.

Rodeo!
Rodeo Grounds, Gerry
Roping and riding.

Travers Stakes
Saratoga Race Course, Saratoga

Corn Festival
Avon
Native American crafts and music.

New York State Fair
Syracuse
The oldest in the country.

September

Iroquois Indian Festival
Iroquois Indian Museum, Howes Cave
Crafts and lacrosse competitions.

Genundawa Night
Canandaigua
Bonfires around Canandaigua Lake.

Scottish Games
Altamount
Pipe bands and dancers.

Shinnecock Pow-Wow
Shinnecock Reservation,
Southampton
Dances, ceremonies, crafts.

Lake George Jazz Festival,
Lake George

Barn Festival of the Arts
Remsen
Music, crafts, food.

Apple Fest
Endicott
Food, crafts and music.

October

Fall Flower Show
Planting Fields Arboretum,
Oyster Bay

Feast of St Francis
Cathedral of St John the Divine,
New York City
Blessing of the Animals.

Giant Pumpkin Party
Grahamsville
Hayrides, apple-baking.

Long Island Fair,
Old Bethpage Village Restoration,
Old Bethpage

Clermont County Fair
Germantown
Re-enactment of 19th-century fair.

November

New York City Marathon.

Thanksgiving at the Farmers' Museum
Farmers' Museum, Cooperstown
Old-time food and games.

Macy's Thanksgiving Day Parade
New York City

Christmas Forest
Binghamton
Through Christmas.

Christmas Star Show
Hayden Planetarium/Museum of Natural History, New York City

December

The Nutcracker
New York City Ballet at Lincoln Center, New York City

Christmas Tree at Rockefeller Center
New York City

Giant Hannukah Menorah
Grand Army Plaza, Brooklyn,
New York City

First Night Celebrations
All around the state
New Year's Eve; alcohol-free dances, concerts and other events.

New Year's Eve Celebration
Times Square, New York City

Children

Long Island
Adventureland
2245 Broadhollow Rd, Rte 110,
Farmingdale
Tel: (631) 694-6868
One of New York's largest
amusement parks, with assorted
kiddie and adult rides.
**Bullwinkle's Family Entertainment
Center**
655 Long Island Ave, Medford
Tel: (631) 475-1771
Has carousels, a roller coaster,
mini-golf, and a dinner theater with
"Moosetronic" characters (9-acres).
Empire State Carousel
Brookwood Hall, East Islip
Tel: (516) 277-6167
Hand-carved carousel; takes
passengers on Sat.
SportsPlus
110 New Moriches Rd, Lake Grove
Tel: (631) 737-210
A huge indoor family entertainment
center, houses a 48-lane bowling
alley, 18-hole golf course and
driving range, Iwerks Motion Master
Theater, Laser tag, rock climbing,
virtual reality games, and more.

The Catskills
Catskill Laser Tag, Inc.
Shedrake Plaza, Loch Sheldrake
Tel: (845) 436-1320
Activities include laser tag, wall
climbing, and arcade games.
Kaatskill Kaleidoscope
5340 Rte 28, Mount Tremper
Tel: (845) 688-5300
Has the world's largest
kaleidoscope and other related fun.
Supersonic Speedway Fun Park
Rte 145, East Durham
Tel: (518) 634-7200
Go-carts, mini-golf, rides and more.

Capital-Saratoga Region
Hoffman's Playland
608 Loudon Rd, Rte 9, Latham
Tel: (518) 785-3842
Has 16 rides and an arcade.
**OTB Tele-Theater Racing and
Sports Center**
711 Central Ave, Albany
Tel: (518) 438-0127
Simulated indoor golf, dancing,
bowling, and batting cages, in
addition to betting.
Sherman's Park
Rte 10/29, Caroga Lake
Tel: (518) 725-9717
Features carousels.

Hudson Valley
Fun Central
Rte 9, Wappingers Falls
Tel: (845) 297-1010
Miniature golf, bumper boats,
batting cages and a virtual reality
roller coaster.
Playland Park
Rye
Tel: (845) 921-0370
45 major and Kiddyland rides,
entertainment; hand-carved carousel.

The Adirondacks
Frontier Town
Rte 9, Blue Ridge Rd, North Hudson
Tel: (518) 532-7181
A frontier theme park, with a rodeo,
stagecoaches, and Wild West rides.
**Great Escape and Splashwater
Kingdom**
Rte 9, Queensbury,
Tel: (518) 792-3500
Over 125 rides and a waterpark.
Lake George Ride and Fun Park
Rte 9, Lake George

Central Park

Central Park in New York City has
an entire children's district,
including a zoo, an antique
carousel and a marionette
theater (tel: 212/988-9093).
Sat morning storytelling
sessions take place in summer
at the statue of Hans Christian
Andersen near the Conservatory
Water (East 74th St). It is also a
popular spot for motor boat
racing (tel: 212/794-6564).

Tel: (518) 668-5459
Some 22 rides, go-cart courses,
and shows.
Santa's Workshop
Whiteface Mountain Memorial Hwy,
Wilmington
Tel: (1-800) 835-2251
Santa Claus and his live reindeer
are in residence here.
Wild West Ranch
Bloody Pond Rd, Lake George
Tel: (518) 668-2121
Horseback riding and Wild West
shows.

Central-Leatherstocking
Broome County Carousels
Tel: (607) 772-0660 ext. 255
Six antique carousels in parks
throughout the Binghamton area.
Cooperstown Fun Park
Rte 28, Cooperstown
Tel: (607) 547-2767
Has miniature golf, bumper boats,
go-carts, and an arcade.
Doubleday Batting Range
Cooperstown
Tel: (607) 547-5168
Has batting cages and an arcade.

Thousand Islands & St
Lawrence Seaway
Old McDonald's Children's Village
North Harbor Rd, Sackets Harbor
Tel: (315) 593-5737
Features a farm with hay and pony
rides and more than 200 animals.
Thunder Island
Wilcox Rd, Fulton
Tel: (315) 598-8016
Has water slides, go-carts,
miniature golf, and carnival rides.

Finger Lakes
Sciencenter
601 First St, Ithaca
Tel: (607) 272-0600
A hands-on museum and science
playground, water flume, and more
than 100 exhibits.
Seabreeze Amusement Park
4600 Culver Rd, Rochester
Tel: (716) 323-1900
or (1-800) 395-2500
Over 75 rides and a water park.
Woolamby Sheep Ranch
8228 Center Port Rd, Port Byron
Tel: (315) 776-4927
Musical hay rides and a storytime.

Greater Niagara
Lockport Cave and Underground Boat Ride
210 Market St, Lockport
Tel: (716) 438-0174
Martin's Fantasy Island
2400 Grand Island Blvd,
Grand Island
Tel: (716) 773-7591
Rides, shows, and a waterpark.
Six Flags Darien Lake
9993 Allegheny Rd, Darien Center
Tel: (716) 599-4641
Over 100 rides and attractions.
Wintergarden
Old Falls St, Niagara Falls
Tel: (716) 286-4940
A glass-enclosed tropical park.

Chautauqua-Allegheny
Midway Park
Rte 430, Springs
Tel: (716) 386-3165
Has rides, go-carts, a beach,
miniature golf and antique carousel.
Pumpkinville
4844 Sugartown Rd, Great Valley
Tel: (716) 257-5870
Harvest season storyland, hayrides,
a corn maze and petting zoo.

Aquariums

New York City
New York Aquarium
West 8th St and Surf Ave,
Coney Island
Tel: (718) 265 3474.
Hundreds of exotic fish.

Greater Niagara
Aquarium of Niagara
701 Whirlpool St, Niagara Falls
Tel: (716) 285-3575
or (1-800) 500-4609
More than 1,500 aquatic animals.

Water Parks

Long Island
Splish Splash Water Park
Splish Splash Dr, Riverhead
Tel: (631) 727-3600
The largest water park in the tri-state
area, with rides for the entire family.

Hudson Valley
Splash Down Park
2200 Rte 9, Fishkill
Tel: (845) 896-6606
Waterslides and miniature golf are
among the features at this multi-
activity family waterpark

The Catskills
Zoom Flume
Shady Glen Rd, East Durham
Tel: (1-800) 888-3586
The Catskills' largest waterpark,
with two 300-ft (90-meter) water
slides, bumper boats, and a "river".

The Adirondacks
Enchanted Forest/Water Safari
3183 Rte 28, Old Forge
Tel: (315) 369-6145
Has 23 water rides.

Zoos

New York City
Bronx Zoo
Tel: (718) 367-1010
Worth an entire day's adventure.
Prospect Park
Brooklyn
Tel: (718) 399-7399
Includes a wonderful children's
zoo.

Long Island
Animal Farm Petting Zoo
184A Wading River Rd, Manorville
Tel: (516) 878-1785
Compact and perfect for small
children.
Long Island Game Farm
Chapman Blvd, Manorville
Tel: (516) 878-6644
With a variety of barnyard animals
as well as larger animals including
bears, and camels, and several
rides including an antique
carousel.

Hudson Valley
**Bear Mountain Trailside Museums
and Wildlife Center**
Bear Mountain State Park
Tel: (845) 786-2701, ext. 263
Four trailside museums and
numerous outdoor exhibits.

The Catskills
Catskill Game Farm
400 Game Farm Rd, Catskill
Tel: (518) 678-9895
Exhibits more than 2,000 animals.

Ted Martin's Reptile Land
5464 Rte 32, Catskill
Tel: (518) 678-3557
From the big to the small: features
snakes, lizards, turtles and
crocodiles.

Capital-Saratoga Region
Adirondack Animal Land
Rte 30, Mayfield
Tel: (518) 883-5748
Has a petting zoo, Western town,
and hundreds of birds and animals.
Berkshire Bird Paradise
43 Red Pond Rd, Petersburg
Tel: (518) 279-3801
or (1-800) 349-7150
Home to more than 150 species of
exotic birds.

Central-Leatherstocking
**Fort Rickey Children's Discovery
Zoo**
Rte 49, Rome
Tel: (315) 366-1930
Has a petting zoo, native and
exotic animals, and a water play
area.
Lolly Pop Farm and Petting Zoo
Rte 28, Cooperstown
Tel: (607) 293-7766
or (1-800) 959-CAMP
More than 25 species of animals
and a large aviary.
Ross Park Zoo
60 Morgan Rd, Binghamton
Tel: (607) 724-5461
Over 150 exotic animals and a
carousel.
Utica Zoo
Steel Hill Rd, Utica
Tel: (315) 738-0472
More than 200 animals and sea
lion shows.

Thousand Islands & St
Lawrence Seaway
Aqua Zoo
43681 Rte 12, Alexandria Bay
Tel: (315) 482-5771
Displays include more than 30
water-related exhibits from around
the world.
**Thompson Park Conservancy and
Zoo**
1 Thompson Park, Watertown
Tel: (315) 782-6180
Has a children's zoo, playground,
and swimming pool.

Finger Lakes
Burnet Park Zoo
1 Conservation Pl, Syracuse
Tel: (315) 435-8511
Over 1,000 animals and birds.
Fullagar Family Farms and Petting Zoo
3202 Bath Rd, Penn Yan
Tel: (315) 536-3545
Includes nature trails and pony rides.
Seneca Park Zoo
222 St Paul St, Rochester
Tel: (716) 336-7200
More than 250 animals live in naturalistic settings.

Museums

New York City
Brooklyn Children's Museum
145 Brooklyn Ave
Tel: (718) 735-4400
The world's first museum for children, founded in 1899.
Children's Museum of Manhattan
212 West 83rd St
Tel: (212) 721-1234
Interactive exhibits. Suitable for all age groups.

Long Island
Long Island Children's Museum
550 Stewart Ave, Garden City
Tel: (516) 222-0207
Interactive exhibits for all ages.
Queens County Farm Museum
73–50 Little Neck Pkwy, Floral Park
Historic working farm; hayrides.

Capital-Saratoga
Junior Museum
282 Fifth Ave, Troy
Tel: (518) 235-2120
Interactive exhibits in science, history and the arts; planetarium and live animals.

Central-Leatherstocking
Children's Museum
311 Main St, Utica
Tel: (315) 724-6129
Interactive exhibits.

Finger Lakes
Strong Museum
One Manhattan Sq, Rochester
(716) 263-2700
Impressive array of hands-on displays; world renowned collections.

Shopping

Shopping Areas

Although New York City is famous for many things, thousands of people come here for the shopping alone – and with good reason. It's always been a shopper's paradise, and the saying, "If you can't find it in New York it doesn't exist," is usually true.

For one thing, New York City happens to be home to some of the world's largest and most famous department stores, ranging from **Bloomingdale's** (Lexington Ave at 59th St) and **Henri Bendel** (712 Fifth Ave) to **Macy's** (151 West 34th St). Other reliable stores are **Saks Fifth Avenue** (611 Fifth Ave), **Lord & Taylor** (Fifth Ave and 39th St) and glittering **Bergdorf Goodman** (754 Fifth Ave).

But besides this sort of one-stop shopping there is a fantastic wealth of smaller specialty stores offering wide selections of almost anything you can think of. Boutiques selling avant-garde fashions, original gifts and souvenirs, children's fashions, toys, and other essentials can be found along **Columbus Avenue**, and also Amsterdam Avenue between 66th and 84th streets. The city's jewelers are concentrated on 47th Street, in the section of it known as "**Diamond Row**". The **Village** and **Soho** have dozens of eccentric stores with unusual window displays; many of the city's galleries are here as well as in **Chelsea**. Sundays are busy on **Orchard Street**, on the Lower East Side: this is a good place for discount clothing, shoes and leather goods. Further downtown, discount designer wear and goods are the specialty at **Century 21**, on Cortlandt Street near the World Trade Center.

Upstate, your best bet for finding something is in one of the numerous shopping malls and outlet centers located in and around the larger towns and cities. But the more interesting buys are probably in the less-populated areas where you can still pick up relative bargains at places like country auctions, flea markets, antiques shops, or from one of the smaller craft stores along the road.

Antiques

New York City
Antiques can be found in Greenwich Village along Bleecker Street and on side streets off University Place; along upper Madison Avenue on 60th Street near Third Avenue; and on Lafayette Street below Houston Street. There are also a few outdoor malls around the city, including **Manhattan Art and Antiques Center** (105 Second Ave, tel: 212/355-4400), **Metropolitan Art and Antiques Pavilion** (110 West 19th St, tel: 212/463-0200) and the **Chelsea Antiques Building** (110 West 25th St, tel: 212/929-0909).

Long Island
The Emporium (176 2nd St, Saint James, tel: 516/862-6198) exhibits art and antiques in a refurbished vaudeville theater.

Hudson Valley
Several towns up and down the Hudson River have a large number of antiques shops. The Main Street of Cold Spring (Antiques Dealers Association, Inc., tel: 845/265-6366) is lined with antiques shops. Among the numerous shops in Cornwall-on-Hudson is **Butter Hill Antique Shop** (211 Hudson St, tel: 845/534-2361), which specializes in antique furniture.

The Catskills
Antique Center of Callicoon (58 School St, Callicoon, tel: 914/887-5918) is a multi-dealer shop. **Ferndale Marketplace Antique Center** (Ferndale, tel: 914/292-8701) has 13 rooms of antiques on three floors. **JA-CO Antique Center**

(41 Jefferson St, Monticello, tel: 914/794-7060) has eight shops in four buildings filled with furniture, bric-a-brac and jewelry. **Canal Town Emporium** (Sullivan St, Wurtsboro, tel: 914/888-2100), an early 1800s general store, is filled with antique reproductions, collectibles and penny candy. **Antique Center of Orange County** (2 North Main St, Florida, tel: 845/651-2711) has collectibles, general and rare antiques. **J. Gardner Antiques** (4 South St, Port Jervis, tel: 845/856-0900), specializes in 18th- and 19th-century American furniture, architectural and garden objects.

Capital-Saratoga Region
Salem Art and Antique Center (4337 Rte 22, Salem, tel: 518/854-7320) has 35 dealers. **Whitehall Antique Center** (Rte 4, Whitehall) has 50 dealers. **Regent Street Antique Center** (153 Regent St, Saratoga Springs, tel: 518/584-0107) represents 20 dealers.

The Adirondacks
Shops of every description dot the landscape throughout the region. **Wildwood Arts & Antiques** (85 Park St, Tupper Lake, tel: 518/359-2336) represents 75 consignors. The **Market Barn** (East Main St Rd, Malone, tel: 518/483-9341) has more than 70 booths. **Train Brook Forest** (Paul Smiths, tel: 518/327-3498) sells ornamental ironwork and 18th- and 19th- century trunks.

Central-Leatherstocking
There are antique shops along every highway and byway in the region, including along the Route 28 corridor, and in major cities including Binghamton. Among them: **Cooperstown Antique Center** (73 Chestnut St, Cooperstown, tel: 607/547-2435); **Wood Bull Antiques** (Rte 28, Cooperstown, tel: 607/286-9021); **Bobbi Von Dehmlein Antiques** (Rte 80, Springfield Center, tel: 607/858-0232); **Colliersville Cottage Antiques** (Rte 7, Colliersville, tel: 607/432-7427); **Iroquois Antique Confederacy** (5 Walnut St, Bainbridge, tel: 607/967-3244); and **The Mad Hatter**

(284 Clinton St, Binghamton, tel: 607/729-6036).

Finger Lakes
Craft Antique Co-op (10 Canning St, Hilton, tel: 716/392-3456 or 1-888/711-3463) has more than 130 craft and antique stores.

Greater Niagara
Canal Country Artisans (435 Main St, Medina, tel: 716/798-4760), **Cobbleridge Antiques** (Rte 98/104, Childs, tel: 716/589-2312). **Canal Antiques and Collectibles** (6 East Bank St, Albion, tel: 716/589-0197). **McMullen's Antiques** (7724 Buffalo Ave, Niagara Falls, tel: 716/283-2900).

Chautauqua-Allegheny
The Rose Garden (82 East Main St, Rte 20, Brocton, tel: 716/792-9036) has statuary, fountains and birdbaths and a Victorian home filled with antiques. **The Olean Antique Center** (269 North Union St, Olean, tel: 716/372-8171) houses several dealers.

Books

New York City
New York City is awash with bookstores, but most notable are **Barnes and Noble** (105 Fifth Ave; tel: 212/807-0099) and **Rizzoli** (31 West 57th St; tel: 212/759-2424).

There are also some excellent antiquarian and second-hand bookstores around town, especially the **Strand Book Store** (828 Broadway at 12th St, tel: 212/473-1452) which claims to have two million volumes in stock and is a wonderful place to browse. (There is also a Strand branch at South Street Seaport, 95 Fulton St, tel: 212/732-6070).

Other notable independent bookstores include:
Biography Bookshop, 400 Bleecker St. Histories of the famous and infamous.
Books of Wonder, 16 West 18th St. Good assortment of Children's books.
Gotham Book Mart, 41 West 47th St. A great place to browse.

Clothing Chart
The variation in measuring sizes in America, Britain and Europe can be very confusing. This table compares US, European and British clothing and shoe sizes. It's advisable to try clothes on before buying as sizes can vary.

Women's Dresses/Suits

US	Europe	UK
6	38/34N	8/30
8	40/36N	10/32
10	42/38N	12/34
12	44/40N	14/36
14	46/42N	16/38
16	48/44N	18/40

Women's Shoes

US	Europe	UK
4.5	36	3
5.5	37	4
6.5	38	5
7.5	40	6
8.5	41	7
9.5	42	8
10.5	43	9

Men's Suits

US	Europe	UK
34	44	34
–	46	36
38	48	38
–	50	40
42	52	42
–	54	44
46	56	46

Men's Shirts

US	Europe	UK
14	36	14
14.5	37	14.5
15	38	15.5
15.5	39	15.5
16	40	16
16.5	41	16.5
17	42	17

Men's Shoes

US	Europe	UK
6.5	–	6
7.5	40	7
8.5	41	8
9.5	42	9
10.5	43	10
11.5	44	11

Long Island

Good Times Bookshop (150 East Main St, Port Jefferson, tel: 516/928-2664) specializes in rare and out-of-print volumes.

The Catskills

Read it Again Bookstore (33 Lakewood Ave, Monticello, tel: 914/794-0017) and **The Bookmark** (Main St, Margaretville, tel: 914/586-2700) sell used books.

Capital-Saratoga Region

Antiquarian shops include: **Salem Old Book and Paper Emporium** (197 Main St, Salem, tel: 518/854-7988 or 1-888/534-5578) and **Lyrical Ballad Bookstore** (7 Phila St, Saratoga Springs, tel: 518/584-8779).

Finger Lakes

Book Barn of the Finger Lakes (198 North Rd, Dryden, tel: 607/844-9365) houses more than 75,000 used books.

Chautauqua-Allegheny

Chautauqua Bookstore (Chautauqua Institution, Bestor Plaza, Chautauqua, tel: 716/357-2151). **The Book Worm** (135 East Fairmount Ave, Lakewood, tel: 716/763-2828). **Barbara Berry's Bookshop** (3943 Rte 394, Stow, tel: 716/789-5757).

Crafts

Hudson Valley

Webatuck Craft Village (Rte 55, Wingdale, tel: 845/832-6601) is a working craft village where the buildings date back to the 18th century; glass blowing, stained glass, and pottery. Master Swedish craftsmen demonstrate their skills at **Arnold Larson** (Rte 55, Poughquag, tel: 914/724-5502).

Chautauqua-Allegheny

Stowbridge Village-Good Morning Farm (Stow, tel: 716/763-1772) has 20 shops in a converted 18th-century barn. **The Depot** (Depot St, Cherry Creek, tel: 716/296-5697) sells Amish goods, crafts and antiques.

Factory Outlets & Shopping Malls

Long Island

There are almost 200 stores of designer and brand name manufacturers at **Tanger Factory Outlet Center** (Tanger Dr, Riverhead, tel: 1-800/4-TANGER).

A number of the island's villages have extensive shopping districts, including: Huntington Village, Northport, Cold Spring Harbor, Oyster Bay, Stony Brook, and Port Washington. Long Island malls include: the 215-store **Roosevelt Field** (Old Country Rd, Garden City, tel: 516/742-8000); the 130-shop **Broadway Mall** (Rts 106/107, tel: 516/822-6336); the 110-store **Walt Whitman Mall** (Rte 110, Huntington Station, tel: 631/271-1741); 250 shops and restaurants at **Great Neck Plaza** (Great Neck, tel: 1-800/244-5148); and **Smith Haven Mall** (Nesconset Hwy, Lake Grove, tel: 631/724-1433) with 150 stores.

Hudson Valley

At **Woodbury Common Premium Outlets** (Rte 32, Central Valley, tel: 845/928-4000) 220 designer manufacturers sell their wares in a Colonial village setting. The **Poughkeepsie Galleria** (tel: 845/297-7600; Rte 9) has 150 shops.

The Catskills

Apollo Plaza (Rte 17, Monticello, tel: 845/794-2010) has more than 30 stores. **Catskill Corners Festival Marketplace** (5340 Rte 28, Mt Pleasant Rd, Mt Tremper, tel: 1-888/303-3936 or 845/688-2451), home of the world's largest kaleidoscope, also has seven country shops in a renovated barn. The 1830s restored **Canal Towne Emporium** (169 Sullivan St, Wurtsboro, tel: 845/888-2100) has gifts, furniture, collectibles and food.

Capital-Saratoga Region

Latham Factory Outlet Stores (400 Old Loudon Rd, Latham, tel: 518/782-0085 or 1-888/548-8375). **Colonie Center** (Wolf Rd and Central Ave, Albany, tel: 518/459-

9020) has 120 upscale shops. **Crossgates Mall** (1 Crossgates Mall Rd, Albany, tel: 1-800/439-2011) has 230 stores, 30 cinemas and 6 restaurants. **Rotterdam Square Mall** (93 West Campbell Rd, Schenectady, tel: 518/374-3713) has major retail chains.

The Adirondacks

The Lake George area has numerous outlet malls. For information, contact **Factory Outlets on The Million Dollar Half Mile** (tel: 1-800/748-1288). **The Market Barn** (East Main St Rd, Malone, tel: 518/483-9341) has 80 shops, antiques, and crafts. **Miromar Factory Outlet Center** (40 Miromar St, Champlain, tel: 518/298-3333) has 28 factory stores. There are 90 stores and a movie theater at **Champlain Centres** (60 Smithfield Blvd, Plattsburgh, tel: 518/561-8660).

Central-Leatherstocking

Great Labels (Rte 28, Cooperstown, tel: 607/547-7226). **Silver City Plaza** (606 Sherrill Rd, Sherrill, tel: 315/361-3661).

Thousand Islands & St Lawrence Seaway

There are five major department stores at **Salmon Run Mall** (21182 Salmon Run Mall Loop West, Watertown, tel: 315/788-9210 or 1-800/786-6255). **Sangertown Square Mall** (Rts 5/5A, New Hartford, tel: 315/797-8520) has 100 stores.

Finger Lakes

Finger Lakes Mall (2000 Clark St Rd, Auburn, tel: 315/255-1188) has more than 50 stores, theaters and restaurants. **Arnot Mall** (3300 Chambers Rd South, Horseheads, tel: 607/739-8704) has 100-plus stores. **Pyramid Mall-Ithaca** (40 Catherwood Rd, Ithaca, tel: 607/257-5337) has more than 70 stores and a 10-screen cinema. There are more than 150 stores at **Marketplace Mall** (One Miracle Mile Dr, Rochester, tel: 716/424-6220). **Carousel Center** (9090 Carousel Center Dr, Syracuse, tel: 315/466-7000) has 170-plus shops and an antique carousel. **Prime Outlets at Waterloo** (655 Rte 318, Waterloo, tel: 315/539-1100 or 877/GO-OUTLET) houses more than 95 stores.

Greater Niagara
Walden Galleria (Galleria Dr, Buffalo, tel: 716/681-7600) has 200-plus stores. **Melton's Factory Outlet** (56 Havester Ave, Batavia, tel: 716/343-8750) sells clothing, gifts and crafts; **Outlet Center** (1881 Ridge Rd, Buffalo, tel: 716/674-8920) has more than 20 stores. **Prime Outlets at Niagara Falls USA** (1900 Military Rd, Niagara Falls, tel: 716/297-2022 or 1-800/414-0475) has 150-plus brand-name outlets.

Chautauqua-Allegheny
Chautauqua Mall (318 East Fairmount Ave, Rte 394, Lakewood, tel: 716/763-1823).

Farm Stands

Long Island
Farm stands all around the island sell fresh-picked produce in season. **Briermere Farms** (Rte 48, Riverhead, tel: 516/722-3931) specializes in freshly baked fruit pies. **Peconic River Herb Farm** (310-C River Rd, Calverton, tel: 631/369-0058), a working riverfront farm, has more than 700 varieties of unique plants, including herbs, vegetables, native island plants and 22 display and trial gardens.

Hudson Valley
Overlook Farm Market (Rte 9W, Newburgh, tel: 1-800/291-9137) sells fresh fruit and has a petting zoo.

The Catskills
There are many farm stands in and near the towns of Pine Island and Warwick. Among them, Pine Island onions and other Orange Country produce are on sale at **Sudol Farms** (762 County Rte I, Pine Island, tel: 845/258-4260). Free wagon rides, puppet shows, and U-pick apples and pumpkins at **Applewood Orchards** (82 Four Corners Rd,

Warwick, tel: 845/986-1684). **Catskill Morning Farm** (tel: 914/482-3984; Livingston Manor) sells organic vegetables, herbs and perennials. **Davenports Circle Farm** (Rte 28, Boiceville, tel: 914/334-9004) sells farm produce including tomatoes and watermelons.

Central-Leatherstocking
Cradle Valley Farms (Cranehill Rd, Unadilla, tel: 607/369-3909) has U-pick berries and pumpkins. **Fly Creek Cider Mill and Orchard** (Goose St, Fly Creek, tel: 607/547-9692) sells cider, apples, cheeses, and baked goods. **Annutto's Farm Stand** (East Main St, Rte 7, Oneonta, tel: 607/432-7905) has fresh produce, and maple syrup.

Finger Lakes
More than 100 vendors, farm produce, crafts, and a food court are at **Hanna Junction Farm and Craft Market** (4375 Rte 21N, Canandaigua, tel: 716/394-7740). **Windmill Farm and Craft Market** (Rte 14A, Penn Yann, tel: 315/536-3032) has more than 240 vendors and sells Mennonite and Amish specialties.

Greater Niagara
The roadsides are dotted with fruit farms, which are particularly lively at fall harvest. Among them: **Watt Farms Country Market** (3121 Rte 98, Albion, tel: 1-800/274-5897); **Brown's Berry Patch** (14264 Roosevelt Hwy, Waterport, tel: 716/682-5569); and **Smith's Family Farm Market** (4362 South Gravel Rd, Medina, tel: 716/798-2656).

Chautauqua-Allegheny
More than 50 vendors sell homemade and homegrown products at **Cross Roads Farm and Craft Market** (County Rd 21, Westfield, tel: 716/326-1997). **Blueberry Ski Farm Winery** (10243 Northeast Sherman Rd, Ripley, tel: 716/252-6535) makes fruit wines and has U-pick berries. **Busti Cider Mill and Farm Market** (1135 Southwestern Dr, Jamestown, tel: 716/487-0177) makes cider, maple products and sells fruits and vegetables.

Markets

New York City
For an eclectic mix of antiques, head over to the weekend flea market on Sixth Avenue between 25th and 26th streets. Another flea market (one of several around the city) is held every Sun on the Upper West Side, on the corner of Columbus Avenue and 77th Street.

The Catskills
Sat and Sun are flea market days at the **Annual Flea Market** at Monticello Raceway (Rte 17B, Monticello, tel: 845/796-1000).

Thousand Islands & St Lawrence Seaway
Great Lakes Cheese of NY (23 Phelps St, Adams, tel: 315/232-4511 or 1-800/932-4337) sells cheddar cheese and other local products. **Ameri/Can Market** (42685 Rte 12, Alexandria Bay, tel: 315/622-2720) has an outdoor mall and flea market, mini golf, and food.

Finger Lakes
Tioga Park Marketplace and Grand Stand (2384 West River Rd, Nichols, tel: 607/699-0022) houses a large indoor marketplace and hosts festivals, carnivals, rodeos and concerts.

Specialty Shops

Capital-Saratoga Region
Eagle Mills Cider Company (Eagle Mills Rd, Broadalbin, tel: 518/883-8700) has a waterwheel-powered cider mill and nature walks. **Steiniger's** (Main St, Salem, tel: 518/854-3830) makes chocolates and other confections.

Central-Leatherstocking
Collector's World (139 Main St, Cooperstown, tel: 607/547-5509) sells baseball-related, autographed items. The **Christmas Barn** (Goose St, Fly Creek, tel: 607/547-2637) is packed with tons of Christmas accessories and country gifts. **Doll Artisan Guild** (35 Main St, Oneonta,

tel: 607/432-4977) sells porcelain dolls. The **Ribbon Mill Store** (17 Willard St, Greene, tel: 607/656-7122), one of the last working ribbon mills in the northeast, sells one-of-a-kind pieces, seconds, and mill ends.

Finger Lakes
Wizard of Clay Pottery (Rte 20A, Bristol, tel: 716/229-2980) sells handcrafted clay items and demonstrates pottery making. **Nadal Glass** (20 Phoenix St, Canandaigua, tel: 716/394-7850) and **Vitrix Hot Glass Studio** (77 West Market St, Corning, tel: 607/936-8707) sell glass items and have glassblowing demonstrations. **Heluva Good Cheese Country Store** (6152 Barclay Rd, Sodus, tel: 315/483-2223 or 1-800/445-0269) sells cheeses and specialty foods.

Greater Niagara
Oliver's Candies (211 West Main St, Batavia, tel: 716/343-5888 or 1-800/924-3879) sells homemade candy. More than 40 vendors sell ethnic foods at **Broadway Market** (999 Broadway, Buffalo, tel: 716/893-0705). **Ridge Road Station & Christmas Shop** (16131 Ridge Rd, Holly, tel: 716/638-6000) sells LGB-grade trains and Christmas-related items.

Chautauqua-Allegheny
Cuba Cheese Shoppe (53 Genesee St, Cuba, tel: 716/968-3949 or 1-800/543-4938) has 100 varieties of imported and domestic cheeses. **Anderson's Maple Products** (1510 Southwestern Dr, Lakewood, tel: 716/664-5393) produces maple syrup and related products. **Webb's Candy Factory** (Rte 394, Mayville, tel: 716/753-2161) has tours. **Kabob Bear Country** (6359 South Stockton-Cassadaga Rd, Sinclairville, tel: 716/962-4647) has tours of their hand-made teddy bear factory. **Sugar Sack-Vinewood Acres** (7904 Rte 5, Westfield, tel: 1-888/563-4324) makes homemade fruit syrups and maple products. **Candle-Escents** (Rte 430, Findley Lake, tel: 716/769-7874) is the region's largest candle gift house. **Wegman's** (945 Fairmount Ave, West Jamestown, tel: 716/483-9900) has a deli, European bakery, Fisherman's Wharf, and kids' fun center.

Toys

New York City
FAO Schwarz, 767 Fifth Ave. At the corner of Central Park is the Fifth Avenue flagship of America's most famous toyshop.

Wineries

Long Island
There are more than 21 full-time wineries and 50 vineyards on the North and South Forks. For a complete listing write: **Long Island Wine Council**, 104 Edwards Ave, Calverton, NY 11933.

Hudson Valley
The Valley has several excellent vineyards, including: **Benmarl Vineyards and Museum** (156 Highland Ave, Marlboro, tel: 845/236-4265); **Millbrook Vineyards and Winery** (Wing and Shunpike Rds, Millbrook, tel: 1-800/662-9463); and **Rivendell Winery** (714 Albany Post Rd, New Paltz, tel: 845/255-2494).

Finger Lakes
The Finger Lakes is the premier wine-growing region in the eastern United States. More than 25 wineries are located on the shores of Seneca Lake alone, including **Lakewood Vineyards** (4024 Rte 14, Watkins Glen, tel: 607/535-9252) and **Glenora Wine Cellars** (5435 Rte 14, Dundee, tel: 607/243-5511). For a complete listing contact the **Seneca Lake Winery Association**, Keuka Business Park, Suite 100, Penn Yan, NY 14527, tel: 877/536-2717). Another good winery in the region is **Casa Larga Vineyards** (2287 Turk Hill Rd, Fairport, tel: 716/223-4210).

Chautauqua-Allegheny
Many of the region's fine wineries are on or near Rte 20.

Outdoor Activities

New York City

New York's numerous parks offer varied facilities for the sports-minded. In New York City, Central Park offers the most attractions, although there are large parks in the other boroughs, including Pelham Bay Park (the largest) in the Bronx and the Greenbelt, 2,300 acres of woods on Staten Island.

You can rent horses at the **Claremont Riding Academy**, (175 West 89th St, tel: 212/724 5100; there is ice skating at both the **Wollman** and **Lasker Rinks** in Central Park (Oct–Apr) and year-round skating (along with roller-skating, horseback riding, rock-climbing and other sports) at **Chelsea Piers** (West 23rd St and the Hudson River, tel: 212/336-6100 or 212/336-6666). There are also dozens of baseball and softball diamonds in parks throughout the city, as well as jogging tracks.

The **New York Road Runners Club** maintains a running center (9 East 89th St, tel: 212/840-4455). For information about golf, tennis and other sports in the city, call the **Parks Department** at (212) 360-8133.

New York State

BEACHES & SWIMMING

Long Island
Beach volleyball is a popular island sport, and visitors are often able to join in pick-up games. Beaches where they're particularly popular include: **East Quogue** in the Hamptons, **Jones Beach** in Wantagh, and **Robert Moses State Park** on Fire Island.

Capital-Saratoga Region

Cherry Plain State Park (off Rte 22, Black River Pond, Cherry Plain, tel: 518/733-5400). **Grafton Lakes State Park** (Rte 2, Grafton, tel: 518/279-1155). **Brown's Beach** (Rte 9P, Saratoga Springs, tel: 518/587-8280).

Central-Leatherstocking

Many – if not all – of the state parks have bathing beaches, including: **Glimmerglass State Park** (Rte 31, Lake Otsego, tel: 607/547-8662); **Gilbert Lake State Park** (County Rd 12, Laurens, tel: 607/432-2114); and **Delta Lake State Park** (off Rte 46, Rome, tel: 315/337-4670).

Finger Lakes

Park Station Recreation Center (2 West Beaver Pond, Elmira, tel: 607/739-9146). **Long Point State Park** (Rte 430, Long Point, tel: 716/386-2722). **Buttermilk Falls State Park** (Rte 13, Ithaca, tel: 607/273-5761).

Greater Niagara

Many municipal and state parks have public swimming areas, including: **Long Point State Park** (Lake Rd, Aurora, tel: 315/497-0130); **Beaver Island State Park** (213 West Oakfield Rd, Grand Island, tel: 716/773-3271); and **Evangola State Park** (Shaw Rd, Irving, tel: 716/549-1760).

Chautauqua-Allegheny

Most communities on the water have public beaches. In addition, the state parks have good beaches. A few: **Lake Erie State Park** (5905 Lake Rd, Rte 5, Brocton, tel: 716/792-9214); **Allegheny State Park** (2373 ASP Rte I, Salamanca, tel: 716/354-2182); and **Long Point State Park** (Rte 430, Bemus Point, tel: 716/ 386-2722).

BIKING

The Catskills

Mountain biking at Pearson Park on **Walnut Mountain** (tel: 914/292-7960) has 265 acres with single track and paths for all levels, and bike rentals.

Capital-Saratoga Region

The 35-mile (56-km) **Mohawk-Hudson Bikeway** (tel: 518/447-5660) travels along the Hudson and Mohawk rivers and connects Albany, Troy and Schenectady. **Troy RiverSpark Visitor Center** (251 River St, Troy, tel: 518/270-8210) rents bikes.

The Adirondacks

The *Adirondack North Country Association Bikeways Map* (tel: 518/8911-6200) is a guide to biking in the region. **Lake Champlain Bikeways** (tel: 518/597-4646) offers a map of the route around the lake.

Mountains Unlimited (Rte 2, Lake George, tel: 1-888/240-6976) rents mountain bikes as well as equipment for whitewater rafting, hiking and climbing. **Gore Mountain** (Peaceful Valley Rd, North Creek, tel: 1-800/342-1234) rents equipment and transports riders (and hikers) to the top of the mountain via the chair lift.

Central-Leatherstocking

Cranks from Cooperstown: 50 Bike Rides in Upstate New York (PO Box 568, Cooperstown 13326, tel: 607/547-2726) provides directions and maps for around 50 backroads biking tours in the Leatherstocking region.

Thousand Islands & St Lawrence Seaway

Lakeshore Bicycle Touring (Oswego, tel: 315/343-0687) organizes cycling trips. **T.I. Cycle** (Gananoque, Ontario, Canada, tel: 613/382-5144) rents bicycles.

Chautauqua-Allegheny

The 30-mile (45-km) **Chautauqua Rails to Trails** (tel: 716/483-2330) between Brockton and Sherman is just one of the many fine places in the region to go biking (it's also popular with hikers). There's also a paved trail at **Long Point State Park** (Rte 430, Bemus Point, tel: 716/386-2722). **Water Jet Rental** (Lakeside Dr, Bemus Point, tel: 716/484-7810) rents bikes (and jet skis).

BOATING

Long Island

Strong's Marine (Mattituck, tel: 631/298-4770) rents motorboats. Sailboats and paddleboats are rented at **Fort Pond** (Montauk Hwy, Montauk, tel: 631/668-4473).

Hudson Valley

Great Hudson Sailing Center (Dock St, Kingston, tel: 845/429-1557) gives cruises and has rentals.

Hudson Highland Cruises (Haverstraw Marina, West Haverstraw, tel: 845/446-7171) sails from West Point's South Dock and West Haverstraw for cruises up the Hudson River. **Hudson River Adventures** (tel: 845/782-0685) sails from Newburgh Landing for cruises along the river. A Mississippi River paddlewheeler plies the Hudson River via the **Hudson River Boat Company** (tel: 845/762-4564).

The Catskills

Gene's Speed Boat Rentals (Rte 55, White Lake, tel: 845/583-9787) rents waverunning jets, speedboats, rowboats and pontoons.

The Adirondacks

Blue Mountain Lake Boat Livery (Blue Mountain, tel: 518/352-7351) rents boats. **Shoreline Marina** (2 Kurosaka Lane, Lake Placid, tel: 1-800/242-7837) rents boats and wave runners. **Clark's Marina** (4th Lake, Inlet, tel: 315/357-3231) rents jet skis, water skis, and pontoon boats. **Northwind Sailing Charters** (Chic's Marina, Bolton Landing, tel: 518/644-2797) has captained sailing charters.

Central-Leatherstocking

Knott's Motel (Goodyear Lake, Oneonta, tel: 607/432-5948) rents rowboats and canoes. **Sam Smith's Boat Yard** (Lake Rd, Rte 80, Cooperstown, tel: 607/547-2543) rents everything from fishing skiffs to pontoon barges.

Thousand Islands & St Lawrence Seaway

Meandering through the islands is a delightful way to spend a day or a week. Visitors can rent a wide variety of vessels, from a jet ski to a houseboat. **Aqua-Mania** (tel: 1-800/439-4FUN; Alexandria Bay) rents jet boats and ski, pontoons, fishing boats, and runabouts. **Remar Houseboat Rental** (510 Theresa St, Clayton, tel: 315/686-3579) rents Sea Doos and houseboats. **Martin's Marina & Motel** (28491 County Rte 6, Mud Bay, Cape Vincent, tel: 315/654-3104) has boat rentals and fishing guides. **Schermerhorn Marine Center** (71 Schermerhorn Landing Rd, Hammond, tel: 315/324-5966) rents pontoon and motor boats, canoes, and paddleboats.

Finger Lakes

East Shore Sailing (1000 East Shore Dr, Ithaca, tel: 607/273-2560) rents sailboats, windsurfers, catamarans and canoes. **Pier Action Sports** (City Pier, Canandaigua, tel: 716/396-9000) rents fishing boats, paddleboats, sailboats, jet skis and canoes.

With its numerous lakes, it's no surprise that there are a huge number of charter boats plying the waters of the Finger Lakes. Among them: the 19th century paddle-wheel steamboat replica *Canandaigua Lady* (169 Lakeshore Dr, Canandaigua, tel: 716/394-5365), the 150-passenger paddlewheeler *Seneca Dreamer II* (Lakeshore Park, Geneva, tel: 315/781-1026). The *Colonial Belle* (6 North Main St, Fairport, tel: 716/377-4600) cruises the Erie Canal, as does the paddlewheeler *Fairport Lady* (10 Liftbridge Lane West, Fairport, tel: 716/223-1930). The restored, 1917 *M/V Manhattan* (702 West Buffalo St, Ithaca, tel: 607/272-4868 or 1-800/591-5901) tours Cayuga Lake. **Mid-Lakes Navigation Co.** (11 Jordan St, Skaneateles, tel: 315/685-8500 or 1-800/545-4318) offers overnight tours of the Erie Canal.

Greater Niagara

Miss Buffalo/Niagara Clipper Cruise Boats (79 Marine Dr, Buffalo, tel: 716/856-6696 or 1-888/625-4509) sail along Buffalo Harbor, Lake Erie, and Niagara River. **Grand Lady Cruises** (Holiday Inn, 100 White Haven Rd, Grand Island, tel: 716/774-8594) cruise the Niagara River and through the locks. **Miss Apple Grove Erie Canal Boat Tours** (Apple Grove Inn, Medina, tel: 716/798-2323 or 1-800/564-2323) has mule-drawn packet boat tours. **Maid of the Mist Boat Tours** (Niagara Falls State Park, tel: 716/284-8897) goes to the base of the Falls. **Lockport Locks & Erie Canal Cruises** (210 Market St, Lockport, tel: 716/433-6155 or 1-800/378-0352) travel through Lockport Locks. **Whirlpool Jet Boat Tours** (The Riverside Inn, 115 South Water St, Lewiston, tel: 1-888/438-4444) travel through Niagara Gorge.

Chautauqua-Allegheny

We Wan Chu Cottages (Rte 394, Chautauqua, tel: 716/789-3383) rents fishing and pontoon boats. **Chautauqua Marina** (Rte 394, Mayville, tel: 716/753-3913) rents fishing boats, jet skis and tubes. **Lakeside Auto Court** (Rte 394, Stow, tel: 716/789-3951) rents fishing boats; **Lake's End Marina** (130 Maple Ave, Cassadaga, tel: 716/595-2152) rents boats and canoes. **Summer Wind Lake Cruises** (Lucille Ball Memorial Park, Celoron, tel: 716/763-7447) and the 19th-century, steam-powered stern wheeler *Chautauqua Belle* (Rte 394, Mayville, tel: 716/753-2403) sail Chautauqua Lake.

CANOEING/KAYAKING

Long Island

The island's four major rivers are popular with canoeists. Among the most popular stretches: the 5 miles (8 km) of the Carmans River in Brookhaven, the lower 3 miles (5 km) of the Connetquot River in Oakdale, 8 miles (11 km) of the Peconic in Riverhead, and a 5-mile (8-km) stretch of the Nissequogue in Smithtown. Rentals are by the hour, day or week. **East End Kayak Tours** (Montauk Highway, Wainscott, tel: 1-800/564-4386) has sea kayak rentals and conducts group excursions. Canoes and kayaks can be rented at **Setauket Harbor** (30 Shore Rd, East Setauket, tel: 516/751-2706).

Hudson Valley

Loric Sports, Inc. (912 Rte 9, Staatsburg, tel: 845/889-4320) rents canoes and kayaks. **Whaley Lake Marina** (Rte 292, Holmes, tel: 914/855-1363) rents boats, paddleboats and canoes.

The Catskills

A few places rent canoes and kayaks and/or offer rafting tours on the Delaware: **Lander's Delaware River Trips** (Narrowsburg, tel: 1-800/252-3925 or 914/252-3925); **Wild and Scenic River Tours & Rentals** (Barryville, tel: 1-800/836-0366 or 914/557-8783), and **Silver Canoe-Raft Rentals** (tel: 1-800/724-8342 or 914/856-7055). In other areas: **Town Tinker Tube Rental** (Phoenicia, tel: 845/688-5553; Rte 28), and **Whitewater Willies** (Pond Eddy, tel: 1-800/233-RAFT), **Town Tinker Tube Rental** (Rte 28, Phoenicia, tel: 845/688-5553) **FS Tube and Raft** (4 Church St, Phoenicia, tel: 914/688-7633). **Indian Head Canoe** (Rte 97N, Barryville, tel: 1-800/874-BOAT).

Capital-Saratoga Region

Battenkill Sports Quarters (937 Rte 313, Cambridge, tel: 518/677-8868 or 1-800/676-8768) has canoeing, kayaking and tubing. **Adirondack Wildwaters** (Corinth, tel: 518/696-2953) runs rafting trips.

The Adirondacks

With more than 3,000 lakes and 6,000 miles (9,600 km) of rivers and streams, and Lake Champlain, the Adirondacks is a paddler's paradise. The **Adirondack Waterways** (ARTC, PO Box 2149, Plattsburg 12901, tel: 518/846-8017 or 1-800/ITS-MTNS) is a guide to paddling in the region. **Woods and Water Touring** (PO Box 144, Blue Mountain Lake, tel: 518/352-7306) rents canoes and organizes tours. **Lake George Kayak Company** (3 Boathouse Lane, Bolton Landing, tel: 518/644-5295) has rentals and gives guided kayak tours.

St Regis Canoe Outfitters (Rte 30, Lake Clear, tel: 518/891-1838) organizes paddle trips. **Rivett's Marine Recreation and Services** (South Shore Rd, Old Forge, tel: 315/369-3123) rents canoes on the Fulton Chain. **Tickner's Moose River Canoe Trips** (1 Riverside Dr, Old Forge, tel: 315/369-6286) has rentals.

Thousand Islands & St Lawrence Seaway
Mad River Unlimited (744 Rte 47, Redfield, tel: 315/599-7328) rents canoes and kayaks.

Finger Lakes
Endless Adventures (145 East Main St, Penn Yann, tel: 315/536-0522 or 1-800/968-8735) rents kayaks and organizes tours. **Oak Orchard Canoe Experts** (40 State St, Pittsford, tel: 716/586-5990) organizes canoeing and kayaking on Erie Barge Canal.

Greater Niagara
Zoar Valley Canoe/Rafting (175 Water St, Gowanda, tel: 716/724-7238 or 1-800/724-0696). **Up-the-Creek Canoe Rental** (11302 Slade Rd, Medina, tel: 716/798-5772). **Oak Orchard Canoe Experts** (2133 Eagle Harbor Rd, Waterport, tel: 716/682-4849).

Chautauqua-Allegheny
Canoeing spots include: Cassadaga Creek, Conewango Creek, Cassadaga Lakes, Findley Lake, and Chautauqua Lake at Jamestown. **Lakes End Marina** (130 Maple Ave, Cassadaga, tel: 716/595-2152) and **Hickory Hills Canoe Rental** (Mosher Hollow Rd, New Albion Lake, tel: 716/257-9812) rent canoes.

CLIMBING

The Catskills
High Angle Adventures (178 Hardensburgh Rd, Ulster, tel: 1-800/777-2546).

Capital-Saratoga Region
Ascents of Adventure (147 Cherry Ave, Delmar, tel: 518/475-7519).

The Adirondacks
Adirondack Mountain Club (818 Goggins Rd, Lake George, tel: 518/668-4447) has extensive information about hiking and climbing. **Adirondack Alpine Adventures** (Rte 73, Keene, tel: 518/576-9881) provides instruction and guide service for rock and ice climbing, backcountryskiing and, of course, mountaineering.

Thousand Islands & St Lawrence Seaway
Vertical Dream (1 Market St, Potsdam, tel: 315/265-3178) organizes climbing, hiking, rafting, canoeing and kayaking.

Finger Lakes
Endless Adventures (145 East Main St, Penn Yann, tel: 315/536-0522 or 1-800/968-8735) organizes tours. **Rock Ventures** (1044 University Ave, Rochester, tel: 716/442-5462) has indoor climbing.

FLYING, GLIDING AND HOT-AIR BALLOONING

Long Island
Sky Sailors, Inc. (Suffolk County Airport, Westhampton Beach, tel: 631/288-5858) offers balloon, glider and biplane rides, as well as parachuting. **Adventures Aloft** (27 Claremont St, Deer Park, tel: 516/595-9213) has hot air balloon flights over Eastern Long Island.

Hudson Valley
Blue Sky Balloons (246 Mountain Rd, Pleasant Valley, tel: 1-888/999-2461) gives balloon rides from Apr–Oct. **Above the Clouds** (Randall Airport, Airport Rd, Middletown, tel: 914/692-2556) soars above the Hudson Valley.

Ellenville, the state's paragliding capital, has several centers that give lessons and rent equipment. Among them are: **Eastcoast Paragliding Center** (150 Canal St, tel: 845/647-3377), and **Sky's the Limit** (41 Navajo Dr, Orange County Airport, Montgomery, tel: 914/457-9252), where first-time parachutists jump the same day.

The Catskills
Glider and plane rides are offered at **Wurtsboro Airport** (Rte 209, Wurtsboro, tel: 914/888-2791), the country's oldest soaring site.

The Adirondacks
Payne's Air Service (Seventh Lake, Inlet, tel: 315/357-397). **Adirondack Flying Service** (Rte 73, Lake Placid Airport, tel: 518/523-2473) and **Helms Seaplane Service** (Rte 30, Long Lake, tel: 518/624-3931) offer plane rides. **Adirondack Balloon Flights** (Aviation Rd, Glens Falls, tel: 518/793-6342) and **A Beautiful Balloon** (47 Assembly Point Rd, Lake George, tel: 518/656-9328) offers hot air ballooning over the region.

Central-Leatherstocking
Susquehanna Flight Park (Cooperstown, tel: 607/866-6153) offers hang gliding.

Thousand Islands & St Lawrence Seaway
Thousand Islands Aviation Services (Rte 26, Maxson Airfield, Alexandria Bay, tel: 315/482-4024). **Champagne Balloon Adventures** (27 James St, Alexandria Bay, tel: 315/482-9356). **Thousand Islands Helicopter Tours** (Rte 12N, Alexandria Bay, tel: 315/482-4024).

Finger Lakes
Sunset Adventures (Beech Tree Rd, Auburn, tel: 315/252-9474). **Liberty Balloon Company** (6730 Barber Hill Rd, Groveland, tel: 716/243-3178 or 1-800/777-2FLY). **Balloons over Letchworth** (Letchworth State Park, tel: 716/237-2660).

Greater Niagara
Rainbow Air (454 Main St, Niagara Falls, tel: 716/284-2800).

Chautauqua-Allegheny
Dart Airport (Rte 430, Mayville, tel: 716/753-2160) offers plane rides. **Balloons Over Chautauqua** (780 Fairmont Ave WE, Jamestown, tel: 716/484-9961 or 1-888/2B-FLYIN). **Sky Sail Balloons** (5673 Rte 380, Sinclairville, tel: 716/326-7245) offer ballooning.

HIKING

Long Island

The **Long Island Greenbelt Trail Conference** (tel: 631/360-0753) has information on trails on the island. The **Nassau Greenbelt Trail** (tel: 631/360-0753) extends for 22 miles (25 km) from Cold Spring Harbor to Massapequa through fields and forest. A 20-mile (32-km) long beachfront **Fire Island Seashore Trail** (tel: 631/289-4810) runs from Davis Park to Smith Point. The **Suffolk Greenbelt Trail** stetches for 34 miles (55 km) from Sunken Meadow State Park south to Heckscher State Park on Great South Bay.

Hudson Valley

The **New York-New Jersey Trail Conference** (PO Box 2250, NY 10016, tel: 212/685-9699) publishes excellent maps. The **Nature Conservancy** (tel: 845/244-3271) oversees numerous reserves throughout the region.

The Catskills

For information on hiking in the Catskill Forest Preserve, contact: **New York State Department of Environmental Conservation** (50 Wolf Rd, Room 438, Albany 12233, tel: 518/457-7433) or the New York-New Jersey Trail Conference as before. **Catskill Hiking Shack** (259 Sullivan St, Wurtsboro, tel: 914/888-HIKE) has maps and guides.

Capital-Saratoga Region

Vischer Ferry Nature Preserve (Riverview Rd, Clifton Park, tel: 518/371-6667). **Dyken Pond Environmental Education Center** (475 Dyken Pond Rd, Cropseyville, tel: 518/658-2055). **Five Rivers Environmental Education Center** (56 Game Farm Rd, Delmar, tel: 518/475-0291). **Hollyhock Hollow Sanctuary** (46 Rarick Rd, Selkirk, tel: 518/767-9051).

The Adirondacks

There are more than 2,000 miles (3,200 km) of hiking trails in the region, ranging from short jaunts to the 132-mile (212-km) Northville-Placid Trail through Adirondack Park. For the guide *Adirondack Great Walks and Day Hikes*, send a check for $3.50 to the **Adirondack Regional Tourism Council** (PO Box 2149, Plattsburgh, NY 12901, tel: 1-800/487-6867).

Central-Leatherstocking

Trails can be found at **Chittenango Falls State Park** (230 Rathbun Rd, Cazenovia, tel: 315/655-9620), **Vroman's Nose/Long Path** (Rte 30, Middleburgh, tel: 518/827-5747) and **Verona Beach State Park** (Verona Beach, tel: 315/762-4463).

Thousand Islands & St Lawrence Seaway

Amboy 4H Environmental Education Center (off NYS Rte. 183, Amboy) has 150 acres of trails. **Oswego County Recreational Trail** (tel: 315/349-8322 or 1-800/496-3200) has 26 miles (42 km) for hiking, biking, horseback riding, and cross-country skiing.

Finger Lakes

Keuka Outlet Trail (Penn Yan, tel: 315/336-3111) has hiking and biking trails.

Greater Niagara

Oak Orchard and Tonawanda (Alabama, tel: 716/948-5182) has trails to view wetlands wildlife. The 10,000-acre **Iroquois National Wildlife Refuge** (State Rte 63, Alabama, tel: 716/ 948-5445) has miles of trails.

Chautauqua-Allegheny

Organized hiking trails include the 19-mile (30-km) **Earl Cardot Eastside Overland Trail** (tel: 716/763-8928) and the 25-mile (40-km) **Fred J. Cusimano Westside Overland Trail.**

HORSEBACK RIDING

Long Island

Deep Hollow Ranch (Theodore Roosevelt County Park, Montauk, tel: 631/668-2744) has pony rides. **Rita's Montauk Stable** (West Lake Dr, Montauk, tel: 631/ 668-5453) has trail and carriage rides.

The Catskills

Saddle Up (355 Woodland Valley Rd, Phoenicia, tel: 914/688-7336) rents horses. Pony rides, hay rides, and horseback riding at **Hadley Riding Stables** (Old Liberty Rd, Monticello, tel: 914/434-9254). Western trail rides on 1,000 acres at **Arrowhead Ranch** (Cooley Rd, Parksville, tel: 914/292-6267). **Bailiwick Ranch** (118 Castle Rd, Catskill, tel: 518/678-0411) offers scenic mountain trail rides.

The Adirondacks

Circle B Ranch (Friends Lake Chestertown, tel: 518/494-4074). **Adirondack Saddle Tours** (Uncas Rd, Eagle Bay, tel: 315/357-4499). **Bennett's Riding Stable** (Rte 9N, Lake Luzerne, tel: 518/696-4444) **Ranch Lake Placid Academy** (Lake Clear, tel: 1-800/613-6033).

Central-Leatherstocking

Edwin Smith LTD (Briar Creek Rd & Rte 7, Otego, tel: 607/988-7959). **Robinson Stables** (Brady Rd, Worcester, tel: 607/397-8275). **Giddy-Up-Go Riding Stables** (5441 Rte 30A, Charleston, tel: 518/875-6233).

Thousand Islands & St Lawrence Seaway

A & J Riding Stable (342 Rte I, Hammond, tel: 315/324-6042). **Horseback Riding @ Lucky Star** (Lucky Star Estate, 13240 Lucky Star Ranch, Chaumont, tel: 315/649-5519).

Chautauqua-Allegheny

R and R Dude Ranch (8940 Lange St, Otto, tel: 716/257-5140) has horseback riding, horse-pulled sleigh/hay rides, swimming and dogsledding. **Double D.A.B Riding Stables** (5811 Welch Hill Rd, Ripley, tel: 716/736-4418) has trail, wagon and pony rides .

WHALE-WATCHING

Long Island

The best time to go on a whale watching cruise is from late Jul–mid-Aug. The **Riverhead**

Foundation for Marine Research and Preservation (tel: 631/369-9840) sponsors whale watch cruises out of Montauk, as does Okeanos Oceah Research Foundation (tel: 516/728-4522).

WHITE-WATER RAFTING

he Adirondacks
The Adirondacks have some of the state's finest whitewater rafting, which begins in early spring and continues through fall. Numerous companies offer guided trips, including: **Adirondack Rafting Company** (Main St, Indian Lake, tel: 518/523-1635 or 1-800/510-RAFT); **Middle Earth Expeditions** (Rte 73, Lake Placid, tel: 518/523-9572); the **Hudson River Rafting Company** (Main St, North Creek, tel: 1-800/888-RAFT), **Whitewater Challengers** (Rte 28, North River, tel: 1-800/443-RAFT); and **Adirondack River Outfitters** (Rte 28, Old Forge, tel: 1-800/525-7238).

Thousand Islands & St Lawrence Seaway
Adirondack River Outfitters (140 Newell St, Watertown, tel: 1-800/525-RAFT) runs Class III–IV whitewater rapids trips. Also: **Whitewater Challengers** (Foster Park Rd, Dexter, tel: 315/639-6100 or 1-800/443-RAFT).

Finger Lakes
Adventure Calls (Letchworth State Park, tel: 716/343-4710) organizes trips through the Gorge.

Sport

Fishing

Long Island
The waters around the island offer some of the East Coast's best sport fishing, which explains why there are so many charter boats. Among the major ports: Bay Shore, Mattituck, Sag Harbor, and the queen of them all – Montauk. No license is required for recreational saltwater fishing, but there are minimum size requirements and daily catch limits for some species. A few charters are: **Captree State Park** (tel: 631/669-6484); **Viking Fishing Fleet** (Montauk, tel: 516/668-5700); and **Marlin V** (Montauk, tel: 516/668-5343).

The Catskills
For information on licenses, regulations and where to fish, contact the Department of Environmental Conservation as before. For supplies and guides contact: **Fly Fishing with Bert & Karen** (1070 Creek Locks Rd, Rosendale, tel: 914/658-9784). **Beaverkill Angler Fly Fishing School** (Stewart Ave, Roscoe, tel: 607/498-5194) sells Orvis tackle and gives lessons. **Gone Fishing Guide Service** (PO Box 230, Narrowsburg, tel: 914/252-3657) offers half- and full-day drift boat charters on the Delaware River.

The Adirondacks
With an abundance of lakes, rivers, and streams, the Adirondacks offers some of the country's finest fishing. Fishing information, hot spots, licensing and water conditions are available from 24-hour hot lines: **Northern Adirondacks**, tel: (518) 891-5413; **Southern Adirondacks**, tel: (518)

623-3682. For a list of the numerous charter boat services in Oswego County (Lake Ontario), contact: **County of Oswego Dept. of Promotion and Tourism** (County Office Building, 46 East Bridge St, Oswego 13126, tel: 315/349-8322).

Hudson Valley
For information on licenses, permits, and where the good fishing is, contact: **Department of Enviromental Conservation** (21 South Putt Corners Rd, New Paltz 12561, tel: 845/256-3161).

Thousand Islands & St Lawrence Seaway
Some of the greatest fishing in the world is in the Thousand Island Region. *1000 Islands International Boaters' Guide* (tel: 1-800/847-5263) is a free guide to American Canadian ports and marinas on the St Lawrence River and Lake Ontario.

Finger Lakes
The many lakes, rivers and streams of the Finger Lakes offer excellent fishing for rainbow, brook and brown trout, walleye, pickerel, large and smallmouth bass and panfish.

Greater Niagara
Lake Ontario and its tributaries teem with trout, salmon and bass (record-size brown trout thrive here). The **Orleans County Fishing Hotline** (tel: 716/589-3220) tells what's biting when. There's fishing at **Orleans County Marine Park** (Point Breeze Rd at Oak Orchard Harbor, Kent, tel: 716/682-3641 or 1-800/724-0314). Numerous companies offer charter boat fishing, including: **Bait Master Charters** (117083 Gulf Rd, Holly, tel: 716/638-5799); **Buc-A-Roo Charters** (2384 Peter Smith Rd, Kent, tel: 716/659-8130); and **Sunrise Sportfishing Charters** (PO Box 127, Albion, tel: 1-800/236-8659 or 716/682-5563).

Chautauqua-Allegheny
There are bait and tackle shops, boat launches and marinas in every corner of the region. Fishing licenses (seasonal or short-term) are required, and can be purchased

in stores and from village clerks. Fishing Hotlines: **Chautauqua Lake** (tel: 716/763-9471 or 716/386-4275); **Lake Erie** (tel: 716/679-3743); **NY Department of Environmental Conservation Offices** (tel: 716/851-7000).

Golf

Long Island
There are more than 100 golf courses on Long Island, and more than half are open to the public. The Robert Trent Jones-designed **Montauk Downs State Park** (South Fairview Ave, Montauk, tel: 631/668-5000) is rated one of the top 50 public courses in the nation by *Golf Digest* magazine.

The Catskills
The 18-hole **Stamford Golf Club** (Taylor Rd, Stamford, tel: 607/652-7398) offers a challenging course and mountain views. **Delhi College Golf Course** (Arbor Hill Rd, Delhi, tel: 607/746-GOLF) has 18 holes.

Capital-Saratoga Region
Among the many courses open to the public in the region: **New Course** (65 O'Neil Rd, Albany, tel: 518/489-3526); and **Town of Colonie Golf Course** (418 Consaul Rd, Colonie, tel: 518/374-4181) are particularly recommended.

The Adirondacks
Golf is a major sport in the Adirondacks, and most of the courses are open to the public, including the 18-hole **Bluff Point Golf and Country Club** (Plattsburg, tel: 1-800/438-0985) and the 9-hole **Lake Pleasant Golf Course** (tel: 518/548-7071) in Lake Pleasant.

Central-Leatherstocking
Leatherstocking Golf Course (Otesaga Hotel, Cooperstown, tel: 1-800/348-6222) is one of the most challenging and scenic courses in the east. The 9-hole **Otsego Golf Club** (West Lake Rd, Springfield Center, tel: 607/547-9290) is one of the oldest courses in the US.

Thousand Islands & St Lawrence Seaway
With more than 30 public courses, the region is a golfers' paradise. Among them: the 9-hole **Alexandria Bay Municipal Golf Course** (Old Goose Bay Rd, Alexandria Bay, tel: 315/482-2127); the 18-hole **C-Way Golf Club** (37093 NYS Rte 12, Clayton, tel: 315/686-4562); and the 36-hole **Thousand Island Golf Club-Lake Course** (Oak Ridge Dr, Wellesley Island, tel: 315/482-4699). **Green Valley Golf Course/Greenview Country Club** (NY Rte 49, West Monroe, tel: 315/668-2244) has 36 holes.

Greater Niagara
The region is also great for golfers. Among courses open to the public: the 18-hole **Hickory Ridge Golf and Country Club** (Holly, tel: 1-888/346-5458) and the 18-hole **Kis-N-Greens Golf Course** (Alden, tel: 716/937-4741).

Chautauqua-Allegheny
Among the many fine courses that are open to the public are: the 18-hole **Allegheny Hills Golf Course** (Rushford, tel: 716/437-2658); the 9-hole **Bemus Point Golf Club** (Bemus Point, tel: 716/386-2893); and the 18-hole **Holiday Valley Resort** (Ellicottville, tel: 716/699-2345).

Skiing

Hudson Valley
Mount Peter (off Rte 17A, Warwick, tel: 845/986-4992), with a vertical drop of 400 ft (120 meters), has two chair lifts, eight slopes and, off-season, mountain biking.

The Catskills
Belleayre Mountain Ski Center (Rte 28, Highmount, tel: 914/254-5600), Catskill's highest peak, has 33 trails for skiing and boarding. **Hunter Mountain Ski Bowl** (Rte 23A, Hunter, tel: 518/263-4223) has 11 lifts and 53 slopes and offers snow tubing. **Ski Plattekill Mountain Resort** (Plattekill Mt Rd, Roxbury, tel: 607/326-3500 or 1-800/NEED-2-SKI) has skiing and snow boarding.

The Adirondacks
Gore Mountain (Peaceful Valley Rd, North Creek, tel: 1-800/342-1234). **Whiteface Mountain Ski Center** (Rte 86, Wilmington, tel: 518/948-2223 or 1-800/462-6236). **McCauley Mountain** (Old Forge, tel: 315/369-3225). **Titus Mountain** (Malone, tel: 518/483-3740). **Big Tupper Ski Area** (Tupper Lake, tel: 1-800/709-4895). For a map of cross-country trails, contact the **Adirondack Ski Touring Council** (tel: 518/5323-1365).

Central-Leatherstocking
Osceola Tug Hill Cross-Country Ski Area (Osceola Rd, Camden, tel: 315/599-7377).

Greater Niagara
Cockaigne Ski Area (143 Thornton Rd, Cherry Creek, tel: 716/287-3404) has 15 trails/slopes. **Holiday Valley Resort** (Holiday Valley Rd, Rte 219, Ellicottville, tel: 716/699-5204) has 52 trails and slopes. **Ski Tamarack** (7414 State Rd, Rte 240, Colden, tel: 716/941-5889) has 15 trails/slopes.

Watersports

Long Island
East End Jet Ski (91 Foster Ave, Hampton Bays, tel: 631/728-8060) rents skis. **Swim King Dive Shop** (572 Rte 25A, Rocky Point, tel: 516/744-7707) rents equipment and organizes dive excursions.

Capital-Saratoga Region
Diving Discovery Scuba Center (1629 Central Ave, Albany, tel: 518/456-8146).

The Adirondacks
Diamond Divers (217 Stagecoach Rd, Chestertown, tel: 518/494-2066) and **Morin's Dive Center** (20 Warren St, Glens Falls, tel: 518/761-0533 or 1-800/924-DIVE) organize dive charters in the Lake George region. **Adirondack Water Ski School** (Lake George, tel: 518/668-2937) and **Daggett Lake Camp and Ski** (Glen Athol Rd, Warrensburg, tel: 518/623-2198) give waterski and tubing rides.

Thousand Islands & St Lawrence Seaway

Hunt's Dive Shop (40782 Rte 12, Clayton, tel: 315/686-1070) and **1000 Islands Diving Adventures** (335 Riverside Dr, Clayton, tel: 1-800/544-4241 or 315/686-3030) organize diving trips and tours.

Finger Lakes

East Shore Sailing (1000 East Shore Dr, Ithaca, tel: 607/273-2560) rents out boats and windsurfing equipment.

Spectator Sports

When you're tired of hiking and fishing or swimming and sailing, there are plenty of opportunities to sit back, relax and enjoy some of the country's most exciting sports as a spectator (*see page 69*).

In New York City, locals are understandably proud of their top-rated baseball teams, the Mets and the Yankees, who play (April–Oct) at (respectively) Shea Stadium in Flushing, Queens, and Yankee Stadium, in the Bronx.

The New York Knickerbockers (or "Knicks") play basketball (Oct–May) at Madison Square Garden, while the New York Giants and the New York Jets play football (Sept through the end of Dec) at Giants Stadium located in Rutherford, New Jersey, at Meadowlands Sports complex.

Madison Square Garden is a major venue for boxing events, as well as ice hockey; the Stanley-Cup-winning New York Rangers play here, while the Islanders play at Nassau Coliseum on Long Island.

Tennis fans also find plenty of action at Madison Square Garden – as well as at the National Tennis Center, in Flushing, Queens, where the US Open takes place every fall in Sept.

Elsewhere in the state, teams of note include the major league Buffalo Bills (football), who play at Rich Stadium; and the National Hockey League's Buffalo Sabres, who play at Buffalo's Memorial Auditorium.

HORSE RACING

Long Island

Belmont Park (Hempstead Turnpike, Elmont, tel: 516/488-6000 or 1-888/285-5961) has thoroughbred racing (May–Oct).

If you have a free weekend, watch polo at **The Meadowbrook Polo Club** (Bethpage State Park, tel: 631/669-1000, ext. 247; every Sun, May–Oct).

Capital-Saratoga Region

Saratoga Polo Club (Whitney Field and Lodge Field, Saratoga Springs, tel: 518/584-8108). The **Saratoga Equine Sports Center** (Crescent Ave, Saratoga Springs, tel: 518/584-2110) has harness racing and simulcasting. **Saratoga Race Course** (Union Ave, Saratoga Springs, tel: 518/584-6200 or 1-888/285-5961) has world-class thoroughbred racing.

Central-Leatherstocking

Vernon Downs Race Track (Stuhlman Rd, Vernon, tel: 315/829-2201) has harness racing.

Finger Lakes

Thoroughbred horse racing at **Finger Lakes Race Track** (5857 Rte 96, Farmington, tel: 716/924-3232 or 1-800/875-7191).

Greater Niagara

Batavia Downs Racetrack and Exposition Center (8315 Park Rd, Batavia, tel: 716/343-3750) has horse shows and off-track betting; **Buffalo Raceway** (5600 McKinley Park, Hamburg, tel: 716/649-1280) has harness racing.

MOTOR RACING

Long Island

Riverhead Raceway (Rte 58, Riverhead, tel: 631/842-RACE) has stock car racing on Sat nights (May–mid-Sept).

Hudson Valley

Yonkers Raceway (Yonkers Ave and Central Ave, Yonkers, tel: 914/968-4200) has nighttime harness

racing. DIRT sanctioned stock car racing and a NHRA. sanctioned drag racing are held at **Lebanon Valley Speedway & Dragway** (Lebanon, tel: 1-800/700-1320).

The Catskills

Spring cars, modifieds and karts tear up the dirt oval at **Accord Speedway** (Whitfield Rd, Accord, tel: 914/626-DIRT) Wed and Fri evenings and Sat afternoons, (Apr–early fall). There's pari-mutual harness racing year-round at **Monticello Raceway** (Rte 17/17B, Monticello, tel: 914/ 794-4100).

Central-Leatherstocking

Afton Raceway (Rte 41, Afton, tel: 607/639-1966) has dirt track racing.

Thousand Islands & St Lawrence Seaway

Can-Am Speedway (Rte 411, La Fargeville, tel: 315/658-4431). **Evans Mills International Speedway** (Rte 11, Evans Mills, tel: 315/629-RACE). **Fulton Speedway** (Rte 57, Fulton, tel: 315/593-6531).

Finger Lakes

Brewerton Speedway (60 US Rte, Brewerton, tel: 315/668-6906) a 3/8 clay dirt oval. Modified stocks, sportsman and street stocks at **Canandaigua Speedway** (Ontario County Fairgrounds, Canandaigua, tel: 716/739-0961). **Watkins Glen International Raceway** (Rte 16, Watkins Glen, tel: 607/535-2481) hosts world-class auto racing.

Greater Niagara

Lancaster National Speedway (57 Gunville Rd, Lancaster, tel: 716/759-6818) has NHRA drag racing and asphalt stock car racing.

Further Reading

Most of the following titles are in print; for those that aren't, try the search services offered by online booksellers, or check titles on auction websites.

General

Country Days in New York City by Divya Symmers. Country Roads Press, 1993.
Country Towns of New York by Bill Kauffman. Castine, ME, 1994.
Low Life by Luc Sante. Vintage/Random House, 1991.
The New Chinatown by Peter Kwong. Hill & Wang, 1987.
New York Handbook by Christiane Bird. Emeryville, CA 2000.
New York: A Guide to the Empire State by Writers' Program of the [...] Administration. New

[...] *ay*

[...] **art of the City** by J.P. [...]allard Press, 1990.
[...] **City and State** by David [...]aca, NY, 1979.
[...] *e II,* **State: Folktales,** *has* **and Ballads** by Harold W. [...]n. New York, 1967.
[...] **gers Beckon** by Archie Interlaken, NY, 1992.
Grows in Brooklyn by Betty Harper & Row, 1968.

[...]tory

Adirondacks: A History of [...]erica's First Wilderness by Paul [...]hneider. Henry Holt, 1997.
Eighty Years and More: Reminiscences 1815–1897 by Elizabeth Cady Stanton. Boston 1993.
The Great Bridge: The Epic Story of the Building of the Brooklyn Bridge by David McCullough. Simon & Schuster, 1983.
Here Is New York by E.B. White. Little Bookroom, 1999 (originally published 1948).
A History of New York by Diedrich

Knickerbocker, by Washington Irving. 1809.
The Hudson by Carl Carmer. Fordham University Press, 1993 (originally published 1943).
Manhattan '45 by Jan Morris. Oxford University Press, 1987.
New York: An Illustrated History by Ric Burns. Knopf, 1999.
O Albany! Improbable City of Political Wizards, Fearless Ethnics, Spectacular Aristocrats, Splendid Nobodies, and Underrated Scoundrels by William Kennedy. Viking, 1985.
The Power Broker: Robert Moses and the Fall of New York by Robert A. Caro. Knopf, 1974.
Up In the Old Hotel by Joseph Mitchell. Vintage, 1993.
Upstate: Records and Recollections of Northern New York by Edmund Wilson. New York: 1971.
The WPA Guide to New York City Federal Writers Project Guide to 1930s New York. Pantheon reprint, 1982.

Fiction

The Age of Innocence by Edith Wharton. Simon & Schuster 1998 (originally published 1920).
The Bonfire of the Vanities by Tom Wolfe. Farrar, Straus, & Giroux, 1990.
The Deerslayer by James Fenimore Cooper. State University of New York Press, 1987 (originally published 1841).
Diedrich Knickerbocker's History of New York by Washington Irving. Heritage Press, 1968 (originally published 1809).
Drums Along the Mohawk by Walter D. Edmonds. Syracuse University Press, 1997 (originally published 1936).
Guys & Dolls: The Stories of Damon Runyon. Penguin, 1992.
The Last of the Mohicans by James Fenimore Cooper. Bantam, 1982 (originally published 1826).
The Sunlight Dialogues by John Gardner. New York, 1972.
Washington Square by Henry James. Wordsworth Editions, 1998 (originally published 1881).

Arts & Culture

George Balanchine, Ballet Master by Richard Buckle, in collaboration with John Taras. Random House, 1988.
Knights of the Brush: The Hudson River School and the Moral Landscape by Frederick Turner. Hudson Hills Press, 1999.
The Lincoln Center Story by Alan Rich. American Heritage, 1984.
Literary Neighborhoods of New York, by Marcia Leisner. Starhill Press, 1989.
The Movie Lover's Guide to New York by Richard Alleman. Perennial Library/Harper & Row, 1988.
Poet in New York by Federico Garcia Lorca. Farrar, Strauss, Giroux 1988.

Architecture

Buffalo Architecture: A Guide by Reyner Banham. MIT Press, 1981.
Great Camps of the Adirondacks by Harvey Kaiser. David R. Godine, 1996.
History Preserved: A Guide to New York City Landmarks and Historic Districts by Harmon H. Goldstone and Martha Dalrymple. Schocken Books, 1976.
Hudson Heritage: An Artist's Perspective on Architecture by Karl B. Smith. Salmagundi Press, 1989.

Natural History

Contested Terrain: A New History of Nature and People in the Adirondacks by Philip G. Terrie. Syracuse University Press, 1997.
The Finger Lakes Region: Its Origin and Nature by O.D. Von Engeln. Cornell University Press 1988.
The Hudson: An Illustrated Guide to the Living River by Stephen P. Stanne. Rutgers University Press, 1996.

Other Insight Guides

There are over 190 Insight titles covering destinations around the world. These include *Insight Guide: New York City*, *Insight Pocket Guide: New York City* and *Insight Compact Guide: New York City*.

ART & PHOTO CREDITS

Al Bello/Allsport 73
The Antique Boat Museum 242T
Ardea London 84, 85, 86, 87L/R, 88, 89
Natasha Babaian 155, 158T, 162T, 298T, 302
Bruce Bernstein/Courtesy of Princeton University Library back cover top right, 16, 17, 18, 22, 25, 26. 27, 28L/R, 29, 32, 40, 75
Bettman Associates/UPI 46
The Bridgeman Art Library 41, 62, 199
Corbis 259
Donna Dailey/Apa 43, 54R, 80, 91, 93L, 93R, 94, 176T, 219T, 220, 221, 233T, 249, 250T, 251, 252, 252T, 262, 263, 267T, 268, 268T, 270T, 273, 275, 276, 277T, 278, 292, 292T
Jonathan Daniel/Allsport 69
Dunkirk Historical Lighthouse and Veteran's Park Museum 297
Elmira College Center for Mark Twain Studies 273
Mary Evans Picture Library 19, 20/21, 24, 36, 37, 39, 42, 63, 65L/R, 66
Christian Heeb/Look 81, 163, 165T, 198, 236, 236T, 283
Herschell Carousel Factory Museum 289
Karen Tweedy-Holmes 176, 179, 181
Ithaca/Tompkins County Convention & Visitors Bureau 271
Henryk T. Kaiser/Rex Interstock LTD 83, 154
Wolfgang Kaehler 185T
Catherine Karnow 1, 8/9, 10/11, 67, 77, 111, 120, 122, 125, 130, 134, 138, 141, 143, 168, 169, 173, 173T, 180, 186, 188, 189, 191, 191T, 192, 192T, 193, 197, 208T, 216, 256, 256T, 278T
Mary Ann Lynch 54L, 113T, 211, 211T, 212, 214, 214T, 217
Buddy Mays/Travel Stock 79, 178, 185, 230, 231, 232, 266, 269, 270, 274, 301, 301T
Darren McGee/NYS Dept of Economic Development 74, 224
Kelly/Mooney Photography front

flap top, 4BL, 12/13, 47, 48/49, 82, 96/97, 110, 113, 132L/R, 145, 146, 161, 165, 166, 167, 202, 219, 229, 235L, 235R
Museum of the City of New York 45
The New York Public Picture Library Collection 38, 44L/R
Richard Nowitz 4BR, 172, 174, 177, 203, 218, 238, 239, 240, 241T, 244, 245, 282, 290, 291, 299
NYC & CO 148
Andy Olenick 184, 205, 209, 257, 258, 267, 287, 287T, 288, 288T
Mickey Osterreicher back cover left, 30
Tony Perrottet 4/5, 6/7, 100/101, 157T, 161T, 162, 179T, 182T, 183, 190, 228T, 230T
Tony Perrottet/Apa front flap bottom, back flap top & bottom, back cover centre, 5B, 64, 92, 112, 114, 114T, 116T, 117, 119T, 120T, 122T, 123, 126, 126T, 127, 128T, 131, 131T, 132T, 133, 135, 135T, 141T, 142T, 145T, 146T, 149, 149T, 197T
Pictures Colour Library 70, 215
Ellen Rooney 208, 210, 233
Jim Schwabel/NESP 14, 90, 98/99, 280/281
Peter Serling 50, 52L
Ezra Shaw/Allsport 71
Mathew Stockman/Allsport 72
Topham Picturepoint 23, 33, 35, 187

INSIGHT GUIDE
New York State

Cartographic Editor **Zoë Goodwin**
Production **Linton Donaldson**
Design Consultants
Carlotta Junger, Graham Mitchener
Picture Research **Hilary Genin, Natasha Babaian**

Vautier-de Nanxe back cover right, 51, 52R, 53L, 53R, 55, 119, 121R, 129, 139, 144
Joseph F. Viesti 2B, 2/3, 34, 58, 59, 60, 61, 76, 78, 115, 152/153, 160, 164, 182, 194, 195, 196, 207, 222/223, 225, 228, 234, 237, 241, 242, 243, 254, 255, 260, 261, 286, 293, 295, 298, 300, 304
The Viesti Collection 158, 159, 175, 213, 246/247, 248, 272, 296
Todd Warshaw/Allsport 68
Bill Wassman 95, 116, 121L, 124, 128, 140, 147, 150, 151
Bill Wrenn 279, 303
Yaddo 212T

Picture Spreads

Page 56/57
Top row, left to right: Viesti Collection, Michael Okoniewski/Empire Expo Center, Mary Ann Lynch, Donna Dailey/Apa. *Center row, left to right:* Andy Olenick, Viesti Associates. *Bottom row, left to right:* Buddy Mays/Travel Stock, Catherine Karnow, Viesti Collection.
Page 136/137
Top row, left to right: Tony Perrottet, Tony Perrotet, Catherine Karnow, Marcus Wilson-Smith. *Bottom row, left to right:* Topham Picturepoint, Catherine Karnow, Topham Picturepoint, Tony Perrottet.
Pages 200/201
Top row, left to right: Princeton University Library, Donna Dailey/Apa, Pictures Colour Library, Andy Olenick. *Center row, left to right:* Viesti Collection, Andy Olenick, Andy Olenick. *Bottom row, left to right:* Wolfgang Kaehler, Andy Olenick, Mary Evans Picture Library.

Map Production Colourmap Scanning Ltd.
© 2001 Apa Publications GmbH & Co. Verlag KG (Singapore branch)

Index

*Numbers in italics refer to
photographs*

A
C
D
E
F
G
H
I
J
a
b
d
e
f
g
h
i
j
k
l

" I was first drawn to the Insight Guides by the excellent "Nepal" volume. I can think of no book which so effectively captures the essence of a country. Out of these pages leaped the Nepal I know – the captivating charm of a people and their culture. I've since discovered and enjoyed the entire Insight Guide series. Each volume deals with a country in the same sensitive depth, which is nowhere more evident than in the superb photography. "

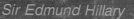

Sir Edmund Hillary

INSIGHT GUIDES

The world's largest collection of visual travel guides

Insight Guides – the Classic Series that puts you in the picture

Alaska	China	Hungary	Munich	South Africa
Alsace	Cologne			South America
Amazon Wildlife	Continental Europe	Iceland	Namibia	South Tyrol
American Southwest	Corsica	India	Native America	Southeast Asia
Amsterdam	Costa Rica	India's Western	Nepal	Wildlife
Argentina	Crete	Himalaya	Netherlands	Spain
Asia, East	Cuba	India, South	New England	Spain, Northern
Asia, South	Cyprus	Indian Wildlife	New Orleans	Spain, Southern
Asia, Southeast	Czech & Slovak	Indonesia	New York City	Sri Lanka
Athens	Republics	Ireland	New York State	Sweden
Atlanta		Israel	New Zealand	Switzerland
Australia	Delhi, Jaipur & Agra	Istanbul	Nile	Sydney
Austria	Denmark	Italy	Normandy	Syria & Lebanon
	Dominican Republic	Italy, Northern	Norway	
Bahamas	Dresden	Italy, Southern		Taiwan
Bali	Dublin		Old South	Tenerife
Baltic States	Düsseldorf	Jamaica	Oman & The UAE	Texas
Bangkok		Japan	Oxford	Thailand
Barbados	East African Wildlife	Java		Tokyo
Barcelona	Eastern Europe	Jerusalem	Pacific Northwest	Trinidad & Tobago
Bay of Naples				Tunisia
Beijing				Turkey
Belgium				Turkish Coast
Belize				Tuscany
Berlin				
Bermuda				Umbria
Boston				USA: On The Road
Brazil				USA: Western States
Brittany				US National Parks: East
Brussels				US National Parks: West
Budapest				
Buenos Aires				Vancouver
Burgundy				Venezuela
Burma (Myanm				Venice
				Vienna
Cairo				Vietnam
Calcutta				
California				Wales
California, Nor				Washington DC
California, Sou				Waterways of Europe
Canada				Wild West
Caribbean				
Catalonia				Yemen
Channel Island				
Chicago				
Chile				

Compl
G

Insight Pocket
ight Maps